Enemy Brothers

Enemy Brothers

Socialists and Communists in France, Italy, and Spain

W. Rand Smith

ROWMAN & LITTLEFIELD PUBLISHERS, INC.
Lanham • Boulder • New York • Toronto • Plymouth, UK

Published by Rowman & Littlefield Publishers, Inc.
A wholly owned subsidiary of The Rowman & Littlefield Publishing Group, Inc.
4501 Forbes Boulevard, Suite 200, Lanham, Maryland 20706
www.rowman.com

10 Thornbury Road, Plymouth PL6 7PP, United Kingdom

British Library Cataloguing in Publication Information Available

Library of Congress Cataloging-in-Publication Data

Smith, W. Rand, 1947-
Enemy brothers : socialists and communists in France, Italy, and Spain / W. Rand Smith.
p. cm.
Includes bibliographical references and index.
ISBN 978-1-4422-1898-7 (cloth : alk. paper) — ISBN 978-1-4422-1900-7 (electronic) 1. Social-
ism—France—History. 2. Socialism—Italy—History. 3. Socialism--Spain--History. I. Title.
HX704.S65 2012
320.53'1094—dc23

2012026586

☺™   The paper used in this publication meets the minimum requirements of American
National Standard for Information Sciences Permanence of Paper for Printed Library
Materials, ANSI/NISO Z39.48-1992.

Printed in the United States of America

Contents

Figures

Tables

Acknowledgments

This is my third book-length project, with each successive one adding another national case for analysis. Such an approach presents its challenges, most notably the need to acquire competence in new languages, become more knowledgeable about specific national contexts, and develop new research contacts. These challenges, I freely admit, provide the greatest pleasure and source of satisfaction despite their retarding effects on published output. As with my two previous books, the learning curve was steep, but I never tired of the subjects, settings, and people.

I am grateful for much help along the way. For starters, I am indebted to my home institution, Lake Forest College, where I have spent most of my academic career. A small liberal arts college offers some wonderful attractions for an academic. Not only does one enjoy small classes and close ties with students and colleagues, but one also has room to roam intellectually, with much institutional encouragement to develop new teaching and research interests. In the course of my career, I have developed courses on environmental and energy policy, the Vietnam War, comparative communist systems (when such existed), Latin American politics, and even American folk music. In none of these did I have formal training, but I learned the material by teaching it. In the process, I have taught with English, French, and Spanish professors, chemists, economists, and philosophers. As I approach (at least formal) retirement, I look back on my Lake Forest years as a continual liberal arts education. Warm thanks go to several helpful administrators, most notably former presidents Eugene Hotchkiss and David Spadafora and deans of the faculty Bailey Donnally, the late Steven Galovich, and Janet McCracken. I especially appreciate the support and encouragement of our visionary current president, Stephen F. Schutt.

Beyond the Lake Forest campus, field work sites in France, Italy, and Spain have drawn me back repeatedly. "Work sites" is perhaps an over-stretched term for my most frequent haunts abroad, namely, research centers and libraries, but I have also spent time on the road, tracking down interviews and documents in factories, party offices, union halls, cafés, and even homes. In addition to the roughly forty scholars and political figures interviewed for this project, I wish to recognize the following people in particular. In Paris, I benefited from the counsel and ideas of Roland Cayrol, Guy Groux, Jean-Daniel Reynaud, and Pierre-Eric Tixier. In Madrid, I enjoyed another research stay at the Center for Advanced Study in the Social Sciences, a unit of the Juan March Institute, and would like to thank its director Ignacio Sánchez-Cuenca, as well as José Ramón Montero and Andrew Richards, for their hospitality and willingness to share ideas. Finally, in Italy I was fortunate to find a research base at the European University Institute in Fiesole (near Florence), where, among others, Roberto D'Alimonte, Donatella Della Porta, Michael Keating, the late Peter Mair, and Alessandro Pizzorno helped me clarify concepts and generate contacts. In Bologna, Gianfranco Pasquino gave a particularly insightful interview. At the University of Turin, Alfio Mastropaolo provided several useful introductions to local political figures, including the former communist mayor of that city.

On this side of the Atlantic, several people aided me greatly. Stephen Hellman of York University deserves special mention. Steve, whose work on the Italian communists remains essential, was unfailingly generous in providing research contacts in Italy. He also gave the initial draft of the manuscript a critical reading that stimulated a summer's worth of revisions. Chris Howell of Oberlin College also provided an incisive critique of the first draft. To Steve and Chris, I am in your debt and can only hope, somehow, to repay your generosity one day. A former professor of mine at the University of Michigan, Samuel Barnes, suggested several useful contacts in Florence and Bologna, while Robert Fishman of the University of Notre Dame and Sebastián Royo of Suffolk University were very helpful in sharing contacts in Spain. To all, *grazie mille, merci beaucoup, muchas gracias.*

Finally, I must thank my cousins, John Thurmond and Frances McNair, for their generous use of the "Thurmond Farm," a 160-year-old farmhouse surrounded by 160 acres of pasture and piney woods near the crossroads hamlet of Mount Lebanon in northwestern Louisiana. For this project, I spent two monthlong writing stints at the farm where, apart from the clicking of computer keys, I mainly heard the mooing of cows and the rumbling of lumber trucks. The solitude did little to develop my social skills but amply provided two precious resources: time and quiet. As always, I am grateful for a supportive family circle, especially my wife, Janet Kelsey; our children, Caleb and Ellie; and my parents, Hurren and Margaret Smith.

Abbreviations

FRANCE

CFDT	Confédération Française Démocratique du Travail
CFTC	Confédération Française des Travailleurs Chrétiens
CGT	Confédération Générale du Travail
CGTU	Confédération Générale du Travail Unitaire
FO	Force Ouvrière
PCF	Parti Comuniste Français
PS	Parti Socialiste
PSU	Parti Socialiste Unifié
RPR	Rassemblement pour la République
SFIO	Section Française de l'Internationale Ouvrière
UDF	Union pour la Démocratie Française

ITALY

CGIL	Confederazione Generale Italiana del Lavoro
CISL	Confederazione Italiana Sindacati Lavoratori
DC	Democrazia Cristiana
DS	Democratici di Sinistra
PCI	Partito Comunista Italiano

PD	Partito Democratico
PDS	Partito Democratico della Sinistra
PLI	Partito dei Lavoratori Italiani
PRC	Partito della Rifondazione Comunista
PSI	Partito Socialista Italiano
UIL	Unione Italiana del Lavoro

SPAIN

CCOO	Comisiones Obreras
CNT	Confederación Nacional del Trabajo
IU	Izquierda Unida
PCE	Partido Comunista de España
PP	Partido Popular
PSOE	Partido Socialista Obrero Español
UCD	Unión de Centro Democrático
UGT	Unión General de Trabajadores

I

Introduction

Introduction

It is quality rather than quantity that matters. Do a good job.
—Fortune cookie, House of Peking, Highwood, Illinois, December 12, 2009

It could be better, but it's good enough.
—Fortune cookie, House of Peking, Highwood, Illinois, March 27, 2011

My interest in Socialist and Communist parties in Western Europe stems in large part from personal experience over the past four decades. One event, in particular, stands out in my mind as formative. The context was the French city of Grenoble in the fall of 1973. I was in that alpine city carrying out fieldwork for a dissertation on the contemporary French labor movement. Like many young Americans at the time, I had been fascinated by the upsurge in worker militancy taking place in France, Italy, and elsewhere in Western Europe in the late 1960s and early 1970s, so I had decided to study French unions firsthand. My specific focus was the country's second-largest union confederation, the French Democratic Confederation of Labor (CFDT), an erstwhile Catholic union, in four Grenoble firms. A decade earlier, the CFDT had severed its formal ties with the Church, changed its name, and moved steadily to the left. In the May–June "events" of 1968, the union was in the forefront of the workers' strikes, and, at the time of my research, it was considered close to the Socialist Party led by François Mitterrand.

For several months, I attended weekly meetings of the CFDT *section syndicale*, the local union in each of the four plants. As in most sizable firms in France, workers in these plants were represented by several unions—as many as five or six in some cases—including the largest confederation, the General Confederation of Labor (CGT), which had long been affiliated with the French Communist Party. Unions were thus enmeshed in a complex game of competition and cooperation. Sharing an overarching goal of repre-

3

senting workers' interests against management, unions also competed against each other for members and influence. Even though both the CFDT and the CGT strongly identified with the Left, this did not prevent them from coming into frequent conflict.

By law, management in each plant had to provide every union its own meeting room on plant property. In most cases, these rooms were dismal affairs: drafty, ramshackle quarters often located in "temporary" outbuildings that had somehow become permanent. One walked into a grim space of unpainted walls, rickety tables, mismatched schoolhouse chairs, and the pervading stench of Gitanes *brunes* cigarettes. In one particular plant, the "suite" of union rooms had only a single entrance that opened into the first of three or four rooms. So, to reach, for example, the third room, one had to walk through the first two rooms. It happened that the CFDT had the first room with the entry door and that the CGT had the third room.

The germinating moment for this project occurred one afternoon during the CFDT section's weekly meeting. The meeting was in full swing, and, as was often the case, the CFDT *militants* were loudly denouncing one or another perfidious action on the part of the local CGT section. Suddenly, there was a knock on the door, and the leader of the CGT section walked in. Instantly, all conversation stopped, and the room grew silent. With some embarrassment, the CGT leader excused himself, explaining that he was passing through on his way to his own union's *locale*. A couple of CFDT activists said a perfunctory "*salut*," but most of the dozen or so CFDT *militants* in the room said nothing. Some eyed the sudden intruder a bit warily, while others seemed to be exploring the cracks in the floor as the CGT leader walked quickly through the room. Thus, in less than five seconds, the CGT leader had entered the building, passed through the CFDT's room, and closed the door behind him. Once he had exited and closed the door, the CFDT members looked at each other with relief. Someone cracked a joke about the awkward moment, then the discussion resumed where it had left off: in a string of denunciations of the CGT and the Communist Party.

I quickly realized that this fleeting moment had revealed something basic about the French Left. I had witnessed an almost comic but real display of distrust and division within a group of leftists who were ostensibly comrades in the class struggle. Although virtually all CGT and CFDT *militants* identified with "*la gauche*"—the long tradition of the French Left that traces back to the revolution—these activists apparently held very different views of what the Left represented.

This event was my introduction par excellence to a chasm within the French Left. For nearly ninety years, the main forces on the Left—the Socialist and Communist parties as well as labor unions close to the two parties—have been, in effect, "enemy brothers."[1] On the one hand, both the Socialist and the Communist traditions derive from the same roots and share a common struggle. Both claim the mission of transforming, if not destroying, capitalism. Both traditions have their origins in a conviction that the capitalist system, whatever its positive aspects in terms of stimulating innovation and economic growth, is fundamentally unstable, crisis prone, exploitative, and unjust and therefore that it must be fundamentally altered. On the other hand, Socialists and Communists are also political competitors—at times, even enemies—seeking to achieve conflicting, even incompatible visions of what the Left should stand for and of how capitalism should be transformed. In that clarifying moment in Grenoble, I was struck not so much by the fact of the French Left's division into competing camps—after all, I had spent the late 1960s on large university campuses and knew about divisions among groups identifying with the Left—as by the depth and intensity of those divisions.

In individual interviews with Socialist-leaning CFDT and Communist-aligned CGT *militants* in Grenoble, I gained even more insight into the gulf that separated them.[2] For example, one CFDT member described this division as a cultural difference:

> The CGT is a different culture. Even at the level of rank-and-file members, there is a difference of mentality. The CFDT is more critical, more intellectual, they ask questions, but the CGT members in the *ateliers* (on the shop floor), they believe. They believe the lies—there are a lot of lies in *L'Humanité* (the Communist newspaper)—but for them, it comes from on high, it's the word, it's the truth.

Not surprisingly, CGT activists had their own critiques of the CFDT. One CGT *militant* remarked,

> The CFDT will sometimes defend a certain position when it talks with management, and a different one when it addresses the workers. . . . I'd have to say [the CFDT] is dishonest. They follow the reformist current—whatever they think workers want to hear and will support at a given moment. They don't care if the *patron* wins as long as they can attack us and advance themselves. It's not unionism. It's not honest. The CFDT will tell workers certain things, knowing it's not possible to do them.

This initial research in 1973 was not only intriguing, it was also puzzling in that this was the high period of cooperation between the Communist and Socialist parties. Just a year earlier, the two parties had established a formal alliance, the Union of the Left, which featured a "common program" of economic and political reforms. Moreover, the two labor confederations were attempting to practice "unity of action" at the national level in their approach to wages, working conditions, and other labor market questions. If the two Left parties and their union allies were so cooperative at the national level, why did such rancor exist at the local level? I could only conclude that below the strategic peak level there coexisted some fundamental organizational and even cultural differences between the two parties. In subsequent work on French labor, I was able to explore the nature and consequences of these differences (Smith 1981, 1984, 1987).

Later, as I expanded my research interests beyond France, the issue of Socialist–Communist relations continued to draw my interest. In a project comparing the economic and industrial policies of Socialist governments in France and Spain during the 1980s and 1990s, I quickly recognized that, as in France, Spanish politics during the past century has been heavily influenced by the two parties' relationship (Smith 1998). Divisions between Spanish Socialists and Communists go back to the 1930s—to the ill-fated Second Republic and the Civil War—and the four subsequent decades of shared opposition to Francoism did not completely efface these splits. Even though Socialists and Communists supported the democratic transition following Franco's death in late 1975, the two parties refused to cooperate with each other. Once the Socialists came to power in 1982, the Communists maintained a drumbeat of opposition to the Socialist government's economic policies for well over a decade.

Most recently, a yearlong teaching opportunity in Italy enabled me to deepen my understanding of the Left in that country. As in France and Spain, the relationship between the two main Left parties has influenced the course of politics since their initial break in the early 1920s. As in many things Italian, the history of Socialist–Communist is complicated. Unlike the Spanish case, where cooperation between the two parties has been rare and fleeting amidst a general climate of hostility and/or indifference, Italian Socialists and Communists engaged in complex cycles of cooperation and conflict, especially since World War II. The Italian case has the added twist that in the past two decades the historic Socialist and Communist parties ceased to exist, the Socialists having imploded through scandals and a majority of Communists having cast off their Leninist heritage.

In summary, fieldwork in France, Spain, and Italy during the past four decades has taught me a fundamental fact: for most of the past century, relations between Socialists and Communists have crucially shaped the fate of the Left in these nations and thereby the course of politics more generally. In essence, this is the motivating factor driving this study. Since their initial split in 1920–1921 (see chapter 1), Communists and Socialists have not simply gone their own way. Unlike two people in a divorce who simply divide up the belongings, pay the lawyers, and "move on," the two left parties have remained intimately tied, if only because they cannot move away and move on. They must, in some fashion, continue to deal with each other. Since their own divorce, the two parties have vied against each other. They have competed for votes and influence in the workplace and the labor market. More generally, they have waged a contest over the superiority and effectiveness of their respective political visions. Thus, ties between the two parties have often been tense and tenuous; at worst, they have been durably and unremittingly hostile. But that is not the whole story. Socialists and Communists have also cooperated in a range of activities, including resistance movements, parliamentary campaigns, strikes, national-level pacts, and governments at local, regional, and national levels.

How have Socialist–Communist relations mattered for politics in these countries? One way to assess this question is to consider some counterfactual situations. In the French case, for example, what if the French Socialists had *not* assented to the Union of the Left with the Communist Party (PCF) in 1972? Without a prior alliance with the PCF, would Mitterrand and the Socialists have been able to build both a presidential and a legislative majority by 1981? Perhaps, but one can make a strong case that the Union of the Left played an important role in shaping the direction of French politics in the 1970s and the decades thereafter.

In the Italian case, what if the Communists and Socialists had been able to bury their differences and develop a unified bloc as an alternative to the manifestly corrupt and ineffective Christian Democrats in the late 1970s? Could an alliance between the Partito Comunista Italiano and the Partito Socialista Italiano have provided a better response to the economic and political crises besetting Italy during that period? Again, a certain response is impossible, but an affirmative answer to the question is certainly plausible.

Finally, in Spain, what if Prime Minister Felipe González had "done a Mitterrand" in 1982 and brought the Communists into his governing tent instead of keeping them at arm's length and excluded from power? Certainly, cooperation between the two parties would have changed the dynamics of the Socialists' industrial reconversion and other economic policies during the 1980s. The point is not that Socialist–Communist relations are the fundamental driving force of politics in all three nations; that would be too strong a claim. Rather, the assertion is that different patterns of cooperation and conflict between these two parties might well have produced different political outcomes in all three nations, and for that reason, it is important to analyze and explain the patterns that have occurred.

The analytical challenge—the purpose of this book—is to make sense of these patterns. At its most basic, this book addresses three central questions. First, how have Socialist and Communist parties in France, Italy, and Spain changed over time in response to changing political conditions? Second, how have relations between the two parties varied both over time within in each country and cross nationally? Finally, what factors best explain this variation?

I address these questions using a framework that combines historical narrative and analytical comparison. This book intends to combine the complexity and nuance of the "long view" of history—the long view in this case being the nine decades of Socialist–Communist coexistence since 1920—with an analytical structure that is explicitly comparative and explanatory.

That structure, laid out in chapter 1, is built around the concept of critical junctures and stresses the impact of three main explanatory variables: institutional context, party culture, and leadership. Following this chapter, the book is organized in two major sections.

Part II consists of case studies, with individual chapters on France (chapter 2), Italy (chapter 3), and Spain (chapter 4). Each of these chapters traces the development of the Socialist and Communist parties and their interrelations since 1920, with an emphasis on the last five decades. My intention in these chapters is to "tell the story" of the Left within the historical context of each nation. In so doing, I have organized these narratives according to major phases in both Socialist–Communist relations and national history. The goal is not to write a complete history of the Left in each country but rather to convey to the reader the main dynamics of that history, especially the major strategic turns of the two parties and the results of those turns. At the end of each chapter, I relate the national case to the central critical juncture argument and to the three main explanatory variables.

Part III builds from part II, extending the analysis in two main ways. The first is by comparing how these parties have addressed two essential tasks. It is axiomatic that all (or virtually all) political parties must take on certain operational tasks. Parties vary greatly in the manner in which they carry out these tasks as well as in their relative degree of success, but carry them out they must. To do so requires that parties make strategic choices about how they will do so. The use of the term "choice" needs to be understood contextually. Parties, as individuals and collectivities in general, are rarely unconstrained in the range of possible choices before them. For an organization such as a political party, the degree of choice is almost always bounded by specific circumstances, both external and internal to the organization, that shape or limit alternatives. At issue, then, is the question not only of what strategic choices are made in a given context but also of the *space*—roughly speaking, the room for maneuver—for making those choices. People indeed make their history, as Marx famously pointed out, but not under conditions they choose.

For purposes of this study, I identify two such essential tasks that parties must undertake. The first is *constructing the party organization*, which is the subject of chapter 5. As a purposeful, ordered collectivity, a political party is first and foremost an organizational structure. [3] Therefore, we must inquire as to how Socialists and Communists have sought to construct their organizations. Recognizing that there are many dimensions to party organization, this study focuses on two: membership and authority relations. Regarding the former, we ask, How have these parties changed over time in terms of membership recruitment and activism? Regarding the latter, we inquire, To what extent is decision-making authority within the party concentrated within the top leadership or, conversely, diffused throughout the organization?

The second essential task analyzed here is *building alliances*. No party exists in a complete vacuum, and certainly Socialist and Communist parties have sought to build working partnerships with other organizations. Chapter 6 examines how these parties have sought to do so. This chapter identifies two types of alliances: political alliances and social alliances. The former refers to cooperative efforts with other political parties, and for Socialists and Communists alike, a central question is whether to ally with the other party. Social alliances refers to collaboration with organizations within civil society, including labor unions, women's groups, neighborhood organizations, and issue groups concerned with such questions as the environment, nuclear energy, civil or equal rights (for women, gays, minorities, and so on), and regional autonomy. This chapter focuses specifically on the Socialists' and Communists' relations with the labor movement.

Part III extends the analysis in a second way by applying the explanatory framework to two other Mediterranean nations where Communist parties have been particularly strong and where relations between Socialists and Communists have been marked by cycles of conflict and cooperation: Greece and Portugal. This is part of the conclusion (chapter 7), which also recaps the book's chief themes and reflects on the status of critical junctures as a methodological approach for the study of Left politics.

NOTES

1. The term "enemy brothers" is the translation of a well-known French term *"frères ennemis,"* which has been used in many contexts. To my knowledge, the first use of the phrase was by Racine, whose first play, *La Thébaïde ou les frères ennemis* (1664), popularized the expression.

2. The quotes below are taken from Smith (1987, 156–57, 167–68).

3. In the age of the Internet and mass media, it is now common to speak of the withering away of the political party qua organization, but even a "virtual" party can be considered structured in the sense used here.

Chapter One

Enemy Brothers and Critical Junctures

> Hence it may be said that to write the history of a party means nothing less than to write the general history of a country from a monographic viewpoint, in order to highlight a particular aspect of it. A party will have had greater or less significance and weight precisely to the extent to which its particular activity has been more or less decisive in determining a country's history.
>
> —Antonio Gramsci (1971, 151)

The purpose of this chapter is twofold: first, to provide some broader Western European historical context for the study of Socialist–Communist relations in France, Italy, and Spain and, second, to lay out the book's central argument.

SOCIALISTS AND COMMUNISTS IN WESTERN EUROPE, 1920–2010

That politics in France, Italy, and Spain have featured a dialectic of collaboration and struggle between Socialists and Communists hardly makes these nations unique. Indeed, the coexistence of Socialist (or Social Democratic or Labor) and Communist parties has been common throughout Europe during most of the past century.[1] The context for the initial division between Socialists and Communists was, of course, the 1917 Bolshevik Revolution. Following the revolution, the Soviets established the Third Communist International (Comintern), which sought to coordinate the worldwide struggle against capitalism. At its second congress in 1919, the Third International (read: Lenin) laid down its famous "Twenty-One Conditions," which required supporters of the Soviet Union in all nations to form specifically Leninist-style Communist parties that would look to Moscow for leadership. During the next three years, such parties formed in all twenty-four European nations as well as

11

elsewhere, including the United States (Eley 2002, 178). In most cases, Communist parties resulted from splits within existing Socialist parties, principally over the question of whether, in effect, to surrender the party's independence to Moscow. In almost all these cases, the most notable exception being France, a majority of Socialists elected to remain independent of Moscow, whereupon a minority faithful to the Soviet Union exited to form a separate and rival Communist party. Needless to say, this breakup was wrenching for all concerned. Longtime comrades parted ways, often with mixed feelings of sadness and bitterness. The term "enemy brothers" aptly captures the nature of this traumatic breakup within the erstwhile socialist "family."

For the most part, Communist parties throughout Europe during the interwar years were smaller and less important politically than their Socialist counterparts. Conflict pervaded the two parties' relations during the decade of the 1920s and into the 1930s, as the Third International line held that Socialists and Social Democrats were the "class enemy" along with the bourgeoisie. This dynamic changed, however, in 1934, with Stalin's declaration of the need for a Popular Front between Communists, Socialists, and even "bourgeois" parties to oppose the rise of Fascism. Thus, Communists became important players in Popular Front governments in France, Spain, and elsewhere. During World War II, Communists fought actively in the anti-Nazi resistance, notably in France and Italy, and emerged after the war with newfound strength and popularity (Sassoon 1996, 41, 93–94). For the next forty-five years, until the collapse of Soviet and Eastern European Communism, Communist parties were active in political life throughout Western Europe, although the advent of the Cold War in the late 1940s (and U.S. opposition to Communism) virtually erased the possibility of Communists participating in government.

In the postwar period, party systems in Western Europe were generally organized along a Left–Right dimension, with a set of parties that identified themselves as constituting the left side of the political spectrum. Within this set of parties, one typically found a main party identifying itself as Socialist, Social Democratic, or Labor as well as a party taking the Communist label. Taken together, these two parties averaged over two-fifths of the vote in national legislative elections in Western Europe between 1945 and 1990 (see appendix A).[2] Moreover, these Left parties, especially the Socialists, were able to translate their electoral support into government office. In all sixteen nations listed in appendix A, one or the other of these parties (and, on occasion, both at the same time) joined or led the governing coalition at some time during this period (Sassoon 1996, 284, 467).

Overall, Communist parties between 1945 and 1990 attracted well less than one-third of the votes of their main Socialist counterparts, but the overall average conceals great variation and some notable exceptions. In most instances—nine of the sixteen nations—Communists remained marginal actors with little popular appeal, averaging less than 5 percent of the vote. In five of the countries, however—Finland, France, Greece, Italy, and Portugal—Communists averaged more than 10 percent. The most successful performers were the French and Italian Communist parties, which averaged over one-fifth of the vote; by contrast, Spanish Communists in the post-Franco period performed below the European mean.

An intriguing question is how to account for this variation in Communist strength. Suffice it to say that no single factor or set of factors can explain why Communist parties have been historically strong in certain nations or regions and weak in others. There is clearly a geographic, North–South dimension to the variation; generally, Communist parties have been strongest in the Mediterranean region and much weaker in northern Europe, but the association is not perfect. For example, the average vote of the Finnish Communist Party is nearly triple that of the Spanish Communists. Clearly, specific national conditions as well as broad structural variables play a role in explaining variation in Communist electoral performance.

In perhaps the most exhaustive study of this question, Stefano Bartolini has identified a "syndrome" whereby relative Communist strength can be explained by three sets of variables: socioeconomic conditions (e.g., early vs. late industrialization, homogeneity vs. heterogeneity of the working class), the organizational features of working-class organizations (e.g., strong vs. weak, united vs. fragmented), and political conditions (e.g., integration vs. isolation of working-class and Socialist movements) (Bartolini 2000, 502–45). To summarize, Communist parties have been strongest in nations where three general conditions have applied. First, there was late and halting industrialization such that both industrial and rural workers did not become integrated successfully into the economy and were thus available for Communist mobilization. Second, Socialist movements were historically weak and divided such that Communist organizations were able to penetrate easily into industrial and rural milieus. Finally, there was poor institutional integration of the working class such that Communists could appeal to workers and others on the basis that they were excluded and marginalized by the existing political system.

Bartolini's analysis, while generally convincing, is not the last word on the question. For one thing, his data are largely drawn from the interwar period. Certainly, path dependence is strongly at work here; early Communist parties found fertile ground in certain types of societies and not others, and those initial strongholds persisted into the late twentieth century. But contingency and later events must also be considered. The most obvious example is one mentioned earlier: the great leap forward made by Communist parties in France and Italy during the Resistance and early postwar period. Could French and Italian Communism have attained the long-lasting levels of voter support that they did in the postwar period without the legitimacy and mobilization they were able to achieve during the struggle against Nazism and Fascism? The importance of contingent national circumstances also applies in the Spanish case. Bartolini's syndrome of social, economic, and political conditions would appear to favor the Spanish Communists, yet the Partido Comunista de España, despite having led the anti-Franco opposition during the dictator's last decade, performed poorly once it was legalized in 1977. As we shall see, broad structural factors going back a century fail to provide an explanation. One must take into account such specific political influences as party strategy and the nature of other Left-party alternatives (specifically the Socialist Party).

Whatever the precise explanation for strong versus weak Communist influence in the early and mid-twentieth century, the term "Communist strength" has become an oxymoron in the past three decades. Even before the coup de grâce, the fall of the Berlin Wall in 1989, Communist parties throughout Western Europe had been experiencing declines in membership, activism, and electoral support. Since the collapse of Soviet Communism, Communist parties throughout Western Europe have either abandoned the label or diminished to the point of political insignificance (see appendix B). Overall, average Communist electoral performance declined by well over half compared with the pre-1990 period, but this figure only begins to tell the story of decline. As of 1990, Communist parties no longer existed in five of the sixteen nations, and in four others Communists averaged less than 2 percent of the vote during the next two decades. In the case of the three strongest Communist parties in the 1945–1990 period—Finland, France, and Italy—deterioration and change have been especially dramatic. In the Italian case, as we shall see in chapter 3, a majority of the Partito Comunista Italiano voted in 1991 to abandon the Communist label and heritage altogether. Although surviving Communist parties can occasionally play strategically important roles,[3] there is no question that Communism as an organized force has greatly weakened throughout Western Europe, as it has elsewhere in the world.

As for Socialist parties, while the post-1990 period has not been as harsh as it has been for the Communists, their recent electoral performance compares unfavorably with the earlier period. In ten of the sixteen nations, the average vote of the principal Socialist party declined after 1990; overall, the Socialist vote declined slightly, from 32.6 to 31.2 percent (compare appendix A and appendix B).[4] Taken together, the combined average vote of Socialist and Communist parties throughout Western Europe slipped markedly, from 41.2 percent in the earlier period to 34.4 percent in the more recent one. Granted that such gross averages reveal nothing about trends, party strategies, the performance of other Left parties, and many other relevant factors, these data do paint a broad picture of a recent overall erosion in support for Left parties compared with the pre-1990 era.

To this numerical slippage of the Left must be added what one might call a loss of ideological traction, for the last three decades have not been kind to the classic Socialist project of transforming capitalism. On the contrary, the nearly thirty years bracketed, on one end, by the elections of Thatcher and Reagan in 1979–1980 and, on the other end, by the onset of the severe world recession in 2008 were unquestionably an era of capitalist hegemony throughout the global economy (Eichengreen 2007). Buzzwords became by-words, as terms such as "competition," "deregulation," "privatization," and "globalization" dominated policy discourse. If the cliché holds that "Whoever names it, owns it," then one can say that conservative political forces have largely owned the political space in the advanced capitalist world since 1980. This shift in discursive and policy dominance did not, of course, eliminate the Left, but it significantly narrowed the maneuvering room of Left governments. Basically admitting that "we are all capitalists now," Left governments have been challenged to craft policies that simultaneously support capitalist growth while advancing such bread-and-butter aims as improving social welfare and lowering unemployment. To be sure, achieving both goals has always been the particular mission of Left/Social Democratic governments over the past century (Berman 2006). But for a host of much-discussed reasons—including, to name a few, slower global growth since the first oil crisis of 1973, the rise of newly industrializing competitor nations, the growing scale and dominance of multinational corporations, and the need for economic cooperation and coordination within the emerging European Monetary Union—that mission became much harder to accomplish.

FRAMEWORK AND ARGUMENT

How does the present analysis of Socialist–Communist relations in France, Italy, and Spain fit within this context? Before developing the book's central argument, let us situate the topic within the scholarly literature on the Western European Left. Here one finds a surprising lacunae: in what is generally a vast literature—much larger, in fact, than the comparable body of scholarship on the Western European Right—the topic of Socialist–Communist relations in the postwar period is largely neglected terrain. To survey the English-language literature briefly, there are many excellent studies of the Western European Left in general, including at least three encyclopedic histories (Sassoon 1996; Bartolini 2000; Eley 2002). A sizable literature exists on the non-Communist Left in general: Socialist, Social Democratic, and Labor parties (e.g., Scase 1977; Paterson and Thomas 1986; Padgett and Paterson 1991; Scharpf 1991; Piven 1992; Gillespie and Paterson 1993; Bell and Shaw 1994; Kitschelt 1994; Thomson 2000; Glyn 2001). The same is true specifically for the non-Communist Left in France, Italy, and Spain (e.g., Barnes

1967; Wilson 1971; Bell and Criddle 1988; Gillespie 1989). On Western European Communism, there are several useful overviews (Waller and Fennema 1988; Bell 1993; Wilson 1993; Bull and Heywood 1994) as well as monographs on the French, Italian, and Spanish parties (Tiersky 1974; Mujal-León 1983; Jenson and Ross 1984; Hellman 1988; Bell and Criddle 1994a, 1994b; Kertzer 1996). Only a handful of books address any of these Communist parties from a cross-national perspective (Blackmer and Tarrow 1975; Guiat 2003).

There are a small number of studies that examine Communist–Socialist relations or that compare the two subcultures in some fashion, yet these typically concern specific countries with little or no cross-national comparison (e.g., Johnson 1981; De Grand 1989; Gaffney 1989; Fishman 2004). Finally, for the European labor movement, which in its majority (though not its totality) identifies with the Left, there are useful surveys (e.g., Western 1997; Martin, Ross, et al. 1999) along with examinations of labor movements in France, Italy, and Spain (e.g., Ross 1982; Kesselman 1984; Golden 1988a, 1988b; Fishman 1990; Howell 1992; Bedani 1995). Despite this wealth of knowledge about various aspects of Left politics, no study, to my knowledge, addresses the issue of Socialist–Communist relations from a comparative perspective. Yet, for reasons suggested in the introduction to this book, this issue merits scholarly attention.

At stake in this analysis is the question of strategic choice. Specifically, this study aims to explain the main strategic choices of Socialists and Communists in our three countries. Although this book adopts a long historical perspective encompassing the full period of the parties' coexistence since the early 1920s, the emphasis is on the period from the 1960s through the first decade of the twenty-first century. The rationale for this emphasis is twofold. The first is to put these three nations into a commensurate temporal and analytical framework. Given Spain's status as a dictatorship until 1975, it would make little sense to compare Socialist–Communist relations in that country to the French and Italian cases prior to Spain's democratization. By the mid-1960s, however, Spain was rapidly modernizing, and by the end of that decade, cracks were beginning to show in the Francoist facade. Although still illegal, dissent against the regime was becoming increasingly mobilized and vocal, and major organizational and ideological changes were taking place within both Left parties. Therefore, one main reason for focusing on the period since the 1960s is to facilitate comparison of the parties within fairly similar democratic contexts.

The second reason for selecting the 1960s as a starting point is related to the central argument of this book. Herein, I argue that beginning in that decade and throughout the following one, political parties across the political spectrum faced major challenges to "business as usual." That I have chosen to focus on parties of the Left does not gainsay the fact that a series of economic, social, and political changes—both long term and immediate—forced parties everywhere to reconsider strategies that they had long employed. Essentially, their choices came down to status quo versus change. Parties had to decide whether to persevere with their current strategies, notably in terms of ideology and alliances, or to adapt their strategies to shifting, even transforming economic, social, and political conditions. As we shall see, how these parties responded followed no set or uniform script in either their timing or the strategic choices themselves. The only common element among these responses was that they proved crucial in determining the long-term prospects of each party.

How can one best analyze the nature of these challenges and the character of the parties' responses? The answer, I contend, is through the conceptual lens of "critical junctures." The concept of critical junctures, in the succinct definition of Collier and Collier (1991), refers to "watersheds in political life, . . .transitions [that] establish certain directions of change and foreclose others in a way that shapes politics for years to come" (27). The Colliers employ the concept to explain processes of labor incorporation in Latin America; other scholars have applied the concept to a range of settings, processes, and actors.[5] This study uses the concept of critical junctures to analyze the strategic responses of Socialist and Communist parties in France, Italy, and Spain during the past five decades.

In simplest terms, the concept of a critical juncture when applied to political parties implies three interconnected elements: cause, response, and outcome.[6] First, the element of cause refers to the appearance of new conditions that create a challenge or crisis for the party. Such conditions can come from outside the party—from what I term the party's "operating environment"—or from within it. Whatever the source of the changed conditions, the party, as mentioned above, finds that business as usual no longer works as before. Conventional strategies and mode of operation are called into question. It should be understood that the term "cause" as used here does not imply singular causation; indeed, in most situations, the conditions that create challenge and crisis are in most cases multiple and interrelated.

Second, the concept of a critical juncture encompasses a strategic response to the challenge or crisis on the part of the party. Again, the term "response" may refer to multiple and interrelated actions, but the basic point is that the party must confront and respond to the challenge or crisis. The qualifying adjective "strategic" implies that the party undergoes a self-reflexive process in which it either reconfirms current practices or changes them, including organizational structures, ideology, and policy positions.

Finally, the term "outcome" refers to the ultimate effects of the party's strategic response. As the definition quoted above implies, a critical juncture can be identified only post hoc, that is, in terms of its eventual impact. To employ the Colliers' language, only when the outcome of a party's strategic response can be identified as having "establish[ed] certain directions of change and foreclose[d] others in a way that shapes politics for years to come" can one fully specify a critical juncture. Phrased differently, a critical juncture in relation to a party has this sine qua non: the party's strategic response establishes a path dependency that shapes and even determines the party's subsequent fortunes. This is not to imply that a critical juncture has an indefinite "shelf life." History is nothing if not flux such that, over time, changing conditions in a party's operating environment or in its own internal processes will likely impose further critical junctures. Thus, any argument or analysis regarding critical junctures must be historically specific as to the duration of its impact.

On the basis of this analytical framework, this book develops three main arguments. The first is that beginning in the 1960s and extending throughout the 1970s, Socialist and Communist parties in France, Italy, and Spain experienced critical junctures as defined by the three main elements of cause, response, and outcome. The second is that of all the strategic responses that these parties made to the challenges they faced during this period, the most critical in terms of shaping the parties' ultimate fortunes was their alliance strategy. Finally, the book argues that, of the various factors that shaped the responses of these parties during their critical junctures, the three most important were institutional context, party culture, and leadership. Let us consider each of these claims in turn.

CRITICAL JUNCTURES: CAUSE, RESPONSE, OUTCOME

With regard to the first argument, the defining elements of a critical juncture—cause, response, and outcome—were evident for each of the Left parties during the period spanning the early 1960s to the late 1970s. To consider, first, the element of *cause*, Socialists and Communists faced conditions, both externally (in their operating environment) and internally, that required them, in effect, to rethink their operational repertoires and to make strategic decisions about how to address the challenges and crises. At the most general external level, the 1960s, particularly in the later years of that decade, marked the beginning of a pivot point in Western economies, as the "thirty glorious years"—a "golden age" of largely uninterrupted growth following World War II—came to an end (Fourastié 1979; Marglin and Schor 1990). The course of the 1970s, it need hardly to be recalled, witnessed two oil shocks, in 1973 and 1979, and the advent of stagflation—an unprecedented combination of recession coupled with inflation—as well as a downturn in business profits (Brenner 1998). With slowed growth came, inevitably, a rise in unemployment.[7]

For many analysts, these negative trends signaled not only a temporary recession but also the exhaustion of a specific type of growth model based on mass industrial production, full employment, and extensive welfare provision (see, e.g., Bell 1973; Piore and Sabel 1984; Boyer 1986).[8] Whatever the description used—the coming of postindustrial society, the second industrial divide, or the end of Fordism—observers agreed that basic shifts in occupational and class structures were taking place in advanced industrial societies, pushed along by automation, new sources of international competition in mass-produced goods (notably Japan), and demands by employers for technically trained workers in emerging fields using advanced technology. One obvious change was that male-dominated, low-skilled jobs in mature, high-volume manufacturing sectors were generally declining, whereas growth was occurring among "new" middle- and working-class occupations, including technicians, researchers, designers, general office workers, teachers, and public sector service workers.[9] An important aspect of this shift was the increasing participation of women among these latter occupations. As Crouch (2008) remarks, "In general the mid-1970s constitute the peak of male industrial employment and the mid-twentieth century forms of politics associated with it" (19).

These shifts in the global economy were accompanied by a number of shared political trends in Western societies, notably a growing public disaffection in relation to traditional politics. This disaffection took various forms, including a loss of trust in public officials, a drop in citizens' sense of political efficacy, a decline in levels of party identification, and a rise in such theretofore unconventional forms of political participation as protests, demonstrations, and boycotts (Barnes, Kaase, et al. 1979; Dalton 2004). While these trends affected all Western countries—creating, according to the Trilateral Commission, a "crisis of governability"—their impacts varied because of the adaptive capacity of national economies and political systems.

Predictably, the kinds of broad systemic changes just mentioned raised challenges for political parties as well. For parties of the Left generally, these changes posed at least two fundamental quandaries. The first was programmatic. Some of the new trends—especially the manifest inability of economies to ensure strong growth, stable prices, and full (or near full) employment—provided ammunition for the classic Left critique of capitalism's failures. But what about the logical next step? What alternative(s) could the Left propose? What margin of maneuver did the Left have to transcend or transform "really existing capitalism"?

A second quandary related to the Left's mobilization capacity. Specifically, the systemic trends noted above—especially the decline of large-scale manufacturing occupations along with a decrease in class voting—tended to erode the Left's support among its historically most important support base: industrial workers (Kitschelt 1994, 45). Moreover, the broad rise in political alienation and unconventional protest constituted a two-edged sword. Public disaffection could fuel a rejection of the status quo that might favor the Left, but it was not a given that protests, strikes, and other forms of direct action would necessarily work to the Left's benefit. Apart from the programmatic question, then, there was also the strategic problem: how could the Left take advantage of both long-term shifts and immediate crisis conditions in capitalist societies in order to build and mobilize new bases of support?

These challenges applied to virtually all Left parties in advanced capitalist societies during the 1960s and 1970s, but any attempt to address these issues had to be carried out in specific national contexts. Thus, in assessing causes of critical junctures, one must take account of national differences. As we shall see, the political and economic context in France, Italy, and Spain differed greatly during this period. There is, however, one common thread that analytically unites these countries: all experienced what I will label "regime crises" during these decades. In various ways, these crises posed both risks and benefits for Left parties.

In France, the regime crisis grew out of the threat to Gaullist hegemony resulting from the mass strikes by students and workers in the so-called events of May and June 1968, which nearly brought down the Fifth Republic along with President de Gaulle himself (Touraine 1971). At root, the strikes were a protest against a political-economic system that many perceived to be economically unjust, dehumanizing, and authoritarian. Although de Gaulle managed to resolve the immediate crisis and save both the regime and his tenure by calling new elections, he badly misjudged the public mood the following year by calling a referendum on which he staked his presidency. On losing the referendum, he gave up the presidency. In new presidential elections in 1969, a longtime Gaullist loyalist, Georges Pompidou, won, leaving the Gaullist system intact but greatly weakened. For the Left, the strategic challenge was how to take advantage of the regime's vulnerability in a system designed by de Gaulle to keep the Right in power.

In Italy, the regime crisis was more general (Tarrow 1985). Although Italy experienced no real equivalent of May–June 1968—a single dramatic moment of system-threatening mass mobilization—the nation by the late 1960s was undergoing a crisis perhaps even more profound. In simplest terms, Italy was experiencing a prolonged crisis of the entire postwar political-economic order built on the twin foundations of Catholicism and anti-Communism. Italy shared with France many of the negative aspects of rapid postwar modernization—including exploitative working conditions, housing shortages, and inadequate and/or ill-adapted educational systems—but its government was demonstrably less efficient and more corrupt than the Gaullist regime. Italy's government had been largely ruled since 1948 by the largest party, the Christian Democratic (Democrazia Cristiana [DC]) Party; however, since the DC could not gain a majority of parliamentary seats on its own, it had to garner support from several smaller parties. This resulted in a pattern of "stable instability" in which governments would fall with regularity—the average tenure of DC-led governments was about nine months—but the new government that reemerged would feature many of the same personnel in a game that resembled musical chairs. Although the DC governed precariously, it was still the permanent, indispensable party, and so it came to basically inhabit the state, turning the bureaucracy into a party-directed spoils system.

For the Italian Left, the key strategic question was how to deal with the DC. For the first fifteen years of the postwar Italian republic, that question had no answer. The DC drew its allies exclusively from centrist and conservative parties, while the Communists and Socialists were excluded from government—a fact that effectively disenfranchised over one-third of the nation's voters. That situation changed in 1963 when the Socialists finally joined a DC-led cabinet, but the DC–Socialist relationship was rocky from the outset. The Communists, on the other hand, remained forever locked out of the political game. As Italy experienced a growing cycle of worker unrest and radicalization on both the Far Left and the Far Right in the late 1960s and early 1970s, the strategic question for both Left parties came down to what kind of accommodation, if any, was possible with a dominant party aligned with the Church.

Finally, the regime crisis in Spain was obviously that of the fate of the Francoist system following El Generalissimo's death in November 1975. From the standpoint of that moment, it was not at all clear whether Franco's appointed heir, King Juan Carlos, would oversee the continuation of that authoritarian system or would seek to effect a movement toward democracy. For both Left parties, emerging from over three decades of clandestinity and exile, the strategic question was what approach to take toward the king and the regime he had inherited (Maravall 1982).

The foregoing discussion has specified the first element of a critical juncture, namely, cause, in terms of both the general external context and the diverse national conditions that the Left parties faced. With regard to the second element, *response*, these parties made critical strategic choices about such questions as organizational structure, ideological orientation, policy programs, and alliances. In all cases, these choices largely broke with inherited patterns and set these parties on new and lasting organizational trajectories.

The consideration of the parties' strategic choices leads to the second main argument of this book: of all the responses that these parties made during this period, the most crucial was the choice of alliances, for this was the most important factor in shaping the parties' long-range prospects. Moreover, in terms of comparative analysis, the most decisive difference among the three cases was in their alliance behavior.

To summarize the basic patterns, in 1972 the French Socialists and Communists formed an electoral alliance and a "common program" for governing. This was a huge gamble on the part of both parties since it represented an unprecedented level of cooperation since the Resistance and Liberation period of 1944–1947. For the previous twenty-five years, the two parties had been either de facto opponents, as during most of the Fourth Republic (1946–1958), or on-again, off-again collaborators, as in national elections in the 1960s. The 1972 Union of the Left pact promised to bring both parties to power in a more or less equal partnership. The end result was far from equal, however, as the dynamics of this alliance produced the systematic advance of the Socialists at the expense of the Communists.

In Italy, by contrast, there was no such alliance; rather, the parties sought partners elsewhere. Breaking their de facto postwar cooperation that lasted from 1948 to the early 1960s, the two parties sought an alliance with their erstwhile nemesis, the Christian Democrats. The first to do so was the Socialist Party, which, as mentioned above, joined a DC government in 1963. Later, beginning in 1973, the Communist Party as well courted the DC in an alliance that would reconcile Italy's two grand blocs of Catholics and secular leftists.

In the Spanish case, there is a surface resemblance to the Italian case: Socialists and Communists rejected cooperation and kept each other at arm's length throughout the 1970s. The two cases differed in a key respect, however. As Spain democratized following Franco's death, both parties rejected not only alliances with each other but also party alliances altogether. Historical enmities dating back to the Second Republic and the Civil War blocked any real rapprochement between the two Left parties. Moreover, the Socialists' early popularity, easily outstripping the appeal of the Communists, largely obviated the party's need for any alliance.

Despite subsequent changes in leadership, electoral performance, and other aspects of party life, the strategic choices that Left parties in all three countries made at various points during the 1960s and 1970s had long-term effects that carried down through subsequent decades. This is the third essential element of a critical juncture: *outcome.* In France, the Socialist advance by 1977 proved fatal to the Union of the Left, as the Communists chose to break off the alliance rather than continue as a junior partner. The Socialists' dominance did not doom all cooperation between the two parties, but the Union of the Left experience gave the Socialists an electoral advantage over the Communists that has proven lasting. Although the Socialists' fortunes have risen and fallen (at times dramatically) over time, the party's surge in the 1970s enabled it to overtake its Communist rival decisively and permanently.

In Italy, attempts by both Socialists and Communists to form an alliance with the Christian Democrats ultimately proved harmful to each party, albeit for different reasons. In the Socialists' case, partnership with the DC, initiated in the 1963 "opening to the Left," brought inclusion into an increasingly corrupt spoils system. Over time, the Partito Socialista Italiano became a comfortable creature within this environment, especially after the young Milan leader Bettino Craxi took over the party in 1975. Although Craxi's prowess at deal making and empire building brought the Socialists to power in the 1980s (despite the fact that they never surpassed 15 percent of the vote), both the party and Craxi were brought down in the "Clean Hands" anticorruption campaign of the early 1990s. As for the Communists, their proposed "Historic Compromise" alliance with the DC was never fully consummated. In the late 1970s, the DC maneuvered to keep the Communists committed to supporting the DC-dominated government while denying them cabinet positions and effective influence. Co-opted but without responsibility or power, the Partito Comunista Italiano shared the blame for Italy's crisis but lacked the leverage to shape policy—a toxic combination from which the party never recovered.

Finally, in Spain, the rejection of any alliance on the part of both Left parties proved highly advantageous for the Socialists but disastrous for the Communists during the first years of the post-Franco era. By the early 1980s, the two parties had in essence changed places in just a few short years. At the time of Franco's death, the Communists had far more members and activists than the Socialists, and it was assumed that the former would dominate the latter in the post-Franco period. The exact opposite turned out to be the case in considerable measure because of the two parties' alliance strategies. Socialist dominance on the Left has continued to the present.

The preceding summary indicates that the key strategic responses—and thus the critical junctures—occurred at various moments for each party. Although broad contextual forces were at work, country-specific and even party-specific conditions more strongly shaped the three elements of cause, response, and outcome. Table 1.1 provides a summary of the approximate dates of each party's critical juncture. Within each country, one sees considerable temporal overlap in the two parties' critical junctures, especially in France and Spain. One would expect such overlap given the salience of the question of intra-Left alliances during moments of regime crisis. But the correspondence is not perfect; these parties also made strategic decisions according to their own internal decision-making processes. This is particularly true in the Italian case. The Italian Socialists, in fact, experienced two distinct albeit related critical junctures—the first in 1962–1963, when the Partito Socialista Italiano decided to participate in the "opening to the Left," and the second in 1976–1980, during the early period of Craxi's ascendancy as party chief. As for the Italian Communists, their critical juncture extended throughout the 1973–1980 period when they sought and failed to realize their Historic Compromise with the Christian Democrats.

EXPLAINING STRATEGIC RESPONSES: INSTITUTIONAL CONTEXT, PARTY CULTURE, LEADERSHIP

The foregoing specification of critical junctures highlights the importance of parties' strategic responses at key historical moments. The logical next question is, How can such responses be explained? This leads to the third main argument developed herein, namely, that, as mentioned above, three factors were especially important: institutional context, party culture, and leadership. The first of these, institutional context, is an external factor in the sense of constituting a major element in the parties' operating environment, whereas the two other factors are internal in that they are endogenous to the parties themselves.

Institutional context refers to the arrangements determining the main governmental and electoral systems. These are the rules of the political game that establish a set of incentives and disincentives for all actors, including parties. These cases reveal that the specific configuration of the principal institutions strongly influences party behavior. One such example was that France's decision in 1958 to discard the parliamentary system of the Fourth Republic in favor of a new constitutional order based on a strong presidency completely transformed the dynamics of party politics. It did so by giving primacy to a party's ability to promote a single leader capable of winning the presidency. This change had the effect of creating a new incentive system for parties. From a single focus on winning parliamentary seats and exerting influence within the legislature, parties henceforth had a new preoccupation: fielding and promoting a credible presidential candidate. As we shall see, this alteration of the basic governing rules ultimately influenced the Socialists' and Communists' alliance behavior in the 1970s in a way that worked to the advantage of the Socialists over the Communists.

The second explanatory factor is what I label *party culture*, which refers to the set of elements—norms, symbols, collective practices, and collective

Table 1.1.   Left Parties and Critical Junctures: France, Italy, and Spain

	France	Italy	Spain
Socialist Party	1972–1977 Union of the Left— from inception to breakup	1962–1963 Opening to the Left 1976–1980 Craxi's rise	1976–1979 Democratization and first post-Franco elections
Communist Party	1972–1977 Union of the Left— from inception to breakup	1973–1980 Attempted Historic Compromise with DC	1976–1979 From democratization to PCE electoral disaster

memory—that constitute a party's identity, or what Panebianco (1988) labels a party's "genetic model." That identity—specific to every political party—is what compels most members to join a given party in the first place. Once one is a member, a party's culture acts as a powerful socializing influence. The new member undergoes a kind of initiation process, discovering not only typical party practices ("this is how we do things") but also characteristic ways of thinking specific to the party ("this is how we view the world"). Generally, party culture acts as a kind of "default mode" for party strategy and behavior. Once set, party norms and practices do not change easily, and thus party culture is highly inertial and path dependent.

This is not to say, however, that a party's strategic response in a given crisis situation can simply be "read out" from past behavior or responses— far from it. Party culture, though indeed inertial, is never fixed or static. A key issue for the comparative analysis of party cultures is the organization's capacity to engage in critical self-reflection. This capacity is akin to the concept of social learning, which refers to the ability of an organization—in this case, a political party—to adjust current behavior and/or strategy on the basis of an evaluation of new information, including the consequences of past actions and experiences (Heclo 1974; Hall 1993; Freeman 2006). Just as individuals can assimilate new information as well as "learn from past mistakes," so too can collectivities, including governments and political parties, alter their actions purposely in order to respond to changed conditions or to avoid negative outcomes that have occurred in the past.

The clearest example of social learning in this sense was the behavior of virtually all key Spanish political actors in the 1970s—and, most notably, Communist and Socialist leaders—who approached the post-Franco transition determined *not* to repeat the internecine fights of the 1930s. By contrast, other party cultures demonstrated relatively low capacity for social learning. For example, the French Communist Party in the 1970s rhetorically embraced an alternative, pluralist model of Communism labeled "Eurocommunism," but it did so without a fundamental change in its decidedly nonpluralist culture. Ultimately, the external embrace of pluralism and democracy clashed with a party culture that remained wedded to Leninist principles of democratic centralism. The result was an organizational crisis that ran from the grassroots to the top leadership levels and helped speed the party's decline after 1980.

The final explanatory factor is one that is often neglected in studies focusing on structures and organizations: *leadership*. There is no denying that leadership and party culture are inseparable. Parties, like any complex organization, get the leaders they produce. That statement is not a tautology, for party cultures tend to reward—and promote—certain types of leaders and not others. But that is not to conclude that party leaders are the predictable byproduct of organizational processes. This analysis, then, leaves explanatory room for the independent effect of party leaders, for the history of the Left in these countries during the past century clearly demonstrates that individual leaders often played a decisive role in the formation of parties' strategic responses. The 1970s, in particular, saw the emergence of several innovative leaders, among both Socialists—Mitterrand in France, Craxi in Italy, and González in Spain—and Communists, notably Berlinguer in Italy. While few would label Communist leaders Marchais (France) and Carrillo (Spain) as innovative, there is no doubt about their impact on their parties' strategies during this decade. A key issue in examining the impact of these leaders is their relationship with the previous factor: party culture. The central question is, did these leaders seek to change or transform party culture, or did they seek to preserve and perpetuate it?

Taken together, these three factors, this book contends, largely account for the strategic responses of Socialist and Communist parties as they faced critical junctures during the 1960s and 1970s. As we shall see, there was much variation in the parties' responses and in the impact of those responses. This fact has direct implications for the status of the explanatory factors in any given context. Just as the parties' responses varied, so too did the relative importance of these factors vary in individual cases, as we shall see in part II, which traces the trajectory of the Left in each nation.

NOTES

1. For simplicity's sake, I will henceforth employ the term "Socialist" to encompass parties that use the label "Socialist," "Social Democratic," or "Labor." I recognize, of course, that there may be significant ideological and programmatic differences among these parties.

2. Obviously, these two parties do not make up the complete universe of those parties identifying with the left side of the political spectrum. Depending on national context, other members of the Left "family" might include center-left (e.g., Social Democrats in Italy and Left Radicals in France), "new left" (e.g., Parti Socialiste Unifié in France), ecology, and extreme left (e.g., Trotskyist and Maoist) parties.

3. In the French case, in the 2002 French presidential election, the Communist candidate Robert Hue drew nearly 1 million votes (3.3 percent) in the first round. If one assumes, reasonably, that without a Communist candidate at least one-third of Hue's voters would have supported the Socialist candidate Lionel Jospin, then Jospin would have placed second in the first round—instead of the Far Right's National Front candidate Jean-Marie Le Pen—and gone on to contest the runoff against the incumbent, Jacques Chirac. That contest might well have produced a new Socialist president instead of an easy Chirac triumph over Le Pen.

In the Italian case, the successor to the Italian Communist Party, the Refounded Communists (Rifondazione Comunista), played a direct role in bringing down Prodi's Olive Tree government in 1998. Although part of the center-left Ulivo coalition, the Rifondazione Comunista, led by Fausto Bertinotti, defected from the coalition over minor policy differences, thereby reducing the coalition to minority status and prompting the resignation of Prodi's government.

4. For reasons indicated in appendix B, I have excluded Italy from this comparison.

5. According to James Mahoney (2001, 285), the concept of critical juncture in the social sciences was first used and developed by Lipset and Rokkan (1967). In addition to the Colliers' monumental study cited in the text, other works that have employed the concept of critical juncture include Mahoney (2001) and Lange, Ross, and Vannicelli (1982). One of the major

introductory texts in comparative politics—Kesselman, Krieger, et al. (2009)—also uses a variant of the concept. Although the term "critical juncture" is not used explicitly, a number of major works in comparative history and political economy employ an analytical framework that features path-dependent development stemming from "determining" historical moments, or critical junctures. See, for example, Moore (1966); Gordon, Edwards, and Reich (1982); and Luebbert (1991). See also the useful essay by Katznelson (2003), which surveys trends in comparative historical studies of critical junctures and path dependency.

6. To be totally clear, I am making no claim that a critical junctures perspective applies only to Left parties or to the specific cases at hand. On the contrary, I see no a priori reason why, in principle, the concept cannot be applied to parties and organizations of virtually all types. My interest, however, is limited to explaining the cases at hand.

7. The following statistics (annual averages) for six large industrial nations (the United States, the United Kingdom, France, Germany, Japan, and Italy) give a summary picture:

	1950–1973	1973–1983
Real gross domestic product (average % annual change)	4.5	1.8
Consumer Price Index (average % annual change)	4.0	11.2
Unemployment (average annual % of workforce)	3.1	5.3

Source: Calculated from statistics from the Organization for Economic Cooperation and Development (various years).

8. Often overlooked in assessments of the economic crisis in advanced industrial societies during the 1970s is the fact that this period also marked the beginning of long-term economic decline in the Soviet Union and its Eastern European empire (Bunce 1984).

9. One indicator of these trends is the relative proportion of industrial sector employment compared with agriculture and services. The following figures are the average percentage of the workforce employed in industry in eleven Western European countries for the periods indicated:

Early 1950s	Early 1970s	1985–1987
37.7	40.3	31.2

Source: Calculated from Kitschelt (1994, 43).

II

Cases

Chapter Two

France: Impossible Victory

> If the Socialist Party is too weak, and especially electorally weak, then the Left cannot obtain a majority in France. If the Socialist Party is regarded by the Communist Party as being too strong, then it will be opposed to the success of the Union. Thus, victory is never possible.
> —Lionel Jospin, speech to Socialist Party congress, 1980 [1]

In this succinct statement, Lionel Jospin, later to become prime minister in a government that included Communists, perfectly captured the historical dilemma of the French Left. The statement contains within it three crucial points. First, the Socialists and Communists are forever locked in competition. Whatever their attachment to the ideals of "*la gauche française*," the two parties are first and foremost rivals not only at the ballot box but also in the hearts and minds of French leftists. Each party claims to defend France's oppressed masses: industrial and rural workers, the lowly paid, the unemployed, and anyone else excluded from power and privilege. Rivalry between the parties is joined, then, not only at the polls but across civil society as well, extending into internecine struggles among affiliated groups, notably within the labor movement.

A second point follows from this basic fact: given the Left's division into two large blocs, neither party can gain a majority on its own, and thus cooperation provides the only hope for achieving power. But what kind of cooperation and under what conditions? Here Jospin expresses the third and most important point: cooperation depends on what the French call "*rapports de forces*," or the relative strength of each competitor-partner. On the one hand, the Socialists must be strong, he claims, in order for the Left to amass its full electoral potential. On the other hand, they cannot be too strong, or the Communists will scuttle any alliance, refusing to play the role of junior partner. Thus, while competition is always present, cooperation hinges on the precarious achievement of parity between the parties.

Whatever else one can say about competition and cooperation between French Socialists and Communists, the two parties have had a lot of practice. During the nine decades between the *"grande scission"* of 1920 and the present day (2011 as of this writing), France has maintained a democratic system in all but the five war years of 1940–1944. Throughout this long period, there have been a total of twenty-two national parliamentary (or constituent assembly) elections as well as countless local and regional elections. Under the Fifth Republic (1958 to the present), there have been eight direct presidential elections. Finally, since 1979, there have been six elections for the European Parliament. In all these contests, Socialists and Communists have had to decide whether to engage in alliances or electoral agreements with the other party. More broadly, on questions bearing on general policy orientations, the parties have faced the choice of seeking convergence or stressing differences. What decisions have the parties made? What have been the main trends, turning points, and patterns in their relationship?

This chapter examines the dynamics of this competition/cooperation between Socialists and Communists with an emphasis on the critical juncture for both parties that was framed by the rise and fall of the Union of the Left from 1972 to 1977. To both contextualize this crucial moment and trace its impact, this chapter proceeds as follows. The next section provides an overview of the full period since 1920, noting secular tendencies in party strength as well as identifying periods of cooperation and conflict. The following five sections examine the dynamics of these periods with an emphasis on the Fifth Republic. The first of these sections provides the historical background from 1920 to 1958, the end of the Fourth Republic. The second analyzes the rise and fall of the Union of the Left driven by the strategic vision of François Mitterrand during the first two decades of the Fifth Republic (1958–1978). The third focuses on the years just before Mitterrand's stunning election as president in 1981 and on the early years of his presidency (1978–1984). The next two sections bring the analysis down to the present by assessing two long periods, the first of conflict (1984–1993) and the most recent one of cooperation (1993 to the present). Finally, the conclusion restates the critical juncture argument for the French left and assesses the impact of the three main explanatory factors: institutional context, party culture, and leadership.

THE BIG PICTURE: SOCIALIST–COMMUNIST RELATIONS, 1920–2010

To recall Jospin's insight, the ability of the French Left to achieve power depends not only on their total electoral strength but also on the power balance between Socialists and Communists. What does the historical record tell us about the Left's capacity in this regard? The parties' performance in parliamentary elections is not the only measure of their power-gaining efficacy, but it is, prima facie, an important one, and it has the advantage of being a consistent and constant gauge of party strength over time. Figure 2.1 displays the vote percentages for Socialist and Communist candidates in all twenty-two parliamentary and constituent assembly elections between 1919 and 2007. This figure reveals two basic points. First, in less than one-quarter of these elections—a total of five (1945, 1978, 1981, 1988, and 1997)—did the Left as a whole (including smaller parties such as Trotskyist and Green parties) obtain a majority (or near majority) of votes. Moreover, in only two elections (1945 and 1981) did Socialist and Communist votes combined exceed 50 percent. The least one can say is that, for the Left, achieving political power defined as a majority vote in legislative elections has proven precarious and fleeting.

Second, the postwar period since 1945 has seen a dramatic reversal of Communist and Socialist fortunes. Coming out of its important and often heroic role in the Resistance, the Parti Comuniste Français (PCF) enjoyed enormous popularity; in the 1945, 1946, and 1951 elections, in fact, the party received more votes than any other party. Although its vote declined during the following decade, the Communists continued to attract over 20 percent of the vote throughout the 1960s and early 1970s. As table 2.1 indicates, in all ten elections between 1945 and 1973, the PCF outpolled the Socialists, often by margins of 10 percent or more. Beginning in the 1967 elections, however, the Communist advantage narrowed, and by 1973 its edge virtually disap-

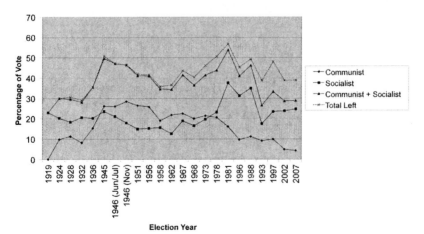

Figure 2.1.   Socialists, Communists, and the Left: French Legislative Elections, 1919–2007

peared. Just as significantly, the electoral system adopted by the Fifth Republic drastically disadvantaged the PCF to the Socialists' benefit in terms of
parliamentary representation. Beginning in 1958, even though the Communists consistently outpolled the Socialists in five successive elections, the
Socialists dominated the PCF in terms of the number of legislative seats (see
table 2.1).

The 1978 elections marked the first time since 1936 that the Socialists
bettered the Communists at the polls, and the Parti Socialiste (PS) has kept an
unassailable lead since then. Although the Socialists have been rather inconsistent performers—ranging between highs of over 30 percent in the 1980s to
an abysmal 17 percent in 1993—they have easily outpolled the PCF in all
eight of the post-1973 elections. As for the Communists, they have been in
fairly continuous free fall during the past three decades, plummeting from 21
percent in 1973 to slightly over 4 percent in 2007. The PCF now draws less
than one-fifth the number of votes as the Socialists. In the 2007 elections, the
PCF even failed to win the requisite twenty seats needed to form a parliamentary group.

Just as the two parties' vote totals have undergone great change over time,
so have their relations oscillated between cooperation and conflict. Jospin's
dictum regarding party parity notwithstanding, the history of Socialist–Communist relations shows no automatic correspondence between relative party strength and conflict/cooperation patterns. Clearly, other variables
besides party strength are also at play, the two most obvious being Soviet
policy (until 1990) and the impact of de Gaulle and the institution of the Fifth
Republic after 1958. On the most general level, an analysis of the full period
indicates an intriguing "parity" in cooperation-versus-conflict patterns as
measured by both the number of periods and the number of years in which
either pattern has dominated. As table 2.2 reveals, in the ninety-one years of
their coexistence between 1920 and 2010 (inclusive), there have been five
separate periods of conflictual relations totaling forty-three years and an
equal number of cooperative periods totaling forty-eight years.

The remainder of this chapter examines these periods in more depth, but
let us pause to comment on two contrasting patterns during the past six
decades, beginning in 1948. This postwar period can be divided evenly into
two thirty-year cycles. The first of these, 1948–1977, featured a long period
of conflict (the fourteen years between 1948 and 1961), followed by an even
longer period of growing cooperation (the sixteen years from 1962 through
1977). Broadly, these three decades correspond to the onset of the Cold War
and the Communists' isolation in the Fourth Republic, followed by the
"peaceful coexistence" thawing of East–West relations along with the establishment of the Fifth Republic under de Gaulle. Both long periods—of conflict and of cooperation—had a distinct and definite logic that tended to "lock
in" consistent behavior patterns on the part of the two parties. By contrast,

Table 2.1. The Left in France: Election Results (National Assembly, Lower House), 1919–2007

Year	Communist Party (PCF)	Socialist Party (SFIO–PS)	PCF vs. SFIO–PS
	% Vote (% Seats)	% Vote (% Seats)	% PCF Vote/ SFIO–PS Vote
			(% PCF Seats/% SFIO–PS Seats)
1919	—	21.2 (11.1)	—
1924	9.8 (4.5)	20.1 (17.9)	0.49 (0.25)
1928	11.3 (1.8)	18.1 (16.6)	0.62 (0.11)
1932	8.3 (1.7)	20.5 (21.8)	0.40 (0.08)
1936	15.3 (11.8)	19.9 (24.4)	0.77 (0.48)
1945	26.2 (27.5)	23.4 (25.6)	1.12 (1.07)
1946 (June)	25.9 (26.1)	21.1 (22.0)	1.23 (1.19)
1946 (November)	28.2 (29.6)	17.8 (17.0)	1.58 (1.74)
1951	26.9 (16.1)	14.6 (17.1)	1.84 (0.94)
1956	25.9 (25.2)	15.2 (16.6)	1.70 (1.52)
1958	19.2 (2.1)	15.7 (9.3)	1.22 (0.23)
1962	21.7 (8.5)	12.6 (13.7)	1.72 (0.62)
1967	22.5 (15.0)	19.0 (23.8)	1.18 (0.63)
1968	20.0 (7.0)	16.5 (11.7)	1.21 (0.60)
1973	21.4 (14.9)	20.8 (20.6)	1.03 (0.72)
1978	20.6 (17.5)	22.6 (21.2)	0.91 (0.83)
1981	16.2 (9.0)	37.5 (54.0)	0.43 (0.17)
1986	9.8 (5.9)	31.2 (34.6)	0.31 (0.17)
1988	11.3 (4.7)	37.0 (45.2)	0.31 (0.10)
1993	9.2 (4.0)	17.6 (9.4)	0.52 (0.43)
1997	9.9 (6.6)	23.5 (41.8)	0.42 (0.16)
2002	4.8 (3.6)	24.1 (24.4)	0.20 (0.15)
2007	4.3 (2.6)	24.7 (32.2)	0.17 (0.08)

Sources: 1919–1936: *France Politique* (http://www.france-politique.fr); 1945–2010: *Parties and Elections in Europe* (http://www.parties-and-elections.de).

**Table 2.2.   Socialist–Communist Relations in France: Conflict versus Coopera-
tion, 1920–2010**

Period	Conflict versus Cooperation	Number of Years
1920–1933	Conflict	14
1934–1938	Cooperation	5
1939–1941	Conflict	3
1942–1947	Cooperation	6
1948–1961	Conflict	14
1962–1977	Cooperation	16
1978–1980	Conflict	3
1981–1984	Cooperation	4
1985–1993	Conflict	9
1994–2010	Cooperation	17

Note: 91 total years (inclusive): conflict: 43 total years/five separate periods; cooperation:
48 total years/five separate periods.

the recent thirty-year period has seen less consistency and more volatility in
conflict/cooperation patterns, with two periods of conflict totaling twelve
years (1978–1980 and 1985–1993) and twenty-one years that can be generally described as cooperative (1981–1984 and 1994–2010).

What difference does being in power make in Socialist–Communist relations? A final consideration in this overview is the relationship between the
exercise of political power and patterns of interparty cooperation and conflict.[2] What is immediately apparent is that there is no clear relationship
between incumbency and relations between the PCF–Section Française de
l'Internationale Ouvrière (SFIO) and the PS. Periods in which at least one of
the parties has exercised power have featured both cooperation and conflict,
the best example being the Mitterrand years (1981–1995), when the two
parties initially cooperated (1981–1984), then clashed (1985–1993), and then
began cooperating again (1994–1995). The same back-and-forth pattern is
true of periods in which both parties have been out of power; for example,
during the first twenty-three years of the Fifth Republic (1958–1980), a
period dominated by Gaullists and their conservative allies, Socialists and
Communists initially opposed each other (1958–1961), then cooperated during the Left's "long march" toward unity (1962–1977), and finally broke
their alliance in 1977.[3] Obviously, the dynamics of being in the government
or the opposition do not drive the parties' decision to cooperate with or to
oppose each other. As we shall see, those determinants lie elsewhere.

HISTORICAL BACKGROUND, 1920–1958

The Socialist Party's 1920 congress in Tours may have provided the stage for the dramatic split between Socialists and Communists, but division on the French Left was nothing new. From the origins of a workers' movement in the 1830s, internal conflicts had robbed the movement of cohesion and unity. By the late nineteenth century, when new ideologies, such as Marxism, revolutionary syndicalism, and Bakunian anarchism, had gained adherents, one could count five socialist parties, ranging from revolutionaries to reformers (Noland 1956; Willard 1965; Wohl 1966). Out of these groups emerged two leaders, Jules Guesde and Jean Jaurès, who in many ways embodied polar tendencies within French Socialism that carried down through the twentieth century. Lichtheim (1966) remarks on these tendencies when he states that the socialist movement "was already born with the internal contradictions which subsequently propelled it along: the tension between patriotism and internationalism, between reform and revolution, between working-class solidarity and the claims of the national community (33).

Guesde (1845–1922), a man of "dogmatic" and "imperious" temperament who formed the Parti Ouvrier Français in 1882, preached an orthodox Marxism emphasizing "violent revolution, party discipline, and international revolution issuing out of war" (Wohl 1966, 4, 5, 15). In Guesde's early view, the inevitable uprising of the working class made any political activity that would support the democratic parliamentary system or work toward reforming capitalism unnecessary, irrelevant, and outright harmful to the cause. Such a stance put him at odds with Jaurès (1859–1914), whose Socialist vision embraced republicanism, democracy, and the possibility of incremental reforms that would gradually transform capitalism into Socialism. Not surprisingly, such competing visions of "what is to be done?" were common in pre-1914 European Socialist circles, so the Guesde–Jaurès dispute had its analogue in debates between Karl Kautsky and Eduard Bernstein in Germany and Enrico Ferri and Francesco Merlino in Italy and elsewhere (Berman 2006). Although Guesde and Jaurès eventually reconciled their differences and came together in 1905 to form the Unified Socialist Party (later renamed the SFIO), many of the same doctrinal differences surfaced after the 1920 split.

As mentioned in the introduction to this book, Lenin's decision in 1919 to self-ordain the Bolshevik Revolution as the model on which all socialists should base their efforts led directly to permanent splits within virtually every European socialist movement. According to Sassoon (1996), the famous "Twenty-One Conditions," which all loyal supporters of the revolution were to follow, came down to this: "Expel all reformists and centrists, accept the discipline which the new international organization will demand, support the Soviet Republic, be prepared for illegal political work and call yourselves communist" (32–33). Among socialists in most European countries, including Italy and Spain, these conditions were embraced by a minority of leaders, activists, and members. In France, however, a large majority of Socialist delegates, newly radicalized by the strikes and economic upheavals of the immediate postwar period, supported the call (Judt 1986, 123–24). On December 30, 1920, at a special congress in Tours, three-quarters of the delegates voted to affiliate with the Comintern and change the SFIO's name to Communist, a decision that prompted the minority of dissenting delegates to walk out and, in short order, reclaim the party name. Almost immediately, bitterness and recriminations poisoned the relationship between the two groups. Although Socialist leaders referred to the Communists as "enemy brothers" as if their split were a family affair, Communists denounced their supposed siblings as class enemies—supporters of the hated bourgeoisie (Bell and Criddle 1994a, 183).

The next fourteen years brought no improvement in the two parties' relations, which ranged, according to one scholar, "from veiled antagonism to overt hostility" (Raymond 2005, 24). For their part, the Communists gradually "Bolshevized" by 1924, adopting democratic centralism as its internal operating procedure and purging those considered too soft (including one of the initial Communist leaders, Oscar Frossard). More important for the long-term implications of Socialist–Communist relations, the party subordinated its domestic strategy to the cause of "proletarian internationalism" as defined by the Soviet Union. As Tiersky convincingly argues, "The *grands tournants* of French Communist history have unfailingly reflected changes in Soviet policy and attitudes" (Tiersky 1974, 371). Thus, in 1928, on orders from Stalin, the party adopted a "class-against-class" strategy calling for Communist parties to go all out for revolution and to isolate Socialists as "social fascists" (Tiersky 1974, 372; Raymond 2005, 29; Kowalski 2006, 157). By 1932, Communist leader Maurice Thorez was proclaiming, "If the working class wants to get rid of the bourgeoisie, it should first and foremost get rid of its principal social support, the Socialist Party" (quoted in Bell and Criddle 1994a, 176).

The Communists' divide-and-denounce approach failed to build the party, however. Membership declined from 118,000 in 1921 to 42,000 in 1933, while the party's vote share stagnated at around 10 percent in the legislative elections of 1924, 1928, and 1932 (Raymond 2005, 7–8; Ross 2006, 9; see also table 2.1). As for the Socialists, although the split cost the prewar SFIO about two-thirds of its assets and much of its radical Marxist Left, the party managed to regroup and perform creditably in the previously mentioned elections, gaining around 20 percent of the vote. The Communists could still exert leverage on the Socialists, however. Fearing Communist denunciations of selling out, the Socialists refused to join Radical-led governments (even while supporting such governments from the sidelines) (Bell and Criddle

1994a, 169). The result was that by the early 1930s, the French Left, now split into two well-organized camps, was strong enough to gain nearly one-third of the total vote, yet its political influence was weakened by internal conflicts.

This dynamic changed suddenly in 1934 when, on orders from the Comintern, the Communists called for a "popular front" with the SFIO, along with the center-left Radicals and Socialist Republicans, in order to fight the growing threat of Fascism throughout Europe. No matter that the PCF's overnight shift smacked of opportunism and foreign direction, it proved a popular move. The PCF abandoned its sectarianism even within the realm that it considered privileged territory: the labor movement. In the early 1920s, the PCF had established its own "transmission belt" within the working class, the General Confederation of Unified Labor (Confédération Générale du Travail Unitaire [CGTU]). Whereas the main labor confederation, the Confédération Générale du Travail (CGT), had long rejected any political affiliation, the CGTU had sought to politicize strikes and promote the goals of the PCF within the workers' movement. For fifteen years, during the 1920s and early 1930s, these two organizations vied for leadership among militant sectors of both craft trades and the rapidly growing ranks of industrial workers.[4] With the new directive to promote unity within all forces on the Left, the CGTU's Communist leadership worked toward an eventual merger with the CGT that occurred in 1936.

This charm offensive by the Communists to unite the Left paid off handsomely. In the 1936 elections, the PCF nearly doubled its vote share over the previous elections—from 8.2 to 15.3 percent—and, more important, increased its number of parliamentary seats from eleven to seventy-two. The Socialists continued to hold their own in the 1936 elections with over 20 percent and with 142 seats remained the largest bloc within the Left. Altogether, the Left parties—including the Socialists, Communists, and the center-left Radicals—held two-thirds of the National Assembly seats, and for the first time a Socialist, Léon Blum, became prime minister in May 1936. Although the Communists declined Blum's invitation to join the government, they vowed to support it.

Despite the promise of Left unity, the Blum government foundered within a year amid labor unrest, economic crisis, and the growing threat of Nazism. The Socialist-led government followed through on popular worker-friendly measures, such as restoring pensions (which had been cut) and instituting a forty-hour workweek and four weeks of annual vacation, but these steps exacerbated existing problems of inflation, lagging productivity, and budget deficits. After just fourteen months marked by strikes and worsening economic conditions, the Blum government was forced to resign in June 1937.

Historians have long debated the Communists' ambiguous role in this ill-fated government.[5] For much of the period, the PCF played a classic inside–outside game. On the inside, within parliament, Communist deputies voted for the governments' measures and never broke with the government. On the outside, however, the party sought to maintain a certain level of social unrest in order to burnish its revolutionary credentials. The ambivalence of the PCF's stance is perfectly captured by this statement by a Communist official that appeared in *L'Humanité*, the party's newspaper: "At the side of the government of the Left, supporting it, assuring its stability, [the Communists] will exercise from outside a sort of ministry of the masses, with the participation of the most ardent and most disciplined members of the Popular Front" (May 12, 1936, quoted in Tiersky 1974, 83).

What is not ambiguous is the positive impact of the PCF's strategy on the party's fortunes, for the Popular Front gave the party a significant parliamentary presence, a massive influx of supporters (party membership grew from 28,000 in 1933 to more than 300,000 in 1937), and a firm base within the working class and the labor movement. Most important, no matter how two-faced in its execution, the Popular Front strategy enabled the party to assert a plausible claim as a defender of French republicanism, thereby countering its critics who accused the party of being the stalking horse of the Soviets (Hazareesingh 1994, 297). This experience did not mean that the Communists had forever renounced revolution in favor of reformism, but it implied to most observers that the party henceforth would pursue its long-term strategy—however that might be defined by the Soviet Union or by the party itself—as a supporter of French national interests.

All the PCF's gains during the 1934–1938 period—not to mention the fragile sense of left-wing unity developed during the Popular Front—were undermined by the machinations of the major powers as they prepared for war. Specifically, the August 1939 Nazi–Soviet Non-Aggression Pact instantly turned Communist parties everywhere into defenders of Soviet appeasement toward Hitler. For the PCF, this meant a direct repudiation of the anti-Fascist strategy that it had been preaching for the previous five years. Moreover, given growing tensions between the Hitler regime and France, this shift made the PCF suddenly appear treasonous, and indeed the conservative Daladier government quickly outlawed the party. Needless to say, any inclination on the part of Socialists to deepen an alliance with the Communists evaporated, while the pro-Nazi tilt met with great resistance within the PCF itself. Even the French defeat and occupation by the Germans in June 1940 did not force a change in the official PCF line of support for the Soviet Union's neutral policy in relation to Nazi aggression. Only Hitler's invasion of the Soviet Union in June 1941 caused a shift in the PCF's strategy, and it then joined the Resistance that was already well under way under de Gaulle's leadership.

The next seven years—the years from 1941 to 1947 that were framed by the Resistance, the Liberation, and the postwar reorganization into the Fourth

Republic—brought a renewal of the popular-front style of cooperation between the Communists and Socialists. Joining forces in the maquis to fight German occupation forces and the puppet Vichy regime on home ground, activists of the two main Left parties joined with followers of de Gaulle and an emerging Catholic nucleus around Georges Bidault to form the National Council of the Resistance. Working effectively and often heroically together, Socialists and Communists helped organize a potent anti-Nazi movement that became the basis for a new government following the Liberation in August 1944. Such was the level of cooperation between the two parties that the SFIO even seriously proposed a merger, or "organic unity," of the two organizations. Although this initiative met with little interest on the PCF's part, the parties collaborated, along with Bidault's newly formed Church-inspired Popular Republican Movement (Mouvement Républicain Populaire), in a tripartite government that ushered through a new Fourth Republic constitution and then tackled the challenges of economic recovery and the colonial crisis in Indochina.

It would be difficult to exaggerate the importance of the Resistance and Liberation periods for the long-term prospects of the Communist Party and indeed the Left in general. Two main points are to be underlined. First, both Communists and Socialists emerged from the wartime experience with enhanced popularity. As can be seen in table 2.1, the two parties' combined vote percentage jumped from 35 percent in the 1936 elections to 49 percent in the first postwar elections in 1945. At least in the short run, the Left profited greatly from a sea change in public perception. Whereas the old conservative elite had disgraced itself by collaborating with the Germans, a young generation of Communists and Socialists had actively fought against the Nazis. Second, while both parties gained in popular standing, the PCF did so even more than the SFIO. The 1945 election marked a watershed in the two parties' relative position. For the first time since the 1920 *scission*, the PCF was now the stronger of the two parties, an advantage that the Communists would hold for the next three decades.

The Socialist–Communist entente, forged in war and maintained in the need to fill the postwar political vacuum, finally came unglued as a casualty of the Cold War in the spring of 1947. To be sure, there were already policy tensions within the tripartite government, but with growing American pressure on moderates within the government to isolate the Communists, coupled with corresponding Soviet pressure on the PCF to counter American influence, the fragile alliance of Christian Democrats, Socialists, and Communists could no longer hold. The precipitating event was a strike for higher pay by Renault workers in April 1947. Although the government had agreed to keep wages blocked until later in the year, PCF leader and vice prime minister Maurice Thorez declared his support for the workers and refused to endorse the government's economic policy. This blatant lack of solidarity eventually led Socialist prime minister Paul Ramadier to dismiss the Communists from the government. From that moment on for the next fifteen years, Socialist–Communist relations reverted to the initial pattern of mutual hostility. The outright Manichaeism of the Cold War was perfectly captured in Thorez's declaration: "There could only be two parties in France, the 'American' party stretching from the Socialists to the Gaullists and the party that refused to submit to the domination of American capitalism" (quoted in Raymond 2005, 22).

The hardened lines between Socialists and Communists continued throughout the dozen years of the Fourth Republic (1946–1958). With Socialists participating regularly in various musical-chairs governments while Communists were permanently ostracized, cooperation and even dialogue between the two parties were largely nonexistent. The main battleground between them took place within the labor movement. The Communists' relationship with the largest confederation, the CGT, during the 1920–1947 period had been uneasy, especially given the CGT's traditional disdain for politics and political affiliation. It will be recalled that, after 1920, the newly formed PCF, desiring an organizational base in the labor movement, had formed its own competing federation, the CGTU. Also recall that during the Popular Front, the Communists had merged the CGTU into the CGT. Following the Hitler–Stalin pact, however, Communist leaders were expelled from the CGT, but by the end of World War II, they were allowed to rejoin. By 1947, the Communists had succeeded in gaining control over the CGT, a power grab that prompted anti-Communists within the confederation (with encouragement from the Central Intelligence Agency) to split off and form a competing organization, Confédération Générale du Travail-Force Ouvrière (usually referred to as simply the FO). Although the FO was officially politically independent, many of its leaders were SFIO supporters. Thus, Communist–Socialist competition during the Fourth Republic found expression in the workplace as well as at the ballot box.

In both of these arenas, the Communists developed a formidable advantage despite (or perhaps because of) its political isolation. Indeed, in retrospect, the 1950s were the golden era for the PCF. In the electoral arena, the party's "heroic" role in the Resistance vastly increased its following, especially in rural areas where the Resistance had been strong (Raymond 2005, 22). As table 2.1 indicates, in all five of the major elections between 1945 and 1956, the Communists outpolled the SFIO, averaging 26.6 percent to the Socialists' 18.5 percent. Moreover, the PCF was remarkably consistent in holding onto one-fourth of the electorate, whereas the Socialists slipped from a high of 23.4 percent in 1945 to 15.2 percent in 1956. The SFIO lost much of its working-class base to the Communists, becoming increasingly a party with a shrinking base in small rural towns (Johnson 1981, 143). In terms of membership and activism, the differences were even starker. It can be fairly said that during the 1950s, the PCF rode the wave of France's "Fordist" modernization, as firms in burgeoning basic industries such as steel and automobiles recruited unskilled and semiskilled workers who became the recruiting base for the PCF and the CGT. The Communist Party came to constitute a "counter-society" (Courtois and Lazar 2000, 293–99). As Pierre Nora (1996) remarks,

> French Communism was a closed, self-sufficient world, with its local roots, its deeply ingrained customs and souvenirs, its rites, its codes, its traditions, its symbols, its language, its repetitive rhythms, its liturgy of the quotidian, its mental reflexes, its celebrations, and its key sites. . . . Its principle was the principle of happiness: a history in which nothing happens, a suspension of time, a reality of unrivaled intensity sheltered from all other realities. (221–22)

Scholars have noted a paradox in the Communist Party's impact on French society and politics and society during the early postwar boom. On the one hand, the party, deep in its practice of "militant autonomy" (Ross 1992, 47), was often a force of instability in an already fragmented political system. Within parliament, Communist deputies "were always available to overthrow governments but never to install new ones" (Wilson 2002, 264). Outside parliament, in the streets and the factories, the PCF and CGT sought to maintain a high level of antisystem mobilization through strikes and demonstrations, all the while exhibiting extreme ideological rigidity (Ross 1982, 49–82). For example, party leader Maurice Thorez continued to denounce the "pauperization" of the working class even as living standards steadily climbed. On the other hand, despite its isolation, the party also performed an integrative, system-legitimizing role. Most notably, the PCF served as an instrument of working-class integration (Lavau 1981b; Schain 1990). In a nation in which the working class had historically been comparatively small, fragmented, radicalized, and politically excluded, the Communist Party "offered workers a kind of alternative community in which they felt valued and empowered: it made them into citizens" (Sa'adah 2003, 115).

TOWARD UNION OF THE LEFT, 1958–1978

The year 1958 is a monumental date in twentieth-century French history because it brought an end to the unstable and ineffectual Fourth Republic and the birth of what has proven to be France's most successful political regime, the Fifth Republic. Along with these institutional changes came a new political dynamic that continues to structure the nation's political life down to the present. The central element—the fulfillment of de Gaulle's political dream—was the creation of a strong executive: a political sun around which parliaments and parties were expected to orbit. This innovation—in effect, a reversion back to more monarchial times—posed a fundamental challenge to all the existing parties, but especially to the Socialists and Communists, as the two parties sought to work out a new political logic based on the "presidentialization" of the political system.

The new constitutional order was not the only change in the political environment that affected the two parties beginning in the late 1950s. Two others were especially important. One was the easing of the Cold War, as Khrushchev, seeking to distance himself from the Stalinist legacy, announced a new era of peaceful coexistence with the United States and the West. At a minimum, such a policy implied that the Soviet Union would stop seeking to sow disruption and instability in such targets of opportunity as France. (In any case, it quickly became apparent that, as a counterweight to American influence in Europe, President de Gaulle would do just fine.) Within the French context, given the Soviets' influence on the PCF, peaceful coexistence translated into the Communists seeking to improve their relations with the Socialists.

A second key change was France's postwar economic recovery, which was in full takeoff mode by late 1950. The country's modernization was bringing urbanization, consumerism, secularization, mass higher education, and increased class mobility—in essence, a host of social changes that were not only altering patterns of class formation, religious practice, and the like but also creating new values and expectations that France was becoming more educated, less religious, more urban, and more middle class. Although the precise impact of these changes on politics was unclear, the least one could say was that they tended to undermine conventional political loyalties (Fourastié 1979; Berstein 1989; Mendras and Cole 1991).

Taken together, these shifts of the late 1950s—the presidentialization of politics, the easing of the Cold War stalemate, and socioeconomic modernization—created a new set of challenges and opportunities for all political parties. In terms of the Left parties' responses to these shifts, the Communists reacted first, but the Socialists reacted most effectively. The story of the two decades following 1958 is one of growing unity between the two parties accompanied by electoral progress; however, that progress occurred on terms that systematically favored the Socialists over the Communists. Jospin's post hoc reflection that "if the Socialist Party is regarded by the Communist Party as being too strong, then it will be opposed to the success of the Union" perfectly captures the dynamic that eventually produced the union's implosion in 1977.

The PCF responded early on to the new political reality. In an effort to counter de Gaulle's and the conservatives' domination of the political arena by the early 1960s, the party began seeking to ally with the Socialists in local and national elections. The main mechanism was a policy of "*désistement*," or standing down in runoff elections. The driver of this policy was France's voting system for parliamentary elections, which can be described as a single-member district system with a runoff provision (technically termed *scrutin majoritaire uninominal à deux tours*). In the typical pattern in this "new–old" electoral system,[6] parties could run candidates in single-member electoral districts. If a candidate gained a majority of the vote, he or she would win the seat outright. If no candidate won a majority, the election would proceed to a runoff round, with eligibility limited to candidates who had received a minimum percentage (initially 15 percent but later changed to 12.5 percent) in the first round. In practice, most contests—on average about 85 to 90 percent—proceeded to a runoff. This system had both an express purpose and an operational logic. The former was to marginalize smaller parties, especially those on the left and right extremes, who could not clear the eligibility bar to contest the runoffs; the latter was to encourage like-minded parties to combine their votes at the second round so as to maximize the chances of winning the seat.

Accordingly, the Communists initiated, in the 1962 legislative elections, a practice of standing down ("desisting") in the second round in favor of Socialist candidates who had outperformed the Communists in the first round. The PCF also proposed that the two parties craft a "common governmental program of democratic unity," but the SFIO majority controlled by party leader Guy Mollet rebuffed the proposal (Lavau 1981b, 151). To carry cooperation a step further, for the 1965 presidential election, the Communists threw their support behind François Mitterrand, who at that time headed a small center-left party, the Convention des Institutions Républicaines. By the mid-1960s, then, the Communists had clearly opted for an inclusive alliance strategy with Socialists and their sympathizers. Underlying this strategy was the PCF's determination to play the "vanguard" and controlling role in a broad anti-Gaullist movement.

Such a strategy appeared sound given the strength of de Gaulle and his movement, but the Communists failed to come to grips with a simple fact: the big political prize in the new Fifth Republic was now the presidency, not parliament, as in the Third and Fourth Republics. Thus, any political party aspiring to power needed to have its own *"présidentiable"*—a leader who would make a plausible presidential candidate. In this context, the PCF's fatal handicap was that the bureaucratic party machine, with its organizational impulse to squelch any "cult of personality" tendencies, was incapable of producing such a candidate. On the other hand, François Mitterrand, an enigmatic independent socialist who had served in eleven Fourth Republic governments, emerged in the 1965 presidential election as just such a leader. Mitterrand shocked the political establishment by forcing de Gaulle into a humiliating runoff and then garnering a respectable 46 percent in a direct face-off with the incumbent.

From that point on, Mitterrand displayed, more clearly than anyone on the Left, an understanding of how to achieve power. The key was to build a political coalition that could bear him to the presidency. Such a coalition had to meet three conditions: 1) it had to be led by a rejuvenated, restructured Socialist Party; 2) the coalition had to include the Communist Party; and 3) in order to attract the Communists, the coalition had to have a distinctly left-leaning program. During the decade following the 1965 election, despite some missteps and setbacks, Mitterrand managed to assemble such a coalition.

In terms of the first condition just mentioned, Mitterrand's strategy was to rebuild the non-Communist Left not around the increasingly moribund SFIO but rather around a new structure in which Mitterrand himself would serve as power broker and standard-bearer. In a series of complex maneuvers extending over the period 1969–1974, Mitterrand succeeded in taking control of a reorganized SFIO—now rebaptized the PS—and then incorporating other smaller parties, notably Michel Rocard's "New Left" Parti Socialiste Unifié.[7] Central to understanding this "new" Socialist Party is the fact that Mitterrand's position within the party was more akin to a shepherd than a king. From the beginning, as an outsider effecting what many old SFIO members regarded as a hostile takeover, Mitterrand had to herd a variety of factions, or *courants*, that competed to promote their own leaders and policy preferences. Factional representation, in fact, was built into the party's statutes.[8] Four major factions competed for influence: a left-leaning, pro-PCF faction led by the CERES group; a right-leaning, promarket faction headed by the previously mentioned Rocard; a so-called Social Democratic faction led by regional leaders Pierre Mauroy of the Nord federation and Gaston Deferre of the Bouches-du-Rhône federation; and, finally, Mitterrand's own faction (Charzat et al. 1975; Hamon and Rotman 1980, 1982; Hanley 1986). Although Mitterrand was the unchallenged party leader and his faction was always the linchpin of any leadership majority, "the Florentine," as the wily Mitterrand was often called, always had the difficult task of placating and balancing these contending factions.

The second and third conditions of Mitterrand's presidential coalition strategy involved building an alliance with the Communist Party that had both an electoral and a programmatic component. To complement the systematic practice of *désistement* and mutual support in legislative elections (and, of course, the recognition of Mitterrand as the Left's sole candidate in presidential contests), the two parties would craft a "common program" for governing the country. Such a program, in Mitterrand's vision, needed to be unambiguously "leftist" in orientation. To mobilize the base of both parties, the program had to promise some classic Left reforms, such as new social programs and nationalizations of several large corporations. Mitterrand's intention was not only to attract the Communist *Party* into a beneficial alliance but ultimately to attract Communist *voters* to the Socialist camp. On this point, Mitterrand was clear: "Our fundamental objective is to rebuild a great socialist party on the terrain occupied by the Communist Party itself, and thus to show that of the five million Communist voters, three million can be brought to vote socialist" (quoted in Johnson 1981, 170). As for the Communists, although their leaders expressed misgivings over Mitterrand's blatant ambitions, they also believed that the PCF could largely move the alliance in their direction in terms of program and long-term advantage, especially in terms of expanding the PCF's electorate beyond the shrinking base of industrial workers (Bergounioux and Grunberg 2005, 264). With their interests apparently converging, the two parties agreed on a "Common Program of Government" in June 1972, along with a formal electoral pact providing for mutual support. Thus was born the Union of the Left.

The first test run of the Union of the Left came the following year, with promising results. In 1973 legislative elections, with systematic *désistements* taking place in all electoral districts, both parties boosted their overall vote percentages over the previous election in 1968, with the PCF's 21.4 percent slightly bettering the Socialists' 19.7 percent. In presidential elections a year later, Mitterrand ran with PCF support as the sole Left candidate and only narrowly lost to Giscard d'Estaing. Ominous indicators, however, soon emerged as it became clear that the alliance was working systematically to the Socialists' advantage and that if those trends continued, the Communists would find themselves a trailing junior partner. For one thing, Mitterrand and the Socialists were benefiting from the image of a modern, dynamic, but still resolutely left-wing party that the "new" PS projected. This positive image had a tonic effect on the party's organization, as membership nearly doubled, from 70,000 to 137,000 members between 1970 and 1974 (Bergounioux and Grunberg 2005, 402). Moreover, the economic crisis precipitated by the 1973 oil shock hastened the "deproletarianization" already well under way, further eroding the PCF's natural voter base within the industrial working class. Finally, in elections themselves, a combination of Communist discipline and Socialist defection worked to hobble the PCF's performance. Throughout a series of national, regional, and local elections between 1972 and 1977, Communist voters supported the electoral pact more consistently than did the Socialists. In runoff elections where a Socialist remained as the Left's sole candidate, about 90 percent of first-round PCF voters supported the Socialist candidate. By contrast, Communist candidates in runoff situations garnered the vote of just two-thirds of first-round Socialist electors (Cayrol 1978a, 54; Johnson 1981, 222). Needless to say, Communists became increasingly disillusioned with the direction in which the Union of the Left was taking their party.

By the mid-1970s, then, the PS and PCF were on diverging paths. On the one hand, the Socialists under Mitterrand had emerged, in only five years, as a potent force. The PS had become a true "catchall" party in that its voters closely resembled the profile of the electorate as a whole. Unlike the SFIO of the early 1960s, which had its strongest roots in the anticlerical petit bourgeois classes in rural and small-town areas of the south, the PS had become a multiclass party with broad geographic strength. One important factor in this evolution was the decline of Gaullism, which had rivaled the PCF in appealing to industrial workers. With the sudden retirement of President de Gaulle himself in 1969 followed by the untimely death of his Gaullist successor, Georges Pompidou in 1974, the Gaullist party lost its attraction to many working-class voters, who moved increasingly to Left parties, especially the Socialists (Johnson 1981, 100). Moreover, the PS was attracting voters among some of France's fastest-growing occupational groups, including liberal professionals, middle- and upper-level managers, small business owners, and office workers. By the late 1970s, these groups constituted 37 percent of the labor force and an equal percentage of PS voters (Smith 1998, 58–59). Finally, in terms of the geography of Socialist support, the party not only held on to its traditional southern base but also drew new voters in the strongly Catholic eastern and western regions. Overall, the party's support across age-groups, socioeconomic groups, and gender groups came to reflect the composition of France's changing national population (Judt 1986, 265–66; Bell and Criddle 1988, 197).

In only one respect was the PS's development problematic from the standpoint of a party seeking to lead the Left. Despite its growing ability to attract working-class voters, the Socialist Party remained notably elitist with only tenuous organizational ties to the working class. To be sure, the party's largely middle-class ethos was nothing new; since the early 1950s, the industrial working class and the largest union confederation, the CGT, had been largely the preserve of the Communist Party. But the PS under Mitterrand failed to reverse this pattern in two major respects. First, within the PS itself, the party hierarchy reflected the social hierarchy: the higher the level in the party hierarchy, the higher the socioeconomic status. For example, whereas only 9 percent of Socialist voters were upper-level professionals (*cadres supérieurs*), over 40 percent of the party's delegates (to party congresses) came from this stratum. By contrast, whereas blue-collar workers made up nearly one-quarter of Socialist voters, this group constituted just 2 percent of party delegates (Rey and Subileau 1991, 76).

Second, the PS failed to develop close ties to organized labor. Although about two-thirds of Socialist members were union members, their memberships were scattered across various industrial confederations as well as the main teachers' union, the National Education Federation (Fédération d'Education Nationale) (Cayrol 1974, 937; Portelli 1980, 186–87). As far as the major confederations—the CGT, CFDT, and FO—the Socialists had no formal links with any of them. Socialists typically held one or two seats on the Communist-led CGT's top decision-making body, the Bureau Confédéral, but their presence was mainly symbolic. The second-largest union, the CFDT, had the largest number of Socialist members and was the closest to the PS ideologically, but its leader, Edmond Maire, got along poorly with Mitterrand, while the third largest, the FO, resolutely maintained its political independence. Although the Socialists vowed that "the first task of a Left government will be to organize the effective power of workers in the firm," their ability to do so, given an elitist organizational structure and weak ties with organized labor, was limited (Cayrol 1978b, 296). According to one observer, the Socialist Party represented "socialism without the workers" (Kesselman 1983).

As for the Communists, the problem was not so much having a weak working-class base but having *little else but* a working-class base. The PCF throughout the 1970s could credibly claim its self-assigned role of "tribune" of the working class—the mouthpiece and defender of the less fortunate—but its identity was largely that of a party defending this particular group rather than a party capable of attracting a wide range of voters and governing in the general interest of all the French (Johnson 1981, 152). Moreover, as mentioned earlier, "postindustrial" trends were generating job growth in occupations not traditionally favorable to Communist appeals: office workers, technically trained professionals (technicians, engineers, and so on), service sector workers, and the like. Thus, the party's core electorate was a shrinking asset, and the PCF demonstrated a limited ability to expand beyond it.

At least two other major problems hampered the Communists' ability to compete on an equal footing with the Socialists. One was the poor image of party leadership, specifically that of the general secretary, Georges Marchais. As the Union of the Left proceeded in the 1970s, Mitterrand's wager that the PCF would fail to put forward a credible *présidentiable* proved prescient. Mitterrand himself expressed disdain for the Communist leaders: "My great luck is the intellectual mediocrity of the Communist leaders. Look at them: Marchais, Plissonier, Laurent, and the others. Not one of them is better than the others. All their reactions are predictable. They're programmed. If I had to deal with leaders like the Italian Communists, things would have been much more difficult" (quoted in Tiersky 2000, 115).[9] Although Marchais's brusque, proletarian style played well with many working-class voters, on television he came across as bombastic, angry, and defensive, and his popularity rating remained the lowest of all major French politicians.

A second problem derived from the PCF's "solidarity" with the Soviet Union, for that association proved increasingly negative in French public opinion. The Czech invasion of 1968 and the 1973 publication of Aleksandr Solzhenitsyn's *The Gulag Archipelago* sparked widespread revulsion against the Soviet system, which in turn tarnished the PCF's image. Ironically, the high period of Left unity—a strategy designed to make the Communists more popular—produced a decline in the PCF's overall image.[10]

In an attempt to create a more positive public image that would complement its Union of the Left alliance strategy, the PCF experimented for a brief time in the mid-1970s with "Eurocommunism," a more open and independent version of Communism being pushed by Enrico Berlinguer and Santiago Carrillo, leaders, respectively, of the Italian and Spanish Communists. At the time, as we shall see in the following chapters, the Italian Communist Party was seeking a "historic compromise" with the center-right Christian Democrats, and the Spanish party was strongly backing its nation's post-Franco democratic transition. In both cases, Eurocommunism implied a commitment to building long-term alliances with other democratic parties, be they centrist or leftist in orientation. Eurocommunism also recognized that "the path to socialism" was not a single road defined by Moscow but rather a process that accorded with specific national conditions (Hobsbawm and Napolitano 1977; Boggs and Plotke 1980). Obviously, the PCF's Union of the Left strategy was in line with the Eurocommunist approach, but the PCF tried to go farther. Thus, between 1975 and 1977, the PCF took several steps to distance itself from the Soviet Union, including public criticism of the latter's treatment of dissidents. In its Twenty-Second Congress in 1976, the party also abandoned the concept of the "dictatorship of the proletariat," thereby asserting a "Socialism in French Colors" (the official slogan of the congress) not beholden to Soviet orthodoxy. Finally, the PCF participated in a high-profile Eurocommunist summit with Italian and Spanish Communist leaders in March 1977 (Ross 1992, 49; Bell and Criddle 1994a, 103–4). Despite these measures to create a distinct "national" Communist identity, the question remained how genuine the PCF's conversion really was.

By March 1978, the answer was clear: the PCF's more open, alliance-oriented strategy was only temporary. It came down to this: the strategy of openness and alliance building had not produced the electoral results expected, and rather than gain victory and serve as a secondary partner in a Socialist-led government, the Communists preferred to terminate the alliance. Municipal elections in March 1977—ironically the same month that the PCF was touting its newfound Eurocommunist line—proved decisive in the PCF's decision. Although the Left overall did well in those elections—amassing over half the vote and gaining control of 155 of the 221 towns and cities with a population of at least 30,000—the Socialists outperformed the Communists. Polls suggested that in the legislative elections to be held a year hence, the Socialists would likely poll around 30 percent versus the PCF's 20 percent. Johnson (1981) remarks, "The Communists had huffed and puffed but the Socialist house showed not the remotest sign of falling down; rather the reverse, in fact" (182).

From that point on, the Communists took a hostile and confrontational approach with the Socialists. The two parties met during the summer of 1977 to "update" the Common Program in view of upcoming parliamentary elections in March 1978, but the parties failed to resolve some major policy differences, notably over the scope of nationalizations to be carried out. Finally, in September 1977, the parties announced that the Common Program was dead. The two parties would continue to practice *désistement* in the runoff ballots in the legislative elections, but in effect, the formal alliance was finished. Socialist leaders claimed that the Communists pushed extremist positions in order to force the Socialists to say no, whereas PCF officials denounced the PS's betrayal and moderation.

With the alliance in tatters, the Left went to the polls already defeated, and the results ratified their loss. From a clear majority of votes in municipal elections just a year before, the combined PS–PCF total was only 44 percent. The Communists, with 20.6 percent, fell from their 1973 total by nearly a percentage point. The Socialists fared better, improving from 19.7 percent in 1973 to 23.2 percent. In the aftermath of these elections, when the Left seemed to have snatched proverbial defeat from the jaws of victory, it was clear that the Mitterrand strategy had worked only too well. It had certainly rebuilt and revivified the Socialist Party, and it had done so by first attracting and then siphoning off Communist voters. The Socialist Party itself, now France's largest party, appeared capable of bearing its leader to the presidency. But the conditions of Socialist dominance served to undermine the unity of the Left and thus ensure that the Left had no solid majority. Whether Mitterrand, once elected as president, would be able to amass and govern with a parliamentary majority appeared unlikely.

FULL CIRCLE: FROM CONFLICT TO COOPERATION TO CONFLICT, 1978–1984

During the next six years, the PS and PCF maintained the same electoral trajectories put in motion by the Union of the Left. On the one hand, the Socialists continued to advance, with Mitterrand winning the presidency in 1981, quickly followed by the Socialist Party gaining a majority of legislative seats. On the other hand, the Communist Party's decline accelerated, falling in the 1981 elections to its lowest point in the postwar period. In this sense, the period 1978–1984 is one of continuity. What changed during this period was not only the fact of the Left's coming to power for the first time in the Fifth Republic's twenty-three-year history but also a bewildering "full-circle" alternation in Socialist–Communist relations. During six short years, the parties went from a period of mutual recriminations and hostility (1978–1981) to an interregnum of cooperation under the early Mitterrand–Socialist government (1981–1984) to an acrimonious rupture during the summer of 1984.

The events of 1977–1978 that produced the breakdown of the Union of the Left had a dual effect on the PCF. On the one hand, the party's leadership grouped around Georges Marchais pulled back into what might be termed "orthodox" mode. The party hardened its rhetoric toward the PS, denouncing Mitterrand and the perfidious Socialists at every turn. For three years, between the disappointing parliamentary elections of May 1978 and the presidential election of May 1981, there were virtually no official contacts between leaders of the two parties. Not only did Marchais challenge Mitterrand (unsuccessfully) in the first round of the 1981 election, but he gave, at best, lukewarm support to Mitterrand in the runoff ballot with conservative incumbent Valéry Giscard d'Estaing (see below). "Orthodoxy" also returned in terms of the PCF's relationship with the Soviet Union, as the party supported various Soviet policies, including its 1979 invasion of Afghanistan.

On the other hand, the disaster of 1977–1978 produced a backlash against the PCF's leadership from dissident elements in the party. To some extent, this was chickens coming home to roost since the party had earlier vaunted its "Eurocommunist" openness and diversity. Almost immediately after the 1978 elections, a chorus of dissidents came forward to denounce the leadership's rigidity and failure to reform. Chief among them were intellectuals Louis Althusser and Jean Ellenstein, who published articles in *Le Monde*. The following year, Henri Fiszbin resigned in protest from the Central Committee and was later expelled from the party (Raymond 2005, 97–98). Disagreement was not just an affair of intellectuals and some top leaders; disaffection and dismay reverberated throughout all levels of the party as grassroots leaders questioned why the party had suddenly abandoned its Eurocommunist promises (Jenson and Ross 1984). These were just the first of several revolts within the PCF that took place throughout the late 1970s and the 1980s (Hazareesingh 1991).

The breakup of the Union of the Left was not without repercussions on the Socialist Party as well. Despite the PS's respectable showing in the 1978 elections, many activists and leaders felt that the Mitterrand strategy had failed in the most important respect: producing a united Left majority victory. As in the case of the PCF, the PS's own critics quickly surfaced. The loudest was Michel Rocard, the former leader of the Unified Socialist Party, who looked with disdain on the Communists and, indeed, on the *étatiste* leanings of the Common Program. Challenging Mitterrand indirectly, Rocard brashly declared that he would stand for president as the PS's candidate in the event that Mitterrand decided not to run. He also intimated that Mitterrand was too old and out of touch to lead the party any longer. This leadership fight culminated at the Metz congress in 1979 when Mitterrand successfully isolated Rocard by forming an alliance with the left-pulling and

pro–Union of the Left *courant* CERES. With the CERES now joining Mitterrand and his supporters as the official party leadership, the PS continued to
hew to the "unity" line, even in the absence of a partner. Even though the
PCF was now going its own way, the Socialists claimed that they would
remain committed to the particulars of the Common Program and would
practice "unity for two."

As mutual recriminations between Socialists and Communists played out
in party circles in the late 1970s and early 1980s, an analogous struggle took
place within the Left parties' allies in the labor movement. As mentioned, the
largest confederation, the CGT, had close ties to the Communist Party, and as
part of the broad Union of the Left strategy, the CGT had been directed by
the party to practice "unity of action" with the other major confederation that
had a generally leftist orientation, the CFDT. Although there were misgivings on both sides, especially at the plant level, the two confederations maintained generally cordial relations and signed several formal "unity pacts"
during the 1970s. The breakup of the Union of the Left had a direct and
immediate negative effect on relations between these two confederations.

The CGT officially backed the PCF position of accusing the PS of "betrayal" of the Union, but disappointment with the breakup was so great at the
grassroots that several leaders began calling for the CGT to distance itself
from the PCF and to focus on strictly trade union concerns instead of politics.
Thus, internal dissent within the CGT paralleled that arising within the PCF.
The eventual result was that the pro-PCF "hard-liners" in the CGT won this
internal struggle, meaning that continued unity of action with the CFDT was
impossible (Mouriaux 1982; Labbé and Andolfatto 1997). As for the CFDT,
the union began to engage in a severe "*auto-critique*," with leader Edmond
Maire claiming that the confederation had focused too heavily on an electoral
victory by the Left and not enough on concrete workplace issues. The result
was a "recentering" of CFDT strategy on workers' everyday concerns, with
collective bargaining playing a central role. For the CGT, this turn in the
CFDT's strategy represented "class collaboration" and thus an end to further
cooperation (Groux and Mouriaux 1989).

These interorganizational fights were just the background, however, for a
more fundamental challenge to the labor movement: a dramatic drop in union
membership that became evident in the late 1970s. Although union "density"
(the proportion of the eligible workforce that is unionized) in France has
usually been low by Western European standards, all the major confederations saw their rolls drop by as much as one-quarter to one-third in just three
or four years. Part of the problem owed to the post-1973 stagflation that
produced a fivefold increase in unemployment—from 400,000 to
2,000,000—between 1973 and 1980. Not only were many erstwhile union
members no longer employed, but the employment crisis had a dampening
effect on workers' willingness to join unions in the first place. Technological

changes also played a role, with blue-collar jobs—the core occupations of traditional industrial unions—being gradually replaced by white-collar positions. Finally, a contributing factor in the membership drop was a certain loss of trust in the unions' capacity to defend their interests. For many workers, the major unions had indeed become too politicized (Gallie 1983; Mouriaux 1983).

Thus, the presidential elections of 1981 took place in a context of division, demoralization, and demobilization on the Left. Such a context made Mitterrand's stunning victory over incumbent Giscard d'Estaing all the more surprising. Even more surprising was that in the parliamentary elections called by Mitterrand after his victory, the Socialist Party emerged with an absolute majority of seats. Riding Mitterrand's coattails with nearly 38 percent of the vote, the PS took a great leap beyond the 21 percent it had gained just three years before. In both of these elections, cooperation between Socialists and Communists was nil. For the Communists, the results were as negative as the Socialists' were positive. In the first round of the presidential contest, Marchais, never missing a chance to lump Mitterrand with Giscard d'Estaing as agents of bourgeois capitalism, polled poorly, with only 15.3 percent (vs. Mitterrand's 25.8 percent). Thus eliminated from the runoff, Marchais proceeded to endorse Mitterrand but without enthusiasm, claiming, "We can't play the game of the Right; we will have to call our supporters to vote for Mitterrand," even as he denounced "the shameful duet" that Mitterrand and Giscard were playing (Favier and Martin-Roland 1990, 28–29). The real shock for the Communists came in the legislative elections, in which the party gained only 16.1 percent, nearly a one-quarter drop from its 1978 performance. With just forty-four seats versus the Socialists' 285 in the National Assembly, the Communists found themselves in the weakest position in relation to the Socialists since the early 1930s. The harsh math meant that Mitterrand and the Socialists had no need of the Communists in order to govern France for the next five years.

The new president did not disregard political reality, however. An isolated, alienated Communist Party could still stir up much trouble for a government it opposed, so Mitterrand decided to bring the PCF "into the tent" by naming four Communists as ministers. The ministries themselves—Professional Training, Health, Public Administration, and Transportation—were considered far less prestigious and important than Economy and Finance or Foreign Affairs, but they were strategic from a political viewpoint. All these ministries included many unionized public sector workers, and thus the Communist ministers' role, at least in the eyes of the Socialist leaders, was clear: keep the workers calm; we do not want a replay of the Popular Front strikes. For the first three years of the Mitterrand government, this arrangement worked fairly smoothly. Even though the PCF often sought to incite worker strikes and protests via the CGT, the Communist ministers faithfully did their job.

It is clear enough why Mitterrand would want to keep the PCF close, at least initially as the government set out an ambitious reform agenda. But what about the Communists? Why did they agree to join a government led by a man and a party that they had pilloried for the preceding three years? One reason was that in the wake of the elections, Mitterrand made all the "right sounds," vowing even before the election, "Communists must not just produce, work, pay taxes, and die in wars. . . . If they join a parliamentary majority based on a popular movement (*rassemblement populaire*), of course I will work with them" (quoted in Favier and Martin-Roland 1990, 83). Although Communist leaders deeply distrusted Mitterrand, they could not accuse him of deserting them. Moreover, Mitterrand and the Socialists promised to adhere to most of the reforms laid out in the Common Program, and thus the PCF had no basis to claim betrayal. Strictly political calculations also played a role. The Communist strategy of opposing the Socialists since 1978 had not only sapped the party's popularity with voters but also led to much contention within the party. Those trends would likely only worsen if the PCF stayed petulantly on the sidelines throwing brickbats at an erstwhile partner who had won an impressive victory. Given these factors, joining the government, even in a relatively minor role, was preferable to any other alternative.

The first two years of the Mitterrand government have been famously labeled the "Socialist experiment." Facing a stalled economy that had an inflation rate of over 13 percent in 1980, the new government under Prime Minister Pierre Mauroy launched an economic program that has been labeled "redistributive Keynesianism" (Hall 1986, 193). Its centerpiece was a huge boost in government spending intended to stimulate consumer spending, especially, it was hoped, for domestically produced goods. Thus, in its first year, government spending jumped 27 percent, which went into such items as pensions and family, maternity, and housing allowances as well as direct public sector job creation. Accompanying this demand-side strategy was a supply-side approach that aimed at creating or, at least, saving jobs. Here, the focus, in line with the Common Program's promises, was to nationalize some of France's largest firms. A total of twelve industrial groups, thirty-six banks, and two finance companies were taken over by the state and given orders (and funds) to restructure and recapitalize in such crucial sectors as energy, electronics, and chemicals. The purpose of all these measures was, in a phrase used often by Mauroy and his government, to "reconquer the domestic market."[11]

Its grand ambitions notwithstanding, this grand experiment ultimately fizzled. The various stimulus measures worked well enough in the sense of spurring consumption, but growing demand also failed to quell inflation; by

1982, France's inflation rate of 11.8 percent well exceeded the European Union average of 10.9 percent, according to statistics from the Organization for Economic Cooperation and Development. French consumers also tended to buy the "wrong stuff": too many imported goods and not enough locally produced ones. The result was a huge increase in the trade deficit, especially with European Union partners such as Germany, and this in turn triggered a slide in the value of the franc. All this was occurring in a context of world recession, and it became obvious within a year that France could not continue swimming against the tide—trying to stimulate its economy while all others were stagnating and even contracting. After a wage–price freeze in June 1982—packaged as a temporary "pause" in the economic program—came a series of devaluations of the franc within the European Monetary System.

Finally, with these measures having effected no change in the fundamentals and the Socialists having performed poorly in municipal elections in March 1983, the government engaged in an intense internal debate over the future course to follow. On one side, a group led by Prime Minister Mauroy and Economy and Finance Minister Jacques Delors advocated a policy labeled "rigor": an austerity aimed at reducing consumption, inflation, and deficits. Arguing against such a turn were advocates of continued expansion and income redistribution. This so-called other policy, championed by several top government ministers as well as Mitterrand's own friends, such as industrial Jean Riboud, even envisioned pulling France out of the European Monetary System in order to pursue reflation. After nearly three weeks of debate, Mitterrand was finally persuaded to back the "rigor" group. Henceforth, the policy would be one of economic orthodoxy: rein in government spending, balance the budget, encourage private investment, and reduce inflation.[12]

For these first two years of the Mitterrand government—that is, until the adoption of the new policy of "rigor"—the Communist Party, at least officially, dutifully played the role of a supportive but distinctly secondary partner. The PCF's role was not without its contradictions, however. For example, the party officially supported the declaration of martial law by General Jaruzelski in Poland in December 1981, even as the Mauroy government—along with its four Communist ministers—condemned it. Moreover, as mentioned, there is also evidence that the PCF, through its control of the CGT, was playing something of a double game: on the one hand, participating in the government while, on the other hand, encouraging workers' struggles at the grassroots, especially in public enterprises as well as in private firms such as Citroën and Talbot, which had repressive managements and right-wing "house" unions (Platone and Ranger 1985).

After March 1983, however, as the austerity measures began to take effect, relations between Socialist leaders and the Communist Party steadily deteriorated. For the next sixteen months, until July 1984, the PCF grew increasingly critical of the government's economic strategy, especially as the Mauroy government sanctioned major restructuring plans for the steel and automobile industries. For example, in an effort to stop massive financial losses in the nationalized steel industry, the government in March 1984 announced a reorganization plan that would eliminate 40,000 jobs. With major strikes breaking out in the Lorraine region, the heart of the steel industry, both the PCF and the CGT went into open opposition; CGT head Henri Krasucki accused the government of "industrial surrender" (*Le Monde*, January 17, 1984). Although the Communist ministers did not resign at that moment, it was apparent that the Socialist government and the Communist Party had reached the breaking point.

That moment finally came four months later, in July, when Mitterrand changed prime ministers, replacing Mauroy with a young technocrat, Laurent Fabius, whom the Communists viewed with great suspicion. In reaction, the PCF pulled its ministers out of the government. Did the Communists quit, or were they "fired"? Both elements were at play. On the one hand, the PCF initiated the break because its leaders refused to continue the double game of participating in the government while Communist and CGT leaders and rank-and-file members in the steel and automobile industries were openly resisting government-sponsored restructuring plans that were laying off masses of workers. On the other hand, the Socialist government made no attempt to keep the PCF in the government and even encouraged their departure. By this point, the Mauroy government had firmly chosen its course of *rigueur* and was not about to turn back in midstream. Moreover, from the Socialists' viewpoint, the Communists were an expendable force, especially after the PCF's dismal performance in the June 1984 European Parliament elections in which the party gained just 11 percent (Smith 1998, 82; Ross 1992).

The Communists' departure from the Mitterrand–Socialist government in July 1984 marked the end of a strained period of cooperation between the two parties. This moment also completed a complex "double turnaround" in PS–PCF relations that had taken place over the previous seven years. From the relatively harmonious days of early 1977 to the bitter breakup of 1984, the two parties had gone through four permutations: close cooperation and agreement on a program of governing (pre–September 1977), breakup and division (September 1977–June 1981), tense but functioning cooperation in governing the country (June 1981–July 1984), and, finally, a second breakup over fundamental policy choices.

CONFLICT, 1984–1994

For a decade following the 1984 split, relations between Socialists and Communists remained hostile. With rapprochement between the two parties virtually impossible at the national level, the two parties went their own ways—in two senses. Not only did the parties largely ignore each other (when they were not openly quarreling), but their trajectories could not have been more divergent. Whereas the Socialists generally prospered, the Communists continued to spiral downward, deserted by erstwhile supporters and weakened by internal turmoil. Only when the Socialists themselves experienced electoral disaster in the 1993 elections did the prospect of interparty cooperation return.

As long as Mitterrand remained president—and his reelection in 1988 assured him of another seven-year term—the Socialists could make an actual or plausible claim to be a governing party. Once the Communists left the government in July 1984, the new Fabius-led government pursued its economic-rigor-cum-restructuring strategy consistently until the end of the National Assembly's five-year term in 1986. By that time, the public had long jettisoned any illusion that the Socialists were going to "change life" ("*changer la vie*") as they had promised in the 1981 campaign. Despite this disenchantment, the Socialists performed creditably in the 1986 legislative elections with a 31 percent vote share; however, they were unable to retain their parliamentary majority, as the Gaullist party and their allies, headed by Chirac, won a majority. For the first time in Fifth Republic history, a president of one party or tendency had to "cohabit" with a parliamentary majority of another party or tendency. The new twist on constitutional arrangements produced a tense working relationship between the two leaders, which ultimately worked to Mitterrand's advantage. In the 1988 presidential elections, Mitterrand soundly trounced Chirac and then dissolved the legislature and called new elections. In those elections, the PS, again riding the president's coattails as in 1981, won 276 seats, only thirteen short of a bare majority.

Theoretically, with support from the Communists' twenty-seven seats, the Socialists could have put together a governing coalition. But Marchais and the Communists refused to support the newly designated prime minister Michel Rocard, whose disdain for the PCF was well known. The only alternative for Rocard was to search for allies toward the center, so several centrist politicians close to former prime minister Raymond Barre were brought into the government. As one observer remarked, "Composite as it was, the Rocard government was not a real coalition; it was rather a Socialist government with non-Socialist participation" (Friend 1998, 118).

During the next five years, from 1988 to 1993, the Socialists were able to retain control of government based on this fragile arrangement. The achievement was all the more notable given the fact that three Socialist leaders— Rocard (1988–1991), Edith Cresson (1991–1992), and Pierre Bérégovoy (1992–1993)—served as prime minister, each becoming more unpopular than the previous one. Although there were different policy emphases in each administration, there were important continuities reminiscent of the "*ri-*

gueur" years under Mauroy and Fabius, notably a focus on keeping inflation low and budgets balanced via a "strong franc" strategy that kept interest rates high and dampened consumer spending. In this respect, this second five-year period of Socialist government can be judged successful: the inflation gap that France had long experienced in relation to Germany was eliminated. On the other hand, the strategy, by discouraging demand, did nothing to address the growing unemployment problem; by 1993, the unemployment rate had grown to 12 percent of the workforce (Smith 1998, 83–88). Beset by internal campaign finance scandals, the Socialists approached the 1993 elections with little hope of retaining control of parliament.

Despite the travails of this period, the Socialists refused to renounce their relations with the PCF. The Socialists continued to claim that their political anchor was firmly on the Left and not in any kind of Third Force alliance with centrist parties. Their attitude was, "We are always ready to cooperate with the Communists, if and when they decide to return to the table." The rationale for this stance resided, of course, in the logic behind the refounding of the "new" Socialist Party in 1970. That logic derived from the *présidentialisation* inherent in the Fifth Republic and the subsequent need for a successful party to field a competitive presidential candidate. Mitterrand's goal in taking over the PS had been to establish himself as such a candidate, one capable of amassing broad support across the whole Left spectrum, and that implied an alliance with the largest extant party on the Left, the Communists. To have denounced the latter in favor of a center-moving strategy, even with the PCF in weakened condition, would have jeopardized what had proven to be a winning strategy. As Bergounioux and Grunberg (2005) remark, "The Union of the Left was the central element of the Epinay refoundation [of the Socialist Party]. . . . The Socialists did not know how to define their leftist identity and in particular their strategy without reference to the Communist Party" (342).[13] At a minimum, this meant a refusal to engage in alliances with centrist parties while leaving the door open to possible future cooperation with the PCF.

As for the Communists, their isolation only worsened their decline. The 1986 elections were especially disastrous, with the party plummeting to under 10 percent. The party rebounded slightly in 1988, with 11.2 percent, but then fell in the 1989 European Parliament elections to 7.7 percent. Increasingly, the PCF was becoming a fringe party, something that could be measured by taking a one-decade snapshot: whereas in 1978 the PCF could boast eighty-eight deputies from thirty-three departments, in 1988 it had only twenty-four deputies representing eleven departments (Hazareesingh 1991, 4). A parallel decline can be seen in the membership and influence of the Communist-affiliated labor confederation, the CGT.[14] There is no doubt that the PCF's electoral decline was linked to a range of factors beyond its immediate control, including the "postindustrial" transition that was decimating the party's core base of blue-collar workers, the decline of Marxism as an intellectual force on the Left, the failure of Soviet-model Communism, and even the growth of the Far Right National Front as a competing pole of attraction for working-class protest voters. But there is also no question that part of the Communists' wound was self-inflicted.

Most critically, the PCF continued to demonstrate two fundamental problems: an incapacity to field its own *présidentiable* and an inability to manage internal debate and effect reform. As an example of the former problem, in the 1988 presidential election, the PCF leadership, knowing that its own leader, the unpopular Marchais, stood no chance, put forward André Lajoinie, a Marchais ally, as their candidate. Far from improving on Marchais's poor 1981 performance, Lajoinie did much worse, drawing just 6.7 percent in the first round—half of Marchais's earlier total. As for the question of internal debate and reform, the voters' disenchantment produced a corresponding dissatisfaction within the party over the leadership's sectarianism and blind support of the Soviet Union. Party figures such as Pierre Juquin and Marcel Rigout (who had been one of the four Communist ministers in the early Mitterrand government) called for the party's "renovation": greater openness and democracy within the party, a rapprochement with the Socialists and other groups on the Left, and a more critical stance toward the Soviet Union. Successive waves of so-called reconstructors and refounders—small groups of dissidents grouped around disgruntled party leaders in opposition to Marchais—came forward in the late 1980s but ultimately to little avail (Ross 1992, 51–54). Marchais, who, according to Bell and Criddle (1994b), had "a tragic genius for missing the self-evident (119)," responded by seeking to quell any and all opposition.

A grand irony of the PCF's travails is that by the late 1980s even the Soviets, then in high Gorbachevian reform mode, criticized the PCF for its rigidity. According to an *Izvestia* editorial, "The [French] Communists have neither a program nor even a slogan which could appeal to wider popular masses. Their strategy and tactics are completely outdated in relation to the new conditions created by the *perestroika* of modern capitalism" (quoted in Hazareesingh 1991, 4).

COOPERATION AND THE "PLURAL LEFT," 1994–2007

The year 1994 marked another turning point—in this case, a rapprochement—in Socialist–Communist relations. With both parties languishing in the opposition, after disastrous showings by both in the 1993 legislative elections and the 1994 European elections, new leaders on both sides began exploring the prospects for cooperation. Thirteen years later, in the wake of the 2007 presidential and parliamentary elections, interparty cooperation had proven at least durable albeit contentious and inconsistent. During this peri-od, Socialists and Communists managed to cooperate through two periods of exclusion from power—1993–1997 and 2002–2007—as well as a five-year period of cohabitation (1997–2002) in which Socialist prime minister Lionel Jospin headed a "plural left" government of Socialists, Communists, Greens, and other small parties.

While there were triggering events within each party that drove the two parties to seek cooperation in 1994, there were also longer-term trends at work, notably shifts in the party system itself, that made cooperation an attractive, indeed necessary, condition for each party's electoral viability. Those shifts can be judged by examining a side-by-side comparison of the results of the 1981 and 1993 elections (see table 2.3). One sees, to be sure, elements of stability. Most notably, the two main Right parties—the conser-vative Gaullists (Rassemblement pour la République [RPR]) and the center-right Union for French Democracy (Union pour la Démocratie Française [UDF])—held their own, with fairly similar vote percentages. Taken togeth-er, these two parties decreased somewhat, from 42.9 to 39.5 percent. What changed was just about everything else, starting with the two major Left parties. The PCF fell below 10 percent—a loss of nearly 40 percent of its 1981 result. The outcome, at least proportionally, was even worse for the Socialists, whose total of 17.6 percent was *less than half* of its winning percentage in 1981. The 1993 election was widely interpreted as a negative referendum on the Socialists' five years in office. The general perception was that three successive Socialist prime ministers had failed to reenergize the French economy while allowing the government and the party to become mired in corruption scandals. Clearly, massive desertions were taking place on the Left.

Three other notable shifts can be seen in these results. The most obvious and notorious was the rise of the Far Right National Front, which had already come to prominence beginning with the 1984 European elections. The party of Jean-Marie Le Pen, appealing directly to working-class voters and bran-dishing an anti-immigrant, anti-Europe rhetoric, siphoned votes not only from the RPR and UDF but also from the PS and PCF. A second change was an impressive advance by the Green movement. Although fractured into four competing parties, the various Green parties drew over 11 percent of the vote.

Finally, as suggested by the Greens' progress even as the movement split into four rival groups, the 1993 elections featured a profusion of new parties. Whereas in the 1981 election the "*quadrille bipolaire*" (bipolar foursome) of the PS, PCF, RPR, and UDF gained 97 percent, in 1993 their total was just 66 percent. The difference is explained by the growth of new parties across the political spectrum. In 1981, aside from the four major parties (and vari-ous "miscellaneous" or unaffiliated candidates), there were only three other

Table 2.3. French Party System Changes, 1981–1993, First Round, National Assembly Elections

Party	1981 % Vote	1993 % Vote
Extreme left (Trotskyists etc.)	1.3	1.1
Greens[a]	1.1	7.6
Other ecology parties	—	3.5
Communist Party (PCF)	16.2	9.2
Socialist Party (PS)	37.5	17.6
Union for French Democracy (UDF)	21.7	19.1
Gaullists (RPR)	21.2	20.4
National Front (FN)	0.2	12.4
Other	0.8	9.1
Total	100.0	100.0

[a] 1981: Greens only; 1993: Ecology Alliance (Greens + ecology generation).
Source: *Parties and Elections in Europe* (http://www.parties-and-elections.de).

national parties (the extreme-left Lutte Ouvrière, the Green Party, and the National Front) that together garnered less than 3 percent of the vote. In 1993, by contrast, the comparable figure was a total of nine parties gaining 34 percent of the vote.

The dismal 1993 legislative results for both the PS and PCF, as well as the parties' equally poor showing in the 1994 European elections, triggered intense debates within both parties over leadership and strategy, especially the issue of alliances. For the Socialists, these debates also revolved around the question of who would succeed Mitterrand as the party's *présidentiable* since Mitterrand's second term would end in 1995. In interminable maneuverings that stretched over two years, Jospin eventually won that struggle over Laurent Fabius and Michel Rocard, but it was immediately clear that Jospin would need support from other groups on the Left, including the Communists, if he hoped to win the next presidential election. Even though the PCF had severely declined during the previous decade, it still constituted an important potential ally for the Socialists, and there were obvious reasons for the Socialists to seek cooperation. As for the PCF, the manifest failure of its "autonomist" line since 1984 had brought the party to a fractious dead end. Ceding to the inevitable, Marchais retired as general secretary in 1994. He was replaced by a cautious reformer, Robert Hue, a longtime party *permanent* but one disposed to a French-style version of perestroika and cooperation with other Left forces. Both parties, then, had motives to renew their cooperation.

The question was what kind of cooperation. A full-blown replay of a 1972-style "common program"—a detailed framework for governing—was never seriously considered. The euphoric hopes of the early 1970s were a distant memory, whereas recollections of the 1977 blowup remained fresh. In any case, the dynamic of cooperation could not be the same. The Common Program/Union of the Left was built on the basis of rough parity, but now the two sides were of vastly different potential. The Socialists, for all their problems, were far stronger than the Communists. This was especially true after Jospin's surprisingly strong candidacy for the presidency in 1995, when he forced Chirac into a runoff and then posted a respectable 47.4 percent. Jospin now stood as dominant figure in a relatively united PS. As for the PCF, even though Hue polled a surprisingly strong 8.7 percent in the first round, the party leadership was well aware of the PCF's comparative weakness and was wary of being submerged by the Socialists. Both sides agreed that it was best to proceed in modest, confidence-building steps. The first step was to collaborate in local elections. Thus, in the June 1995 municipal elections, united lists of PS and PCF were struck in three-quarters of the 742 towns with populations of more than 10,000 (*Le Monde*, June 3, 1995). The results were sufficiently positive for the two parties to undertake a series of public meetings to explore further cooperation. Also included in these meetings were other possible allies, including the Greens, Jean-Pierre Chevènement's Citizens' Movement (Mouvement des Citoyens [MDC]), and the Left Radicals.

The core issue for the Communists throughout this period was whether, in effect, to seek allies to the left or to the right. A sizable contingent within the party wanted to move leftward by forming a "radical pole" (*pôle de radicalité*) that would be a counterweight to the Socialists. Such a pole would encompass several small parties, including the Greens and extreme-left parties such as the Trotskyist Revolutionary Communist League (Ligue Communiste Révolutionnaire [LCR]). Although such a coalition would have no chance of winning either the presidency or a parliamentary majority, it would enable the PCF to remain ideologically "*pur et dur*" (pure and hard) and act as a left-pulling force on the larger Socialists.

The other major option for the Communists would be to move toward the right by seeking a coalition with the PS. Such a move would run two risks. One would be to become a very junior partner in a Socialist-led alliance. The other would be to compromise on its program, especially its opposition to privatizations and European monetary union—both of which the Socialists supported. In the end, the Communists chose the rightward option, but Hue, though obviously dealing from a weak position, took pains to assert the PCF's autonomy within the alliance while warning the Socialists against "partitioning" the Left into a single voice headed by the PS (*Le Monde*, July 9, 1996).

By the time of the 1997 legislative elections, the various components of the Left, with the exception of the extreme-left LCR, had put together both a "common declaration" and an electoral support agreement (*Le Monde*, April 30, 1997). In those elections, which were marked more by disaffection for the incumbent conservative majority than by enthusiasm for the Left alternative,[15] the "plural Left" (as the alliance called itself) gained a total of 45.6 percent of the vote versus the mainstream Right's total of 36.5 percent. The Left vote translated into a clear parliamentary majority of 317 seats, and Jospin was named prime minister.[16] Once installed, Jospin tapped various leaders of the associated parties to cabinet posts.[17]

This plural Left coalition, in cohabitation with President Chirac, governed France for the next five years. In assessing this government, one can distinguish its policies from its politics. In terms of the former, the plural Left government carried out what has been termed a "Left Realism" strategy: an approach that recognized the inescapability of "external constraints" but that provided social protection and redistribution measures favoring those whose livelihoods were harmed by economic adjustment (Clift 2005, 132). Thus, the Jospin government, with the "lessons of 1983" regarding the perils of excessive economic voluntarism firmly in mind, took few risks that might elicit the opposition of the private sector. Moreover, given France's commitment to the Stability and Growth Pact of the European Union, the key component paving the way for the launch of monetary union in 1999, Jospin had to ensure that the nation's inflation, budget and trade deficits, and debt levels met the stringent criteria. The result was a generally hands-off, "business-friendly" approach to the private sector, along with a decidedly non-*dirigiste* stance in relation to public firms. For example, far from reprising the Common Program's and the early Mitterrand government's emphasis on nationalizations, the government actually pursued privatizations with steady commitment (Bergounioux and Grunberg 2005, 452). By 2002, this government had actually privatized more assets than the previous conservative government (*Les Echos*, November 21, 2000). On balance, the Jospin government maintained the trend that began with the Socialists' 1983 U-turn and continued on through governments of the Left (1988–1993) and the Right (1986–1988, 1993–1997), namely, the gradual dismantling of the interventionist instruments and reflexes of the postwar French state (Levy 1999, 2000).

In assessing the economic policies of the Jospin government (and its predecessors), it is important not to equate the move away from *dirigisme* as an embrace of neoliberalism. While respecting the need for macroeconomic stability and promoting a hands-off policy toward both private and public firms, the government also used fiscal policies to enact progressive tax cuts, increase minimum-income guarantees and the minimum wage, extend health care coverage, and create new jobs. A centerpiece of reform was the reduction of the legal workweek to thirty-five hours, something that was intended to encourage job creation. In terms of overall impact, one can credit the strategy with cushioning the income loss and dislocations of unemployment while helping to reduce unemployment itself from 12.5 percent in 1997 to 8.6 percent in 2002 (Clift 2005, 175). On the less positive side, the various measures were enormously expensive; as a percentage of gross domestic product, France's expenditures on labor market measures rose to equal those of Sweden (more than 3 percent). Moreover, these measures were tilted toward "passive" measures to maintain income rather than active measures aimed at getting people back to work, such as job training, relocation assistance, and affordable public child care (Levy 2005, 177, 181).

That the Jospin government was able to achieve a respectable economic policy record is all the more notable given the internal politics of the Plural Left government, for Jospin also had to engage in the political equivalent of herding cats. The daily work consisted of trying to placate one or another of the various elements of the coalition. All parties could easily agree on the various social welfare measures mentioned above, but there were frequent tensions over other issues. For example, the PCF and Chevènement's MDC opposed both the European Monetary Union project and NATO strikes in Kosovo, whereas the Jospin government supported both (*Le Monde*, June 11, 1999). The Greens, along with their leader Dominque Voynet who served as environment minister, opposed a plan pushed by Jospin to develop a new underground nuclear waste storage (*Le Monde*, September 13, 2000). Unlike the Fourth Republic, however, when a disaffected party often withdrew from the governing coalition over a specific issue and brought down the government, all parties recognized the high stakes in doing so and avoided open splits. That did not prevent the small parties from playing the inside–outside game, however, with their deputies remaining in solidarity within parliament but the party organizations and various activist groups applying pressure "in the streets." For example, in October 1999, the PCF, two Trotskyist parties, the Greens, the MDC, and various associations of the unemployed staged a large demonstration in Paris protesting a government bill to raise taxes on employee stock options (*Le Monde*, October 20, 1999).

With the approach of the 2002 elections, in which, for the first time under the Fifth Republic, both presidential and legislative terms ended in the same year, the Plural Left coalition became increasingly frayed, with the various parties unwilling to support Jospin as the Left's sole presidential candidate. Thus, each party tried to distinguish itself from the Jospin government not only by critiquing specific policies but also by proposing its own candidate for president. Especially critical of government policy was PCF leader Robert Hue, who had announced his own candidacy for president. Not being a deputy much less a member of the government, Hue had considerable latitude of action, and though he had no hope of equaling Jospin's total in the first round, he was facing pressure from his left, namely, the perennial Trotskyist candidate Arlette Laguiller. This growing cacophony of voices ultimately spelled doom for the Plural Left. In the presidential first round, Jospin was beaten by the National Front leader, Jean-Marie Le Pen, and failed to place in the top two and thus was eliminated from the runoff. While it is true that Jospin ran an uninspiring campaign, the real reason for Jospin's stunning and humiliating loss is not hard to find: the multiplicity of Left candidates—four from the Plural Left coalition alone—siphoned off votes that otherwise would have gone for Jospin. In the irony of ironies, Jospin had assembled a governing coalition that, in the end, unwittingly did him in.[18]

Not surprisingly, with the wind knocked out of their presidential sails, the Socialists and the rest of the Left did poorly in the follow-on parliamentary elections. PS secretary François Hollande attempted to fashion a "united Left" strategy in which the four remaining elements of the Plural Left—the PS, PCF, Greens, and Radical Socialists—would run only a single candidate in all 577 electoral districts; negotiations produced just thirty-four such candidacies (Clift 2005, 54). The erstwhile Plural Left majority of 320 seats in 1997 fell by almost half, to 178, while on the Right, the Gaullist Union for a Popular Movement (Union pour un Mouvement Populaire) gained 357 seats.

These elections defined the Left's status as a powerless minority until the next elections five years hence.[19] Forced into self-examination for its failure, the parties of the Left engaged in endless rounds of recriminations. Not only were potshots fired across party lines, but leadership squabbles and rank-and-file grumbling were rife within all the Left parties. A sampling of headlines during the following years indicates the state of the Left's interparty relations:

"The Left Shipwrecked" (*Libération*, July 17, 2003)

"PS-PC Relations Are at a Dead Point" (*Le Figaro*, August 2, 2003)

"The Ex-Plural Left Puts Its Disagreements on the Table" (*Le Monde*, September 10, 2003)

"The Question of Europe Sows Discord in the French Left" (*Le Monde*, September 12–13, 2004)

"The Left between Fractures and Schism" (*Le Monde*, March 20, 2005)

"The Left in Its Labyrinth" (*Le Monde Diplomatique*, May 2005)

Within the Left parties themselves, the five years following the 2002 debacle brought internal tensions to the surface. For example, shortly after the election, both the Communists and the Greens replaced their leaders, with Marie-George Buffet taking over from Hue in the PCF and Gilles Lemaire succeeding Dominique Voynet in the Greens.[20] As for the Socialists, the party weathered both leadership struggles and critiques of the leadership by the rank and file. Divisions within the leadership came to a head in 2007 in the party's "primary season" to designate a candidate for the upcoming presidential election. With the tarnished Jospin virtually hiding in retirement and the party's *présidentiable* designation up for grabs, a fierce struggle for support pitted hopefuls Dominique Strauss-Kahn, Laurent Fabius, and the eventual candidate, Ségolène Royal, against each other. Within the party's rank and file, many activists complained of the leadership's elitism and isolation from the masses. One claimed, for example, "The PS no longer reflects our society. Where are the leaders who've come from the unions, from the world of voluntary associations, or even from the provinces?" Another decried the "cultural fracture between the techno-left of the Sixth Arrondissement and the real country" (*Libération*, October 18, 2002). These critiques echoed an outpouring of both journalistic and scholarly analyses underlining the growing *embourgeoisement* of the Left in general and the Socialists in particular.[21]

The Left's prospects failed to fundamentally alter in the 2007 elections, which included back-to-back presidential and legislative elections. In all, these elections confirmed the Left's status as a "structural minority" tendency (Grunberg 2007). For the third presidential election in a row, the Left's main candidate lost, and in the legislative elections a month later, the combined results of all Left parties fell below 40 percent for the second election in a row. The larger perspective was even more alarming for the Left, for the 2007 legislative contest was the sixth successive one in which the Left's combined score fell below 50 percent. Whereas Left parties drew 55.6 percent of the vote in the 1981 election, in the six subsequent elections they averaged just 41.5 percent, compared with the Right's combined average of 53.3 percent (Grunberg 2007, 64). The Socialist Party could take some comfort in having increased its vote percentage and number of parliamentary seats over 2002. With nearly one-fourth of the vote and one-third of the National Assembly seats, the PS constituted the country's second-largest party. On the other hand, the party was more divided than ever, with no uncontested leader, much less a consensus *présidentiable.* For the rest of the Left, however, the 2007 elections were little short of disaster. The combined vote percentage of the non-Socialist Left—including the extreme-left LCR, Left Radicals, PCF, the two ecology parties, and "independent Left" candidates—was 15.0 percent. For the second election in a row, the Communists failed to draw 5 percent of the vote.

CONCLUSION

This chapter began with Lionel Jospin's astute analysis of Socialist–Communist relations as they stood in 1980, the end of a momentous and formative decade for the French Left. Recall that Jospin framed the Left's eternal dilemma, namely, that the Left would never achieve a majority—and thus victory would never be possible—if either the Socialists or the Communists were significantly stronger than the other party. Jospin's hypotheses perfectly explained the dynamics of the decade that had just passed. In the early 1970s, the Socialists were indeed far weaker than the Communists, and the prospect of a Left majority appeared impossible. By the late 1970s, however, the two parties' relative *rapports de force* had completely reversed—the Socialists had found a growing audience, whereas the Communists were declining—and yet the Left still appeared far from victory, principally because, as Jospin recognized, the PCF was "opposed to the success of the Union." The bitter breakup of the Union of the Left in 1977–1978 was essentially caused by the Communists' unwillingness to share power with the Socialists if that meant playing a subordinate role.

Events of that decade—specifically the years 1972–1977—constituted a critical juncture for both the Socialist and the Communist parties. It will be recalled from chapter 1 that a critical juncture has three interrelated components: cause, response, and outcome. The cause in this case was a set of what I have labeled crisis-inducing conditions. At the most general level, the backdrop for this critical juncture was a crisis in the Gaullist regime that exploded in the Events of May–June 1968. That regime did some things well; notably, it promoted rapid industrialization and economic growth during the 1960s. But it did other things poorly; specifically, it failed to reform rigid, outdated institutions in such areas as education and industrial relations (Howell 1992, 61–81). The result was a comparatively dynamic economy that was, however, ill adapted to the needs and expectations of millions of students and workers, many of whom viewed de Gaulle and his government as distant and authoritarian. While few observers predicted the timing and scale of the students' and workers' strikes of 1968, in retrospect this *explosion de colère* hardly seemed surprising.[22]

Despite the massive mobilization by students and workers and the damage inflicted on the Gaullist regime's image, the Events were ultimately a defeat for the Left. From a critical juncture perspective, then, the main crisis-inducing condition was the negative fallout from the Events. For the PCF especially, the Events proved to be a no-win situation, as the PCF's role in the students' and workers' strikes during those weeks was highly criticized from both the Left and the Right. On the one hand, various "new Left" and student groups denounced the Communists for having sought to control, dampen, and channel the militancy in the factories and streets, while, on the other hand, Gaullists and other conservative groups accused the party of fomenting revolution. As for the Socialists, they appeared divided and ineffectual. Their titular leader, Guy Mollet, was largely invisible during the Events, whereas François Mitterrand, who at that time was not a member of the Socialist Party, tried to play a spokesman's role for the non-Communist

Left but was roundly critiqued for appearing overly eager to oust de Gaulle and install an interim government composed of all parties (including Communists) (Bell 2005, 55).

In the legislative elections of June 1968 that effectively brought a conclusion to the Events, a Gaullist-led wave of reaction crushed the Left. A year later, in presidential elections following de Gaulle's sudden resignation, no Left candidate was able to gain the runoff round. Mitterrand, temporarily eclipsed because of his misplay during the Events, did not run, and the non-Communist Left's main candidate, Gaston Deferre, drew only 5 percent in the first round. As for the Communists, although their presidential candidate Jacques Duclos performed creditably in the first round with 21.5 percent, he was in no sense a serious candidate to win a majority in the unlikely event that he could make the runoff. Thus, both the Socialist and the Communist parties entered the 1970s seeking alternative strategies to break out of a status quo, which appeared to consign both parties permanently to the political sidelines.

The two parties' response to this unfavorable context constituted the second component of this critical juncture. The centerpiece of both parties' strategic response was the Union of the Left. We have reviewed the ultimately failed trajectory of the Union between 1972 and 1977, along with the main reason for its failure, noted above: the PCF's unwillingness to continue it because the Union was working to the party's disadvantage. The question that needs to be addressed is, How can one account for the two parties' strategic responses during this critical juncture? Chapter 1, to recall, proposed three explanatory factors that help us answer this question: institutional context, party culture, and leadership. Let us briefly review the impact of each of these factors.

Institutional Context

It is difficult to exaggerate the extent to which the still relatively new institutional arrangements of the Fifth Republic impacted the actions of the French Left after 1958. Two modifications, in particular, stand out: a strengthened presidency and a parliamentary election system based on single-member districts with a runoff provision. The first of these, a constitutionally empowered president, put the focus on the executive at the expense of parliament, thereby reversing nearly a century of strong parliamentary government.[23] A critically important revision of the constitutional provisions regarding the presidency occurred in 1962 with the adoption of an amendment providing for the direct election of the president.[24] In effect, beginning with the 1965 presidential election—the first such direct election under the Fifth Republic—the chief goal of any individual and/or group desirous of holding the most powerful political position in France was to win the presidency. This institutional change created a powerful incentive system that operated at both the individual and the collective level. Individuals seeking to become president would need to become the standard-bearer of a party and/or coalition capable of mobilizing a voting majority; at the same time, any party striving to hold power would need to promote an individual capable of attracting a majority of voters.

The second institutional change under the Fifth Republic was the reinstitution of the single-member district, two-ballot electoral system for legislative elections (see note 6). As we have noted, this system provided strong incentives for parties to form coalitions in one of two ways. The first is that two or more parties agree to put forward a single candidate in each district for the first round, thus maximizing that candidate's chances of winning an outright majority and thus obviating a runoff. This option has been largely rejected by French parties. Not only is the task of agreeing on a single candidate in every district enormously complicated, but this option provides no test of individual party strength while it blurs the identity of the participating parties. From a party-organizational viewpoint, this option is, to say the least, unattractive. More appealing to most parties is a second option whereby parties practice *désistement*, or mutual withdrawals in the runoff round. Not only does each party in the coalition get to assess its popular support in the first round and thus promote its own distinctive identity, but the principle of mutual withdrawals is extremely simple to apply: only the leading candidate within the coalition in the first round proceeds to the runoff; all others withdraw. As Jospin noted, however, there is a potential fly in this ointment: this runoff withdrawal option is likely to remain attractive only if each of the parties participating in the coalition is able to elect a satisfactory number of its own candidates. That can happen only if the voters of the participating parties, when called on to do so, faithfully transfer their votes to other coalition candidates in the runoff round.

Within the changed institutional context of the Fifth Republic, both Socialist and Communist leaders had incentives to cooperate. During the 1960s, they began to do so; the PCF supported Mitterrand as the Left's sole presidential candidate in 1965, and the parties practiced *désistement* beginning in 1962. But, as mentioned, the unfavorable political environment resulting from the dual electoral defeats in 1968 and 1969 gave these parties added reasons to extend their cooperation. The basis of that cooperation was an unspoken quid pro quo—in effect, a wager by each party that a moderate risk could produce a high reward. The quid pro quo was that the PCF would recognize Mitterrand as the Left's sole *présidentiable*, while the Socialists, in implicit exchange, would virtually allow the Communists to write the Common Program of the Left. If all went well and the Union of the Left benefited both parties as planned, the reward would be the winning of both heights of power, the presidency and parliament. In this best-case scenario, the Communists wagered that they could continue to play their self-appointed "vanguard" role by bending Mitterrand and the Socialists to their will. The Socialists bet that by moving to the left ideologically and committing themselves to an alliance with the PCF, they could simultaneously draw defecting Communist voters, marginalize and "housebreak" the PCF, and thereby attract centrist voters who feared Communism.

Party Culture

When accounting for strategic responses on the part of Socialists and Communists, one must remember that those responses arose from distinct organizational cultures. On the most obvious level, the Communists, both sociologically and rhetorically, were much more "workerist" (*"ouvrièriste"*) than the more bourgeois (and even *haut* bourgeois) Socialists. More directly relevant for explaining the two parties' strategic responses in the early 1970s were two other distinctive characteristics that I will label organizational continuity and cohesion. In simplest terms, the Socialists lacked these qualities, whereas the Communists possessed them.

The Socialists at this time, one must remember, were not a recycled version of Guy Mollet's SFIO, even though the latter formed the "trunk" onto which were grafted Mitterrand's followers from the Convention des Institutions Républicaines, Rocard's Parti Socialiste Unifié, and other smaller leftist groups. As indicated by its rechristened name, Le Nouveau Parti Socialiste, the PS in the early 1970s was looking to reinvent itself in terms of ideology and identity. Coupled with this relative organizational *dis*continuity was the fact that the PS was a party of contentious, competitive factions. The party's main source of cohesion was the figure of Mitterrand himself, who was the one leader acceptable to all factions—at least until Rocard's direct challenge in 1979. These two qualities of the PS's culture—organizational discontinuity and lack of cohesion—proved functional in the 1970s because they endowed the party with a great deal of ideological flexibility (some might argue opportunism). Not only were party leaders open to new ideas— for example, self-management (*autogestion*) and governmental decentralization—but the factional divisions produced shifts in ideological and/or programmatic positions according to the balance of factional forces at a given moment. This kind of protean identity proved attractive to new audiences, including workers and, especially, the professional middle classes. It also enabled the PS to appear unambiguously leftist as well as "modern."

Communist Party culture, by contrast, demonstrated considerable continuity and cohesion, although these qualities ultimately worked to the party's disadvantage. Continuity could be seen most clearly in the PCF's emphasis on its historic identity as the organizational expression of the industrial working class, even as "postindustrial" change was beginning to transform the class structure and reduce the ranks of factory workers. While continuing to embrace that identity, the party did part with tradition in two ways: first, the Union of the Left demonstrated the party's willingness to cooperate and potentially share power with other progressive forces, and, second, the party's short-lived embrace of Eurocommunism. Ultimately, these programmatic and ideological departures fell apart because they clashed with the party's other distinctive quality: its emphasis on cohesion.

In contrast with the Socialists' factionalism, the PCF's culture emphasized solidarity, unity, hierarchy, and discipline—in a word, conformity—which found organizational expression in the practice of democratic centralism. These traits not only tended to produce leaders who were classic organization men (see below) but also served to legitimate the other main principle of Leninism: the party as "vanguard" of the working class. Ultimately, the party's refusal to collectively question these founding principles meant that the attempt to embrace innovation through the Union of the Left or Eurocommunism could go only so far. Implacable party logic dictated not only that democratic centralism had to be preserved at the expense of internal party pluralism (as Eurocommunism at least implied). Even more crucially, party logic said, in effect, If we, the party, cannot lead the Left, then better to withdraw from compromising alliances and wait for more favorable conditions. As we have seen, this became the PCF's operative logic in 1977–1978. In the end, the party's incapacity to transform its own culture made its actions in that period both predictable and self-destructive.

In all, as one compares the two parties' strategic responses during the critical juncture of 1972–1977, the distinctive aspects of each party's culture help explain differences in their capacities to engage in the kind of self-reflective organizational change that scholars have termed social learning. As defined in chapter 1, social learning refers to the ability of an organization to adapt or alter its behavior and/or strategy on the basis of new information, changes in its operating environment, or an evaluation of the consequences of past actions and experiences. In its capacity to reinvent itself, promote new generations of leaders, anticipate social trends (including the interests of emerging middle-class groups), and adapt to the opportunity structure of the Fifth Republic, the Socialist Party proved relatively successful, whereas the PCF was a dismal failure. Socialist Party culture demonstrated a considerable capacity for social learning, whereas Communist culture did not.

Leadership

At first glance, differences in party culture as just described might appear to leave little room for the role of individual leaders in explaining Socialist-versus-Communist strategic responses in the 1970s. Yet it would be simplistic to conclude that Mitterrand and Marchais were mere products of their respective party cultures and thus irrelevant. Such a conclusion would be to ignore the fundamentally dialectical relationship between leadership and party culture. Party cultures indeed tend to reward and promote certain types of leaders—and thus "produce" them in that sense—but leaders, in turn, can decisively shape a party's strategic response in a given situation. This was certainly true in the French case: the Socialists' and Communists' responses were strongly molded by their respective leaders, Mitterrand and Marchais.

In assessing their impact, it is evident that Mitterrand's grasp of the dynamics of Fifth Republic politics was far more sophisticated and farsighted than Marchais's. As became clear by 1977, Mitterrand's calculated risk that the Union of the Left would work to the Socialists' advantage proved correct. Marchais, by contrast, not only badly misjudged the costs of coalition to his own party but then compounded his strategic error by torching the Union in 1977–1978 and declaring virtual scorched-earth warfare on the Socialists in the run-up to the 1981 presidential election. When Mitterrand and the Socialists emerged victorious in elections that year, the Communists became politically superfluous. Under humiliating conditions, the party had little choice but to accept the Socialists' invitation to join the government as a minor partner. Although the handwriting of the PCF's decline was already on the wall, the 1981 electoral defeats were devastating, marking the start of a dramatic secular decline from which the PCF never recovered. One can reasonably argue that Marchais and the Communists made a historic mistake in 1977 by breaking the Union. By sticking with the Union, the Communists would likely have come to power as a still strong partner. They could then have pushed Mitterrand (who would certainly have become prime minister in a cohabitation government) to carry out the Common Program, while President Giscard d'Estaing would have resisted it. As Ross (2006) contends, "The party might then have maximized its strength and minimized that of Mitterrand and the PS, reversing the trend of the earlier 1970s" (22).

That outcome, of course, did not happen. The chief result was that the two parties' responses to the challenges of the late 1960s and early 1970s put them on divergent electoral and organizational paths that have lasted to the present. In that sense, the years 1972–1977 were indeed, to use the Colliers' term, a "watershed" for both parties. Events of this period in no way cast the fate of the Socialists and Communists in some predictable fashion. Parties, like all living organisms, have a survival instinct and thus an impulse to adapt behavior to changing environmental conditions. Both the Socialists and the Communists demonstrated such an instinct and impulse in various ways after 1980, and one could make a plausible case that both parties faced subsequent critical junctures, for example, the Socialists in 1982–1983 when they reversed their economic policy course and the Communists in 1993–1994 when Hue tried to rescue the party from the wreckage wrought by Marchais. But, in retrospect, the parties' responses between 1972 and 1977 stand out as the crucial ones, as the influences of institutional context, party culture, and leadership combined in such a way as to establish new, definitive directions for both parties.

NOTES

1. Jospin, quoted in Pickles (1982, 42).
2. For present purposes, "exercising political power" is defined as one or both parties participating in the governing of parliament (i.e., being a member of the government) or (after 1958) controlling the presidency.
3. There is a slight tendency for cooperation to be more prevalent when the two parties are *out* of power. For example, in the ninety-one years under consideration, Socialists and/or Communists were not part of government for a total of fifty-two years. During those "out" years, the two parties generally cooperated a total of thirty-three years, or 56 percent of the time. By contrast, of the thirty-six years that Socialists and/or Communists participated in the government, cooperation was the rule slightly less than half the time—seventeen years, or 47 percent of the time.
4. A third competing national confederation, albeit a moderate one espousing a Catholic-inspired doctrine of class conciliation, was formed in 1919: the French Confederation of Christian Workers (Confédération Française des Travailleurs Chrétiens), which, with its main following among office workers and other white-collar professionals, did not compete effectively with the CGT and CGTU among blue-collar workers.
5. The literature on the Popular Front, in English as well as French, is huge. In English, see, for example, the extensive analyses in Colton (1966), Brower (1968), Greene (1969), Tiersky (1974), and Jackson (1988). Essential French sources include Lefranc (1965) and Bodin and Touchard (1986).
6. The two-round system herein described was also used during most of the Third Republic (1870–1940) but was jettisoned in favor of a one-round proportional representation system during the Fourth Republic. Thus, the Fifth Republic's "new" electoral system was largely a reprise of the earlier practice.
7. Excellent accounts of these maneuvers can be found in, inter alia, Portelli (1980), Johnson (1981), Bell and Criddle (1988), and Bergounioux and Grunberg (2005).
8. Article 5 of the PS's statutes basically institutionalized the existence of recognized *courants*. Different groups within the party could present their own political motion at the party's biennial congress. Assuming that a particular motion gained at least 5 percent of the total vote on political motions, then the group presenting that motion would be guaranteed proportional representation at the local, federal, and national levels of the party (Sawicki 1998, 72).
9. Marchais's feelings for Mitterrand were mutual. He is reported to have said, "Every time I see Mitterrand I'm tempted to put my hand over his mouth" (quoted in Tiersky 2000, 115).
10. Whereas in 1973 the percentage of French people holding a "bad opinion" of the PCF was 48 percent (vs. 33 percent holding a "good opinion"), by 1977 the "bad opinion" figure had risen to 55 percent (vs. 30 percent "good opinion") (Bell and Criddle 1994a, 223).
11. Scholarly interest in the 1981–1983 French "Socialist experiment" has been intense, generating a huge scholarly literature. My intent here is to not to recount once again the events of this period but rather to give its basic outlines within the broader narrative of Socialist–Communist relations. For more complete accounts of the "experiment," see, inter alia, Fonteneau and Muet (1985); Hall (1986); Ross, Hoffman, and Malzacher (1987); Cameron (1988); Singer (1988); Smith (1990, 1998); and Schmidt (1996). This and the following paragraph are based on these and other sources.
12. Essential sources for this internal policy struggle include Bauchard (1986), Favier and Martin-Roland (1990), and Pfister (1986). For a summary, see Smith (1998, 74–78).

13. Epinay is the city in the Paris suburbs where the PS's founding congress was held in 1970.

14. Between 1970 and 1990, CGT membership dropped by more than two-thirds, from 1.87 million to 600,000. In roughly the same time period (1968–1988), the CGT's percentage of votes in works council (*comité d'entreprise*) elections declined from 47.9 to 26.7 percent (Bell and Criddle 1994b, 129–30).

15. A poll taken two years earlier, in 1995, indicated that 70 percent of the public agreed with the statement, "Whether the Right or the Left is in government, the result is the same" (Knapp 2004, 137).

16. In these elections, the PS increased its vote share to 23.4 percent (vs. 17.5 percent in 1993), while Communists held their own at 9.9 percent. The other components of the Plural Left coalition—the Greens, Chevénement's MDC, Bernard Tapie's Radical Socialists, and various unaffiliated Left candidates—gained 12.2 percent.

17. Jospin's cabinet featured three Communists (including the future party head, Marie-George Buffet), one Green (party leader Dominique Voynet, named minister of the environment), two Left Radicals, and one MDC (party leader Chevènement as minister of the interior).

18. In the first round of the 2002 presidential election, the four non-PS candidates from the Plural Left coalition gained a total of 16.3 percent. Compare that to the total of 12.0 percent achieved by just two non-PS Plural Left candidates in 1995. The other major difference in the two elections, in terms of the impact of other Left parties on the PS candidate, was that in 2002, the two extreme-left candidates—Laguiller of Lutte Ouvrière and Besancenot of Ligue Communiste Révolutionnaire—gained a total of 10.0 percent, whereas in 1995 only one extreme-left candidate (Laguiller) drew 5.3 percent. Taken all together, the non-PS Left vote in 2002 was a surprising 26.2 percent—larger any single candidate in the race—whereas in 1995 the corresponding figure was only 17.3 percent. Assuming that non-PS Left voters would be more likely to vote for Jospin than Le Pen in the absence of other choices, it is obvious that a smaller "supply" of non-PS candidates in 2002 would have virtually assured Jospin of a runoff spot.

19. In 2001, presidential terms were reduced from seven years to five. Given that the maximum term of a legislature is also five years, this modification in the presidential term established the possibility that presidential and legislative elections could occur in the same year without dissolving parliament and holding new elections.

20. Lemaire, in turn, was replaced in 2005 by Yann Wehrling.

21. The following are two representative headlines on this theme: "How the Left Lost the People" (*L'Express*, May 30, 2002); "The Deproletarianization of the Left" (*Le Monde*, June 2–3, 2002). The best study of the erosion of the Left's support among the "popular classes" (workers and nonprofessional office workers) is that of Rey (2004).

22. The Events of May–June 1968, as with the other major moment of twentieth-century mass worker mobilization, the Popular Front, have generated a huge literature. A very small sampling includes Singer (1970), Dubois et al. (1971), Touraine (1971), Feenberg and Freedman (2001), Ross (2002), and Seidman (2004).

23. More accurately, the Fifth Republic constitution "grafted a powerful presidency on to the traditional form of parliamentary government" (Pierce 1995, 4).

24. The 1958 Fifth Republic constitution mandated presidential selection by an electoral college of local officials.

Chapter Three

Italy: Historically Compromised

> The Communist and Socialist parties are natural allies, bound by their common hostility to the existing capitalist society, yet they were also natural enemies, competing for the allegiance of the same workers.
> —Alexander De Grand (1989, xi)

At first glance, Socialists and Communists in Italy seem to share many similarities with their French counterparts. As in France, the two parties have cooperated for extended periods, for example, during the Resistance against Fascism and the early postwar Liberation and Reconstruction governments. There have also been periods of fierce rivalry and even outright hostility between the two parties that parallel the French case, most notably during the 1980s when Socialist prime minister Bettino Craxi rarely missed an opportunity to castigate the Communists. Despite these surface parallels, however, the dynamics of Socialist–Communist relations in Italy have been distinct from those in France. The chief differences stem from two aspects of the domestic political context: the nature of the political opposition the Left has faced and the impact of institutional and electoral arrangements.

The Italian Left has historically faced a political opposition of daunting and even forbidding strength. Most obviously, Italy was ruled by a Fascist dictatorship for over twenty years beginning shortly after the schism between the two parties in early 1921. During the Mussolini reign, both parties were first harassed, then banned and repressed; much of the Socialist and Communist leadership was either imprisoned or went into exile. The suppression of "normal" democratic politics between 1922 and the end of World War II meant that the early identities of the Partito Comunista Italiano (PCI) and the Partito Socialista Italiano (PSI) were forged in clandestine struggles rather than electoral contests. By contrast, until the German army overran the country in 1940, France maintained a contentious but functioning democracy for the whole interwar period, and, as we have seen, both the Socialists and the Communists had a role in governing during Léon Blum's Popular Front government in 1937–1938.

Italian leftists continued to face implacable opposition after World War II. The early years of Italy's fledging republic were heavily influenced by the Cold War and American support for the Christian Democrats (Democrazia Cristiana [DC]). By strongly playing the anti-Communist card, the DC gained the upper hand in the 1948 elections. Thereafter, for the next forty-five years, the DC resisted every Communist attempt to gain a share of national power despite the latter's campaign for a "historic compromise" in the 1970s. Thus, in its entire seventy-year history, from its 1921 founding until its transformation into a "post-Communist" party in 1991, the PCI never had a representative in a governing cabinet other than during the short-lived Liberation government of 1945–1947. The Socialists fared better in the post-war period, although they too were initially excluded from DC-led coalition governments. Only in the early 1960s were they able to enter the charmed circle of the "inner party system," the collection of smaller parties with which the DC was willing to form coalitions (Morlino 1986; Bosco and Gaspar 2001). Moreover, even though the Socialist Craxi served as prime minister from 1983 to 1987, the PSI was always a minority in governments dominated by the DC. Again, the contrast with the French case is stark. As we saw in the previous chapter, the Parti Comuniste Français (PCF), although excluded from office from 1947 to 1981, joined the governing coalition, in association with the Socialists, for two periods: 1981–1984 and 1997–2002. As for the French Socialists, beginning in the early 1980s, they were a far more potent political force than their Italian counterparts. To state the distinction most simply, in Italy conservative and/or authoritarian opposition proved much more repressive, resistant, and durable than in France. This fact, as we shall see, significantly affected both Left parties individually as well as the relationship between them.

The other major aspect of the political setting that has shaped the strategies of the Communists and Socialists—and therefore their interrelations—is what I have termed the institutional context, that is, the arrangements determining the main governmental and electoral systems. In the French case, we have already seen how the Fifth Republic's presidential system affected party behavior, as all parties after 1958 had an incentive to produce or coalesce behind a single leader capable of leading a party or coalition to power. The key to the Left's finally gaining power in 1981 was Mitterrand's ability to exploit this system by becoming the undisputed candidate of all the Left forces. By contrast, Italian politicians generally and Left politicians in particular have resolutely rejected a presidential type of system—largely out of fear that direct election of the president might produce another authoritarian leader in the Mussolini mold—in favor of a parliamentary regime in which parties, not individuals, tend to dominate politics.[1] The result has been a tendency toward party fragmentation and division rather than consolidation as in the French case.

Coupled with a strong parliamentary system has been an electoral system that also reinforced fragmentation. Italy has been a classic example of "Duverger's law," according to which proportional representation (PR) systems promote the proliferation of smaller parties and thus multiparty systems, whereas single-member-district (or "first past the post") systems tend to foster two-party or two-coalition systems (Duverger 1959). From 1948 to 1994, Italy used a "permissive" PR system in which parties with as little as 2 percent of the vote could gain parliamentary seats.[2] With such a low threshold for securing parliamentary seats, parties had little incentive to merge into larger formations or form coalitions. In only one instance—the initial postwar parliamentary elections of 1948—did Communists and Socialists fully cooperate by forming a single bloc list, and the results were disastrous. In every one of the subsequent ten legislative elections until 1994, the two parties went to the polls as competitors. By contrast, as we have seen, Fifth Republic France's institution of a single-member-district system with a runoff provision encourages interparty cooperation and coalition formation.

Clearly, then, context matters in any comparison of the Italian and French Left. But this is not to conclude that context determines all. In the end, parties make their own histories, just as individuals do. Thus, the perennial question for both Socialists and Communists has been, Conflict or cooperation? As in the previous chapter, the present discussion analyzes how the two parties have answered this question, as we examine the trends, turning points, and patterns in their relationship. The next section surveys the full period, 1921–2010, focusing on fluctuations in party strength and phases of cooperation and conflict. The following four sections provide a narrative of interparty dynamics, with a focus on the period since the early 1960s. The first of these sections provides historical background from 1921 to 1962. The latter date is chosen because it represents a dramatic departure: the first moment since 1921 (again, excepting the exceptional immediate postwar period, 1945–1947) when one of the major Left parties, the Socialists, entered a government cabinet. From that moment on, a new, largely negative dynamic was established between Socialists and Communists that continued to play out over successive decades.

The second section, covering 1963–1980, examines the Socialists' experience in government along with Communist attempts in the 1970s to reach a so-called Historic Compromise—a power-sharing agreement with the Christian Democrats. As we shall see, this period encompassed critical junctures for both the PSI and the PCI. For the Socialists, there were two distinct but related critical junctures: first, the initial decision in 1962–1963 to "cross the Cold War line" and end its alliance with the Communists and then, in

1976–1980, a drive by Craxi to isolate and marginalize the PCI while establishing the PSI as the system's essential power broker. As for the Communists, the years 1973–1980 were a critical juncture, as the Historic Compromise never came to fruition and ended with the party in a downward trajectory.

The third section surveys the period 1980–1994, an era of crisis and transformation not only of the Socialist and Communist parties but also of the entire party system. By the end of this period, Italy's "First Republic" had imploded in the wake of massive corruption scandals.[3] The final section analyzes the 1994–2010 period during which leaders on the Left sought to forge a new political force out of the splinters and remnants of the Socialists and Communists, which either disappeared (PSI) or were transformed (PCI) in the tumultuous events of the early 1990s.

THE BIG PICTURE: SOCIALIST–COMMUNIST RELATIONS, 1921–2010

Any discussion of Socialist–Communist relations in Italy must begin with an assessment of the parties' relative strength. As noted in the previous chapter, a key indicator of party strength is electoral performance, which is best measured by the parties' vote percentages in national parliamentary elections. Such an assessment is complicated in Italy by two historical realities. First, for virtually the entire twenty-five years that followed the split between Socialists and Communists in 1921, the two parties were illegal and driven underground. Given those conditions, one simply cannot measure relative party strength with any confidence, and therefore we must focus on the postwar period. This points to a second reality: by definition, measures of relative party strength can extend only as long as the parties exist, and thus such an assessment must end with the 1987 elections, the last time that the two parties went head-to-head under their traditional banners.

Figure 3.1 portrays the Left parties' electoral performance for all twenty parliamentary elections from 1919 to 2008.[4] For analytical purposes, one can identify three clusters of elections. A first cluster of three (1919, 1921, and 1924) were the pre-Fascist or early Fascist elections, in which the fledgling Communist Party struggled to assert itself against the historically dominant Socialists.[5] A second group was the eleven elections between 1946 and 1987 in which Socialists and Communists coexisted. In these elections, the Left as a whole—including extreme-left, center-left, and Green parties as well as the Communists and Socialists—demonstrated the consistency of a strong but permanent minority, averaging nearly 45 percent and obtaining only a bare majority of 50 percent on just two occasions (50.0 percent in 1976 and 50.6 percent in 1987). The constant drama of the Left, of course, was its inability to pool its components into a single party or coalition, and thus its overall potential remained forever unfulfilled. The third set of elections consists of the six contests held between 1992 and 2008 in a new and still evolving party system environment, featuring new patterns of intra-Left competition and cooperation, without, as mentioned, the existence of its classic pillars, the PSI and PCI.

During the core period, 1946–1987, one sees a striking similarity in relative Communist–Socialist strength in Italy and France. In both countries, the Communists emerged in the early postwar period as the more popular party, a position they maintained during the next three decades. As figure 3.2 indicates, Communists consistently outpolled Socialists, the former averaging 26.5 percent and the latter 13.1 percent.[6]

In terms of interparty relations, while there were, as in France, periods of both cooperation and conflict, the pattern differs in two major respects (see table 3.1.). First, in Italy the wartime cooperation between Communists and Socialists, born out of the resistance to Fascism, not only survived the onset of the Cold War but continued into the early 1960s. Throughout the 1950s, the PSI and PCI formed the core of the permanent opposition to the triumphant Christian Democrats. This cooperation contrasted with the French case, as the East–West conflict drove a wedge early on between the PCF and the Section Française de l'Internationale Ouvrière (SFIO). One need only recall that, in France, it was the *Socialist* premier Paul Ramadier who banished his five Communist ministers from government in May 1947. Thereafter, the SFIO formed one of the usual suspects in successive Fourth Republic governments, whereas the PCF remained excluded and isolated.

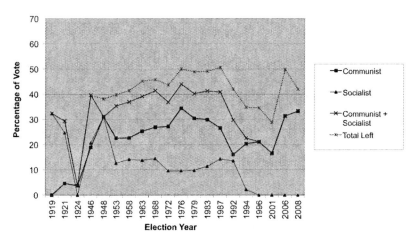

Figure 3.1. Socialists, Communists, and the Left: Italian Legislative (Chamber of Deputies) Elections, 1919–2008

Year	Communist (and Post-PCI) Party % Vote (% Seats)		Socialist Party % Vote (% Seats)	PCI vs. PSI % PCI Vote/% PSI Vote (% PCI Seats/% PSI Seats)
1919	—		32.3	0
1921	4.6		24.7	.19
1924	3.8		10.8[a]	.35
1946[b]	18.9 (18.7)		20.7 (20.7)	.91 (.90)
1948	31.0[c] (31.9)			—
1953	22.6 (24.2)		12.7 (12.7)	1.78 (1.91)
1958	22.7 (23.5)		14.2 (14.1)	1.60 (1.67)
1963	25.3 (26.3)		13.8 (13.8)	1.83 (1.91)
1968	26.9 (28.1)		14.5[d] (14.4)	1.85 (1.95)
1972	27.2 (28.4)		9.6 (9.7)	2.83 (2.93)
1976	34.4 (36.0)		9.6 (9.0)	3.58 (4.00)
1979	30.4 (32.0)		9.8 (9.8)	3.10 (3.27)
1983	29.9 (31.4)		11.4 (11.6)	2.62 (2.71)
1987	26.6 (28.1)		14.3 (14.9)	1.86 (1.89)
1992	16.1[e] (17.0)	5.6[f] (5.6)	13.6 (14.6)	1.18[g] (1.16)
1994	20.4 (17.3)	6.0 (6.2)	2.2 (2.2)	9.27 (7.86)
1996	21.1 (27.1)	8.6 (5.5)	—	—
2001	16.6 (21.7)	5.0 (1.7)	—	—
2006	31.3[h] (35.7)	5.8 (6.5)	2.6 (2.9)	—
2008	33.2 (34.4)	3.1[i] (0.0)	1.0 (0.0)	—

Source: Ignazi (2002, 234); *Parties and Elections in Europe* (http://www.parties-and-elections.de).

[a] Combined result of Unified Socialist Party and Italian Socialist Party.
[b] Elections for Constitutional Assembly.
[c] PCI and PSI had combined candidate list called *Fronte Popolare*.
[d] PSI and PSDI reunited as *Partito Socialista Unificato* (PSU).
[e] Post-Communist party: PDS (1992, 1994, 1996), DS (2001, 2006), PD (2008).
[f] *Partito della Rifondazione Comunista* (PRC).
[g] Ratios based on PDS vote only.
[h] DS ran in single list as *Unione* coalition in 2006.
[i] PRC ran in "Rainbow Coalition" with Greens and other parties.

Figure 3.2.   The Left in Italy: Election Results (Chamber of Deputies—Lower House), 1919–2008

Second, once the PSI "defected" from the PCI–PSI alliance by joining a DC-led cabinet in 1963, the two parties were never able to heal the breach, except for a brief rapprochement in the early 1970s. Some level of cooperation did continue between the two parties at subnational levels—in cities and regions—but Socialist and Communist leaders publicly carried out disputes for most of the three decades from 1963 to 1992. There was simply no Italian equivalent of a French-style Union of the Left or of coalition governments led by Socialists, Communists, and other Left forces, as in 1981–1984 and 1997–2002. The Italian pattern, then, is paradoxical: a long phase of cooperation (1942–1960) in which many observers accused the Socialists of being virtual lapdogs of the Communists, followed by an even longer period during which the two parties, as it were, fought like dogs. After such a long, close collaboration, why did things fall apart so definitively and permanently? We return to this question later in the chapter.

HISTORICAL BACKGROUND, 1921–1962

The Pre-1921 Context

The 1921 split between Italian Socialists and Communists took place in an ideological context that resembled France in some respects. If the French Left prior to World War I had its Jaurès and Guesde, Italy had its Turati and Serrati: leaders espousing conflicting visions of how the socialist movement should achieve its goals.[7] Filippo Turati, one of the founders of the Partito dei Lavoratori Italiani in 1892, preached the pacific, democratic way. The leading Italian advocate of Eduard Bernstein's concept of evolutionary so-

Table 3.1. Socialist–Communist Relations in Italy: Conflict versus Cooperation, 1921–1992

Period	Conflict versus Cooperation	Number of Years
1921–1933	Conflict	13
1934–1938	Cooperation	5
1939–1941	Conflict	3
1942–1961	Cooperation	20
1962–1969	Conflict	8
1970–1975	Cooperation	6
1976–1992	Conflict	17

Note: Conflict: 41 total years/four separate periods; Cooperation: 31 total years/three separate periods.

cialism, Turati argued that socialism was not possible without democracy. Economic equality had to go hand in hand with political equality; indeed, achieving political equality was the precondition for achieving economic justice. Therefore, for Turati and his followers, such as his longtime lover Anna Kulisciofff and Claudio Treves, the Partito dei Lavoratori Italiani (soon renamed the PSI) had to surrender any illusions of a vast proletarian uprising à la Marx and focus instead on building a political majority led by the working class. If Turati was Italy's Jaurès preaching moderation, Giacinto Serrati was its Guesde, breathing fire and brimstone. As a self-described "maximalist," Serrati, along with followers including Costantino Lazzari and Arturo Vella, argued that Italy's constitutional monarchy dominated by opportunistic Liberals was both illegitimate and incapable of reform and therefore had to be overthrown by revolution.

Prior to 1912, these two natural currents in the socialist movement were able to coexist, with the Turati current generally in control of the PSI.[8] Although it remained a small party with less than 10 percent of the vote in a restricted-suffrage parliamentary system, the Socialists were a vocal albeit perpetually frustrated force for reform. The party's internal center of gravity changed, however, in 1912, when the Serrati revolutionary wing took control of the party. In the process, one of the maximalists' emerging leaders, Benito Mussolini, became the editor of the party's newspaper, *Avanti!* (Kogan 1983, 106). During the following decade, as Italy fought a devastating, futile war and then plunged into economic crisis, the PSI leadership moved ever leftward.[9] As in France and many other nations, the Bolshevik Revolution was another factor that encouraged the revolutionaries within the PSI.

By 1919, the PSI found itself in a precarious and untenable situation. On the one hand, it experienced soaring popularity, especially among a newly enfranchised working class. In parliamentary elections that year, the party won 32 percent of the vote, becoming the largest party in parliament with 156 of 508 seats. On the other hand, the party's radical leadership—now being pressed by an even more revolutionary, pro-Soviet group within the party—refused to play the government game, rejecting a coalition with the other major party, the Catholic-inspired Partito Popolare. According to De-Grand (1989, 34), Socialist leaders "temporized" while Italy's economic and political crises grew ever more dire. During the course of the following year, 1920, a dual process of polarization ensued within Italian society and the Socialist Party itself. Within the society, an eerie dialectic developed between a wave of factory occupations—culminating in the celebrated "workers' councils" in Turin in September—and the growing mobilization of Fascist *squadristi* bent on defeating Socialism and "restoring order." Meanwhile, the PSI endured its own internal struggles among Turatian reformists, the "old" maximalists led by Serrati, and the "new" maximalists—now the party's left wing—headed by a group of pro-Soviet revolutionaries, including

Amadeo Bordiga from Naples and a Turin contingent led by Antonio Gramsci, Angelo Tasca, Umberto Terracini, and Palmiro Togliatti.

1921–1943: Surviving under Fascism

As in France, the denouement among the contending socialist currents played itself out in a party congress. At the January 1921 congress in Livorno, a vote on whether to follow the Lenin script and transform the PSI into a Communist party failed, with only about one-third of delegates supporting affiliation with the Soviets. In predictable fashion, this group promptly left the PSI and formed the Partito Comunista d'Italia with Bordiga as its first head. (The party's name was changed in 1943 to PCI. For simplicity's sake, I will use this appellation and these initials in referring to the Communist Party throughout its existence from 1921 to 1991.) Because the PCI represented only a minority of socialist forces, it found itself initially in a weak position in relation to the PSI. For example, in national elections later that year, the Communists received less than 5 percent of the vote and only sixteen seats versus the PSI's 25 percent and 112 seats (De Grand 1989, 47).[10]

The following years, which saw Mussolini rise to power and consolidate Fascist rule, brought three significant changes for the Left. First, even though the Socialists' most radical faction had departed to form the Communist Party, the Socialists remained divided between reformists—those who were willing to play the parliamentary game—and maximalists who continued to reject the game in favor of revolution (although, of course, maximalists also rejected any subordination of the party to the Third International). Demonstrating its unending capacity for self-division, the PSI split again in October 1922, with the moderate reformists led by Giacomo Matteotti (and including the original reformists Turati and Treves) leaving to form the Unitary Socialist Party. Thus, by the time Mussolini came to power a month later, in November 1922, the once-unified Left consisted of three rival parties. Although Mussolini's triumph owed to several causes, there is no question that the Left's internecine battles, coupled with its inability to engage constructively with moderate democratic forces that could have resisted Mussolini, facilitated Il Duce's rise (Smith 1997, 288–322; Bosworth 2006, 101–20; Duggan 2007, 420–30).

A second change was an important leadership shift within the Communist Party. Responding to the obvious dangers of a divided Left confronting a rising Mussolini, Lenin and the Third International pressured the PCI to put Humpty Dumpty at least partially back together by negotiating a fusion with the Serrati maximalists within the PSI. When the Communist leader Bordiga resisted this pressure, he found himself accused of "ultraleftism" by none other than Lenin himself. The end result was Bordiga's ouster and replacement by party "centrists" Gramsci and Togliatti (Sassoon 2003, 40). This was a fateful move in that it put the PCI under the direction of leaders who were relatively flexible in their approach to alliances with other political forces (Cammett 1967, 165–70). Whereas in France the Third International's impact was to encourage a more sectarian party, in Italy the effect was rather the reverse.

A final change for the Left was its repression, as Mussolini, in his first four years in power, took advantage of the Left's weakness to harass and ultimately outlaw it. Following the banning of all other political formations except the Fascists in November 1926, Left activists were either arrested, driven underground, or forced into exile. The PCI's leader, Gramsci, was arrested that month (and kept in prison until his death in April 1937), while an estimated one-third of all Communist members and half of the party's executive committee were also imprisoned. Togliatti, who became party head after Gramsci's arrest, fled to Paris and eventually Moscow, never returning to Italy until Mussolini's fall in 1943. By the early 1930s, the total number of Communist activists was fewer than 10,000 (Sassoon 2003, 38). The party's fortunes did improve, however, during the 1930s as disillusionment with Mussolini grew. For example, the PCI recruited new members among young intellectuals who had been active in the Fascist youth movement. As for the Socialists, although their activists were subject to the same repression experienced by the Communists, there was at least one bright spot: the reunification, in 1930, of the PSI and its erstwhile reformist wing, the Unitary Socialist Party (now called the Socialist Party of Italian Workers [PSLI]; see below). Thus, for the first time since 1922, Italy had a single Socialist party.

Relations between Socialists and Communists during the Fascist period broadly paralleled those of their French comrades during the 1920s and 1930s, chiefly as a function of Soviet/Third International dictates. In the first few years following its formation, the Third International declared a United Front strategy promoting cooperation between Communists and local allies. As noted previously, during this period, the Soviets engineered the ouster of Bordiga as PCI head, precisely because he rejected any such alliances. This strategy changed, however, in the wake of the power struggle following Lenin's death in 1924. After defeating Trotsky, Bukharin, and other contenders, Stalin in 1928 initiated a "class-against-class" strategy within the Comintern that considered Socialist and Social Democratic parties as objective class enemies and therefore no better than Fascists. This implied that Communist parties should struggle against fascism on their own, rejecting all anti-Fascist alliances with other parties. Although there was considerable resistance to this line within the PCI, including opposition by Togliatti, who, as noted, had succeeded the imprisoned Gramsci as party leader, the PCI finally adhered to the policy (Urban 1986, 52–79). Doing so closed off cooperation with the PSI. For their part, the PSI reciprocated by going its own way, joining with the other Socialist party, the PSLI, and other exile groups to form the "Anti-

Fascist Concentration," a movement that pointedly excluded the Communists (Di Scala 1988, 3–4). This cooperation between the PSI and the PSLI led directly to the reunification of the two parties.

As we have seen in the French case, once Comintern policy reversed course in favor of a Popular Front strategy in 1934, relations between Communists and Socialists dramatically improved. The same was true in Italy, as the Communists signed a Unity of Action pact with the Socialists in August of that year.[11] This new *volontà* of cooperation proved durable. It was renewed in 1937 and remained in effect, with one exception, for the next two decades. The one exception, of course, was during the period of the 1939–1941 Nazi–Soviet Non-Aggression Pact—an agreement that objectively put the Soviet Union on the side of Mussolini and the Fascists. Even a dialectician as skilled as Togliatti could not make that alliance digestible, even to his own members.

1943–1947: Resistance, Liberation, and the Coming of Cold War

Driven largely out of Italy and off the political stage for over two decades, Socialists and Communists received new life with the American invasion of Sicily and the sacking and arrest of Mussolini by King Victor Emanuel III in July 1943. For the next four years, until May 1947, these two parties, as their French counterparts, were key elements in both the Resistance and early postwar reconstruction. Joining first with four other parties, notably the newly born Christian Democratic Party, in the anti-Fascist coalition, the Committees of National Liberation, the PSI, and the PCI formed the backbone of the Partigiani guerrilla movement that took on Nazi troops and soldiers of Mussolini's puppet government in the north. Following Liberation in May 1945, Communists, Socialists, and Christian Democrats formed a tripartite government that established a new republican constitution and began the process of economic rebuilding (Smith 1997, 418).

From the standpoint of an analysis of the Left, there were three important trends of this period. The most notable was the Communists' change in orientation—a sea change in political approach that is termed the "*svolta di Salerno*."[12] On returning to Italy in March 1944 from Moscow, where he had spent much of World War II, Togliatti announced his support of the promonarchy, American-supported Badoglio government headquartered in the southern coastal town of Salerno. This move angered some other members of the Committees of National Liberation, who were forthrightly republican, but for Togliatti (and for the Soviet Union, which backed him), this represented a practical move that anticipated postwar Italian realities.[13] Togliatti's view was that the transition to Socialism would be a long march, requiring new alliances and the building of mass organizations within the capitalist order.

It would be difficult to exaggerate the importance of this *svolta* for post-war Italian Communism, for it provided the template for PCI strategy for much of the next five decades. Togliatti's stance indicated that the party henceforth would not only reject revolution in favor of a parliamentary path to socialism, but it would also seek to cooperate with centrist and even conservative parties, including the Christian Democrats. This implied a consistently conciliatory, moderate stance toward Catholic and conservative sensibilities. For example, in the drafting of the 1946 Republican constitution, the PCI supported the inclusion of the 1929 Lateran Treaty that gave a privileged position to the Catholic Church. Certainly a main reason for this shift was Togliatti's realization that Fascism had been a mass phenomenon with strong middle-class support; therefore, to deny the resurgence of Fascism after the war, it would be necessary to rally at least a critical mass of the middle class to one's side (Hellman 1975, 375–76; Sassoon 2003, 40–41).

A second trend of this period was the definitive emergence of the PCI as the dominant force on the Left. Although both the PSI and the PCI came out of the Resistance with renewed prestige and organizational strength, the Communists, being subject to Third International discipline, were much more unified. The Socialists, by contrast, were divided into four identifiable currents, pulled between a revolutionary Left and a prodemocratic, reformist faction—a division that would soon lead to yet another organizational split (see below).[14] Moreover, the PCI's activism was much broader and deeper in scope than the Socialists. By the end of the war, the PCI had managed to extend its organization to workplaces, peasant cooperatives, women's organizations, and other groups not only in the proletarian centers of the north but also in socially diverse areas of the center. This penetration of civil society was in line with Togliatti's concept of *il partito nuovo*—the "new" Communist Party that would no longer be a small, conspiratorial, Leninist-style organization but rather a mass organization reaching into neighborhoods, workplaces, and people's daily lives (Weitz 1992, 32).[15] Accordingly, the party experienced a surge in membership; from about 5,000 members in mid-1943, the party swelled to 1.7 million members by the end of 1945 (Urban 1986, 189). Although the PCI failed to overtake the PSI in the 1946 Constituent Assembly elections, it drew almost even (see figure 3.2) and clearly bested the Socialists in local elections later that year. In the eternal contest for primacy on the Left, the PCI had momentum in its favor in the early postwar period.

Finally, even though the balance of organizational strength had tipped the Communists' way, this shift did not disrupt the practice of close cooperation between the two parties. As much as any other factor, this cooperation owed much to the personal commitment of PSI leader Pietro Nenni, who went so far as to advocate the reunification of the two parties.[16] Mindful of the disasters caused in the early 1920s by divisions within the Left, Nenni believed in unity at virtually any cost. That cost proved to be high. Nenni's idée fixe of unity with the Communists triggered old fears of Communist domination and ultimately cost the party its conservative wing. In late 1946, as Cold War tensions mounted, the PCI and PSI signed another unity pact, a move that apparently produced poor results for the Socialists in local elections a month later. Concluding that aligning with the Communists was weakening the PSI's independence as well as its popularity, the anti-Communist faction within the PSI, led by Giuseppe Saragat, left the PSI to form the PSLI.[17]

Even as the Communists were reinforcing their position in relation to the Socialists, the coming of the Cold War brought political defeat and exclusion to the Left as a whole. Under pressure from the U.S. government, the Christian Democratic Prime Minister De Gasperi sacked the Socialist and Communist ministers from his tripartite cabinet in May 1947, ending the four-year Resistance and postwar collaboration among the three parties. Thus, onto old Left–Right enmities of class and religion was laid the U.S.–Soviet conflict—a divide that would endure for another forty-five years. While the French scenario was similar to the Italian one in general outline, a big difference is that whereas in France the onset of the Cold War drove a wedge between Socialists and Communists, the same did not occur in Italy: Socialists and Communists remained in solidarity. This unity carried over into parliamentary elections the following year in which the two parties ran together as the Fronte Democratico Popolare (Galli 2004, 68).

1948–1962: Cold War Politics

The 1948 elections, the first held under the new republican constitution, revealed two things about the Left. First, the Left as a whole suffered badly in the new, Cold War–dominated order. The PCI–PSI Fronte received just 31 percent of the vote, compared with a total of nearly 40 percent for the two parties running separately in the 1946 elections. By contrast, the Left's new nemesis, the Christian Democrats, gained an absolute majority in parliament, largely by stoking fears of the Soviet Union. Second, even though the Left as a whole did poorly, the Socialists fared much worse than the Communists.[18] The Socialists now found themselves distinctly inferior to the PCI in terms of organizational strength and popular appeal, as many voters viewed them as being dominated by their Communist partners.

The 1948 elections set a basic pattern that would govern Italian politics until the early 1990s. In essence, the party system was built around the existence of two mutually antagonistic mass parties: the Christian Democrats and the Communists (Barnes 1966). Clearly, the dominant actor was the Christian Democratic Party, although the 1948 elections turned out to be anomalous in that it was only time that the DC gained a majority of seats on its own. From the 1953 elections on, the DC would have to recruit coalition partners to form a governing majority, and these were typically smaller parties, such as the Liberals, Republicans, and Social Democrats. Practicing an informal *"conventio ad excludendum"*—an agreement to exclude the Communists from any consideration as a coalition partner—these parties had trouble agreeing on little else, so governments were typically short lived. For example, between 1948 and 1994, Italy had a total of forty-seven governments but only eleven parliamentary elections; thus the average government lasted about ten months. Despite its inability to establish a stable government, the DC, being by far the largest party in any government coalition, was always the linchpin and thereby became permanently enmeshed in running the government bureaucracy. In this fashion, the DC gradually morphed from a Catholic-inspired movement to a faction-ridden, spoils-generating electoral machine (Bardi and Morlino 1994).

The other mass party, the PCI, had no stake in sharing power at the national level; however, it maintained a vigorous minority presence in parliament and a growing role in local government, where it became known for competent management in such Red Belt cities as Bologna, Florence, and Ferrara (Calise 1994). Beyond these governmental toeholds, the PCI established a highly organized subculture of workplace and neighborhood party cells, labor unions, women's and youth organizations, and sports and social clubs (Kertzer 1980, 26–72; Guiat 2003). As in France, the Italian Communists also maintained an active publishing/propaganda wing, issuing a daily newspaper and various magazines, reviews, and books. The heart of the party, of course, was a core of rank-and-file and activist members that topped 2 million by the mid-1950s (Hellman 1988, 38). For many of them, the PCI was a veritable "counterchurch" that encompassed all aspects of their lives.

Of particular importance in terms of the PCI's capacity to connect to social struggles was the party's influence within the largest labor confederation, the Confederazione Generale Italiana di Lavoro (CGIL). As in France, the labor movement was divided into various confederations based largely on partisan affiliation, and thus the CGIL, as in the case of the Communist-aligned Confédération Générale du Travail (CGT) in France, faced competition in the workplace and labor market from competing unions.[19] Unlike the CGT, however, whose leadership was dominated by Communists in the early postwar period, the CGIL's leadership was a de facto power-sharing arrangement between Communist and Socialist labor leaders, and thus the CGIL never approached the "transmission-belt" model that tended to define the PCF–CGT relationship, especially after 1956, when the PCI officially rejected any such subordination of the union to the party. Moreover, Communist CGIL leaders themselves increasingly insisted on operational autonomy from the party. Nonetheless, the CGIL was an important organizational resource the PCI could draw on to extend its influence (Weitz 1975, 548–49; Lange, Ross, and Vannicelli 1982, 241; Golden 1988b, 36; Bedani 1995).

A major shock to the PCI–PSI partnership occurred in 1956, although its effects were not fully felt for several years. In that year, Khrushchev presented his "secret speech" to the Twentieth Party Congress of the Communist Party of the Soviet Union, denouncing Stalin's errors and excesses. In the same year, the Soviet Union intervened to suppress revolts in Eastern Europe either directly, as in Hungary, or indirectly, as in Poland. These events reverberated through both the PCI and the PSI. For the former, although Togliatti continued to support the Soviet system publicly, he also began to distance his party from the Soviets by speaking of an "Italian Road to Socialism": an approach that would respect Italian political culture and traditions rather than copy the Soviet model (Urban 1986; Sassoon 1990, 90; Agosti 1996; Bracke and Jørgensen 2002, 12–13). It was not coincidental that the party lost 400,000 members between 1955 and 1957 largely, by Togliatti's own admission, because of his members' disgust over Soviet tactics in Hungary (Judt 2005, 321).

The PSI's reaction was considerably more negative and emphatic. Most symbolically, Nenni returned the Stalin Peace Prize that he had won in 1951. Although he maintained a public facade of unity with the Communists and refused to join a DC-led government, behind the scenes he began exploring alternative alliance possibilities with the Social Democrats and the Christian Democrats. While the official parting of the ways with the Communists did not come for several more years, the events of 1956 crystallized Nenni's determination to move the Socialists out of the Communists' large shadow. A fundamental transfer of the Socialists' political loyalties was under way (Sassoon 1996, 266).

ESCAPING THE COLD WAR GHETTO? 1963–1980

The final transfer of Socialist loyalties came in 1963, when the Socialists accepted the offer of DC Prime Minister Aldo Moro to join his cabinet. This *"apertura a sinistra,"* or "opening to the left," was historically significant. Excepting the short-lived and exceptional Liberation period (1944–1947), the opening marked the first time since Italy's 1870 unification that the Socialist Left had participated in a government. The move also constituted the first of two critical junctures that the PSI experienced in the 1960s and 1970s, for it created a new threefold dynamic in terms of party competition and strategy that was to have lasting effects. First, it turned the PSI and PCI into competitors and definitively ended the two parties' long history of collaboration. Moreover, the *apertura* gave the Socialists an opportunity to establish a new identity as independent reformers no longer beholden or subordinate to the Communists. In this endeavor, they could claim some success, although the decision to break with the Communists engendered much internal opposition (and yet another organizational split) as well as electoral decline.

Finally, by tilting Italy's center of political gravity slightly to the left, this new phase provided a space for the Communists, by the early 1970s, to launch their own opening: a bid to collaborate with the Christian Democrats. In the process, the PCI sought to escape the political isolation, the Cold War ghetto, into which both the DC and, after 1963, the PSI had consigned it. The Communists' hope proved futile, however. For the PCI, the story of the 1970s is the party's ultimately failed attempt to bring about a "Historic Compromise" with the DC. From the perspective of 1980, this phase, which began with the Opening to the Left in the early 1960s, not only produced an enduring break between the Socialists and the Communists but also bracketed the frustrated efforts by both parties to cooperate with the Christian Democratic Party.

In the early 1960s, the Socialists became a plausible coalition partner for the DC for three main reasons. One was the increasingly public spats between the Socialists and the Communists, notably PSI leader Nenni's progressively harsh accusations against the Soviet Union for violating human rights and suppressing freedom in Eastern Europe. An important step was Nenni's January 1962 article in the journal *Foreign Affairs* indicating that the PSI accepted Italy's membership in NATO, thus placing the Socialists on the American side of the East–West divide for the first time. Although Togliatti was no vocal defender of the Soviet Union on every occasion, by refusing to criticize Soviet action, he put his party at odds with the Socialists. Thus, the DC saw a golden opportunity to take advantage of the split and co-opt the Socialists.

A second reason for a DC–PSI rapprochement was that several important actors—among them the Kennedy administration, big business, and the liberalizing Catholic Church under Pope John XXIII—signaled their approval of such a move (Di Scala 1988, 115–32; De Grand 1989, 131). Finally, a third reason was simple necessity: the DC needed a significant new coalition partner. The DC vote share had declined from 48.5 percent in 1948 to 38.3 percent in 1963, making the party's ability to muster a majority ever more precarious and dependent on satisfying its smaller coalition partners. [20] In this context, the Socialists could bring in new voters, especially from the working class. The DC recognized that Italy's "Economic Miracle"—its industrial takeoff beginning in the late 1950s—was transforming large numbers of southern peasants into northern industrial workers, and the DC wanted to establish a link to this emerging class. Although the Socialists had far less of an organizational presence among industrial workers than the PCI, the DC wagered that collaboration with the Socialists would still boost the coalition's working-class appeal (De Grand 1989, 129–30; Bardi and Morlino 1994, 247–48).

The opening to the left arrangement lasted, albeit bumpily, from 1963 to 1974. Although the Socialists never held the prime ministership, they held cabinet positions in most of the governments formed during this period. The alliance did produce several reforms—notably nationalization of the electricity industry, a law to eliminate sharecropping, school reform, and a bill of rights for workers—but most of these came early in the collaboration. As a consequence, the Socialists received little long-term credit from the voters, as their vote share slumped from 13.8 to 9.6 percent between 1963 and 1972 (see figure 3.2). Moreover, the decision to join DC-led governments prompted a left-wing faction to leave the party and form a separate party that eventually merged with the PCI.[21]

Despite these problems, as well as continuing tensions between the PSI and PCI at the national level, the two parties cooperated in two important respects during the 1960s. One was in local government, where Socialist and Communist elected officials often joined in municipal and commune-level governing coalitions. By one estimate, of the roughly 2,000 communes under the Left's administration in the 1960s, about three-fourths depended on a coalition of Socialists and Communists (Di Scala 1988, 126).

A second venue was in the labor movement, specifically the largest union confederation, the CGIL, where, as mentioned earlier, Socialists and Communists essentially shared power. Unlike the French case, where the Cold War divided the two parties within the largest confederation, the CGT, and led to the formation of the anti-Communist, pro-Socialist Force Ouvrière, no such split occurred in Italy. In the CGIL, PSI and PCI members held leadership positions and worked collectively. The extent of interparty collaboration within the CGIL should not be exaggerated, however. During the 1960s, all the major union confederations—including the DC-related Confederazione Italiana Sindacati Lavoratori (CISL) and the Unione Italiana del Lavoro (UIL), which was close to the Social Democrats and Republicans (see note 20)—exercised growing autonomy in relation to their "sponsoring" political parties. At the same time, these three confederations increasingly cooperated in advancing their own reform proposals in such areas as wages, labor law, and pensions.

There were several reasons for this double movement by the major unions, among them a growing militancy among industrial workers demanding union unity, the CISL's emergence as an aggressive shop-floor competitor of the CGIL, and a frustration among unionists with the government's lack of responsiveness to their interests. Thus, one of the distinctive aspects of Italy's industrial relations during the 1960s and 1970s is the extent to which the major confederations took on the role of political actors in their own right (Lange et al. 181). Nonetheless, if one defines political cooperation to extend beyond electoral politics and direct interparty relations, then union activity constituted an important site of continued collaboration between the two parties.

By the late 1960s, it was clear that the center-left governing experiment, however innovative politically, had failed to resolve major problems of economic and social modernization. Sluggish growth, coupled with rising inflation and unemployment, were fueling manifestations of protest from students and workers alike. The "Hot Autumn" of 1969 witnessed a huge jump in strike activity, especially by unskilled, newly arrived migrant workers from the south now working in heavy industry in northern cities such as Turin and Milan (Regalia and Reyneri 1978). Strikes and building occupations by university students protesting the Vietnam War, overcrowded classrooms, and poor employment prospects also became daily occurrences. In this context, violent extremist movements mobilized on both the Left and the Right. On the Left, groups such as the Red Brigades not only denounced the DC, the PSI, and other inner-system parties for failing to help the working class but also accused the PCI of passivity and de facto complicity with the current regime. On the extreme Right, groups such as the Fronte Nazionale used violence in hopes of triggering an authoritarian backlash that would somehow "restore order." Both groups employed the repertoire of terrorism—bombings, kidnappings, and murder—with the first such action being the bombing, by extreme rightists, of a bank in Milan and three sites in Rome on December 12, 1969, that killed sixteen people and wounded 105 (Ferraresi 1996, 90–91).[22]

How to respond to these multiple crises became the preoccupying question for both Socialists and Communists. For the PSI, the center-left experience was proving disappointing. On the one hand, the PSI had little influence over the DC; for example, a Socialist-initiated plan to legalize divorce was blocked by the DC, and the two parties could not agree on a university reform plan, even as students clamored for change. On the other hand, the PSI's identification with an apparently paralyzed DC-led government produced voter disenchantment, a trend that, for the Socialists, was all the more disappointing, as the Communists seemed to profit from its outsider status (D'Alimonte 1999, 161).[23] Following the Socialists' poor showing in the 1968 elections, Nenni's opponents within the party sought to scuttle the Socialists' partnership with the DC and seek a rapprochement with the Communists. Factional fights within the party finally led, in July 1969, to Nenni's resignation as PSI president and as foreign minister, thus bringing an end to over five years of continuous PSI–DC collaboration (Di Scala 1988, 164–65). The two parties' partnership was far from dead, however. Over the next five years, the PSI would hold cabinet seats in various DC-led coalition governments even though the relationship between the two parties was often conflictual and elements within the PSI continued to press for a new alliance with the PCI.

As for the Communist Party, the crises of the late 1960s and early 1970s produced a quandary: should the party support the various protests and push for the defeat of the DC, or should it seek some accommodation with the DC in order to preserve the current system? Needless to say, within the PCI, there were fervent proponents of both approaches, but in late 1973, in the wake of the Pinochet coup in Chile, the new party secretary Enrico Berlinguer announced the party's definitive stance: the proposal of a "Compromesso Storico," or "Historic Compromise," in which the PCI would join with the DC in a government of national unity. This new strategy marked the beginning of a critical juncture for the Communists, for the playing out of this strategy over the next few years had a long-term impact on the party's fortunes.

Although analysts have rightly referred to Berlinguer's proposal as a "*svolta*" (turning point), there was a strong element of continuity with both Togliatti's "new party" line of the Tripartite period and Gramsci's concept of the importance of cultural hegemony. Both of these predecessors were well aware of the PCI's need to appeal to loyal Catholics. Berlinguer argued that the DC was a mass party that drew support not only from devout Catholics but also from all sectors of the population; therefore, no definitive change could be effected without the DC's cooperation. While linking his proposal to his party's past, Berlinguer also tied it to the present—specifically Italy's current crisis as well as the "lessons of Chile." Seeking an exclusive coalition with the PSI, which at best could garner a slight majority, would run the risk of further polarization and even the prospect of a military coup. According to Berlinguer (1973), "It would be completely illusory to think, even if the parties and the political forces of the Left succeeded in gaining 51 percent of the votes and seats in Parliament . . . , that this would guarantee the survival and functioning of a cabinet that represented only that 51 percent." Only a coalition with the DC, he argued, would have the necessary public support to avoid a right-wing backlash (Hellman 1988, 22–23; Eley 2002, 410). Berlinguer also wagered that, with sufficient Communist pressure, the DC could be pushed to enact progressive reforms.

Given the DC's fractiousness—the party counted six organized factions—as well as its record for corruption and policy paralysis, Berlinguer's bet was a long shot at best. The compromise strategy obviously put Berlinguer and the Communists in an ambiguous position. How could a party professing loyalty to Moscow and a commitment to Socialism also defend a system run by a manifestly opportunistic and largely anti-Communist party with strong ties to the United States? This uneasy if not completely contradictory combination of the PCI's long-term goal of Socialist transformation and its short-term aim of shoring up the status quo drove Berlinguer into a classic double discourse. Seeking to appear reasonable and accommodating to the outside world and especially to the Christian Democrats, he showed a more traditional Communist face to the party's own members. A telling example was a June 1976 interview given to the daily newspaper *Corriere della Sera* in which Berlinguer claimed that he wanted Italy to remain in NATO; in fact, he added that he "felt more secure being on this side." When the interview was published in the PCI daily *L'Unità*, however, this statement was excised (D'Alimonte 1999, 168).

Whatever the contradictions of the PCI's stance, the party initially reaped only gains: an influx of new members, growing voter popularity, and a reputation for "responsibility." Between 1968 and 1976, the party grew from 1.5 to 1.8 million members; by the late 1970s, over half of all PCI members had joined since 1969, with nearly one-third of these under the age of thirty (Pasquino 1988, 42; Lange, Irvin, and Tarrow 1990, 22). The party's surging appeal was reflected in regional elections in 1975 and parliamentary elections in 1976; in the latter, the PCI reached its historic high of 34.4 percent compared with the slumping DC's 38.7 percent. The Socialists, tarnished with the image of dependency on the DC, stagnated at just under 10 percent of the vote. Given these dynamics, the Communists appeared to be in a credible position to negotiate a "grand-coalition" style of government with the Christian Democrats.

The playing out of Berlinguer's compromise strategy took place between 1976 and 1980. To be clear, the PCI's actions during this period did *not* constitute the implementation of the Compromesso Storico strategy as theorized by Berlinguer and the leadership group. But the compromise strategy was the stated long-range goal of the Communists, and the party's behavior in the late 1970s was conditioned by and in line with that programmatic commitment. In any case, there is no question about the outcome. The end result for the Communists was negative in two respects: the strategy did not work as planned, and it cost the PCI dearly in terms of internal unity and electoral viability.

The strategy did not work as envisioned because, although the Communists pushed hard to become an official partner in the government, the DC kept the door closed, forcing the PCI into the worst of all worlds: a position of "support" without portfolio but with no policy responsibility. Between August 1976 and January 1979—a span of two and a half years—the Communists supported two *monocolore* governments (i.e., DC-only cabinets) headed by Giulio Andreotti.[24] In return, the party had little to show for its support. The government passed new laws in such areas as regional government, urban planning, and mental health provision, but implementation was often poor or nonexistent. In the critical area of wages, the PCI, through its influence on the largest union, the CGIL, counseled restraint and discouraged active pressure to keep wages at least in line with inflation. But workers received little *quid* for their *quo*: unemployment continued to rise, and a union proposal to stimulate job growth in the south received little attention.

As Paul Ginsborg (2003a) remarks, "Once again, as in 1945–7, the PCI was unable and unwilling to use its considerable powers of mass mobilization to force the DC into making real concessions" (390).

Not only was the PCI unable to strongly influence a shaky and unpopular government, but the party's image suffered in its handling of one of the most traumatic events in Italy's postwar history: the kidnapping and murder of DC President Aldo Moro by the Red Brigades in the spring of 1978. By taking a hard line against any negotiations with the kidnappers for Moro's release, the PCI was viewed by many as lacking a humanitarian impulse, especially since Moro had been one of the champions of including the PCI in the government (Di Scala 1988, 185). In all, Berlinguer's Historic Compromise, in the sense of a full partnership with the other great "historic bloc," the Christian Democrats, was never realized: the Communists never achieved full partner status, and, although they were consulted regularly, they were never in a position to have a significant impact on policy. At the same time, the party became associated in the public mind with responsibility for the many policy failures.

The question remains as to why the Communists were not given a formal place at the cabinet table. Suffice it to say that there was resistance from many quarters. The DC itself was torn on the question of Communist participation. Party leader Aldo Moro favored inclusion of the PCI into the governing majority, but he proceeded cautiously because of internal opposition from some of the party's more conservative factions. Opposition also came, albeit expressed *sotto voce*, from the Carter administration, which viewed with alarm the prospect of Communists being privy to NATO-related security information and even in a position to veto deployment of nuclear-armed cruise missiles in Western Europe (Gardner 2005, 214–15). Resistance came as well from the Socialist Party, now under the leadership of a brash young leader, Bettino Craxi, who was seeking to reassert both the PSI's independence from the PCI and its position as the Left's favored partner with the Christian Democrats (Giovagnoli 1996, 178–79). Finally, Moro's death traumatically disrupted the process of rapprochement and removed the PCI's main interlocutor within the DC.

Not surprisingly, the PCI's disappointing Compromesso bid also exacted a cost in terms of party unity and electoral appeal. As Hellman has convincingly argued in his study of the PCI in Turin during this period, the Historic Compromise strategy was poorly understood and received by local-level *militanti*. Hellman's interviews, carried out within the Turin federation in 1978, revealed that only about one-third of party functionaries strongly supported the strategy of aligning with the DC. The rest either opposed it outright or supported it only with qualifications, with many of the latter expressing doubt about the reliability of the DC as an ally and criticizing the PCI's leadership for not being more aggressive toward this prospective "partner" (Hellman 1988, 199).

Much of this disaffection among local party personnel and rank-and-file members can be traced to a generational divide evident in the PCI in the late 1970s. As mentioned earlier, the party had welcomed an influx of new members in the early 1970s, with many of these being educated young people coming from backgrounds in student organizations, women's groups, and the like. Research carried out in the late 1970s demonstrates that many in this cohort had become impatient and even disillusioned with the party's cautious, defensive approach to political change (Barbagli and Corbetta 1982a, 215; Lange et al. 1990, 42).

Such disappointment became all the more difficult to bear given the party's poor electoral performance. In local elections in 1978, the PCI drew just 26 percent and in parliamentary elections the following year just 30.4 percent—down a full four points from its high of just three years before. Given the various disappointments of the PCI's bid for an alliance with the DC, it would not have been difficult to predict yet another *svolta* in the offing. As we shall see in the next section, such a turn was not long in coming.

As with Mitterrand's decision to abandon the *relance* strategy in 1983, there has been an extensive debate over the PCI's Compromesso strategy. Was the strategy the only option for the Communists, given the various crises at the time, the country's polarization, and the party's own isolation? If not, what other possible alternatives existed? Was the strategy well conceived but undone by events, notably the Moro kidnapping and killing? I would argue that, in hindsight, both the strategy and the disappointing results were both logical and even predictable outcomes of the path defined by Togliatti in the 1940s.[25]

That path, the vaunted "*via italiana al socialismo*," was based on a fundamental tension inherent in the party's dual role as both vanguard of change and defender of Italian democracy. On the one hand, the PCI, proclaiming an essential loyalty to the Soviet Union, bore the banner of a party sworn to bury capitalism. This implied a readiness, indeed a desire, to contest the very legitimacy of the capitalist system and those social forces, including other political parties, that supported that system. On the other hand, the PCI, having played a central role in writing the 1946 republican constitution, swore to defend Italy's institutional order both as a "vaccination" against any possible reversion to authoritarianism and as a way of achieving the Gramscian goal of cultural hegemony. The tension in these conflicting roles produced the widely recognized *doppiezza*—a doublespeak of revolutionary rhetoric coupled with cautious, regime-reinforcing behavior that posed no great problem for the party as long as there was no realistic prospect of ever having to exercise power. In essence, the party could eat its revolutionary cake and have it too since the revolution was always "out there" in some undefined future. From 1948 until the mid-1970s, the PCI could credibly claim to be both a party of protest and radical change and a party of order, moderation, and, in the case of local administration, good government.

This formula became untenable, however, in the late 1970s as the party faced the sharpening of its contradictory stance. On one side, the PCI found itself pushed from below by an influx of young activists impatient for change. Push also came from the voters, who viewed the governing parties as incapable of managing the country's polarization. By the mid-1970s, the PCI was a credible contender to join the inner-system parties, and the Historic Compromise proposal was the party's appeal to do so. On the other side, however, the Communist initiative met a push back in the form of the DC's refusal to grant the PCI full partnership, a stance that was encouraged, as we have seen, by the United States.

At that crucial moment, the PCI had no real counterploy, no real vision of what structural changes it would demand in exchange for its support. The key problem was that, for the PCI, the Historic Compromise had become an end in itself, not a tactic for eventually achieving the party's longer-term goals. This was the case in large part because the party *had* no clearly defined longer-term goals. In essence, the party's commitment to defending the flawed democratic system took precedence over its other professed aim of radical transformation. Forced finally to confront the contradictions of *doppiezza*, the party opted for preservation over transformation. As mentioned earlier, one can plausibly argue that the Moro affair closed off the possibility of the Communists' eventually joining the government, and thus the Compromise was ultimately undone by unforeseen events. However, this does not erase the fact that the PCI had already traded away its trump card: the demand that the government commit itself to profound structural changes in return for Communist support.

Just as the Communists were sinking in the late 1970s, the Socialists under Craxi were rising. A supreme Machiavellian who rivaled Mitterrand in his ability to identify and eliminate possible enemies within his own party and to constitute a nemesis to other parties, Craxi had a clear vision: to bring the PSI out from under the Communists' shadow by constituting a "Socialist pole" that would unify all the forces of the non-Communist Left. To counter the movement of Eurocommunism that enjoyed a season of notoriety in the mid-1970s, Craxi posed the idea of Eurosocialism, and he cultivated ties with other Socialist and Social Democratic parties in Germany, Spain, France, and elsewhere (Di Scala 1988, 181). In Craxi's view, this Socialist pole would not just rival the Communists; it would destroy them. In this concept, one sees the driving animus of Craxi's entire tenure as head of the Socialist Party from 1976 until his flight into exile in 1994: an unrelenting anti-Communism. In part, this hostility was personal; Craxi had only disdain for Berlinguer and took every opportunity to goad him about the PCI's subservience to Moscow. Craxi's anti-Communism also had a "revenge-of-the-father" quality, growing out of his father's unhappy experiences with the PCI.[26] The end result was that Craxi's rise created a new dynamic in PSI–PCI relations—one of unremitting opposition—that would endure until the early 1990s. For this reason, Craxi's initial period as PSI chief from 1976 to 1980, when he put his definitive mark on the party's strategy and modus operandi, constituted a second critical juncture for the Italian Socialists.

In all, the period 1963–1980 represented a long phase in which first the Socialists and then the Communists sought to emerge from the political isolation imposed by the Cold War. Given the hegemonic position of the Christian Democrats after 1948, as well as the impossibility of the PSI and PCI ever achieving a consistent electoral majority, the only possible path for ending their isolation was through some kind of alliance with the DC. First the Socialists in 1963 and then the Communists in 1976 attempted such a path.

One can draw three general conclusions from these endeavors. The first is that, as we have seen, ending the Left parties' isolation came at the price of the alliance that the two parties had established during the Resistance period. From the early 1940s until the early 1960s, Socialists and Communists had practiced solidarity. Although that alliance became frayed after the events of 1956, the Socialists still had not "switched sides." That formal break came with the 1963 Opening to the Left—a breach that was never fully healed. Second, the experience of seeking an alliance with the DC ultimately proved negative for the PSI and PCI. Unable or unwilling in both cases to change the basic dynamic of DC dominance, the two parties became tarnished by their association with the Catholic party. Both the Opening and the Historic Compromise initiatives proved harmful to the Socialists' and Communists' image and electoral performance.

Finally, this long phase encompassed critical junctures for both Left parties. Both the Communists and the Socialists, albeit at different times, responded to "crossroads" moments in their history with strategies that had long-term ramifications. For the Communists, the critical juncture was the period between 1973 and 1980, during which the party sought to achieve its Historic Compromise with the DC. This strategy, as just noted, produced confusion and disaffection both inside and outside the party. It would be too strong to argue that the Compromise led directly to the PCI's abandonment of Communism in the early 1990s. Communism was a deteriorating political "brand" worldwide in the 1980s, so the PCI would likely have encountered an organizational crisis in any case. But there is little doubt that the Compromise strategy and its fallout hastened the party's decline, as we shall see in the next section.

As for the Socialists, there were two critical junctures during this period, the first being the 1962–1963 "opening to the left" and the second being Craxi's initial years as party head from 1976 to 1980. The "opening" was a strategic shift for the Socialists, an abandonment of its long alliance with the Communists and an embrace of "the system" as organized by the Christian Democrats. While definitive, this shift, as we have seen, proved frustrating for the Socialists. As a junior partner in DC-led governments, the PSI found its reform efforts thwarted by the DC, the party fared poorly at the ballot box, and factional struggles within the party pitted those who wanted to continue the DC alliance against others who wanted a rapprochement with the Communists. Craxi's rise, in effect, clarified and cemented the PSI's basic direction as an inner-system party and thus, to that extent, represented continuity. But Craxi also brought an original vision: a determination to forge a new kind of Socialist Party that defined itself as not just independent from but *in opposition to* the Communist Party. I contend that this second strategic turn put the PSI on a road that, in the 1980s and early 1990s, led not only to enhanced power for its leader and the party but also to corruption, scandal, and ultimately collapse.

PARTY SYSTEM CRISIS AND TRANSFORMATION, 1980–1994

For an observer surveying the Italian political scene in 1980, it would have been almost impossible to imagine the seismic shocks that were to come in the next dozen years. Even as late as 1987, an expert as knowledgeable as Joseph LaPalombara (1987) claimed, "Italy is fundamentally a healthy, dynamic, democratic country, with little chance of going over the brink and breaking to pieces" (x). Five years later, no one would make such a claim. Perhaps the nation itself did not break apart, but the political system certainly went over the brink. By 1993, the three largest parties—the DC, PCI, and PSI—either no longer existed or were engulfed in crises that would soon bring them down. For the two Left parties specifically, this period brought the disgrace and collapse of one party (the PSI) and a fundamental transformation of the other (the PCI).

For the Socialist Party, its downfall was all the more shocking as the party had recently soared to its postwar zenith in terms of votes and effective power. According to two astute analysts writing in the mid-1980s, "From being a vacillating, faction-ridden, Marxist-Leninist party subordinate to the Communists at the outset of the postwar period, the [PSI] had transformed itself by the early 1980s into a unified, self-confident, moderate-left party in the mainstream of European social democracy" (Spotts and Wieser 1986, 68). This celebratory assessment was written during the prime ministership of Bettino Craxi, who served in that office from August 1983 to April 1987—the longest-running government in postwar Italy to that time. Yet just seven years after leaving office, in April 1994, Craxi fled to Tunisia to escape going to prison on corruption charges; in elections that same year, the PSI drew a risible 2 percent of the vote and soon disbanded.

To understand the party's rise and fall, one is naturally drawn to analyze the central role of Craxi, who, to recall, became PSI secretary in 1976 and immediately sought to carve out an independent power niche for himself and his party. A key to Craxi's rise as party leader was a fearless ambition coupled with a brilliant ability to outmaneuver potential rivals within the party.[27] Within the arena of party politics, Craxi's aim was to erase the traditional postwar bipolarization between a permanent Communist opposition and a permanent DC hegemony, in the process making the PSI the kingmaker in a more fluid system. For this task, Craxi had a jugular-seeking instinct for exploiting the weaknesses of his rivals. We have already mentioned his attempts to isolate the PCI by playing on the anti-Communist theme. Thus, at a time in the late 1970s when the Communists had been stressing their own moderation, Craxi kept up a barrage of anti-Soviet criticism. This in turn forced Berlinguer to reaffirm his Marxist-Leninist and even Stalinist heritage, thus raising doubts within the public as to whether the Communists had truly changed (Di Scala 1988, 188–89). Once the PCI returned to the opposition in 1980, Craxi aligned the Socialists with the DC, but he proved a prickly partner, rarely hesitating to criticize DC leaders even as his party held cabinet positions. Following the 1983 elections, when the Socialists advanced only slightly but the DC fell dramatically, Craxi felt emboldened to demand the prime ministership from his much larger partners.[28] The DC acceded, and Craxi became the first Socialist prime minister in Italian history.

As prime minister, Craxi sought to establish an image as a decisive, "pragmatic" socialist in the mold of Schmidt, Mitterrand, and González. In an economic context in which the inflation rate had consistently exceeded 15 percent for years, Craxi's main economic goal was to restrain wage increases—an aim that enabled him to appear tough on unions, and, not coincidentally, to challenge the Communists. The main way to limit wage gains was to alter and eventually to abolish the *scala mobile* (literally, the escalator): the nationwide cost-of-living adjustment that had been established in 1975 to protect wages from erosion due to inflation. In early 1984, the Craxi government decreed that this wage-indexing regime would be drastically reduced from the previous year. This decision set up a bitter confrontation between the government on the one side and the CGIL and Communists on the other, punctuated by general strikes and a PCI press campaign denouncing the government as "adventurist" and "dangerous." (The other two major confederations, the CISL and UIL, sided with the government.) This conflict lasted for over a year, during which the government's decree was ratified by parliament but then countered by a referendum sponsored by the PCI and CGIL aiming to annul the law. In the end, the referendum failed to pass, formal cooperation among the three major confederations broke down, and the Communists found themselves at odds with most of organized labor, including the Socialist sector within the CGIL. In all, Craxi engineered a clear victory over his Communist nemesis (Lange 1986; Di Scala 1988, 218–22; Golden 1988b, 85–86; Locke 1995, 87–88; Galli 2004, 271–80).

While scoring some spectacular wins such as this one, establishing a reputation as an action-oriented "decider," and amassing considerable personal power, Craxi also presided over a party that was rapidly embedding itself in the traditional spoils system. Thus, any explanation of the Socialists' rise and fall must take into account not only Craxi's individual actions but also the party culture that he helped foster. For example, Bardi and Morlino argue that even as Craxi forced the disappearance of factions at the national level, he allowed the provincial federations greater autonomy: "The national leadership had a free hand in making the major strategic decisions and even in drawing up the lists of parliamentary candidates, but it was seldom able to exercise any real influence on local government alliances or even on single decisions" (Bardi and Morlino 1994, 264). With little by way of an ideological rudder and lacking a mass organization of selfless activists, the PSI under Craxi devolved into a spoils-seeking machine whose mantra seemed to be "*enrichissez-vous*." Ginsborg's (2003b) description provides an evocative image of the "new Socialist man" of the 1980s: "To be a Socialist politician in Italy in these years meant to have a portable telephone and a BMW, to mix with high-flying lawyers and businessmen, to lunch at Matarel or Savini in Milan's Galleria, to have a good line of conversation on information technology and to take exotic holidays" (151).

Craxi's nearly four years as prime minister were not enough to bring about a decisive shift in the traditional *rapporti di forze* among the political parties in favor of the Socialists. In the 1987 elections, the Socialists, as mentioned, did achieve their postwar high, but the Christian Democrats also recovered from their 1983 swoon, putting them in a strong enough position to remove Craxi and impose a DC prime minister. Nonetheless, the Socialists remained in the governing coalition and were thus able to use their entrenched positions to partake of the free-flowing largesse produced by the *sottogoverno*—Italy's highly developed under-the-table system of payoffs, extortion, rigged contracts, and outright theft. All of this, of course, came to an end, however temporary, in the early 1990s as an energized class of Milanese magistrates began vigorously prosecuting flagrant corruption. Swept up in this vast campaign, quickly dubbed "*Mani pulite*" ("Clean Hands") by the press, were hundreds of Socialist and Christian Democratic politicians who were charged with various crimes. The biggest malefactor to go down was Craxi himself, who was charged with forty counts of corruption and illegal party funding (Smith 1997, 483). Exile status as a fugitive from justice in 1994 soon followed, but by then the Socialist Party was largely defunct. Following elections that year, in which the PSI polled a negligible 2.2 percent, the party dissolved, ending its century-long existence.[29]

The fate of the Communist Party during the 1980–1992 period was hardly less dramatic than that of the Socialists, as the party underwent both a makeover and a breakup. By 1992, while the majority of the party decided in favor of jettisoning its Communist affiliation in favor of a blurry "post-Communist" identity, a significant minority split off to form a "refounded" Communist party. The Italian Communists' trauma took place, of course, within a larger crisis of Soviet Communism that ultimately could not be saved through Gorbachev's reform efforts. In that sense, the prospect of the PCI's decline was as predictable as the decline of Communist parties everywhere (Wilson 1993). But the specific causes and outcomes of the PCI's crisis were unique to Italy and thus far from predetermined. The main causal factors were both external and internal, stemming, on the one hand, from the party's isolation and weakening clout within the party system and civil society more broadly and, on the other hand, from demoralization and polarization within the party itself.

In the wake of the failure of the Historic Compromise strategy in 1979, the PCI found itself isolated, without allies to the left or right, and thus became a party in search of a new role. Denied formal membership in the governing coalition, the PCI was too compromised ideologically and entrenched politically at all levels of government to take on the role of radical reformer.[30] That the PCI lacked an alternative strategy following its withdrawal of support for the DC-led government in January 1979 could be seen in the fact that even though the party was now in the opposition, it continued to defend the Compromise strategy for nearly two years. Only in November 1980, in the wake of the governments' inept handling of several horrific earthquakes, did it finally shift strategy. The new line, labeled "a democratic alternative," called for more militant opposition to the status quo, which was expressed chiefly in the party's support of several high-profile labor disputes. The two most notable of these were a long strike over massive layoffs at Fiat in 1980 and the 1984–1985 struggle over the *scala mobile* already mentioned. In both cases, the PCI met defeat, as both campaigns failed to reverse actions harmful to workers. Thus, the Communists found their influence dwindling both within the party system and in labor market struggles.

The PCI's troubles outside, predictably, spelled trouble inside. First, the sudden abandonment of the Historic Compromise strategy generated dismay and demoralization at the grassroots. For years, local party officials, in the tradition of democratic centralism, had dutifully defended the Compromesso line, with, as noted earlier, considerable resistance and incomprehension among the rank and file. With the shift in strategy in late 1980, these officials found themselves, virtually overnight and without any internal party debate, called on to advocate *rejection* of the compromise line. According to two close observers, "If [this change in strategy by the leadership] restored the faith of the members and the militants, even inspiring them to true outbursts of enthusiasm, the leadership's decision was at first received with incredulity and then with hostility by the apparatus of functionaries" (Barbagli and Corbetta, 1982a, 235).

To this demoralization *alla base* was added a second problem: polarization at the top. While the PCI had always had diverse internal tendencies, these were traditionally kept under control by Leninist strictures concerning party discipline. During the 1980s, however, fissures began appearing in the unitary facade. In part, this was due to a certain loosening of party discipline, beginning in 1981, to allow for freer expression of differences within the party.[31] But the splits also derived from the PCI's ideological drift and lack of consensus over how to respond to a changed context in which the party, bereft of prospective allies, faced marginalization. Distinct camps emerged around three prominent leaders: Pietro Ingrao, Giorgio Napolitano, and Armando Cossutta. On the party's left, Ingrao had long advocated a more overtly confrontational, anticapitalist confrontational stance. He now pressed that advocacy with renewed vigor. Staking out a position as a moderate centrist within the party, Napolitano urged the party to hew to a reformist line compatible with other European social democratic parties. Finally, Cossutta argued for a return to Communist orthodoxy. Specifically, he advocated restoring a close relationship with the Soviet Union, especially after Berlinguer denounced the Soviet crackdown in Poland in December 1981 (Bull 1994, 35–36; Hellman 1996, 81).

Parliamentary election results in 1983 (29.9 percent) and 1987 (26.6 percent), while far from catastrophic, clearly indicated that the PCI was on a downward course; in fact, the 1987 performance was the party's poorest since 1963. Similar signs of decline were evident in membership figures.[32] Failing to make inroads into the southern strongholds of the DC, the PCI's geographic base remained centered on its historic bastions: the Red Belt (Tuscany, Emilia-Romagna, and Umbria) and, to a lesser extent, the industrial triangle of Genoa, Turin, and Milan. Reinforcing these worrisome trends was an equally disquieting turnover in leadership. Still massively popular and respected for his image of austere probity, Berlinguer died unexpectedly of a stroke in 1984. He was then followed by the uninspiring Alessandro Natta, who himself was forced to resign for health reasons in 1988. The new leader selected to replace Natta, Achille Occhetto, inherited a divided and isolated party (Hellman 1988, 222–23).

At the outset of his tenure as PCI secretary, Occhetto seemed to follow in the footsteps of the early Gorbachev in seeking to reform the party rather than to transform it. This proved to be a doomed enterprise, however. Within his first year, Occhetto succeeded in dismantling the party's historic practice of democratic centralism by promoting a new statute allowing members to publicly criticize the leadership and by expanding the size of the party's central organs. As in Gorbachev's reign, the short-term effect of these measures, far from unifying the party, was to *increase* division and factionalism within the party (Bull 1994, 37–38). By November 1989, after just eighteen months at the helm, Occhetto was on the verge of losing control over the party. But on November 12, three days after the fall of the Berlin Wall, Occhetto seized the occasion of a ceremony of former wartime *partigiani* in a working-class quarter of Bologna (called "La Bolognina") to espouse a fundamental transformation of the PCI, including the party's name, symbols, and ideology (Lorusso 1992, 225–27; Kertzer 1996, 1–3). In response to a planted question from a journalist of the PCI daily *L'Unità* (November 13, 1989) as to whether the PCI had to change, Occhetto replied,

> I want to remind you that we are living in a time of great dynamism. Gorbachev, before launching his reforms in the USSR, met some veterans and said: you won the Second World War, and now if we don't want to lose what you fought for, we must not just conserve what we have but commit ourselves to immense transformations. From this I draw the motivation not to continue on the old paths but to invent new ones in order to unify the forces of progress.

As Occhetto no doubt expected, his announcement sent a shock wave through the party, arousing immediate opposition. He had reason, however, to expect his initiative to succeed. He was the party's duly elected leader, Communist regimes were collapsing everywhere, and the PCI was floundering—all factors that favored his proposal. During the following fourteen months, Occhetto and fellow proponents of transformation, such as Giorgio Napolitano, squared off in various venues against opponents of the move, chiefly Pietro Ingrao and Armando Cossutta. At issue was nothing less than the basics of the party's culture, what David Kertzer has termed the PCI's "symbolic universe": the rituals, historical references, language, songs, slogans, and graphic representations (notably the hammer and sickle) that made up what it meant to "be a Communist" (Kertzer 1996). While insisting that he honored and cherished those symbols, Occhetto was proposing, in effect, to reframe the party's seventy-year collective memory as outmoded and obsolete. To many in the party, this was the rankest betrayal imaginable.

The issue was finally settled in two party congresses, the nineteenth and twentieth congresses, held in March 1990 and January 1991, respectively. In the former, delegates voted approximately two to one in favor of Occhetto's proposal to dissolve the PCI and enter a "constituent" phase in which a new party would be organized, named, and officially ratified at the next congress. This plan was executed, and the new party, the Democratic Party of the Left (Partito Democratico della Sinistra [PDS]), received its official christening at the twentieth and final congress of the PCI, again by a two-to-one margin (Baccetti 1996, 298). For the new party, a new insignia was created, featuring a large oak tree, a symbol of sturdiness and reliability. To pay homage to the party's historic roots, two small flags—a red and yellow hammer and sickle atop the Italian *tricolore*—were inserted at the base of the tree. Soon thereafter, the PDS was accepted into the Socialist International, a move that constituted the reintegration into the political family that the PCI had abandoned in 1921 (Sassoon 2003, 35).

Occhetto's "*svolta della Bolognina*" remains controversial to the present day (Rhodes 1995, 121–22). On the one hand, many view Occhetto's move as an audacious act that staved off a bigger collapse (Gilbert 1995, 77). According to one knowledgeable analyst,

> In 1991, Occhetto did something that took great courage—nobody else had that courage. If he hadn't pushed this name change when he did, the PCI's decline would have dragged on for a long time. Berlinguer would never have made such a decision—to break with the PCI's whole past. He would never have changed the party's name. No other leader could have found the courage to do what Occhetto did. [33]

On the other hand, some analysts fault Occhetto for lacking any clear vision of what a post-Communist party should be (Hellman 1993, 207; Abse 2001, 65). Others, especially longtime party activists, denounce the way Occhetto made the decision: spur of the moment without consultation. According to the former Communist mayor of Turin, Occhetto's 1989 announcement of his intention to "decommunize" the PCI was made literally on the fly, while the party leader was on a plane flight to Bologna to give a speech. [34] The former mayor concluded, "This decision wasn't discussed with anybody. It was crazy and offensive. I felt offended, not personally, but when I think of all the people, the workers, the men and women, the young, those who'd suffered . . . you see, the party was a family. When I think of all the section meetings, the *l'Unità* festivals. . . . In principle I'm not against changing the party's name if there had been a discussion, a debate. But that's not what happened." [35]

The PCI's transformation remained totally unacceptable to those who had opposed Occhetto's initiative from the outset. While some of the opponents of transformation, notably Ingrao, accepted defeat and chose to remain in the new party, the hard core of the opposition led by Cossutta and Fausto Bertinotti resigned and formed a new party, the Communist Refoundation Party (Partito della Rifondazione Comunista [PRC]). Although the PRC's leaders claimed that the party would represent continuity in relation to the PCI, in fact it broke with the Togliatti–Berlinguer line of moderation and collaboration with other parties. For the next decade, the PRC played the role of antagonist, projecting a purist, anticapitalist image (Baccetti 2003, 36).

Thus, in the early 1990s, the PCI was simultaneously abandoning Communism and splitting apart even as the PSI was self-destructing because of its complicity in rampant corruption. The damage was dramatic all around. In the 1992 elections, the PDS obtained just 16.1 percent and the PRC 5.6 percent—a combined total representing a drop of nearly 5 percent compared with the PCI's previous result. In elections just two years later, following the wave of corruption charges falling on the PSI, the full dimensions of the Left's crisis became apparent, as the PDS, PRC, and PSI polled a combined 28.6 percent—a far cry from the PCI–PSI total of 41.3 percent a decade earlier.[36] Shortly thereafter, the PSI itself formally dissolved. In all, by 1994, the traditional Italian Left had definitively run its course. The classic enemy brothers of the Left—the Communists and Socialists—no longer existed after nearly seventy-five years of competition and cooperation, leaving in their place a set of largely undefined splinter parties searching for programs and voters.

A NEW START? THE UNCERTAIN ROAD OF THE SECOND REPUBLIC, 1994–2010

The redefinition and recomposition of the Left after 1994 took place within a party system that itself was being refashioned. Even though the 1946 Constitution remained in place, the "First Republic" party system dominated by the DC, PCI, PSI, and several other smaller parties was giving way to a new configuration: a "Second Republic" party system with largely new or transformed players. Thus, one cannot assess the trajectory of the Left since 1994 without taking into account the larger shifts within the traditional party system.

One may summarize the big changes in the party system between 1992 and 1994 as follows. A perfect storm of domestic causes and external factors combined to produce both institutional reforms and the collapse (or transformation) of virtually all the traditional postwar parties and the emergence of new political forces. The underlying domestic cause was the virtual paralysis of the party system: a manifest inability of the traditional parties to govern effectively. This, of course, was not a new problem, but it became glaring and intolerable in the light of an immediate domestic cause: the "Clean Hands" campaign by activist magistrates to root out party and governmental corruption, beginning in Milan in 1992. The explosion of political scandals produced revulsion on the part of voters, who began massively deserting the traditional parties. Between 1992 and 1994, the Christian Democrats, Social Democrats, Liberals, and Republicans either dissolved completely or splintered into smaller formations.

Reinforcing this vicious domestic cycle were two external influences: the end of the Cold War and the pressures of European integration. The former removed the raison d'être of the DC—anti-Communism—as a motivation for voters, while the latter produced a lira crisis and the need for austerity measures.[37] One response to this intersection of crises was institutional reform, specifically a revamped electoral system for municipal and parliamentary elections. Another was the appearance of new or transformed parties seeking, on the one hand, to attract voters "stranded" by the collapse of the old parties and, on the other hand, to craft coalitions that would take advantage of the new electoral rules. In this context, Gramsci's (1971) famous phrase seemed especially apt: "The crisis consists precisely in the fact that the old is dying and the new cannot be born; in this interregnum a great variety of morbid symptoms appear" (276).[38]

One can debate whether Silvio Berlusconi, the Northern League (Lega Nord), and the National Alliance (Alleanza Nazionale) constituted morbid symptoms, but there is no question that they indeed appeared—and they remained. Italy's largest media mogul and richest person, Berlusconi, fifty-eight years old in 1994, had never run for political office, but he leaped into the breach and created a new party, Forza Italia, virtually overnight. Several critics have argued that Berlusconi was driven by a desire to protect his business interests, which had become dependent on political connections with Socialist and Christian Democratic politicians. When these parties collapsed in the wake of the corruption scandals, Berlusconi found himself economically threatened and legally exposed and so decided to enter the political fray directly (Ginsborg 2004; Lane 2004; Stille 2006). Whatever Berlusconi's motivations, he sought to attract erstwhile DC and PSI voters by staking out classic center-right positions on such matters as law and order (in favor), relations with the United States (in favor of close ties), personal liberties (in favor), and the role of government in the economy (it taxes too much). Moreover, even though the PCI no longer existed and the split-off PRC drew only a fraction of the former PCI vote, Berlusconi posed as the ardent defender against the Communist menace. Finally, having created and financed the new party single-handedly, Berlusconi made his own persona a central element in Forza Italia's appeal: ebullient, successful, and, above all, *furbo* (shrewd and clever).

Berlusconi not only created a potent contender in a matter of a few weeks but also successfully exploited the new electoral system to maximum advantage. That system, approved in referenda in 1993, reserved three-quarters of the parliamentary seats to contests carried out in single-member districts.[39] This new "first-past-the-post" system put a premium on large, catchall coalitions, and Berlusconi brilliantly assembled such a coalition out of apparently contradictory elements. On the one hand, he co-opted the Northern League, a regionalist, antisouthern and anti-immigrant party with strong roots in the northern regions of Lombardy, Veneto, and Friuli-Venezia-Giulia. Nursing resentment against the old party system that, according to Lega Nord leader Umberto Bossi, took tax money from hardworking northerners and funneled

it to corrupt politicians in Rome (and then on to shiftless Sicilians and Cala-
brians), the Northern League even went so far as to propose a new nation,
Padania, that would secede from the Italian Republic (Gold 2003). On the
other hand, Berlusconi also courted the National Alliance, the "post-Fascist"
successor of the Italian Social Movement (Movimento Sociale Italiano),
whose social base was precisely the shiftless southerners that the Northern
League detested.

These strange bedfellows notwithstanding, Berlusconi's coalition won a
majority in the 1994 elections, thus marking the first time since 1948 that the
governing coalition did not include the Christian Democrats as its largest
element. As for the Left, the PDS patched together its own coalition called
"the Progressives" with their former comrades, the PRC, as well as the
Greens, the rump PSI, and several smaller groups. Although the Progressives
were easily beaten by Berlusconi's coalition, the 1994 elections held at least
some positive news. Not only did the Progressives emerge as a potential
contender for power, with 34 percent of the vote, but both the PDS and the
PRC improved on their 1992 performance (see table 3.2).

The 1994 elections also held an important lesson for the future. If the
remnants of the old Left were to become a viable coalition, they needed to
draw in more centrist voters who had previously supported the Socialists,
Social Democrats, Christian Democrats, and other, smaller parties in the
broad middle. The next step in this process came the following year with the
formation of the Olive Tree coalition (Ulivo), which included a total of four
parties, including the PDS.[40] Although by far the largest party in the coalition, the PDS could not simply dictate terms since the driving force behind
the Olive Tree was not one of their own but rather a former Christian Democrat, Romano Prodi. With the formation of Olive Tree, the Left's way forward clearly lay in the quest for moderate, centrist voters.

If the 1994 elections set the basic template of the "Second Republic,"
subsequent experience refined the outlines of the new party system and the
Left's place within it. In the wake of the 2008 elections, the system could not
be said to be consolidated if only because the electoral rules continued to be
modified. Nevertheless, several distinctive traits emerged. First, as indicated,
the system had a broadly bipolar dynamic, with two large coalitions vying to
form working majorities (Andreatta and Leonardi 2003). Second, while each
coalition had a specific name (which has changed several times), each also
had a commonly employed generic description: center-left and center-right.
These terms indicate that the bipolarity, in the terms Sartori used to describe
the "First Republic," was centripetal rather than centrifugal (Sartori 1966;
Pappalardo 2006, 484). In everyday language, the strategy of each coalition
was to hold onto its base—on the Left or the Right—while appealing catchall
style to floating voters who lacked strong partisan loyalties. Third, whatever
else one may say about this new party system, it demonstrated a flexibility

Table 3.2. Transformation of the Italian Party System: Election Results (Chamber of Deputies, Lower House), 1987–2008

Party	1987	1992	1994	1996	2001	2006	2008
Communist/Post-Communist[a]	26.6	16.1	20.4	21.1	16.6	—	—
Unione/Democratic (PD)[b]						31.3	33.2
Refounded Communists (PRC)	—	5.6	6.0	8.6	5.0	5.8	3.1[c]
Socialist (PSI)	14.3	13.6	2.2	—	—	—	—
Social Democratic (PSDI)	2.9	2.7	—	—	—	—	—
Republican (PRI)	3.7	4.4	—	—	—	—	—
Liberal (PLI)	2.1	2.8	—	—	—	—	—
Daisy (ex-DC)	—	—	11.1	6.8	14.5	—	
Christian Democratic (DC)	34.3	29.7	—	—	—	—	—
Go Italy (FI)	—	—	21.0	20.6	29.4	23.7	37.4[d]
National Alliance (AN)	5.9	5.4	13.5	15.7	12.0	12.3	—
Northern League (LN)	0.5	8.7	8.4	10.1	3.9	4.6	8.3
Other	9.7	11.0	17.4	17.1	18.6	22..3	18.0
Total	100.0	100.0	100.0	100.0	100.0	100.0	100.0

[a] PCI: 1987; DS: 1992, 1994, 1996; PDS: 2001.
[b] Unione (common list of PDS and smaller parties, including Daisy, ex-Socialist, etc.): 2006; Democratic Party (PD = merger of PDS + Daisy + other smaller groups): 2008.
[c] PRC ran in Rainbow Coalition with Greens.
[d] FI + AN common list.
Source: *Parties and Elections in Europe* (http://www.parties-and-elections.de).

and dynamism largely lacking in the First Republic in that alternation of the governing coalition became a regular feature of the system (see table 3.3). Between 1994 and 2008, there were five parliamentary elections. In *every one* of these elections, the governing majority changed hands.

Finally, although the system had an alternating bipolar dynamic, there remained considerable fragmentation and instability. Fragmentation was evident in the sheer number of parties, for while the electoral reform indeed produced a bipolar "clumping," each clump or coalition contained many constituents (Bartolini, Chiaramonte, and D'Alimonte 2004, 10). For example, in the 2006 elections, the incumbent Berlusconi-led Casa della Libertà coalition consisted of twelve parties, while the winning center-left Union coalition headed by Romano Prodi contained fifteen parties—a total of twenty-seven parties. Bardi argues that the reason for the continued proliferation of parties was that while electoral reform encouraged the formation of

Table 3.3. Italy: Alternating Majority Coalitions in Parliamentary Elections, 1994–2008

Election	Majority Coalition
1994	Center-right: Freedom Alliance (FI, AN, LN, UdC, etc.—8 parties total)
1996	Center-left: Olive Tree (PDS, PRC, Greens, etc.—14 parties total)
2001	Center-right: House of Freedoms (FI, AN, LN, etc.—5 parties total)
2006	Center-left: Union (DS, RC, PdCI, Daisy, Greens, etc.—9 parties total)
2008	Center-right: Freedom's People (FI, AN) + LN—3 parties total

Sources: Bull and Newell (2005, 55); Newell (2006, 803); Pasquino (2008, 351).

coalitions, the *lack* of reform within parliament—in terms of procedures and the organization of party groups—still gave even small parties incentives to survive (Bardi 2006, 274). Accompanying this fragmentation was the issue of instability. As Pappalardo (2006) argues,

> [Italy's problem is] not so much a case of too many parties, but rather parties with shallow organizational and political roots, vulnerable to continual electoral fluctuations, capable of banding together and promptly disbanding, through various alliances and coalitions, and often, born and deceased in the course of a single legislature. (486)

This new system shaped a Left that had little in common with its pre-1994 predecessors. Indeed, given the center-pulling tendencies in the system, many analysts questioned whether one could still speak of a clearly demarcated Left other than with respect to a few fringe parties. Gone, of course, were the old stalwarts, the PCI and PSI, along with, for the most part, any ideological or historical references to Marx, Lenin, Bordiga, Gramsci, Togliatti, or Berlinguer as inspirational ancestors. The only residual element of the old Left was the PRC, which averaged 6.2 percent in the five national elections between 1992 and 2006. In the 2008 elections, however, the PRC suffered a sharp decline, as its "Rainbow" coalition—a four-party "alternative Left" group including the Greens—polled only 3 percent and won no seats (Pasquino 2008, 352–53). This is not to say that the PRC's influence has been nil; in fact, it has sometimes played the role of gadfly and even spoiler in relation to other Left parties and governments, as in 1998, when its defection from the governing coalition brought down the Prodi-led Olive Tree government (see below).

The post-Communist PDS has been the central element of the Left, constituting not only the largest party but also the driving force behind endeavors to forge a broader Left coalition. In seeking to redefine itself, the party had to confront three basic questions. The first concerned what kind of party it would become. In essence, two contrasting visions vied for primacy (Baccetti 2003; Giannetti and Mulé 2006). On the one hand, a "Social Democratic" group led by Massimo D'Alema (party leader 1994–1998) advocated the building of a mainstream Social Democratic Party in line with those of other European nations. This party would be the anchor of the Left coalition while maintaining a classic Social Democratic identity. In this view, the Olive Tree coalition would maintain a fairly loose structure of compatible parties, but the PDS would be the dominant guiding force. On the other hand, a second group centered on the mayor of Rome, Walter Veltroni, sought to have the PDS *incorporate* the various elements of the Olive Tree coalition into a broad, catchall center-left party. Veltroni took pains to separate himself from the PDS's (and his own) Communist past, denouncing the "tragedy of communism and the horrors of Stalinism" and identifying with the liberal-socialist tradition of Carlo Rosselli, whom Togliatti considered a "worthless dilettante" (Bellucci, Maraffi, and Segatti 2001, 56). To some extent, the D'Alema and Veltroni models could be reconciled since all PDS leaders naturally favored the party's growth by absorbing compatible smaller formations. The question hinged on which smaller formations. The D'Alema "Social Democrats" sought to draw the line on Catholic-inspired groups, whereas the Veltroni group favored including them.

By 2008, it was evident that the Veltroni model had won the day. This was a victory that came in two stages. The first came in 1998, when the PDS incorporated several smaller parties of the Left and center-left, including the Unitary Communists (who had split off from the PRC), Laborists, Social Christians, and Left Republicans. The new entity, still under the dominance of the PDS structure, was called the Left Democrats (Democratici di Sinistra [DS]). The second stage came in 2007 with the creation of the Democratic Party through the merger of the DS and the other main element of the Olive Tree coalition, the Catholic-inspired Daisy Party (La Margherita), led by Francesco Rutelli, who, like Veltroni, was another former Rome mayor. The formation of the Partito Democratico (PD) represented a milestone in Italian politics by bringing together under one roof the major descendants of both the laical Left—the Communists and Socialists—and the confessional Right, the Christian Democrats. As mentioned, these were historically estranged bedfellows, and there were sharp differences between DS and Daisy activists on such "moral" issues as abortion, divorce, gay rights, and the legalization of drugs (Bordandini, Di Virgilio, Raniolo 2008, 313). Whether such a catchall and programmatically nebulous formation had a viable long-term future appeared doubtful in the wake of the PD's defeat in the 2008 elections. Veltroni, having failed to revive the center-left, resigned as PD head in early 2009, and the party experienced further election losses and leadership turnover throughout the following months.

The preceding organizational history helps answer a second basic question the post-PCI party faced, namely, what kind of program should it embrace? To mix metaphors, to the degree that the PDS–DS–PD enlarged its tent, it also watered its wine. Each successive incorporation of this or that small party blurred the party's identification with classic Left positions such as income redistribution, union rights, and public control over corporate power, not to mention the "moral" issues that traditionally divided Catholics and non-Catholics. The post-PCI's loss of a distinctive Left program owed, to be sure, to other reasons that went beyond the specifics of politics, most notably the constraints inherent in European monetary integration as well as Italy's own stagnant economy and declining international competitiveness ("Addio, Dolce Vita: A Survey of Italy," *The Economist*, November 24, 2005). Nonetheless, the PD's move toward the center, while understandable in strategic terms, risked not only abandonment of a long Left identity but also considerable ideological confusion. As one analyst remarked,

> I've talked with PD leaders who came from the PCI who say "We're not leftists anymore. We're not a left party, we're a democratic party." But in Italy that term means nothing. Within the European Parliament, the PD hasn't yet decided which parliamentary group it will join, because whereas the DS component wants to join the Socialist group, the Christian Democrats who have come from the Margherita have told the PD: no way, never. At this point, the PD is neither Communist, Socialist, Left, Social Democratic, nor Laborist.[41]

The third question the post-PCI party faced was, Who would lead the party? At issue was the question of organizational continuity. By jettisoning the old Communist practice of democratic centralism and incorporating new elements into its structures, would the PDS–DS–PD engage in an extensive "circulation of elites" and the recruitment of new leaders, especially at the local and regional levels? Although the party instituted internal elections and other mechanisms that provide for fuller participation of the rank and file, much of the old PCI structure remained intact (Giannetti and Mulé 2006, 463). According to several analysts, there had been relatively little turnover in the leadership group since the 1980s, and the PCI's latest successor, the Democratic Party, was still dominated by former Communists (Bellucci et al. 2001; Baccetti 2003; Bull 2003). According to one prominent political scientist, who was also a senator on the "Independent Left" list (sponsored by the PCI) in the 1980s and early 1990s,

> It's not true that the PD's leaders have changed. They're all the same as before, except in a few rare situations. The Bologna provincial secretary of the PD was a PCI member. He's about 45 or 50 years old, but he joined the PCI at least 25 years ago. The regional secretary of the PD was first provincial secretary and before in the secretariat of the PCI. Veltroni [the PD leader in 2008]

himself isn't new. He joined the PCI more than 35 years ago—he was also a local secretary, he was PCI vice-president of the municipal council, etc. There's no change? Why? Because the doors aren't open. The leaders decide who can enter. The system works on co-optation. Those who are co-opted are those who are loyal, disciplined, and obedient. [42]

Despite this continuity in party personnel from the pre-1991 PCI period and despite a long-term trend toward amalgamation of various elements of the old Left and center into an umbrella party, the larger picture of the Left under the Second Republic is decidedly mixed. On the positive side, the center-left demonstrated an ability to build a coalition capable of gaining power—something the pre-1992 Left was never capable of doing. In the fourteen years between 1994 and 2008, the center-left coalition formed the governing majority for fully one-half of this period: 1996–2001 and 2006–2008. In the four elections since its founding—1996, 2001, 2006, and 2008—the Olive Tree (and its successor, the Union, in 2006) averaged 44.0 percent of the vote versus the Berlusconi coalition's 45.6 percent. But winning office is only part of the story. Even leaving aside Berlusconi's and the center-right's constant campaign of denunciations, ridicule, and obstructionism—all in an effort to paint the center-left as crypto-Communist and somehow illegitimate—the center-left's experience between 1994 and 2008 was largely one of frustration born of limited policy options and internal fractiousness.

In both of its tenures as a governing majority, the center-left was largely called on to "manage the crisis," that is, put the public accounts in order by cutting fiscal deficits, limiting inflation, and reducing the public debt. This task was especially pressing during the 1996–1998 run-up to the launching of the euro in which all participating nations had to conform to the "convergence" criteria. By all accounts, the first Prodi government performed respectably in meeting the convergence goals, but politically it proved a thankless endeavor that left little room for social reforms. The second Prodi government (2006–2008) faced many of the same limits, this time forced by the global slowdown. Both tenures in office ended in electoral defeat, as voters apparently concluded that the center-left had lost its élan.

Beyond the austere economic conditions that confronted the center-left in both circumstances, the center-left was hamstrung by both weak leadership and its own internal divisions. A major difficulty was that, although Prodi was highly esteemed as an honest, intelligent public servant, he had few "troops." Respected for his economic management skills—he had been an economics professor and head of the state-run industrial conglomerate the IRI—Prodi had no organization behind him. Moreover, he had come from a Christian Democratic background, with no prior links to the Left. There was always, then, an inherent tension between Prodi, the center-left's main leader during most of this period, and the leadership of the coalition's constituent parties. The most dramatic example of this tension was the decision in 1998 by Fausto Bertinotti, the leader of one of the Olive Tree parties, the PRC, to withdraw support from the Prodi government, thereby causing its collapse. Although the Olive Tree was able to cobble together a new governing coalition and remain in office without calling a new election, Prodi's fall revealed the fragility of trying to keep all the constituent parties satisfied without a single commanding leader.

Similar tensions marked the center-left's second period in office in 2006–2008, as Prodi, now back and leading the rebaptized Union coalition, spent most of the two years seeking to placate one or another of his fourteen coalition partners. His authority was also arguably undermined by Walter Veltroni's campaign throughout 2007 to create the Democratic Party, a move that constituted an alternative platform to Prodi's governing program (Pasquino 2008, 348). Finally, Prodi's position went from precarious to untenable in January 2008 when a Union senator who was also minister of justice withdrew his support from the government, ultimately forcing Prodi's resignation and new elections that produced the return of Berlusconi for his third term as prime minister. In all, although the Left could note some successes in its attempt to regroup and reform following the trauma of 1991–1993, it continued to engage in divisive, self-destructive behavior even as it sought to redefine itself.

CONCLUSION

The past three decades have been challenging, to say the least, for the Left in Western Europe. For the Italian Left, they have been downright devastating. Whatever one may say about the vicissitudes of Socialists and Communists in France and Spain since the 1970s, those parties, however shakily, are still standing. The same cannot be said for the Italian Left. For over seventy years, the two great parties of the Left, the PSI and the PCI, carried on an on-again-off-again relationship with each other. They fought together in the Resistance, maintained an alliance during the early Cold War, and shared power within the largest union confederation for four decades after World War II. They also split apart, in the 1960s, over the question of partnering with the Christian Democrats and then fell into outright mutual animosity in the late 1970s and 1980s. Yet, as recently as the mid-1980s, there was every reason to believe that this complex relationship would go on indefinitely.

How to explain why these two parties have either transformed themselves (PCI) or collapsed (PSI)? The historical overview presented in this chapter leads to one central conclusion: the seeds of these dramatic changes were planted in the 1960s and 1970s. For that reason, I argue that both parties experienced critical junctures during this period. For the Communists, the critical juncture occurred between 1973 and 1980, as the party sought and ultimately failed to strike a partnership with its erstwhile opponent during the Cold War, the Christian Democrats. For the Socialists, there were two critical junctures during these two decades: in 1962–1963 when the PSI decided to abandon its alliance with the Communists and join the DC governing coalition and in 1976–1980 when Bettino Craxi consolidated power in the party, in the process giving the party a much more expansive mission.

As in the case of the French Left, one finds evidence of the three essential elements of a critical juncture for each party: cause, response, and outcome. The similarity ends there, however, for the elements themselves differed in the French and Italian cases. First, in terms of cause, the driving factor in the French case was primarily a political challenge to the Left stemming from a resurgence of the Right following the May 1968 Events and the presidential elections a year later. Economic and social factors, while present in France, did not constitute grave challenges to the regime generally or to the Left specifically.

This was not the case in Italy, where the country faced a series of interrelated economic, social, and political crises that came to a head in the 1970s. Unlike France, Italy underwent a full-scale *crisi di regime* during that decade, one that forced all political parties, including the PCI and the PSI, to respond. In a fundamental sense, the roots of that crisis stretched back to 1948 and the onset of the Cold War that drove a seemingly permanent wedge between Left and the Right. Thereafter, Italy's postwar political system became, in effect, frozen into two blocs—on one side a dominant but unstable conservative block organized by the DC and on the other a Communist-dominated Left basically excluded from the parliamentary game. Within this context, the Socialists' 1963 decision to join the governing majority marked a turning point for the party—the first time that Socialists and Communists parted ways in the postwar period. What was less clear was whether this *apertura* constituted a turning point for the political system as a whole. Although it raised the eventual prospect of a more general entente between the main parties of the Left and Right, in the near term the Socialists' inclusion into the inner-party system only bolstered the DC's hold on the status quo.

DC dominance, over time, fostered policy paralysis, as the various DC-headed governments proved incapable of successfully managing the tensions of growth, most notably worker and student unrest. In the wake of the "Hot Autumn" strike wave of 1969, the economy stagnated while unemployment and inflation soared (Salvati 1981, 329–30). These problems, of course, became common throughout Western Europe after the first oil shock of 1973, but Italy's economic downturn started earlier and went deeper than in other advanced industrial nations. Accompanying the country's economic problems was the highest level of strike activity throughout Europe during this period (see data reported in Cameron 1984). By the early 1970s, Italy was increasingly beset by violent extremist groups on the Left and the Right. For both the Communists and the Socialists, the central question became, What role should we play and how should we try to intervene in these intertwined crises?

In examining the two parties' strategic responses to this question, again one finds a principal difference with the French case. Whereas the main response in France was the Union of the Left, in Italy it was a push by both parties to form a coalition not with each other but with the hegemonic party of the postwar period, the Christian Democrats. Such a "grand coalition" style of arrangement was unthinkable in France for several reasons. Perhaps the overriding one was that France in the 1970s simply faced far less severe economic, social, and political challenges than Italy, and thus there appeared to be no compelling argument in favor of a National Unity government to save the country from disaster. Other factors that effectively removed a grand-coalition option in France included the unshakable position of the Gaullists and their allies as well as the PCF's unwillingness to even consider cooperating with the Right.

In Italy, by contrast, compelling arguments for a Left–Right rapprochement abounded. Not only was the crisis itself of sufficient magnitude to encourage cooperation between the Left and the DC, but the Socialists and Communists were also disposed to consider such an arrangement. The Socialists, as we have seen, had already chosen this camp. As for the Communists, Berlinguer's offer of a Historic Compromise with the DC had its roots in the Gramsci–Togliatti vision of the Communist Party as both a vanguard *and* a culturally hegemonic party, something that implied the possibility of reconciliation and accommodation with Italy's conservative, Catholic culture. Thus, the fact that both Socialists and Communists essentially rejected a Union of the Left style of response in favor of an alliance with the DC is not so puzzling when put in its proper historical context. What is puzzling is that both Left parties sought not only to ally with the DC but also to *exclude* the other party in the process. To account for these responses, let us consider the impact of our three main explanatory factors: institutional context, party culture, and leadership.

Institutional Context

As noted at the beginning of this chapter, Italy's governmental and electoral arrangements adopted at the outset of the new Republic in 1946 tended to foster a high level of fragmentation among the political parties. Not only was there no directly elected executive, as in Fifth Republic France, which might have encouraged the building of a presidential majority among two or more parties, but the low-threshold PR system, by permitting even small parties to elect deputies, largely removed incentives for parties to cooperate in parliamentary elections. The result, at least until 1994 when new electoral rules induced a different dynamic, was a large number of parties, none of which could gain a majority on its own. As the largest one, the DC was always in the position of having to find a sufficient number of partners to constitute a governing majority. Thus coalitions were typically put together *after* the elections in order to govern, not before the elections in order to win office.

These arrangements alone discouraged an alliance between the Communists and Socialists. This did not stop the two parties from cooperating in the immediate postwar period, however. Unlike the French Socialists, who remained in the inner-party system even after the advent of the Cold War, the Italian Socialists were ousted from government participation by the DC after 1948. With both the PSI and the PCI being victims of Cold War exclusion, the two parties initially found grounds for cooperating both in the formal political sphere (parliament and local and regional governments) and the labor movement (shared leadership within CGIL). But from the outset of the Republic, there were two important givens that shaped the two parties' options. The first was that the two parties, acting either on their own or conjointly, could never attract a majority of voters and thus could never hope to form a government together. The "conjoint" option, in the form of a common list of "Popular Front" candidates in the 1948 election, failed to attract one-third of the vote, whereas the two parties running separately never received more than 45 percent of the vote. Hence, it was simply not realistic for the two parties to envision a Union of the Left type of government. The second given was that the potential always existed for the DC to drive a wedge between the parties by playing on the anti-Communist theme and co-opting the Socialists, a move that finally occurred in 1963. In sum, while the institutional context did not make an eventual alliance bid with the DC inevitable, it certainly obviated the option of a French-style Union.

Party Culture

In the French case, we saw how party culture affected the strategic responses of the PS and PCF in the 1970s. To recall, the PS's factionalism and ideological flexibility proved to be functional attributes, enabling the party to craft a kind of "left-modernist" identity that opened the way for a coalition with the Communists while also attracting new centrist voters. By contrast, the PCF's organizational rigidity and ideological attachment to the concept of the vanguard party not only constituted an identity albatross that the party could never cast off; these traits also caused the party to abolish its partnership with the Socialists in 1977–1978—an action that sowed internal discord while further tarnishing the party's image. This kind of contrast did not hold in the Italian case for several reasons.

The most obvious is that the Italian Communist Party developed a party culture that, compared with the PCF, was considerably less committed to Communist orthodoxy.[43] In simplest terms, the PCI was both less Leninist and less Stalinist than the PCF. It is important to underline that Togliatti's "new-party" concept, which fixed the organizational template for the postwar PCI, called for a *mass* party as opposed to the Leninist ideal of relatively small cadre of professional revolutionaries. Accordingly, after World War II, the PCI virtually threw open its doors and within a decade counted over 2 million members. By contrast, the PCF went in the opposite direction in the decade following the war, dropping from a postwar high of 800,000 in 1946 to about 300,000 members by the mid-1950s.

The PCI was also less Stalinist than the PCF in the sense of being intellectually more open and tolerant of diverse ideas. It is common among historians to note that the PCF never had the equivalent of a Gramsci or Togliatti—party leaders who were also major intellectuals and theoreticians (e.g., Greene 1968; Lazar 1992). One result was that the PCI possessed a strategic, tactical, and theoretical suppleness by which it was able, plausibly, to square the intellectual circle: professing, on the one hand, its commitment to Marxist principles of class struggle while, on the other, espousing a modus vivendi and even a strategic alliance with Italy's Catholic Party. (The downside of such suppleness, as noted earlier, was that the party also became known for a "double language" [*doppiezza*] of revolutionary rhetoric and reformist practice.) As mentioned above, Berlinguer's Historic Compromise strategy was the logical extension of this party culture. Such a move was simply unimaginable for PCF leaders such as Thorez or Marchais.

For Italian Socialists, alliance with the DC was no stretch in terms of either theory or praxis. Having participated in DC-led cabinets since 1963, the PSI by the 1970s no longer bore any pretensions to radical reform, Marxist or otherwise. Party leaders were long used to negotiating and sharing power with the Christian Democrats. Thus, unlike the French Socialists, the PSI had little in the way of political space that it could occupy in order to recast its identity. It could not, à la the PS, move to the left ideologically at a time when the PCI was not only moderating its program in order to attract the DC but also overtly rejecting a Union of the Left style of alliance. One need only recall Berlinguer's dismissal of the "51 percent solution," a leftist alliance that, in his view, would be fragile and unsustainable. By the mid-1970s, the PSI appeared to be at a standstill. Its party culture projected both intense factionalism and a blurry ideology, while its electoral ceiling stalled at about 10 percent. A testy alliance with the DC was not just a logical choice; it seemed to be the PSI's only choice.

Leadership

The impact of individual party leaders cannot be ignored when assessing Communist and Socialist responses, for both Berlinguer and Craxi were pro-verbial larger-than-life characters who left an enormous imprint on their respective parties' strategies and fortunes. Of the two leaders, Craxi was the more innovative ideologically and organizationally despite the fact that Berlinguer received the world's kudos for espousing Eurocommunism and an end to Italy's Red–White cleavage. Craxi, who was also more ruthless and arguably more politically astute than Berlinguer, sought to develop a "new-look" Italian Socialism built around two main elements: anti-Communism and technocratic modernism. While these were hardly new concepts in and of themselves, they were certainly original in the context of Craxi's own party. De Grand (1989) provides an apt description of the new party culture that Craxi sought to create after becoming party chief in 1976:

> One by one, the old symbols of the party were thrown overboard. The red carnation replaced the old rising run and hammer and sickle. Marx gave way to the Harvard Business School's management theories, as the PSI cast away the heritage of the past to compete for an entirely new electorate of middle-class professional and bureaucrats in the public and private sector. (158)

In both respects—in the rejection of an alliance with the Communists and the embrace of cost–benefit managerialism—Craxi in the late 1970s more close-ly resembled Felipe González than François Mitterrand. Craxi certainly bore no resemblance to Berlinguer. Their differences went well beyond the obvi-ous stylistic ones—the retiring austere Berlinguer versus the brash, ebullient Craxi. More important was their mutual animosity—their palpable disdain for one another—and this factor, too, played a role in the two parties' failure to move toward an alliance in the late 1970s. The grand irony, of course, was that the personal antagonism between these two men widened as the prog-rammatic differences between their two parties narrowed. To be sure, the two leaders' motivations differed greatly. Berlinguer sought a grand coalition National Unity government as a great leap forward in the PCI's long march toward cultural hegemony, whereas Craxi aimed to cut the Communists out of power while setting the stage for his own party to replace the DC as the dominant power broker in the system. But both leaders sought, in essence, the same thing: an alliance with the DC.

In the end, whatever differences existed between Berlinguer and Craxi, one must look to outcomes to determine whether their actions—and, more generally, their parties' strategic responses—constituted a critical juncture. In the case of the Communists, the Historic Compromise initiative, as we have seen, failed on several levels. There were many reasons for the PCI's slide after 1976, not least Craxi's own hostility toward the Communists when he was prime minister. More broadly, one cannot discount the price that the party ultimately paid for its association with the Soviet Union. The 1970s and early 1980s saw a major intellectual shift, especially among Western European leftists, against the Soviet Union in the wake of the crushing of the 1968 Prague Spring, the 1973 publication of Solzhenitsyn's *The Gulag Archipelago*, General Jarulzelski's crackdown on the Solidarity movement in Poland, and other events. Although the PCI sought to distance itself from the Soviets, it never took the ultimate step of breaking completely with them, and its image suffered in the process. But beyond these factors, the PCI's decline owed much to the party's own missteps in the late 1970s, notably its failure to fully achieve the touted Compromesso in 1976–1979, and then its abrupt about-face in 1980. Not only voters but also the party's own activists and members felt confused and even betrayed by the leadership's actions. After 1976, the PCI never again attained the number of voters and members it had in that year.[44]

For the Socialists, the two critical junctures I have identified had two distinct but related effects. The "Opening" decision of 1962–1963 marked the Socialists' definitive abandonment of an alliance with the PCI, while Craxi's rise in 1976–1980 represented a more general abandonment, namely, of the Left as an ideological and programmatic anchoring point. Even more important, Craxi's early tenure was critical in that he set the party on a path that ultimately led to disaster. Craxi thus stands as a key hinge figure, representing both originality and continuity. He was original in that his takeover of the party injected a new dynamism that eventually brought the party to power. Under Craxi's leadership, the PSI began gaining members and voters. Between 1977 and 1987, for example, party membership increased by nearly 30 percent, and the Socialists' share of the vote in parliamentary elections increased from 9.6 percent in 1976 to 14.3 percent in 1987.

On the other hand, Craxi embodied continuity in that he greatly reinforced and deepened extant tendencies within the Socialist Party. Those tendencies chiefly included turning not just a blind eye but a willing hand toward corruption. Long before Craxi, by the 1960s, the DC had basically infiltrated and organized the state to operate as a spoils system controlled by the party. Needing allies to keep its parliamentary majority (and its control over the money spigots) going, the DC established an informal *lottizzazione* system whereby its coalition partners got a cut of the action. Having joined the DC's coalition in the 1963, the PSI was already embedded in the spoils system when Craxi became party leader.

The ambitious Craxi took his party's participation in this system to a new level, especially after he became prime minister in 1983. Within a decade, however, the level of corruption became so great that it could no longer be ignored, and when the judicial hammer came down, it smashed not only Craxi and his party but the whole party system as well. Craxi was not yet "indictable" in the 1970s, but all the personal characteristics that eventually did him and his party in—greed, opportunism, and the pursuit of office for personal enrichment—were present from the beginning of his tenure as PSI chief. In that sense, this second critical juncture for the Socialists stemmed not so much from strategic errors, as in the case of the Communists, as from the development of a culture of accommodation to corrupt power and the selection of a new leadership generation for whom, to paraphrase another leader of Italian origin, power was not everything, it was the only thing.

NOTES

1. Pasquino (2005) provides a penetrating discussion of the fate of various attempts in Italy to adopt a French-style system. He notes in passing that the 1946 Italian Constitution was strongly influenced by the French Fourth Republic Constitution, approved in the same year. Thus, unlike the French, the Italians have kept their postwar constitution despite comparable problems of cabinet instability and policy paralysis that caused the French to abandon theirs after just twelve years.

2. Italy's postwar electoral system can be technically described as a PR system with a low threshold and preference voting. The low threshold—the minimal performance to gain seats in parliament—consisted of a "bar" of just 300,000 votes nationally, or about 2 percent of the vote. (More restrictive systems, such as Germany's, require up to 5 percent or more of the vote nationally in order to obtain *any* seats in parliament.) Electoral districts were multimember, and seats within a district were divided according to the parties' proportion of the vote in that district. Although each party would present a list of candidates, voters were able to indicate their preference for who would be ranked on the list as first, second, and so on. The main critiques of this system are twofold: 1) it encouraged excessive party fragmentation by permitting even tiny parties to gain parliamentary representation, and 2) it promoted the building of personal fiefdoms within parties, as candidates on the party list would stage personal campaigns (complete with promises to loyal voters) in order to move up the list in preference voting.

3. Although Italy is still under the same republican constitution it adopted in 1946, it has become customary among analysts to speak of the country's "First Republic" as the period 1946–1992 and the "Second Republic" as the period since 1992. The distinction has to do with the transformation of the traditional postwar party system beginning in 1992 rather than any fundamental constitutional change. With this distinction understood, I will employ the two terms without quotation marks.

4. I am including the Constituent Assembly elections of 1946.

5. In the 1924 elections, the only elections held under Mussolini's rule, the Socialists and Communists were ruthlessly harassed by Fascist thugs but still managed to garner about 15 percent of the vote between them.

6. I have excluded the anomalous 1948 election, when the two parties ran together in the Popular Front bloc.

7. For much of this section, I have relied on Alexander De Grand's compact but comprehensive survey of the Italian Left. Unless otherwise noted, De Grand (1989) is the principal source.

8. For the sake of brevity, I am simplifying a more complex picture. I am leaving aside earlier manifestations of Socialist thought including revolutionary syndicalism and anarchism. As for the post-1900 PSI, although Turati favored gradual reform, there was another important current in the party that was even more moderate: a group headed by Leonida Bissolati, Ivanoe Bonomi, and Angiolo Cabrini. These "ultrareformists" supported close alliances with middle-class Radical and Liberal parties and thus had no aspirations for an eventual socialist society (see De Grand 1989, 23).

9. Mussolini, on becoming the editor of *Avanti!*, began espousing Italy's engagement on the Axis side (with Germany and Austria). Since this ran directly counter to the party's long-held pacifism and neutrality, he was eventually expelled from the PSI in 1914.

10. This initial *rapporti di forze* between Communists and Socialists contrasted with the French case, in which, as we have seen, a majority of the SFIO delegates voted to transform the party into a Communist one affiliated with the Third International. Such a scenario put the French Communists in a stronger position, albeit still a minority one, in relation to the Social-ists compared with their Italian counterparts. For example, in the first postsplit elections in 1924, the PCF obtained about half the votes of the SFIO (see table 2.1 in chapter 2).

11. In an action that has been largely overlooked (perhaps purposely so) by many observers, the Communists also launched an appeal to residual leftist elements in the Fascist movement. Instructed by the Comintern to reach out to other non-Communist forces that could be enlisted in the struggle against Fascism yet lacking a significant cohort of middle-class democrats, the PCI looked to peel off sympathetic elements in the Fascist movement itself. Appealing to "our brothers in black shirts," Togliatti expressed sympathy with elements of the Fascists' 1919 program that he termed democratic and progressive. Surprisingly, this campaign did meet with some success—for example, several prominent Fascists "converted" to the Communist cause (see De Grand 1989, 72; Adler 2005, 732).

12. *Svolta* means a "turn" or "turning point."

13. De Grand argues convincingly that Stalin opposed radicalization of the PCI at the end of the war. Stalin's main goal was to ensure Allied support for consolidation of the Soviet Union's sphere of influence in Eastern Europe rather than to foment immediate revolution in the West. To have encouraged the PCI in a radical direction in 1944–1945 would have been foolhardy in Stalin's view (De Grand 1989, 88; see also Urban 1986, 190–96).

14. The four currents were a Leninist "left" led by Basso, a "center-left" headed by Nenni and Morandi, a "center" around Sandro Pertini and Ignazio Silone, and a "right" centered on the Critica Socialista group headed by Giuseppe Saragat.

15. Unlike the PCI's *svolta* toward moderation, which the Soviet Union endorsed, the party's mass-organization strategy went against the Soviets' wishes, as it ran counter to the "vanguard" party espoused by Lenin. Again, the "lessons of Fascism" were fresh in Togliatti's mind: a mass party would serve as a strong defensive instrument against any possible resur-gence of Fascism (see Hellman 1988, 16–17).

16. Interestingly, the PSI generally took more militant positions during the 1943–1947 period than did the more cautious, moderate Communists. For example, whereas the Commu-nists supported the Badoglio government, Nenni insisted that Badoglio resign and that the new government swear allegiance to the CLN, not the King—both positions the Communists re-jected (see Di Scala 1988, 28).

17. The PSLI eventually changed its name in 1951 to the Italian Social Democratic Party (PSDI) (see Di Scala 1988, 58–63).

18. The following numbers tell the tale. In the 1946 elections, the PCI gained 104 seats to the PSI's 115 for a grand Left total of 219 seats. In 1948, the two parties' seat total slipped to 183, but the PCI gained seats—going to 141, thus a gain of thirty-seven seats—whereas the PSI won only forty-two seats, resulting in a huge net loss of seventy-three seats (see Di Scala 1988, 76). The PCI's relative success in relation to the PSI can be explained largely by the Commu-nists' ability to mobilize their voters to take advantage of the preference voting aspects of Italy's electoral system (see note 2).

19. Founded in 1944 by the main Resistance parties, the CGIL remained the only national labor confederation until the breakup of tripartism in 1947. In the next two to three years, the Catholic faction within the CGIL, sponsored by the Church and the DC (as well as the Central Intelligence Agency), split off to form a Catholic-oriented confederation, the Confederazione Italiana Sindacati Lavoratori (CISL). During the same period, an anti-Communist but non-Catholic faction within the CGIL, with ties to the Social Democratic and Republican parties, also split off to form the Unione Italiana del Lavoro (UIL).

20. These were principally the Social Democrats (6.1 percent), Republicans (1.4 percent), and Liberals (7.0 percent). Figures are vote percentages for the 1963 elections.

21. This group, headed by Lelio Basso and Tullio Vecchietti, formed the Partito Socialista Italiano d'Unità Proletariana in 1964. The party merged with the PCI in 1972.

22. This is not to say that the tactics were all the same. Generally, the extreme Right carried out bombings—the most notorious being the August 1980 bombing of the Bologna train station that killed eighty-five people—and rarely claimed credit for these actions, whereas the extreme Left used targeted kidnappings and murders and always claimed credit (private communication, Steven Hellman).

23. For example, in the 1968 elections, the PSI and PSDI—now united in the Unitary Socialist Party—gained only 14.5 percent, whereas in the previous 1963 elections, the two parties running separately had gained a total of 19.9 percent (PSI 13.8 percent and PSDI 6.1 percent). Meanwhile, the PCI increased its vote from 25.3 percent in 1963 to 26.9 percent in 1968.

24. The first Andreotti government (July 1976–January 1978) was possible because Communist deputies abstained in a vote of confidence, thus enabling Andreotti to form a government. For the second Andreotti government (March 1978–January 1979), the Communists agreed to participate officially in the government majority, although they were granted no cabinet positions. When the Communists withdrew their support from this government in January 1979, Andreotti was forced to resign.

25. In this argument, I have drawn on some of the analyses of Hellman (1988, 1996) and D'Alimonte (1999).

26. Di Scala recounts that Craxi (b. 1934) became anti-Communist at an early age when his father, a Socialist, ran for parliament in 1948 on the PCI–PSI Popular Front list. Apparently, his father had come away hating the Communists for their duplicity (see Di Scala 1988, 174–77).

27. For an in-depth account of Craxi's maneuverings, see Di Scala (1988, 181–83, 192–94) and Bardi and Morlino (1994, 263–64).

28. In the 1983 elections, the PSI advanced to 11.4 percent (vs. 9.8 percent in the previous elections in 1979), whereas the DC drew only 32.9 percent (vs. 38.3 percent in 1979).

29. Rhodes (1995, 114–21) provides a useful summary of the internal turmoil and leadership struggles within the PSI in the wake of the corruption charges.

30. Hellman (1996, 80–81) argues that the Historic Compromise period did gain the PCI a kind of informal recognition from the inner-system parties, namely, that the PCI was eligible to participate in the spoils game—the informal system of *lottizzazione* (literally, dividing into plots or spoils sharing) being perfected by DC and PSI politicians. Even though elements within the party remained honest—evidencing "communist morality in the best sense, that is moral commitment and abnegation that discouraged illicit behavior"—the party faced growing pressures to raise funds, especially to pay for its various marketing and mass-communication activities.

31. No doubt, this relaxing of "centralism" in favor of "democracy" was linked to the fallout over the closed, authoritarian way in which the strategic shift away from the Compromesso was carried out. Pasquino (1988, 35) notes that beginning in 1981, the party allowed secret voting in elections and on motions at party congresses.

32. In 1986, the party reported 1.55 million members, down from 1.81 million in 1976. Just as worrisome from a long-term perspective, membership in the Communist Youth Federation declined from 74,000 to 45,000 between 1980 and 1984 (see Pasquino 1988, 42–43).

33. Author interview with Professor Carlo Baccetti, University of Florence, October 14, 2008.

34. In an interview, the former mayor, Diego Novelli, told the author, "I know the true story of the Bolognina. Occhetto invented this whole idea during a plane ride from Rome to Bologna. In the plane he meets Arrigo Boldrini, who is one of the legendary figures of the Medaglia d'Oro, the Resistance organization. Boldrini was returning from the Soviet Union, coming from a meeting of old Soviet World War II veterans. And Boldrini spoke about this new secretary of the CPSU [Communist Party of the Soviet Union], Gorbachev, who had initiated glasnost and perestroika. When Gorbachev launched his reforms for the first time, he made a speech before an assembly of Soviet war veterans. This gave Gorbachev the opportunity to draw the greatest contrast between himself and those who were much more rigid. Occhetto said, 'Wow, what a great idea.' When he got off the plane in Bologna he said to the local party secretary who came

to pick him up, 'Listen, during the next two or three days while I'm here, will there be, by chance, an assembly of former partisans?' The local secretary told him later that evening that the next day there was to be a ceremony of former partisans in the Bolognina. Occhetto then said, 'Would you do me a favor? Are there some journalists here from *L'Unità* whom we get could confidentially get to ask me certain questions, which I could then respond to?' So they find a journalist who worked for Lanza and they have him ask, 'Given everything that's happening—the fall of the Berlin wall, etc.—do you think it's a good thing to keep the name Communist?' Occhetto answered, 'I am in favor of changing the Party's name, symbols, the hammer and sickle, etc.'" (author interview, November 5, 2008).

35. Author interview with Diego Novelli, November 5, 2008.

36. The individual party totals were PDS 20.4 percent, PRC 6.0 percent, and PSI 2.2 percent.

37. Specifically, the signing of the Maastricht Treaty in February 1992 committed Italy to put its economic house in order, principally to bring inflation, public spending, and public debt accounts in line with European Union–defined guidelines. With the prospect of the treaty taking effect in 1993, currency speculators concluded what many Italian voters already felt: that Italy's political leaders were incapable of reform. Accordingly, in the summer of 1992, speculators sought to unload lira, driving its value down and prompting Italy to defend it and maintain the country's participation in the European Monetary System or withdraw. Unable to defend the currency sufficiently, Italy withdrew temporarily from the European Monetary System.

38. Writing in 1995 and perhaps in subconscious recollection of Gramsci, the philosopher Norberto Bobbio (1995) wrote that "the First Republic is in protracted agony and the Second is still to come" (198).

39. The purpose of the new electoral system was to reduce party fragmentation by giving parties incentives to form larger parties and/or coalitions. As mentioned, 75 percent of the seats were to be decided in a "uninominal" manner, that is, in single-member district, first-past-the-post contests, while the other 25 percent of seats would be decided by the traditional PR mechanism. This system was used in 1994, 1996, and 2001. In 2005, the Berlusconi government reverted back to a PR system with one new twist: the leading party or coalition would be given a "majority bonus" of additional seats sufficient to ensure a solid working majority of 55 percent. That system was used in the 2006 and 2008 elections. I am grateful to Professor Aldo Di Virgilio of the University of Bologna for explaining this system to me (author interview, October 21, 2008).

40. The Olive Tree included the PDS, the PPI (ex–Christian Democrats), the Greens, and an informal group led by Prodi (see Galli 2004, 413). The coalition did *not* formally include the PRC, although this party agreed to throw its support to Ulivo candidates in runoff situations.

41. Author interview with Professor Donatella Della Porta, University of Florence and European University Institute, October 13, 2008.

42. Author interview with Professor Gianfranco Pasquino, University of Bologna, October 24, 2008.

43. Well before the events of the 1970s, an astute observer of both the PCI and the PCF wrote, "In the case of the French and Italian Communist parties, there no longer should be any novelty to the argument that documents the relative liberalism of the PCI, and the vestiges of Stalinism that still characterize the PCF" (Greene 1968, 3).

44. Not the least of all the ironies of this period is that Berlinguer himself remained highly popular and respected within the party.

Chapter Four

Spain: Transcending History

We shall merit disaster because of our stupidity.
—Socialist leader Indalecio Prieto, 1936

I am a Socialist, but I am no fool.
—Socialist leader Felipe González, 1985 [1]

In relation to our other two cases, the experience of the Spanish Left during the past century—and especially since Franco's death in November 1975—stands in stark contrast. As we have seen, relations between Socialists and Communists in France and Italy have been marked by tensions and hostility, but they have also featured periods of extensive cooperation. The record is not one of unremitting discord. Yet this is largely the story of the Spanish Left. Although there have been instances of cooperation at the local level, in city councils and regional assemblies, these have been largely coalitions of convenience in which local concerns are at stake. At the national level, only the brief, contentious Popular Front period (1934–1938) stands as an example of collaboration between the two main parties of the Left. The reverse image more accurately describes the parties' relationship: since the early 1920s—through one dictatorship, a thwarted republic, civil war, a second dictatorship, and a successful transition to democracy—Socialists and Communists have treated each other with distrust and disdain. If the French and Italian cases reflect "brotherly" instances of comradeship and common struggle, the Spanish experience reflects mainly opposition and enmity.

Broadly speaking, one may adduce two main reasons for this conflict. The first lies in the realm of historical memory, specifically the disastrous experience of the Second Republic (1931–1936) followed by three years of civil war (1936–1939) that ushered in the long Franco dictatorship. As we shall see, Socialists and Communists often worked at cross-purposes in the face of daunting challenges from both internal and foreign opponents. Most historians concur that much of the blame for both the collapse of the Second Republic and the failure of Republican defenders to repel the Nationalist rebels can be laid at the doorstep of the Left. Specifically, the Left's seemingly suicidal fractiousness weakened the Republic's legitimacy and its ability to mount an effective defense against the military's rebellion. This was the "stupidity" to which Socialist leader Prieto was referring in this chapter's opening quote. At the heart of the Left's discord was a struggle for primacy among various elements of the Left, notably Socialists and Communists but also including anarchists and regionalist groups. In the wake of the Republic's final defeat in 1939, mutual recriminations between these parties—now banished in exile or driven underground within Spain—closed off any possibility of a rapprochement.

The second reason stems from simple electoral logic: under most conditions, parties cooperate when their self-interest compels them to do so. Once Spain returned to democracy following Franco's death, such a compulsion vanished, at least for the Socialists. In the 1977 constituent assembly elections—the first democratic contest in over forty years—the Socialists (Partido Socialista Obrero Español [PSOE]) easily outpolled the Communists (Partido Comunista de España [PCE]) to the point that the Socialists instantly became the chief opposition to the victorious center-right party, the Union of the Democratic Center (Unión de Centro Democrático [UCD]). Henceforth, the PSOE could envision becoming a majority party on its own, without electoral allies, something that it did just five years later. Since that clarifying moment in 1977, the Socialists have had little motive to reach out to the Communists, while the Communists have struggled to remain even a marginal political force.

For these reasons, the history of Socialist–Communist relations in Spain is an unhappy picture of fierce rivalry, blame throwing, and mutual contempt. Yet, paradoxically, within the past three decades, division within the Left—now within a context of an established democracy—has brought not weakness but rather strength—at least to the Socialists. Of our three cases, Spain is certainly the most surprising, especially from the vantage point of the mid-1970s. At that time—both the high point of the Eurocommunist initiative and the moment of Spain's return to democracy—few observers would have predicted that the Spanish Socialists would emerge as one of Europe's strongest Left parties during the next generation while their Communist counterparts would struggle mightily to survive. Yet that is what happened.

This outcome has its origins in the first years of the post-Franco regime, for, as just indicated, the performance of the two parties during the early period of Spain's new democracy set a pattern that has endured. For this reason, I identify this period—specifically, the years 1976–1979—as a critical juncture for both Socialist and Communist parties. The goal of this chapter is to trace and explain this outcome. In customary fashion, the chapter first presents an overview of Socialist–Communist relations since the two parties' split in 1920, followed by a section providing historical background to the contemporary period. The current period, defined as the decades since Franco's death, is the subject of the four succeeding sections. These are organized according to distinct phases: 1) democratic transition and consolidation (1975–1982); 2) the four-term Socialist ascendancy under Felipe González that was also accompanied by a full-scale crisis, reorganization, and revival of the Communist Party (1982–1996); 3) a period of the Left in opposition, featuring a renewal of the PSOE and a corresponding decline of the PCE (1996–2004); and 4) the Socialists' rebound in the 2004 elections, followed by their reelection in 2008.

THE BIG PICTURE: SOCIALIST–COMMUNIST RELATIONS, 1920–2008

In broadest terms, the big picture of Socialist–Communist relations in Spain is far simpler and clearer cut than the French and Italian cases. In the latter instances, experience with democracy has obviously been considerably longer, thereby providing more opportunities for interparty cooperation as the fortunes of parties change over time. As we have seen, in France democratic elections have been practiced continuously since 1920, except for the relatively brief hiatus of the Vichy years (1940–1944). Although Italy had a long bout with dictatorship from 1922 to 1943, the country did have a limited but contentious pre–World War I democratic tradition; since 1946, the country has had a functioning republic. In both nations, the relative strength of the Socialist and Communist parties has shifted dramatically over time, and the parties have adjusted their alliance strategies to take advantage of new electoral rules and coalition prospects.

Such flux and complexity are missing in the Spanish case. For one thing, Spain's democratic experience has been much briefer. In the fifty-seven years between the Socialist–Communist schism in 1920 and the first constituent assembly elections in 1977 following Franco's death, Spain held just three elections, all in the five years of the ill-fated Second Republic. In just one of those, the 1936 legislative election, did Socialists and Communists form a coalition. Thus, prior to the return to democracy, there were few opportunities for cooperation or competition in the electoral arena. Moreover, during the Franco regime, the two parties remained illegal and persecuted. This experience makes it difficult to assess the two parties' relative strength prior to 1977. As for their relationship, there is little evidence of sustained cooperation between the two parties. Other than the crisis years of

1935–1939, when both parties fought to defend the Republic against the Franco-led insurgents, the two parties' relationship can probably best be described as hostile.

Of the post-Franco democratic period, the ten national elections held between 1977 and 2008 clearly established the lasting supremacy of the Socialists relative to their Communist counterparts (see table 4.1). Although the PSOE never drew an outright majority of votes, the particularities of Spain's electoral system—a form of proportional representation using the d'Hondt method of apportioning seats—gave the party a parliamentary majority (or near majority) in six of the eight elections beginning with its 1982 triumph.[2] From the outset of the transition to democracy, the PSOE proved to be a popular "brand," not least because of its charismatic young leader, Felipe González, so the 1982 victory represented the culmination of a steady climb in public appeal. That proved to be the party's high point, however, and the five succeeding elections between 1986 and 2000 saw the PSOE's vote percentage decline, although the party did not lose its governmental majority until 1996. Following its relatively poor showing in 2000—with a percentage (34.2 percent) that would be the envy of any of its fellow leftists in France or Italy—the Socialists underwent a generational leadership shift and regained a good measure of their former electoral support.

As for the Communists, the party averaged somewhat less than one-fifth the percentage of votes as the PSOE, with the high point occurring in 1979. As table 4.1 indicates, this differential in the popular vote was compounded by the electoral system, which, as mentioned, systematically underrepresents small parties, including the PCE (see note 2). With an average of 7.2 percent of the vote in the ten elections, the PCE averaged just 3.5 percent of the parliamentary seats. (The corresponding averages for the PSOE are 38.9 percent of the vote and 44.6 percent of the seats.) Although the PCE managed to reduce their vote gap in relation to the Socialists during the 1989–1996 period, as the PCE-led coalition Izquierda Unida (IU) eventually built its totals back up to a respectable 10 percent, the party was never able to reduce the difference to the levels of the late 1970s. After 2000, the PCE/IU lost virtually all the ground it had gained during the 1990s and in the 2008 election drew less than one-tenth the number of voters as the Socialists.

Socialist dominance of the Left in the post-Franco period has rendered the necessity of an alliance with the Communists largely moot, at least at the national level. There was one halting attempt to resurrect an electoral support pact for the 2000 elections—at a moment when the PSOE was embroiled in scandals and leadership struggles while the PCE/IU appeared to be gaining in strength—but by all accounts the pact was badly executed, and the results were disappointing (see below). Relations between the parties are more variable at lower levels, where the two parties often cooperate to build majority coalitions in city and regional councils. But these are exceptions to the gener-

Table 4.1. The Left in Spain: Election Results (Congress of Deputies, Lower House), 1977–2008

Year	Communist Party (PCE) % Vote (% Seats)	Socialist Party (PSOE) % Vote (% Seats)	PCE vs. PSOE % PCE Vote/% PSOE Vote (% PCE Seats/% PSOE Seats)
1977	9.3 (5.4)	29.3 (33.7)	.32 (.16)
1979	10.8 (6.6)	30.5 (34.6)	.35 (.19)
1982	4.0 (1.1)	48.1 (57.7)	.08 (.02)
1986	4.6 (2.0)	44.1 (52.6)	.10 (.04)
1989	9.1[a] (4.9)	39.6 (50.3)	.23 (.10)
1993	9.6 (5.1)	38.8 (45.4)	.25 (.11)
1996	10.5 (6.0)	37.6 (40.3)	.28 (.15)
2000	5.5 (2.3)	34.2 (35.7)	.16 (.06)
2004	5.0 (1.4)	42.6 (46.9)	.12 (.03)
2008	3.8 (0.6)	43.9 (48.3)	.09 (.01)

[a] Izquierda Unida, 1989–2008.
Source: Ministerio del Interior, Dirección General de Política Interior (http://www.elecciones.mir.es/MIR/jsp/resultados/index.htm).

al pattern: Socialists and Communists operate largely independently for the simple reason that Socialists have been able to flourish in Spain's still young democracy without Communist support.

HISTORICAL BACKGROUND, 1920–1975

Spain's transition to democracy following Franco's death fairly dazzled observers by its smoothness and speed (see below). The transition's success was also surprising in that it occurred in such an unpropitious context. For decades if not centuries, the Spanish political pattern had featured cycles of monarchical rule, military intervention, revolutionary stirrings, and civil war, with only two brief, failed attempts to establish liberal democracy. During the six decades prior to Franco's demise, Spain experienced an unpopular monarchy, a crown-approved military dictatorship (1923–1930), a tumultuous and unstable democratic regime (Second Republic, 1931–1936), a civil war (1936–1939), and, finally, Franco's long dictatorship (1939–1975). The reasons for this dismal political record are not hard to find. These include the country's relative economic backwardness based on a privilege-seeking *latifundia* class of large landowners, Spain's intellectual isolation from European currents of liberalism, an entrenched monarchical tradition with democratic politics restricted largely to a small circle of middle-class professionals, and a propensity for military intervention in politics—led by blustering *caudillos*—when civilian politicians failed to maintain order (Crow 1985; Tamames 1992; Tortella 2000).

This syndrome of isolation, economic stagnation, entrenched privilege, and authoritarianism naturally tended to produce its equal and opposite reaction: a left-wing political opposition with a fervent desire to change this system. What prevented desire from becoming reality was the Left's inability to agree on how to bring about that change. In this respect, the Spanish Left reflected the Achilles' heel of the Left throughout Western Europe in the early twentieth century: the classic debilitating split between those who deemed the status quo amenable to reform versus those who espoused its destruction. But the Spanish Left took this split to a new level of contention, spawning fissures not only between but also within the various political formations. The nearly six decades from the end of World War I to Franco's demise provided ample time for these divisions to flower, fester, and ultimately destroy any hope of Left unity.

In surveying this full period, one needs to distinguish the first two decades from the following four, for the dynamics of political opposition completely changed with the crushing of the Left by Franco's Nationalist forces in 1939. During the 1920s and 1930s, Spain experienced more civil strife than any other Western European nation, whereas the Franco regime was notable not only for its longevity but also for its relative stability. Throughout the former period, at least three major lines of fracture plagued the Left and made concerted action highly problematic, even within individual parties.

One line of cleavage within the Left was that between groups favoring a "national" solution to Spain's problem and those espousing alternative versions. Socialists and Communists, for all their differences (see below), fell into the former camp; both sought to keep the Spanish state and nation intact, even while transforming it. Not so for the alternative camp, which included anarchists and regionalists. The anarchist movement, led by its main labor organization, the Confederación Nacional del Trabajo (CNT), had strong followings among landless peasants in Andalusia and workers in Catalonia. Refusing to recognize the legitimacy of the "bourgeois" Second Republic, anarchists pushed for immediate revolution to be followed by a system of autonomous, self-managed workers' communities. The CNT drew no distinction, for example, between the left-center government (which included three Socialist cabinet members) led by the Left Republican Manuel Azaña (1931–1933), the rightist government elected in 1933, and the left-leaning Popular Front government elected in 1936. To anarchists, all were "enemies of the people." Even during the Civil War, anarchists in Catalonia sought to carry out a revolution rather than join with Socialists, Communists, and other forces in defending the Republic against the Nationalist opponents.

Whereas anarchists sought to smash the central state, regionalists sought to dismember it or at least to weaken it. Notably in Catalonia and the Basque Country, opposition to the status quo increasingly took the form of a struggle for regional autonomy and the assertion of regional (Catalan, Basque, and so on) identity as opposed to Spanish (Castilian) identity. The regionalists' relationship with the Left was complicated to say the least; there was certainly no automatic affinity between Catalan and Basque regionalists on the one hand and the Left on the other. In part, this was due to divisions within the regionalist camp. Some regionalist groups sought greater autonomy within a preserved central state, a demand that most elements within the Left found congenial. Other groups, however, sought full independence, something that most leftists rejected. Religious and class differences also divided regionalists and the Left. In the Basque Country, for example, even though the Socialists generally backed demands for limited regional autonomy, the highly Catholic Basque separatist leaders kept their distance from the Socialists because of the latter's anticlericalism (Thomas 1961, 56). In Catalonia, one of the main regional parties, the Partit Radical headed by Alejandro Lerroux, favored greater Catalan autonomy but within the current Spanish state—a stance compatible with the Socialists—but the Partit Radical increasingly drew away from the Left during the Second Republic by seeking to appeal to the moderate middle class (Díez Medrano 1995, 102).

A second major fault line within the Left ran through the Socialist Party itself. For most of the party's first five decades, factionalism was not a pressing problem. Founded in 1879 and then instrumental in establishing the major labor organization, the Unión General de Trabajadores (UGT) in 1888, the PSOE by the 1920s had over four decades of experience in accommodating itself to a monarchy as well as to intermittent dictatorships. Like many Socialist parties of the early twentieth century, the PSOE followed a pattern that could be summarized as "radical discourse, reformist practice" (Gillespie 1989, 24; Heywood 1990, 176). Although the party never gained more than 5 percent of the vote under Spain's limited parliamentary system, its first elected representatives took their seats in 1910 through an electoral pact with Republicans. Thereafter, the PSOE continued to espouse (eventual) revolution even as it proceeded to cooperate not only with Republicans and other middle-class parties but also with strongman governments, such as the dictatorship headed by General Primo de Rivera (1923–1930).

The obvious contradictions between the Socialists' rhetoric and their practice were manageable as long as the austere *padre fundador*, Pablo Iglesias, remained the party's uncontested head and the prospect of revolution remained distant. But Iglesia's passing in 1925 set up a leadership struggle that played out over the next decade, in the process dividing the party into warring blocs. The two main antagonists in this drama were Indalecio Prieto and Francisco Largo Caballero, leader of the UGT.[3] Historians have often portrayed these men as ideological rivals, with the former portrayed as "reformist" and the latter as "radical." But ideology per se was not the determining factor; both men were capable of espousing revolutionary insurrection or collaboration with ideological enemies, depending on circumstances. Rather, personal animosities and organizational factors drove their dispute.[4] At root, Largo Caballero, the head of the UGT, was a union man ever vigilant to protect his organization's autonomy, whereas Prieto was a party man constantly seeking allies. Preston refers to Largo Caballero's leadership style as "leading from behind," meaning that the UGT leader's primary reflex was to ask, What do workers want? (Preston 1977, 122). This tendency gave Largo Caballero a certain tactical flexibility, but it also made him wary of alliances with other parties—whether Communist or Republican—when such alliances might endanger or inhibit the UGT's autonomy (Fuentes 2005). By contrast, Prieto, the party man, was by temperament and experience a conciliator, compromiser, and alliance builder.

These basic tensions remained latent during the first two years of the Second Republic, as the Socialists—including Largo Caballero as labor minister—joined in a coalition government headed by the Left Republican Manuel Azaña. This government launched reforms in the areas of land reform, civil liberties, infrastructure development, regional autonomy, church–state relations, and education; however, many of these reforms—notably the new agrarian law—were executed poorly and served mainly to disillusion the Republic's peasant and working-class supporters while alarming and mobilizing conservative forces.[5] New elections in November 1933 further polarized the country, as rightist parties gained a parliamentary majority. At that point, Left forces of all stripes went into revolt against the government, and a cycle of grassroots mobilization and government repression ensued that ultimately provoked a revolt by the military that launched the Civil War (Jackson 1974, 18).

This polarization directly affected the PSOE, as the Largo Caballero and Prieto wings of the party reacted in opposite fashion to the 1933 electoral loss. On the one hand, Largo Caballero advocated the "bolshevization" of the party and a turn to mass insurrection. Throughout the next year, the union leader backed mass revolt, including a large-scale workers' strike in Asturias (also backed by the CNT). In large measure, Largo Caballero was indeed "leading from behind," as the UGT experienced a massive influx of radicalized members.[6] On the other hand, Prieto urged moderation and the strengthening of alliances with the middle-class Republican Left. The PSOE became, in effect, a house warring within itself. One historian has commented, "What made the Spanish civil war inevitable was the civil war within the Socialist Party" (Salvador de Madariaga, quoted in Preston 1977, 102). During 1934 and 1935, the party continued to pull at cross-purposes, a process fueled by worker discontent that strengthened the labor sector to the point that the UGT became an independent counterpower to the PSOE's executive body (Juliá 1989, 25). By late 1935, according to the PSOE's own official history, "without producing an organic split, the [Socialist Party] was effectively split into two tendencies that were strategically in conflict over the question of its relations with other political forces and with the republican regime" (Tezanos 2004, 86).

Finally, a third major fault line within the Left was between the Socialist and Communist parties. Following the Comintern-induced fracture of the PSOE in 1921,[7] the two parties had virtually no relationship for over a decade. Although the PCE opposed the Second Republic from the outset, thereby putting it at odds with the PSOE during the Republic's first years, the Communist Party remained small and isolated, with pockets of support in Catalonia, Madrid, and Asturias. This situation changed during the last three years of the Second Republic. A confluence of events—including the escalation of mass action against a right-leaning Republican government in 1933–1935, the Comintern's anti-Fascist Popular Front strategy decreed in 1934, and the onset of civil war that drew in Germany, Italy, and the Soviet Union—boosted the PCE's resources and prestige and made it both a potential ally and a competitor for the Socialists.

During its first two decades of existence, the PCE closely hewed to the Comintern line, and thus its actions closely followed the dictates of Soviet foreign policy. As we have seen in the French and Italian cases, a key turning point was Stalin's 1934 decision to confront the growing Fascist threat by building alliances with other parties of the Left and center. In the Spanish context, this shift involved some nimble footwork by the PCE, which went from being a fierce opponent of the Second Republic in 1931 to its most ardent defender following the elections of February 1936 that brought a Popular Front coalition to power. With the outbreak of civil war just six months later, the PCE became a key actor in the Republican government's fight against the Nationalists, especially insofar as it became the conduit for Soviet arms and supplies. Even though numerically the Communists were a minor part of the Popular Front governing coalition,[8] they proved to be effective administrators and organizers, especially of the armed forces. Whatever else one can say about their behavior during the Civil War, the Communists were dedicated to saving the Republic against Franco's forces, even to the point of forcibly repressing other elements of the Popular Front coalition that were pushing revolution in Catalonia, notably the CNT and the "quasi-Trotskyist" Partido Obrero de Unificación Marxista (POUM).[9]

As far as the Communists' relations with the Socialists, although the two parties had a working albeit tense relationship from 1934 to 1939, the ultimate defeat of Republican forces brought bitterness and mutual recriminations that were slow to dissipate over the succeeding decades. The case of Largo Caballero can be taken as emblematic of the complexities and tensions in the PSOE–PCE relationship. As mentioned, after initially supporting the Second Republic, the UGT leader turned against the conservative government that was elected in 1933, thereafter encouraging worker strikes and direct actions such as land seizures by landless peasants. By late 1935, he was encouraging an alliance with the PCE and pushed for the Communists to be included in the Popular Front coalition; he even engineered a merger of the youth organizations of both parties. Less than a year later, in September 1936, he became prime minister in a Popular Front government that included Communists and that was facing open rebellion by the nation's own military as well as a full-scale local revolution in Barcelona and Aragon led by anarchists. Yet just nine months later, in May 1937, he was ousted and replaced by his Socialist archrival, Prieto. Thereafter, Largo Caballero blamed the PCE for his ouster; until his death in exile in 1946, he remained viscerally anti-Communist. Generally, in the wake of the Republic's defeat, Socialists and Communists blamed each other for betraying the Republican cause. The grand irony is that for many Socialists such as Largo Caballero (who by 1936 had moved into the revolutionary camp), the Communists' "betrayal" consisted of being too moderate.

The victory of the Franco-led forces in 1939 brought an abrupt end to the chaos and instability of the preceding decade. The victory also altered the dynamics of political opposition for nearly four decades. Franco, of course, had no use for pluralism, calling political parties "platforms for class conflict and agents of disintegration of national unity." He vowed that "[political parties] will never come . . . because it would mean the destruction, the dismemberment of the fatherland . . . to lose all that has been gained, it would imply treason to our dead and our heroes" (quoted in Linz 1973, 172). Accordingly, Franco banned all independent elements of civil society—parties, labor unions, and so on—while creating a quasi-corporatist system that provided some limited avenues for public participation through state-controlled bodies.

Yet the Franco regime was far from a monolithic leviathan that suppressed all vestiges of opposition. In fact, from the early 1960s on, Spanish society became increasingly dynamic, both politically and economically, such that active grassroots opposition emerged, notably among students and workers. Driving this process was an economic *apertura*, or opening, launched in 1960 that brought growth and modernization.[10] Economic change brought, in turn, social and political mobilization. One indicator of this mobilization is that strike activity increased tenfold between 1966 and 1975.[11] In all, this "return of civil society" during the last fifteen years of the Franco regime helped establish, albeit unwittingly, the conditions for the country's successful democratic transition following the general's death (Pérez-Díaz 1993).

While both Left parties sought to adapt to Spain's growing dynamism in the late Franco years, the Communists were clearly more successful than the Socialists (Preston 1983). By the mid-1970s, the PCE could boast a larger, more vigorous organization and a stronger presence in the labor movement. This relative success was linked to two main factors. The first was a revision of the party's ideological line that broadened the party's appeal. Most notable was a new stance toward Moscow. From its origins, the PCE had been under the thumb of the Soviets, not only during the Popular Front and the Civil War but also during World War II and the early Cold War years. This relationship changed during the 1950s, however, as a new generation of leaders came to power in the PCE. Led by Santiago Carrillo, who became secretary in 1954, the party gradually distanced itself from Moscow. Although the PCE always stopped short of a full break with the Soviets, the party eventually went so far as to condemn the 1968 invasion of Czechoslovakia.[12] Another component of its revised line was the party's "National Reconciliation" policy, adopted in 1956, in which the party renounced its former sectarianism and expressed its willingness to work with any and all groups for the reestablishment of democracy (Preston 1981, 48; Gunther, Sani, and Shabad 1988, 62). These shifts in the party's line were not without contradictions—notably Carrillo's intolerance of internal dissent even as he championed Spain's return to democracy—but they did improve the party's image and served to attract a young generation of activists (Preston 1983, 161–62).[13]

The other factor behind the PCE's emergence as a major force in the anti-Franco opposition by the time of El Caudillo's death was its base within the "official" labor movement. Franco had outlawed free unionism but did permit limited collective bargaining through an official body, the Organización Sindical Española. Beginning in the late 1950s, "workers' commissions" were allowed to form within workplaces in order to handle local grievances. Initially, not only Communists but also independent socialists, Catholic activists, and even liberal members of Franco's Falange movement participated together in these commissions. Eventually, these local activists formed a national confederation of such groups, called the Comisiones Obreras (CCOO), which pursued a strategy of "infiltration and occupation" of the Organización Sindical Española itself.[14] Although the CCOO was outlawed in 1967, it continued to grow and foment resistance to the regime. For the PCE, the CCOO became a principal resource for recruiting members and expanding the party's grassroots base to the point that by the early 1970s the PCE largely dominated what had become the country's main, indeed only, functioning labor organization (Maravall 1978, 60; Mujal-León 1979, 85; Botella 1988, 75–76; Smith 1998, 245–26).

As for the Socialists under Franco, they paled in comparison with the Communists in terms of organization and activism. In part this was due to the party's dispersal. Not only did many leaders and members go into exile after 1939, but they sought refuge and new lives in a wide range of cities and countries.[15] Within Spain, the only surviving nuclei of activists were located in Asturias and the Basque Country. The party also continued to be split into factions, which, following the Civil War, included three distinct groups: a reformist, Social Democratic faction around Indalecio Prieto; a radical but anti-Communist group led by Largo Caballero; and the followers of the last Socialist prime minister, Juan Negrín, who had worked closely with the Communists during the final Civil War years. By 1947, the Prieto wing dominated the party, but the PSOE had only their "almost obsessive anti-communism" to unite it (Mujal-León 1979, 87). By the early 1950s, the party could count just 3,000 members (Gilmour 1985, 90). For the next two decades, the party was dominated by an aging group of exiles based in Toulouse headed by a former Prietista, Rodolfo Llopis.

Beginning in the late 1960s, however, the party began a renewal process that ultimately put it in a stronger position than the PCE once democracy arrived. Change came to the Socialists not from abroad but from within. The driving force was a group of young *"renovadores"* from Andalusia who charged that the exile leadership had lost touch with the social and economic changes that had taken place in Spain during the 1960s. Led by Felipe González, a labor lawyer from Seville, the *renovadores* pushed for official representation of the party's "interior" sector. For thirty years, this sector had been denied a voice in party congresses, which, of course, were always held outside of Spain. In 1970, the twenty-eight-year-old González and his southern comrades managed to gain equal representation for the interior sector. Over the next four years, the southerners developed ties with UGT activists in Asturias and the Basque Country, most notably Nicolás Redondo of Bilbao. In the process, this bloc waged a successful fight against the Llopis-led exiles for party leadership.[16] The coup de grâce for the Llopis faction came in October 1974, when the party's Thirteenth Congress in Suresnes, France, elected González first secretary and Redondo organization secretary.[17] On the eve of Franco's death, then, although the PSOE had fewer than 5,000 members, it had a new élan behind a young "homegrown" generation of leaders.

DEMOCRATIC TRANSITION AND CONSOLIDATION, 1975–1982

Nearly seven years elapsed between Franco's demise in November 1975 and the Socialists' electoral triumph in October 1982.[18] That brief span featured a remarkable series of changes—in effect, a triple transformation of Spanish politics that has proven remarkably durable. The major transformation, of course, was the transition to and consolidation of democracy. During this period, not only did Spain pass from a dictatorship to a parliamentary democracy but control of parliament itself passed from one political bloc to another—the signal mark of democratic consolidation. This transformation came "bundled" in reinforcing ways with two other transformations: basic changes in the structures, programs, and fortunes of the two main left parties, the Socialists and Communists. In an outcome that no one would have predicted at the time of Franco's death, by 1982 the Socialists had forged dramatically ahead of the PCE to the point that the former constituted a majority party on its own, whereas the latter was struggling to survive. Relations between the two parties, competitive if not hostile from the beginning of the transition process, virtually ceased to exist.

The main transformation—the successful remaking of the political system itself—owed to several factors, not least King Juan Carlos himself.[19] Designated personally by Franco at an early age to be his successor, Juan Carlos was expected to restore the monarchy while keeping the Francoist structure intact. But the young king—just thirty-seven years old in 1975—failed to follow the script. Instead, he initiated a democratization process that, within three years, produced constituent assembly elections—the first free elections in forty-one years—and a new democratic constitution.

Beyond Juan Carlos's important shepherding role, two other factors strongly shaped the transition and consolidation. One was Spanish public opinion, which surveys showed to be moderate and supportive of democracy.[20] Among voters, there was little evidence of the age-old Spanish plague: ideological polarization. While most voters tended to self-identify on the basis of a Left–Right framework, the vast majority clustered in a range from left-center to right-center. Classic cleavages such as social class, religion, and region were of little importance in explaining party preference. Surveys also indicated the public's strong belief in democracy as the most desirable form of government and in the legitimacy of the new democratic system. Such attitudes obviously encouraged political actors toward cooperation and moderation.

The other factor that shaped the transition and consolidation process was its inclusive character. The king's appointment of Franco loyalist Adolfo Suárez as prime minister in July 1976 proved decisive in this regard. Suárez, who later proved disastrous as a leader in the early 1980s, was adept at fostering a compromise among the leaders of all major political organizations, including the PSOE and PCE (Gunther 1992). Private negotiations among a relatively small group of elites led to a broad consensus regarding the democratization process, which included a referendum on the government's reform proposal, the legalization of political parties, the abolition of the Franquist Syndical Organization and the regime's National Movement, elections for a Constituent Assembly, and a referendum on the new constitution.[21]

Within a context that fostered compromise and consensus, two other important transformations took place: fundamental changes in the Socialist and Communist parties. The behavior of these parties throughout this period exhibits a clear example of "political learning," which I define simply as the use of experience and collective memory to inform current behavior. By the time of the constituent assembly elections in June 1977, both parties had firmly rejected the polarizing, revolutionary tendencies of the 1930s, opting instead for centrist, gradualist programs that supported the democratic transition. Although there were minority voices in both parties that sought to radicalize the parties' positions, leaders González and Carrillo resolutely steered their parties toward moderation—a clear break with past behavior. Transformation was not just ideological; it was also organizational and electoral. In these respects, however, the outcomes for the two parties could not have been more different. Whereas the Socialists' organizational and electoral makeover spelled expansion and triumph, for the Communists it spelled diminution and defeat.

Of the two parties, the Socialists' transformation was the more complete, entailing major changes in the party's ideology and structure. Specifically, the PSOE moved toward the center while centralizing power in the hands of the party executive. The two processes were related: González's control over the party increased as the party moved politically toward the center (and toward power). Such an outcome was hardly preordained in 1975; however, the dynamics of the democratic transition gradually encouraged such an evolution.

It is important to remember that at the time of Franco's death, Spain's political future was highly uncertain, and several factors were pushing the Socialists leftward. Political parties remained illegal (and would remain so for well over another year), the prospects for a democratic opening were dubious at best, and Felipe González had just become party leader by espousing active resistance to the Franco regime. Moreover, the PCE at that time, having been at the forefront of anti-Franco protests and strikes, appeared as a formidable competitor for primacy on the Left; to challenge the PCE, the PSOE had an incentive to identify with workers and the disadvantaged in general. Thus, the Socialists' ideological center of gravity was well to the left; for example, as late as December 1976, a year after Franco's death, the party congress, for the first time in the party's history, officially espoused Marxism while proclaiming that "the economic subjugation of the proletariat is the primary cause of enslavement in all forms of social misery, intellectual degradation and political dependence" (quoted in Gunther 1986, 16).

The Socialists' left-pulling dynamic shifted in early 1977, however, as their leaders became convinced that Suárez was moving toward democracy.

Behind the scenes, the prime minister had begun consulting with Socialist leaders, and the party was legalized in February. From that time on, the PSOE supported the democratization process, dropping its earlier advocacy of a *ruptura democrática*—an abrupt break with the Franquist regime that would come about through mass protests supporting a process of negotiation. This shift did not preclude the PSOE taking firm stands against the Suárez government's actions in subsequent years; for example, the Socialists continued to stress an anti-imperialist line in foreign policy, while on the domestic front, they advocated greatly increased spending on education and unemployment insurance. In the manner of a loyal opposition, however, these positions reflected policy differences with the Suárez government, not a rejection of the post-Franco system itself (Maravall 1992, 11).

The Socialists' shift toward the center owed to several factors, including the contextual ones already mentioned. The essential centrism of the citizenry convinced Socialist leaders that votes were to be gained by supporting democracy and system stability. Especially was this true after the 1977 elections that saw the Socialists' turn toward moderation rewarded handsomely. Moreover, with Socialists now included in the transition process, the party had a stake in its successful passage. PSOE participation in drafting the 1978 Constitution as well as in negotiating the *Pactos de la Moncloa*—agreements among the major parties regarding such issues as terrorism, inflation, and unemployment—further reinforced their leaders' determination to turn away from the party's radical discourse of the early 1970s. Encouragement in this direction also came from the party's foreign benefactors within the Socialist International, notably the German Social Democratic Party, which provided the PSOE with financial and training support (Ortuño Anaya 2002).

Finally, unfolding electoral dynamics after the 1977 elections also served to move the Socialists toward the moderate center. Not only did the Communists' underwhelming performance in those elections remove them as a serious rival on the Left, but the PSOE's chief opponent, Suárez and his UCD, used the Socialists' earlier radicalism against them to good effect. In the March 1979 elections—at a time when the PSOE's official party line still embraced Marxism—Suárez quoted from the Socialists' 1976 congress resolutions and sought to portray the party as a veritable wolf in sheep's clothing: an organization that was dangerously subversive despite its soothing rhetoric. The fact that the ploy worked—the Socialists' vote stagnated in relation to 1977 and Suárez's coalition was reelected—convinced González of the need to jettison Marxism. The implosion and disintegration of Suárez's coalition in the following two years gave further justification for the Socialists to seek votes in the broad center (Share 1989, 58–59).

The other major change in the Socialist Party during the 1970s—the centralization of power in the hands of the "Andalusians," notably González and fellow southerner Alfonso Guerra—was directly related to the leadership's rightward shift. Not surprisingly, the gradual abandonment of the party's historical legacy of radicalism provoked resistance within. As we have seen, internal disputes based on personal and ideological differences have been a hallmark of the PSOE since the 1920s. Such disputes hardly disappeared with the party's banishment under Franco, and the triumph of the González-led "interiors" over the Llopis exile group was rooted in such struggles. While the Felipistas made good use of internal polemics when they were in insurgent mode in the 1969–1975 period, they found such infighting much less useful during the post-Franco democratization era as the González team led the party away from the Marxist Left and toward the center. Yet the leadership group had ridden the tiger of radicalism to take control of the party and so found it difficult to jump off. As the leaders sought to do so in the 1977–1979 period, they faced criticism from a vocal left wing of the party—informally named the *sector crítico*—who accused the leaders of being soft on Suárez, rejecting alliances with the PCE and other left groups (see below), and centralizing power within the party.

The contention between the González-Guerra "*oficialista*" leadership and the "*críticos*" came to a head in two party congresses in 1979 (Nash 1983; Gunther 1986; Preston 1986b; Share 1989; Juliá 1990; Maravall 2008). In a regular congress in May, González proposed a resolution to sever the party's Marxist affiliation. Defying the leadership's desire to abandon this critical ideological anchor, a majority of delegates rejected the proposal. González then went the delegates one better by resigning as party chief. There was an ironic twist to this conflict between González and the critical sector, however. The May congress also approved procedural changes in delegate selection and voting rules that strengthened the *oficialista*'s control over the party.[22] After several months of confusion, a special congress was called, presumably to select a new party leader. At the meeting in September, González found himself facing not a radical tiger but a paper one. Confronted with the reality of Felipe's resignation, the *sector crítico* failed to propose a candidate—a clear demonstration that González was the only viable leader. The party's left wing having been defeated, the delegates proceeded to remove the PSOE's embrace of Marxism and to exclude all critical-sector leaders from top party posts.[23] Coupled with the effects of the new rule changes, González's triumph was complete. The party's "Bad Godesberg" had also strengthened the hand of the party's most pragmatic, least ideological wing.[24]

What kind of party had the PSOE become by the early 1980s? It had two main traits that, to some extent, pulled in contrary directions, namely, an elitist structure coupled with close ties to the labor movement. On the one hand, the PSOE reflected a trend that has become increasingly pronounced among Social Democratic parties generally: just as we noted in the case of the French Socialists, leadership level within the party correlated highly with occupational status and level of education (Tezanos 1983). As the sociologist

José María Maravall (1992), himself a PSOE education minister in the early 1980s, expressed it, the party exhibited "the rather habitual pattern of easier opportunities for political promotion for educated middle-class members" (12). Maravall's own research during this period found that manual workers made up 37 percent of rank-and-file members but just 7 percent of the parliamentary group and 8 percent of the executive commission. Within those two latter bodies, liberal professionals (doctors, lawyers, professors, and so on) made up 60 and 72 percent of the members, respectively. A similar hierarchical profile applied in terms of education, with over two-thirds of the members of the party's top bodies having a university education, compared with less than one-tenth of Socialist voters and rank-and-file members (Maravall 1992, 12).

On the other hand, the party retained a countervailing pull in the direction of its populist roots: formal "fraternal" ties with the UGT. As we have seen, those ties went back to the early days of the PSOE in the late nineteenth century, and the UGT traditionally constituted a powerful sector within the party even while claiming its formal independence. In the early post-Franco period, there was considerable overlap in the two bodies. By the early 1980s, the UGT's executive committee was largely (though not completely) made up of PSOE members, and over three-fourths of UGT members supported the Socialists. Moreover, PSOE members were obligated by party statutes to join the UGT, although only about half of the members actually did so (Pérez-Díaz 1980, 109; McDonough, Barnes, and Pina 1981, 76; Puhle 1986, 331).

In one key respect, the PSOE demonstrated virtually no change from its Franco days: its opposition to an alliance with the Communists. The reasons for rejecting cooperation had little to do with the kind of visceral anti-Communism that animated Largo Caballero, Prieto, Luis Araquistáin, and other leaders in exile. Rather, rejection had to do, initially, with a fear of domination by the PCE prior to 1977 and then, following the clarifying elections of that year, with the perception that such cooperation would not serve the Socialists' purposes. The initial fear factor stemmed in part from the PCE's much larger membership. At the time of Franco's death, for example, the Communists claimed 20,000 members to the Socialists' 4,000. By late 1977, the PCE reported over 200,000 members, whereas the Socialists, although growing rapidly, still had only one-quarter that number (Verge Mestre 2007, 113). The Socialists' wariness also stemmed from the PCE's working-class presence in the Comisiones Obreras as well as its leadership role in the anti-Franco opposition. The Communists in 1975–1976 appeared positioned to strike their own version of a "historic compromise" with the Suárez government; as Heywood (1994) remarks, "It was natural to assume that, in any post-Franco democratic settlement, the PCE would play a role analogous to that of the *Partito Comunista Italiano* (PCI) in Italy" (58). Thus, the PSOE refused to join a PCE initiative in July 1974 to form a coordinated anti-

Franco opposition called the Junta Democrática—a coalition that included CCOO and several small parties. Instead, the Socialists formed their own organization, Plataforma de Convergencia Democrática, that criticized the PCE-led Junta for being "bourgeois" (Gillespie 1989, 303–4).

Following the 1977 elections, which demonstrated that the PSOE had approximately three times the electoral support of the PCE, the Socialists' impetus to refuse cooperation with the Communists shifted from fear to the lack of necessity. It should be stressed that the Socialists' aversion to collaboration with the Communists did not stem from fundamental ideological conflicts or differences in approach to the democratization process. Such differences may have existed in the late Franco period—when the Socialists considered the Communists as too cautious and the latter viewed the PSOE as too radical—but by 1977 the parties converged in terms of their basic orientations and were competing for the same pool of centrist voters (Maravall 1985, 153–56). In the entire transition and consolidation period between Franco's death in November 1975 and the October 1982 elections, there is only one instance of effective cooperation. For municipal elections in April 1979, the two parties formed joint lists in the major cities, and the results were positive: PSOE–PCE tickets won city council majorities in Madrid, Barcelona, and Valencia and in twenty-seven of the fifty provincial capitals (Camiller 1994, 240). But this proved to be a one-off event driven by temporary factors and was not repeated.[25]

The trajectory of the Communist Party during the transition and consolidation period could not have been more different from the Socialists': while González was leading his party to unexpected heights, the PCE came crashing down. As we have noted, this was a surprising outcome given the state of the two parties at the time of Franco's death. Suffice it to say that the PCE flourished far more as a force of opposition against an aging dictator in the early to mid-1970s than as a legalized "system" party just a few years later. In opposition, the party could draw on decades of experience as a disciplined unit struggling on behalf of those repressed by the Franco regime. The party's combative image also appealed to a rising generation of university and labor activists, and its control of the CCOO gave it a grassroots network. The question is, Why did the party appeal to tens of thousands of anti-Franco activists but not to the millions of Spanish voters, who, as we have seen, favored the moderate middle? This question is all the more puzzling given that the PCE, after its legalization in early 1977, became the very model of moderation.

The answer, in simplest form, is that the PCE failed to establish a convincing image as a moderate, democratic party. Moreover, as its organizational troubles accumulated following its poor initial performance in 1977, even the party's image as a unified body dissolved. It would be overly reductionist to lay the Communists' credibility problem at the feet of its leader;

however, there is little question that Santiago Carrillo did not convince most Spaniards that he was fit to be the country's leader.

Part of Carrillo's problem was strictly "mediagenic": television viewers could instantly see the twenty-five-year age difference between the gruff, graying Communist and his dynamic Socialist counterpart. But the basic problem, in the eyes of most voters, was that although the PCE chief talked like a democrat, he still acted like a Stalinist. In the minds of many citizens— especially those who had been politically socialized under a Franco regime that had made anti-Communism its virtual raison d'être—the terms "organized" and "disciplined" when applied to the PCE translated as "hierarchical" and "authoritarian" (Gunther et al. 1988, 67–70). Communism arrived to most Spaniards as a tainted brand, and Carrillo—a party official since the mid-1930s—did little to alter that image. Carrillo's failure in this regard was not for lack of trying. A driving force in the brief Eurocommunist boomlet of the mid-1970s, Carrillo took pains to distance his party from the Soviet Union, notably in a harsh critique published in 1977 (Carrillo 1977). Counteracting whatever positive impression this publication may have created, Carrillo's old nemesis Jorge Semprún (see note 13), in memoirs published that same year, accused the PCE leader of creating a false image of the PCE as a democratic party when in fact it had devolved into a cult of personality around Carrillo himself (Preston 1981, 38–39).

Whatever the truth of the claim that the PCE had become a "roughneck autocracy" (Camiller 1994, 246), the impression of the PCE as a cohesive force evaporated after the 1977 elections. In effect, the inconsistency of Carrillo's preaching democracy for the country while failing to practice it within the party, coupled with the PCE's weak performance in those elections, brought internal opposition from two sides. On one side was a faction of pro-Soviet loyalists—labeled "Afghans" for their support of the 1979 Soviet invasion of their southern neighbor—who resented not only Carrillo's Moscow bashing but also the party's overly accommodating posture in relation to the Suárez government. This group had problems not with the "discipline" of democratic centralism but rather with the party's ideological drift. On the other side was a faction of *renovadores* who were disenchanted with democratic centralism and wanted more internal party democracy (Heywood 1994, 62). As with many political questions in Spain, these disputes also intersected with tensions between central (Madrid) control versus regional autonomy.[26] By the time of the 1982 elections, the PCF was reeling from internal contention and a hemorrhaging of members.

Those elections demolished Carrillo's vision of a triumphant or even a credible Eurocommunist alternative to the Socialists. In all respects, the PSOE's victory was as impressive as the PCE's was dismal. With 48 percent of the votes and—thanks to the boost provided by Spain's electoral system— 58 percent of the Cortes seats, the Socialists were now positioned to enact their program without trimming their sails for any coalition partners. Nearly doubling its vote total from 1979, the PSOE drew votes away from many erstwhile UCD and PCE voters; by one estimate, nearly 60 percent of Communist voters in 1979 shifted to the PSOE (López-Pintor 1985, 297). The PSOE's electorate remarkably reflected the country as a whole in terms of gender, age, occupational status, region, and type of community—much more so than either the UCD or the PCE (Puhle 1986, 290; Smith 1998, 60). As for the PCE, its vote total shrank to a minuscule 4 percent, and the party gained just four parliamentary seats. In the face of manifest failure, Carrillo resigned his post shortly thereafter. As the definitive sign of Spain's democratic consolidation, González assumed the prime ministership from his conservative opponent, Suárez. For a shining moment, "Felipe" stood as the embodiment of a new Spain: "The son of a cowman, he came across as a son of the people, warm and open, occasionally speaking in a revolutionary manner yet not quite managing to frighten anyone. His good looks, vigor, and natural intelligence gave him tremendous political sex appeal" (Gillespie 1989, 326–27). It remained to be seen how long the new leader could maintain this luster.

SOCIALISTS RISE AND FALL, COMMUNISTS REGROUP, 1982–1996

In comparative terms, González's luster lasted a long time. Holding power through three reelections, the Socialist leader and his party governed for fourteen years—a tenure exceeding Thatcher's and rivaling that of Mitterrand and Kohl as among the longest-serving European leaders of their generation. By contrast, the Communists were never in a position to challenge Socialist supremacy on the Left, and they remained shut out of office for the entire period. While accurate, the preceding summary does not reveal the full story, for the dynamics of this period eventually worked against the Socialists and in favor of the Communists. By 1996, when the PSOE lost control of parliament to José María Aznar's Popular Party (Partido Popular [PP]), the two left parties were headed in different directions. The Socialists' decline, although hardly catastrophic, was marked. Between 1982 and 1996, the PSOE's vote percentage declined gradually but steadily by over ten points, from 48.1 to 37.6 percent. Along with their luster, González and his Socialists tarnished their own reputation for efficient, corruption-free government, as the final years of their reign saw the eruption of financial and other scandals. By contrast, during the same period the PCE managed to regroup, albeit haltingly, and increase its vote percentage in every election. By the end of this period, the PCE had managed to more than double its 1982 percentage and narrow the electoral gap with the Socialists to its lowest point since the late 1970s (see table 4.1). What explains this turnabout in the two parties' fortunes?

For the Communists, the turnabout was born out of the party's response to the disaster of 1982. That response was not immediate; in fact, if anything, the PCE's crisis worsened during the next three years, as leadership fights led, by late 1985, to the existence of *three* Communist parties (Bosco 2000, 148–51). The first fight occurred in the wake of the resignation of Santiago Carrillo as party chief, who willingly left his post after the 1982 defeat. Having resigned his seat but not resigning himself to sit quietly in the party's ranks, Carrillo quickly grew critical of the PCE's new leadership. His successor, Gerardo Iglesias, was no Berlinguer, but he was also no Marchais. That is, while Iglesias envisioned no grand compromise à la Berlinguer—not with the Socialists much less the PP—he did begin to build ties with other groups and movements on the Left, notably peace and environmental groups. In this respect, Iglesias's approach differed from that of Marchais, who single-mindedly defended the PCF's autonomy and "vanguard" role, especially in relation to its core group, the working class. Carrillo, by contrast, espoused a position akin to Marchais's: the PCE should seek to build worker dissatisfaction with the PSOE government's "neoliberal" economic policies. This dispute, building over the course of the three years following the 1982 elections, finally resulted in the former leader's resignation to form a new party, the Revolutionary Marxist Communist Party (PCE Marxista Revolucionaria), later to be renamed the Party of Spanish Workers (Partido de los Trabajadores Españoles). In the meantime, a group of unreconciled "Afghans"—old-line Soviet supporters who resented the PCE's distancing itself from Moscow—also exited to form their own party, the Communist Party of the People of Spain (Partido Comunista de los Pueblos de España) (Botella 1988, 80; Heywood 1994, 68–99; Ramiro-Fernández 2004b, 2–3).

By early 1986, the PCE was perhaps no stronger than before, but party leader Iglesias now had a fairly clear road to take the PCE in the direction he desired, namely, the building of a coalition of various groups to the left of the PSOE. An encouraging road sign for Iglesias was the outcome of a government-sponsored referendum on Spain's NATO membership in March 1986. The government's position, favoring a "yes" vote for Spain's continued membership in the alliance, represented a complete reversal of the PSOE's opposition to NATO membership during the 1982 campaign. For the PCE and smaller groups to the PSOE's left, this flip-flop constituted both a sellout and a loss of credibility. Working together, these groups mounted a "no" campaign that was sufficiently strong with about 40 percent of the vote to encourage the participants to formalize an electoral alliance for upcoming parliamentary elections. Thus was born the United Left (Izquierda Unida [IU]), an unusual type of hybrid coalition. Far from being a coalition of equals, the IU consisted of a dominant party, the PCE, surrounded by a mix of smaller parties and groups led by "notable" individuals.[27] Of the group's claimed membership of 100,000, about 62,000 were PCE members (Heywood 1994, 70). Although the IU's initial foray into electoral politics in 1986 was hardly auspicious—the coalition polled only slightly higher than the PCE's lamentable 1982 total—the prospect of building a Communist-led rallying point well to the left of the PSOE party and government became, perhaps faute de mieux, the party's new strategy.

While the Communists were struggling to surmount their various crises, the Socialists were busy governing Spain. Each of the Socialists' four terms featured its own policy emphases and political momentum. As in all new administrations, the PSOE government's first term, 1982–1986, offered the largest window of opportunity. One might have imagined that the new government would be tempted initially to veer toward a leftist reform program as Mitterrand's Socialists did in 1981–1982. With a dominant parliamentary position, a young charismatic leader, and a certain euphoria surrounding the arrival of the first Left-led government in Spain in over forty years, the Socialists could have been expected to launch a raft of left-leaning reforms.

There were good reasons, however, why González & Co. refused to go in that direction. First, the heralded "Mitterrand experiment" of reflation-cum-nationalizations had, by late 1982, run up against economic reality in the form of mounting trade and budget deficits. For their Spanish counterparts, the French Socialists' reform program served not as a model but as a cautionary tale. Second, the 1982 election gave the new government a "leeway, not a mandate" (McDonough, Barnes, and Pina, 1986a, 448). The Socialists' triumph owed not to massive voter realignment on the Left but rather to a "power vacuum created by a discredited political alternative" (López-Pintor 1985, 311). Public opinion surveys revealed a citizenry that expected the Socialists to provide a greater measure of social welfare benefits—to bring Spain in line with other European countries—but not to undertake fundamental structural changes in the economy (McDonough et al. 1986b, 757). Finally, added to these factors was that the Spanish economy was in no shape for experimentation. With unemployment topping 15 percent and inflation running at nearly the same level, the government faced great pressure to put the economy's fundamentals right. Making this constraint all the more limiting was that Spain was slated to join the European Community (EC) in 1986 and thus needed to prepare for increased competition from and coordination with its European partners.

Thus, the PSOE government's initial economic policy was largely a study in mainstream orthodoxy.[28] To bring down inflation, the government tightened credit, reduced the fiscal deficit, and orchestrated a series of peak-level *pactos sociales* with the two major unions as well as the employers association, the CEOE, to temper wage increases. To encourage the economy's modernization, the government focused on two areas: industrial "reconversion" and reform of the public enterprise sector. The industrial reconversion program provided a framework to facilitate investment and reduce unprofitable capacity and labor for nearly 800 private firms in eleven core industrial sectors. In all, the reconversion program targeted—and achieved—a one-third reduction of the workforce in the targeted sectors. At the same time, the program provided active labor market measures such as retraining while offering various kinds of investment incentives in regions hit by job losses (Montero 2002).

The public sector also came in for modernization, specifically public firms operating under the aegis of the National Institute of Industry (Instituto Nacional de Industria [INI]). Established by Franco in 1941, INI had an initial mission of developing Spain's capacity in industries considered crucial for national defense and economic security, such as armaments, electricity, oil production, basic metals production (steel, copper, and aluminum), and motor vehicles. In the wake of the 1973 oil crisis, however, INI became a huge salvage operation for failing private firms; for example, between 1971 and 1982, INI nationalized twenty-five firms in the steel, automobile, shipbuilding, and other sectors. By the time the Socialists came to power, INI had become a chronic money loser, with its deficits equaling about 1.5 percent of GDP. Through a combination of privatization, rationalization (including major job cuts), and reorganization that continued throughout the decade and into the 1990s, INI was able to improve its performance; by the late 1980s, the entity was actually turning respectable profits. [29]

As the government's economic program took effect, job losses mounted while wage increases lagged behind inflation; between 1982 and 1985, for example, the unemployment rate jumped from 15.6 to 21.1 percent versus an average increase in the European Union from 9.4 to 10.9 percent (Smith 1998, 93). Although the González government sought to be union friendly in the sense of including the major labor organizations in negotiations regarding industrial reconversion, INI reform, and the wage-indexation pacts, by the end of the Socialists' first term the unions were distancing themselves from the government. Increasingly, both major confederations, the UGT and the CCOO, viewed the government's policies as producing more austerity than progress for workers.

In truth, the CCOO had taken that perspective from the outset, not only refusing to participate in the industrial reconversion negotiations but also actively promoting strikes and demonstrations against the program in hard-hit areas in Asturias, the Basque Country, and elsewhere. Although it would be simplistic to claim that the PCE, in transmission-belt style, ordered the Comisiones to take such an adversary stance, the party certainly agreed with and supported the union's opposition. For the fraternal UGT, the divorce from the Socialists came more slowly but, in the end, more bitterly (Gillespie

1990). Initially, the UGT supported industrial reconversion and signed all reconversion agreements; the union also signed wage-indexation pacts in 1983 and 1984. By 1985, however, reacting to growing worker dissatisfaction, UGT leader Nicolás Redondo was publicly opposing the government's proposal to reform the pension system by reducing both the number and the compensation level of pensioners. Henceforth, the government was preoccupied with how to pursue economic modernization while managing the political discontent resulting from the program's unequal distribution of sacrifices and benefits.

Reelected in 1986, the González government faced a second term largely consumed by the issue of economic growth and its discontents.[30] Its record was decidedly mixed. On the one hand, the government, by the end of its term in 1989, could point to some impressive results. Overall economic growth during the period was significantly higher than the EC average: 4.7 versus 3.3 percent. Underpinning this growth was an investment boom that was twice the EC average.[31] Especially impressive was the growth of foreign direct investment, which increased over sixfold—from $1.6 billion in 1985 to $10.5 billion in 1989. Since this term coincided with Spain's entry into the EC, much of this increase in foreign direct investment, especially into the financial sector, came from EC countries. The rate of inflation also slowed markedly—from an annual average of nearly 12 percent in the government's first term to 6.5 percent in the second term. Business profits moved up, and public deficits declined. Even Spain's notoriously high unemployment, which typically was over twice the EC average, began coming down.

On the other hand, from the standpoint of many workers and their unions, the presumed benefits of economic modernization were too slow in coming or were not coming at all. So even though the main economic indicators were moving in a positive direction, indicators of social satisfaction were increasingly negative. Most notably, the UGT ended its support of the government's economic program and joined the CCOO in opposing it. The UGT's motivations for the break were multiple, stemming from policy differences, organizational maintenance imperatives, and even personal animosities.

Chief among the policy differences was the union's critique of the government's poor labor record. Specifically, the UGT charged that government attempts to make labor more "flexible" had led mainly to a growth of part-time and/or temporary jobs, not secure, well-paying jobs.[32] Moreover, from an organizational point of view, the UGT felt that it was no longer benefiting from its partnership with the PSOE government; rather, it was being challenged by the CCOO, whose opposition had put the UGT on the defensive. In the two unions' competition to secure workers' support, the UGT considered that its continued support of the government's economic policies would disadvantage it in relation to the Comisiones.[33] Finally, personal clashes between the old comrades in arms, González and UGT chief

Redondo, appear to have played a role in the union's split with the government.[34] Scholars continue to debate the precise causes of the PSOE–UGT breakup, specifically whether the initiative came primarily from the government's or the union's side.[35] Whatever the precise cause, the result was not only a growing gulf between the two erstwhile allies but also an increasing bond between the UGT and CCOO in opposition to the government policy. The culmination of this conflict came in a massive general strike on December 14, 1988, that UGT and CCOO leaders celebrated as a great success, with about 80 percent of all workers participating.

Despite these expressions of discontent with the government's economic policies, there were still enough citizens happy enough with the Socialists' overall performance—or at least not impressed enough with the conservative alternative—to give the Socialists a third term in early elections called in 1989. But there were clear signals of disaffection, notably a nearly five-point drop in the party's vote percentage—to just under 40 percent—compared with 1986. Only thanks to the distorting effects of Spain's electoral system did the Socialists retain a bare majority of one seat in the Cortes. If anything, this third term, which lasted until 1993, proved even more crisis ridden than the previous one, partly because of a global recession that took the bloom off Spain's booming economy. Of more importance in creating turmoil were two problems of the Socialists' own making.

The first is that the government's economic model came unhinged and contributed to a major currency crisis. In simplest terms, by the early 1990s the government was carrying out a contradictory and ultimately unsustainable economic program that combined restrictive monetary measures with a lax fiscal approach. On the one hand, having joined the EC's Exchange Rate Mechanism (ERM) in 1989, the government opted for a strong peseta policy.[36] This implied a tight monetary policy based on high interest rates. Such an approach had the advantage of dampening inflationary pressures by discouraging consumer borrowing and spending, reducing import prices, and increasing business's financial costs, thereby giving employers strong incentive to resist inflationary wage settlements. High interest rates also served to maintain the flow of foreign direct investment. On the other hand, largely in response to the social discontent mobilized by the unions in December 1988 general strike, the government increased social spending without raising taxes commensurately, thus generating ballooning budget deficits.[37]

In effect, the government was increasing the budget deficit while using high interest rates to finance it—the equivalent of pressing down on the fiscal accelerator while slamming on the monetary brakes. This contradictory strategy worked as long as foreigners were willing to buy pesetas and invest in Spain's banks and businesses; however, the onset of the global recession shook investors' and currency speculators' confidence that Spain could sustain its growth model. This growing lack of confidence ultimately led to a run on the peseta's value, and the government was forced to expend about two-thirds of its foreign reserves defending the currency. Ultimately, between September 1992 and May 1993, the government had to devalue the currency three times for a total of nearly 20 percent. In all, much of the Socialists' third term was consumed in trying to manage the contradictions of their economic policy.

The Socialists' second problem had less to do with economics and more to do with "integrity" in both an ethical and an organizational sense. During this period, the term "Marbella Socialist" was coined by some journalistic critics in an allusion to the chic beach town on the southern coast. Even significant voices within the PSOE itself began to assert that the government had deserted the traditional ethical concerns of socialists. One former PSOE leader and official in the Economy Ministry stated to this author, "The values portrayed by the government are nonsocialist values. They are the values of fast money and speculation, values completely different from socialist ones of solidarity and cooperation."[38] During this period, several government scandals broke out, reinforcing a growing impression that the government was engaging in corruption and abusing its power.[39] Expressions of discontent with the Socialists' manner of governing became widespread both outside the party and within.

These critiques extended to the party's internal practices, specifically its handling of opinion differences within the organization. Much of the controversy surrounded the party's (and the government's) second in command, Alfonso Guerra. It will be recalled that Guerra and González, fellow Andalusians, had been political partners since the Franco days. During the transition period, Guerra had helped engineer rule changes within the PSOE in 1979 that centralized power in the hands of the González-led leadership team. Once González became prime minister, Guerra's position as *número dos* in the party was strengthened, as he oversaw the day-to-day running of the organization. By the early 1990s, however, in the view of many party officials, Guerra had become increasingly autocratic and intolerant of internal dissent. For example, no less a figure than José María Maravall, who had served as education minister from 1982 to 1986, wrote the following in a letter to Felipe González in 1990:

> Internal power is often used ruthlessly. . . . We are ditching a spectacular number of people, generally people that do not belong to the party's machinery and do not accept submission—which is quite different from loyalty. . . . Nobody, however minoritarian, should be afraid of personal political consequences for dissenting. This is not to defend divisions inside the party: only that internal cohesion can only be the result of debates and of accountability. (Maravall 2008, 185)

Ultimately, the controversy over Guerra's role in the party, as well as corruption charges surrounding him and his brother, led to a split between Guerra and González that dragged on for several years, reinforcing the impression that the Socialists had become a divided party.[40]

While the Socialists were struggling to maintain popularity and cohesion in the early 1990s, their Communist counterparts were mounting something of a comeback. The parties' contrasting fortunes were not coincidental: to the extent that the Socialists appeared to be losing popularity and becoming indistinct from any other centrist party, the Communists found growing space on the left side of the political spectrum. As mentioned, the PCE had embarked on a new political formula in 1986: an attempt to rally smaller Left parties around itself to form a larger coalition, the IU. Following the IU's disappointing initial foray in the 1986 election—when the coalition's vote percentage barely exceeded that of the PCE alone in the previous election— PCE leader Iglesias was replaced by a thirty-seven-year-old Andalusian, Julio Anguita, who had been the mayor of Córdoba.

Dynamic and outspoken, Anguita staked out an unabashedly leftist stance that departed from that of the PCE during the previous two decades. First and foremost, Anguita took a harsh line against the Socialists, accusing them of abandoning the Left. In so doing, he emphasized the PCE/IU's roots in Marxism and class struggle. At the same time, he sought to attract "postmaterialist" voters by emphasizing proenvironmental and antinuclear positions (Torcal and Montero 1997, 16–22). This combination of old and new themes began paying dividends in the following elections in 1989, which, it should be recalled, came on the heels of the successful general strike of December 1988. In those elections, the IU doubled the PCE's vote percentage from the previous election. Surveys indicated that the IU succeeded in peeling off erstwhile PSOE voters who had become disillusioned with the government's move to the center; fully one-third of IU voters had voted for the PSOE in 1986 (Bosco and Gaspar 2001, 368). Over the next two elections, in 1993 and 1996, the IU continued to carve out a niche as the main left-wing opposition to the government. While the coalition never came close to realizing Anguita's goal of surpassing the PSOE, the IU gradually increased its electoral appeal, reaching a high point of 10.5 percent of the vote and twenty-one parliamentary seats in 1996.

While the Anguita-led IU leadership could take credit for a respectable comeback of the Communist Party, his tenure failed to resolve several organizational questions. The central one was the nature of the IU itself: Was it a true coalition? A protoparty? A sham creation of the PCE? The relationship of the PCE to its other partners remained unsettled and undefined. According to the most in-depth study of the IU/PCE during this period, the relationship between the party and the coalition evolved over time, largely as a function of the leadership's increasing radicalization. During the organization's first

six years—from its founding in 1986 until 1992—the PCE took a self-effac-
ing role, reducing its own membership and placing itself "in a position close
to disappearance in favour of the IU" (Ramiro-Fernández 2004b, 4; see also
Ramiro-Fernández 2004a). From 1992 on, Anguita and the PCE reversed this
stance, with the party assuming a "vanguard" role and taking a more forthright anti-government—and also antiunion (see below)—position.[41] In addition to the question of the PCE's relationship to the IU coalition, there were
strong voices within the coalition—and even within the PCE itself—that
questioned Anguita's vision. The most vocal of these urged the PCE/IU to
abandon Communism, as Occhetto and the PCI had done in Italy. These
included the leader of the Catalan PCE affiliate (PSUC), Andalusian leaders
of a small IU party (PASOC), and a new current (Neuva Izquierda), headed
by Nicolás Sartorius, that was established within the PCE itself (Heywood
1994, 74–79). Anguita, however, stood firm, making for a contentious coalition that never succeeded in establishing a clear identity.

The most dramatic change in Spanish Communism during this period
came not within the PCE itself, which, despite its internal struggles, never
renounced Communism or changed its name, but rather in the party's relations with the labor movement. It will be recalled that Communists were
instrumental in establishing the Comisiones Obreras, the only active labor-
based opposition to Franco during the 1960s and early 1970s. Following the
transition to democracy, the CCOO challenged the Socialist-affiliated UGT
for leadership of the labor movement, with the two confederations establishing a rough parity in members and worker support as measured in works
council elections. The CCOO had always exercised a certain autonomy in
relation to the PCE, but during the 1970s and 1980s the two organizations
had overlapping leaderships and generally took similar positions (Fishman
1990, 164–65). Moreover, both organizations strongly opposed the González
government's industrial and macroeconomic policies during the 1980s.

This close working relationship changed, however, during the early 1990s
as the CCOO separated itself from the PCE, mainly over strategic differences
between the leaders of the two organizations. CCOO head Antonio Gutiérrez,
who had taken over leadership of the confederation in 1988, had been close
to Anguita's predecessor, Gerardo Iglesias, and never shared Anguita's vision of an unreformed Communist Party or the PCE leader's almost visceral
antagonism toward the Socialists. In fact, Gutiérrez strongly supported Occhetto's transformation of the Italian Communist Party and backed the same
process for the PCE (Heywood 1994, 74; Ramiro-Fernández 2004b, 22).
Gutiérrez also represented a new generation of CCOO leaders who were less
ideological and more open to dialogue with employers and the government.[42]
Given the government's increased propensity to negotiate with unions following the December 1988 general strike, Gutiérrez was even less inclined to
systematically oppose the González government, as Anguita espoused.

The CCOO's changed stance did not preclude the confederation's taking strong positions against specific government policies; for example, the Comisiones and UGT called a general strike in June 1992 to protest a government decree cutting unemployment benefits. But the CCOO leader's stance did make possible occasional agreements between the unions and the government, as seen in an omnibus 1990 accord regarding pensions, unemployment benefits, and other matters (Royo 2008, 134–35). Throughout the first half of the 1990s, Anguita carried out an attack on Gutiérrez's leadership and sought to tighten the PCE's control over the CCOO. The attempt, however, ultimately failed, and the CCOO finally cut all formal ties to the PCE in the confederation's Sixth Congress in 1996 (Van Biezen 1998, 56).[43]

Whatever its internal inconsistencies and tensions in the early 1990s, the IU continued to advance at least modestly. No such fate, however, awaited the Socialists in the 1993 elections. With the party internally divided and mired in various scandals, the economy in recession and unemployment topping 20 percent, and González himself appearing visibly tired and seemingly bored with his job, the party maintained its downward electoral slide, winning less than 39 percent of the vote. For the first time, the PSOE was seriously challenged by an opposition, as the PP, led by their new chief José María Aznar, polled nearly 35 percent. With just 159 seats, the PSOE was well short of the 175 seats needed for a Cortes majority. Numerically, the IU, with eighteen seats, was a possible coalition partner, but González rejected this prospect, holding that policy differences with the Communists were too great (Lancaster 1994, 186). He sought to establish a formal coalition with two regional parties, the Catalan Convergència i Unió (CiU) and the Basque Partido Nacionalista Vasco, but the attempt was unsuccessful. Ultimately, González formed a minority government, which then had to cobble together ad hoc majorities from among the CiU, the Partido Nacionalista Vasco, and other smaller parties in order to pass legislation. The government's dependence on placating the regional parties clearly diminished its power when it came to issues affecting these regions.[44]

Given its lack of a consistent majority after 1993, the government launched few new initiatives, and it was finally forced to call for new elections a year early, in 1996. By that time, the sense of stasis, if not paralysis, in the Socialist Party was palpable after four terms and nearly fourteen years in power. The party continued to be marked by factional fights—notably between González and Guerra factions—as well as charges of corruption. On the positive side, the government's steady economic management had stabilized the currency after the peseta crisis of 1992–1993, and economic indicators improved as the global economy pulled out of the recession of the early 1990s.[45] Nonetheless, with Aznar's reinvigorated PP promoting their leader as a man of "integrity"—as opposed to the now-graying Socialist leader who

had allowed corruption to flourish on *his* watch—the Socialists fully expected to meet defeat in the 1996 elections.

In examining Felipe González's record just a few years before, a journalist for the *Financial Times* (June 1, 1992) wrote, "Mr. González never
wanted to change Spain, just calm it down after so many years of nervous
dictatorship and tumultuous transition. It is his stated aim to raise Spain to be
an average country, with average E.C. incomes, average lifestyles and average output." The statement certainly captures González's innately moderate,
pragmatic governing style. For him, "Socialism" was never about class warfare or transforming the capitalist system. It was always about, first, modernizing the Spanish economy so that Spain could "join Europe" as a full partner
while, second, using the benefits of growth—through higher taxes and redistributive measures—to improve the life chances of citizens. These apparently
modest goals, however, entailed considerable change on the part of the Spanish economy and society. In that sense, the journalist understates the legacy
of the Socialists' four terms in office.

Critics have often charged the González government with following "neoliberal" policies that abandoned socialist principles of social protection, but
such a charge does not capture the complexity of the PSOE government's
economic record (Share 1988b; Petras 1993). At the least, any self-respecting
"neoliberal" government would be expected to hold down public spending,
but the Socialists significantly increased the state budget during their tenure,
ending with a spending record considerably above the OECD average.[46]
While the country's overall economic performance was mixed—during the
entire period, compared with the EU average, Spain's growth rate was higher, but so were its inflation and unemployment levels (Smith 1998, 109)—the
government carved out a distinctive policy focus in two important respects.
First, the government directed spending toward "public capital formation,"
that is, the boosting of supply-side productive factors that would increase
overall economic productivity (Boix 1998b, 113). A principal target was
transport and communication infrastructure, including roads, railroads, air-
ports, and ports. There were also significant increases in spending on water
systems and education. Second, in classic Social Democratic fashion, the
government increased spending on social welfare measures, notably pensions, health care, and unemployment benefits (Maravall and Fraile 1998).
Taking the two categories of public capital formation and social expenditures
together, government spending increased from 24.7 percent of GDP in 1982
to 30.8 percent in 1991 (Boix 1998b, 112). On balance, during the Socialist
years, Spain made considerable progress in reaching González's goal of becoming an "average country."

THE LEFT IN OPPOSITION: SOCIALIST RENEWAL, COMMUNIST DECLINE, 1996–2004

The Socialists met defeat in the 1996 elections and so, for the first time since 1982, found themselves in the opposition. For the fourth election in a row, the PSOE saw its share of the vote decline. Meanwhile, the Communists continued their advance as the lead element of the United Left coalition, topping 10 percent for the first time since the party's high point in 1979. PCE and IU leader Julio Anguita's claim that his coalition would eventually surpass the PSOE appeared to be less of a pipe dream. As we have seen, the parties were heading in different directions. While the larger Socialists were losing steam—and votes—under an aging generation of centrist leaders tainted by scandals, the feisty Communists had carved out a sizable niche on the Left by a confrontational approach stressing their differences with the Socialists on environmental, economic, and foreign policy questions. Alas, political momentum, like political careers, often proves short lived. This was the case for Socialists and Communists during the next eight years, as the political fortunes of the two parties completely reversed. By 2004, the Socialists found themselves back in power, whereas the PCE/IU saw its vote percentage shrink by half and its parliamentary seats decrease from twenty-one in 1996 to just five in 2004. Underlying this shift in fortunes was a series of leadership struggles in both parties that produced, on the one hand, a remarkable generational renovation in the PSOE and, on the other, a divided Communist movement whose vaunted internal discipline had broken down.

For the Socialists, the return to power was anything but smooth, and in fact the emergence of a new post-Felipe generation of leaders came only after the PSOE's resounding loss in the 2000 elections. This protracted process was due to two related factors. The first was the bittersweet nature of the 1996 defeat. The PP's victory in those elections had been presaged by the party's wins in various local, regional, and European elections in the preceding years, and all the polls predicted the party's triumph.[47] For the Socialists, the only surprise was that they lost by *so little*—just 1.37 percent in the popular vote. According to one analyst, "The 1996 result was actually something of a relief. The PSOE showed that it was still competitive. So the elections did not send a clear signal in terms of where the party should go. That explains why the party's reaction was a bit slower and the change less drastic than if the party had lost by a lot."[48] The second factor was the deep split in the party between the González and Guerra factions. Following the elections, González was ready to give up leadership of the party, but he was in no position to simply designate a successor. Moreover, he wanted to prevent the Guerra faction from taking control. This split within the party meant that the process of selecting a successor would likely be drawn out and contested.

Such was indeed the scenario.[49] Just before the next party congress in June 1997, González announced that he would not stand for reelection as general secretary. Guerra also indicated that he would not be a candidate, knowing that he faced too much personal opposition to win the post. At the 1997 congress, a former minister and "Felipista" Joaquín Almunia narrowly won the post with the support of González and his supporters. Almunia, however, felt that he needed to gain greater legitimacy within the party, so the following year he took the risky, unprecedented step of calling for a primary election to determine the PSOE's prime-ministerial candidate for the 2000 elections. To the surprise and confusion of virtually everyone in the party, Almunia lost the primary to another former minister, Josep Borrell. Thus, the party faced the bizarre prospect of having a leader (Almunia) who was, in effect, *not* to be the party's standard-bearer in the upcoming election.

The situation became even more confused in 1999 when Borrell was forced to resign in the face of corruption charges and a lack of backing by other party leaders. As the 2000 elections approached, Almunia had to step in for the disgraced Borrell and become the party's lead candidate. Needless to say, this scenario proved a recipe for electoral disaster. On the night of the Socialists' defeat, Almunia resigned as general secretary, opening the way for a new round of leadership selection. At the party's next congress just four months after the 2000 election, a relatively unknown forty-year-old back-bench member of Parliament, José Luis Rodríguez Zapatero, was able to piece together a minimum winning coalition of Felipistas, Guerristas, and uncommitted younger party leaders. Much of Zapatero's appeal derived from his youth and the sense that he would bring renewal to the party.[50]

Zapatero, whom Guerra had dismissed as "Bambi," proved to be anything but a babe in the woods. In addition to initiating internal party changes concerning membership status and campaign design—all with the goal of building the party's capacity to communicate with and mobilize its members and sympathizers (Méndez-Lago 2006, 428–31)—Zapatero's early tenure was notable in establishing a new identity for the PSOE. Breaking with the González government's general Atlanticism, Zapatero came out strongly against the American-sponsored invasion of Iraq. This stance put him directly at odds with Aznar's backing of the invasion, but Zapatero's opposition clearly coincided with Spanish public opinion. On economic matters, Zapatero espoused no fundamental differences with the modernization emphasis promoted by both the González and the Aznar government, but he did demarcate himself on such noneconomic issues as the extension of civil rights and institutional reform. Having been heavily influenced by British Third Way thinking, Zapatero spoke of "deepening" democracy and citizenship by making institutions more transparent and accountable and by promoting such reforms as gender parity and gay marriage. By the time of the March 2004 elections, Zapatero's leadership had brought the PSOE back into position to directly challenge the PP.

In contrast to this tortuous but ultimately successful organizational renewal on the part of the Socialists, the experience of the PCE/IU during this period was one of internal division and crisis. The summary explanation for the coalition's travails is that its Anguita-inspired, left-leaning strategy of opposition to the governing Socialists was no longer viable once the Socialists themselves were out of power. One observer comments,

> It's one thing to vote for the IU while the PSOE was still in power. It was a kind of protest vote, especially during a period in which the PSOE government was running into many problems—strong growth but growing inequality, the general strike of 1988 and worker protests, corruption scandals, and the rest. It's another thing to keep on voting for the IU once the PSOE was in opposition. After the PP came to power in 1996, many IU voters, knowing that the IU had no chance of ever winning a majority, figured the most useful way to vote was for the PSOE, to bring back the largest Left party. And that's what happened—and the IU's support declined sharply.[51]

The loss of its strategic niche, coupled with Anguita's own retirement in 2000 due to heart problems, triggered, in turn, an internal dispute that ultimately resulted in a leadership struggle more reminiscent of the Prieto–Largo Caballero split within the 1930s Socialist Party rather than the unity and discipline of a classic Communist Party. The result was a PCE/IU with a divided executive that pulled in opposite directions, especially as regards alliance strategy.

The split derived from changes in both the IU's leadership structure and the composition of the IU coalition.[52] First, as regards leadership structure, it will be recalled that Anguita, while active, headed both the IU coalition and its dominant component, the PCE. Following his retirement, the coalition decided to split the roles, with the IU having its own leader separate from the PCE chief. Thus, the coalition created a kind of dual executive, along with the obvious potential for a divided leadership. Division, pitting one Communist leader against another, is precisely what happened. On one side of the struggle were the followers and heirs of Anguita, led by the PCE's general secretary, Francisco Frutos, who continued to espouse the oppositionist line. This tendency did not automatically refuse any and all alliances with the Socialists; for example, it did engage in an electoral pact—albeit a hastily crafted and ineffective one—with the PSOE for the 2000 elections. Any prospective alliance, however, was to be conditional and based on a strict quid pro quo: specific concessions given in exchange for PCE/IU support. In no case would PCE/IU representatives formally enter a government and serve in a governing coalition.

On the other side of the dispute was a tendency led by the head of the IU, Gaspar Llamazares—a fellow Communist who also headed the Asturias federation of the party. The Llamazares faction, displaying a more pragmatic, flexible style, rejected the Frutos faction's hard-line opposition to coalitions. Instead, seeking to make the most of the PCE/IU's limited electoral punch, this faction sought to make the IU a coalition partner, especially at the subnational level, where the IU still had a significant presence in certain regions.

A second factor in the leadership split stemmed from shifts in the IU coalition's composition throughout the 1990s. On the one hand, by 2000, the PCE was the only party left in the IU, all the other original founding groups having left the coalition. On the other hand, the percentage of IU members who were also PCE members decreased over time, from 78 percent in 1992 to 38 percent in 2004.[53] This change in membership patterns meant that the IU qua political organization was evolving independently in its own right since it had its own directly affiliated members who were not PCE members. This membership shift also meant that leadership struggles within the PCE would naturally "spill over" to the IU as a whole. Rival leaders within the PCE had an incentive to appeal to the growing proportion of non-Communist IU members in order to build support for their positions. As head of the IU, Llamazares was able to mobilize behind him not only a portion of the PCE but also most of the non-Communist IU members. Frutos's base, by contrast, was largely the leadership faction of the PCE. Thus, the organization presented the strange, unprecedented, and unexpected spectacle of the PCE leadership acting as the minority opposition or critical faction within the IU coalition. In all, changes in membership patterns altered the relationship between the PCE and the coalition as a whole and enhanced the power of the IU head in relation to the PCE leader.

The end result was that the Llamazares faction had become the dominant one by the end of the decade. As such, it was able to carry through on its aim of engaging in coalitions with other parties. Between 1999 and 2004, for example, the IU entered four regional governments—Asturias, Catalonia, the Balearic Islands, and the Basque Country—as a minority coalition partner. In the first three of these, the IU joined coalitions with the PSOE; in Asturias, the IU's support was even pivotal in the sense of being crucial for the formation of a majority coalition. Although the minority Frutos faction remained unreconciled to this "betrayal" of Communist values, it was in no position to change it. Thus, by 2004, the PCE/IU had undergone great change since its high point in the 1996 elections. From a self-confident unabashedly leftist organization headed by a charismatic leader who disdained the Socialists, the PCE/IU in eight years had lost half of its electorate, become internally fractious, and embraced alliances with Socialists and even nonleftist parties. The future of Spanish "Communism," such as it was, appeared cloudy to say the least.

SOCIALISTS RETURN TO POWER, 2004–2008

The 2004 elections will long be remembered for the terrorist bombings that occurred in Madrid just three days before the voting, and the impact of those bombings on the election outcome will long be debated (Barreiro 2004; Santamaría 2004; Torcal and Rico 2004; Lago and Montero 2005; Michavila 2005). All the major polls before the attacks forecast a victory for the incumbent PP. Although in some polls the PP's edge over the PSOE was within the margin of error, no poll predicted that the PSOE would win convincingly. But that is what happened, as the Socialists' percentage share jumped from 34.2 percent in 2000 to 42.6 percent, while the PP's vote declined from 44.5 percent in 2000 to 37.7 percent. There is little question that Prime Minister Aznar ineptly handled the bombing crisis, producing a combination of vote switching and mobilization of new and previously abstaining voters—all of which strongly favored the Socialists.[54] Still, even with its best performance since 1986, the PSOE fell eleven seats shy of a parliamentary majority and had to seek coalition partners. It did so by striking "support" pacts with the newly available IU (see above) as well as with several regional parties such that these parties pledged to support the government's major bills but were not formally represented in the executive cabinet.

In the four years of his first legislature, Prime Minister Zapatero definitively moved the PSOE past the "Felipe" era by stressing a new set of issues and appealing to new constituencies. Following through on the Blairist-style Third Way approach he had espoused while in opposition, Zapatero stressed reforms in the areas of civil and gender rights, historical memory, church–state relations, and constitutional issues (Kennedy 2007). There was little innovation or experimentation on the economic front, the government being content to follow the footsteps of its Socialist and PP predecessors. In the field of civil and gender rights, the government enacted laws relating to domestic violence, gender equality, same-sex marriage, and assistance for the elderly and disabled. In perhaps his riskiest initiative, Zapatero sponsored a Law for the Recovery of History Memory, which sought to forthrightly address the injustices committed—on all sides—during the Civil War and the Franco period (Encarnación 2008). Although stopping short of a Truth and Reconciliation Commission type of approach and refusing to invalidate the 1977 amnesty law that closed off a public accounting of Franco-era crimes, the law aimed, among other things, to efface all public symbols (e.g., shields, plaques, and statues) that exalted either side in the Civil War, to finance the exhumation and reburial of Civil War victims, and to collect claims of abuse (e.g., torture and murder) related to the Civil War and the Franco dictatorship.

Finally, the Zapatero government addressed selected institutional issues in the areas of church–state and center–periphery relations, both of which then served as flash points for the PP opposition. Regarding the former, the government sought to draw a stronger line between the Catholic Church and the state, for example, by voiding a PP-sponsored 2000 law that made religious instruction obligatory in public schools. With regard to center–periphery relations, the PSOE government sought to be more welcoming in relation to the autonomy aspirations of such regions as the Basque Country and Catalonia. A growing "nationalist-friendly" bias within the Socialist Party was already apparent prior to 2004, but the party's incentive to revise the statutes of Spain's "autonomous communities" was certainly increased by its dependence on the autonomy-minded Catalan ERC to form a parliamentary majority.[55]

By 2008, the PSOE government's record in office was sufficient to convince voters to maintain the party in power. In elections that year, the Socialists boosted both their vote percentage (from 42.6 to 43.9) and number of parliamentary seats (from 164 to 169) from the previous election. As for the IU, the outcome reinforced its continued decline, as the coalition gained less than 4 percent and just two parliamentary seats. Although the IU had continued to seek coalitions at the regional level after 2004—renewing pacts in Catalonia, the Basque Country, and the Balearic Islands—this cooperative behavior produced no payoff at the national level. As for the PP, it surprisingly advanced in both vote share (from 37.6 to 40.1 percent) and number of seats (from 148 to 154).

The 2008 results thus suggested a possibly durable trend in Spanish politics: the growing bipolarization of the system into two dominant parties, the PSOE and PP, with the outcome between them depending heavily on the PSOE's ability to mobilize its base of sympathizers, given that the "median voter" is slightly left of center (Barreiro 2002). Moreover, given that the voting system enables small regionalist parties to concentrate their votes and win seats roughly in proportion to their national vote,[56] it would be difficult for either of the two main parties to gain an outright majority of seats, and thus they would have to rely on forming coalitions with one or more of these regional parties. Such was the case in four of the five elections between 1993 and 2008. With the IU having lost its cohesion and, apparently, its raison d'être, there is little in this dynamic that would encourage the PSOE to promote a reform agenda that earlier Socialists such as Largo Caballero might recognize as remotely "Socialist."

CONCLUSION

In the introduction, it was noted that relations between Socialists and Communists in Spain have differed from those in France and Italy. In the latter cases, the two parties have often been in conflict, but they have also cooperated for extended periods. In Spain, however, there have been precious few instances of such comradeship. During the first five decades, the two parties cooperated only briefly in the Popular Front–Republican government that fought against the Franco-led rebellion in the Civil War, and the outcome of that conflict was such that Socialists and Communists accused each other of betraying the Republican cause. The enmity spawned by defeat in the Civil War continued throughout the Franco period when the two parties were in exile and underground in Spain. There was reason to think that the parties would have drawn closer in the late Franco years, when the logic of "the enemy of my enemy is my friend" might have brought the parties together. But such a rapprochement never occurred, and by and large the separation between the two parties has remained through more than three decades of democracy.

Despite this relative stasis in their relationship, the two parties themselves have undergone profound changes during the past forty years, the most significant of which occurred during what I have identified as the critical juncture for each party between 1976 and 1979. During these first years following Franco's death in November 1975, Spain moved from a *caudillo* dictatorship, governed by the man who had led the rebel forces in the Civil War, to a full-fledged democracy. A greater *ruptura* between one regime and another is hard to imagine, and Spain's accomplishment is all the more impressive in that the democratic transition was engineered by the very people whom Franco himself had designated to carry on his autocratic regime. During this transition, the Socialists and Communists engaged in what were, by any standard, reversals in long-term basic strategy; specifically, they abandoned, in both rhetoric and practice, their commitment to revolutionary change, opting instead to support the conservative-led democratization process.

This strategic shift on the part of both parties was crucial in at least two ways. First, the two parties' willing, constructive participation in Spain's democratization was one of the key reinforcing factors in the success of that process. Moreover, the two parties' strategic responses to the shifting (indeed transforming) politics of that decade had an enduring impact not only on the parties themselves but also on Spanish democracy generally. In all, the two parties' experiences during the 1976–1979 period easily fit the three criteria of cause, response, and outcome that define a critical juncture.

As in our previous cases, the analytical challenge is to specify and explain the strategic responses of the Socialists and Communists. In terms of specifying the responses themselves, the Spanish case presents a paradoxical combination of ideological convergence and mutual antagonism during the 1970s. Even as the two parties softened their erstwhile radical line and embraced the democratic process, they refused to entertain any kind of formal alliance. [57] There is a certain parallel here with the Italian case during the same period. The PCI and the Partito Socialista Italiano, as their Spanish counterparts, were generally moving toward the ideological center during the mid- to late 1970s, yet they also avoided an alliance with each other. But there is a major difference in the two cases: both Italian parties sought an alliance with the largest party, the Democrazia Cristiana, whereas in Spain the PCE and the PSOE avoided party alliances altogether. Thus, the challenge is to explain this paradoxical pattern. To do so, we assess the impact of our three main factors: institutional context, party culture, and leadership.

Institutional Context

It is customary, in accounts of the Spanish democratic transition, to salute the wisdom, farsightedness, and skill of political elites, notably the King and Adolfo Suárez. Rightly so. Certainly, Franco never envisioned democracy as a suitable regime for Spain, and it is difficult to imagine that he would have condoned the process undertaken by two of his most trusted appointees to open up the system to the will of the people. The hallmark of that process has been labeled an "elite settlement" in that the immediate post-Franco leaders reached out to all major political formations, including the Communists and Socialists, in an effort to make them stakeholders in an emerging democratic order (Gunther 1992). Thus, the inclusive nature of the transition tended to obviate the benefits that any party could gain by taking an antisystem stance. On the most basic level, once all parties were legalized and constituent elections held in 1977, ideological moderation, as both Carrillo and González quickly realized, was a functional strategy.

While recognizing that this elite settlement was a key contributor to the country's relatively smooth transition, one must not forget the broader economic and social context that developed during the last two decades of Franquismo. Specifically, the regime's decision in the early 1960s to open the economy to trade and tourism spurred not only economic expansion but also the growth and mobilization of such social groups as industrial workers, independent professionals (lawyers, technical occupations, professors, and so on), and secondary and university students. Thus, as Victor Pérez-Díaz (1993) and others have observed, the late 1960s and early 1970s brought a "return of civil society" that occurred under a rigid regime that resisted reforms as long as Franco remained in charge. By the time of Franco's death, even though Spain was still relatively poor by European standards, the country bore little resemblance to what it had been in the 1950s, much less the 1930s.

These economic and social changes strongly conditioned the nature of the transition process. As noted earlier, survey research in the late 1970s and early 1980s underlined the moderate nature of Spanish public opinion. While the compromising spirit that reigned among political elites—from Communists to ex-Franquistas—certainly reinforced the public's moderation, that moderation owed much to the fact that Spain in the mid-1970s lacked the sharp class and regional divisions that had so polarized the country in the 1930s. Thus, in assessing the impact of institutional context on the strategies of the Socialists and Communists during this period, one must analyze not just formal institutional rules and arrangements but also the nature of Spanish public opinion, an amorphous but real influence that strongly defined the boundaries of viable party strategies. Just as Willie Sutton robbed banks because, as he famously claimed, that's where the money was, the PSOE and PCE moved toward the center because that's where the voters were.

As for the formal rules and arrangements, these had their main effects on the two parties' alliance behavior. Although Spain, like Italy, adopted an electoral system based on proportional representation, the Spanish variant (the d'Hondt system) produced distorting effects that systematically favored large national parties and regionalist parties while underrepresenting smaller national parties (see note 2). The result was consistently to magnify the parliamentary representation of Socialists in relation to their vote percentage while diminishing that of the Communists (see table 4.1). Thus, beginning with the first post-Franco electoral contest in 1977, the Socialists perceived little benefit in allying with the Communists, either before elections (e.g., in crafting joint lists) or after elections, in parliament. That perception went to *no* benefit in 1982, when the Socialists, with 48 percent of the vote, gained 58 percent of the seats. In the two subsequent elections, the Socialists, while losing nearly 10 percent of their vote total, still managed to claim a majority of parliamentary seats. From the early post-Franco period, the Socialists' attitude toward an alliance with the PCE could be succinctly summarized as, Communists—who needs Communists? For the Communists' part, given the Socialists' attitude and the punishing rules of the electoral system, the party had little choice but to go its own way.

Party Culture

Nearly four decades of exile and illegality under Franco brought major changes to the party cultures of both Left parties. One is tempted to refer to this long exile in the political desert as a "time of reflection" for both the Socialists and the Communists—an extended period in which to contemplate and learn from the strategic mistakes of the 1930s. By the time of Franco's death, both parties appeared to have engaged in considerable social learning in the sense of seeking to avoid the kind of organizational and ideological splits that had plagued the Left before and during the Civil War. There was certainly nothing preordained or automatic about the process of social learning in each party; such learning took place amidst internal factional and ideological struggles. But the record of the two parties' behavior in the mid-

and late 1970s indicates that party leaders were mindful not to repeat the errors of the past.

For the Socialists, the chief errors were the party's combination of ideological radicalism and extreme factionalism during the 1930s. Once the younger generation of Socialist leaders led by González and Guerra took control of the party in 1974, this new group carried out a dual process of ideological moderation and centralization of authority. This process played out gradually and fitfully; in fact, until the democratization process was under way and the PSOE was legalized in early 1977, the new leadership maintained a militant stance against the post-Francoist government and continued to espouse a Marxist-style class struggle. But this orientation changed markedly once the Socialists demonstrated their popularity in the first free elections later that year. As we noted earlier, by the end of 1979, the González-Guerra leadership group had moved the party away from Marxism, virtually silenced the party's left wing (the "critical sector"), and asserted control over the party apparatus. These moves later generated their own problems, but from the perspective of the end of the 1970s, Socialist leaders could look back on a set of strategic responses during the previous decade that brought the party considerable success.

As for the Communists, whereas their strategic responses obviously brought much less success than the Socialists', there is nonetheless evidence of significant social learning and thus of adaptation of PCE culture to the seismic political shifts of the 1970s. The prime example is the party's consistent effort to distance itself from Moscow. It will be recalled that the PCE's behavior during the Popular Front and Civil War smacked strongly of servitude to the Soviets; certainly, that perception was a constant theme in critiques voiced for decades by Francoists and Socialists alike. This was a perception that Carrillo was determined to efface even prior to the 1970s but especially during the democratic transition. It was no mere coincidence that Carrillo pushed the short-lived Eurocommunist initiative at the same time as he was trying to build his party's following in Spain's new democracy. Asserting the party's independence from the Soviet Union was an effort to change the public image of the PCE's culture as one based on authoritarianism. Unfortunately for the PCE, this project of image modification did not prove convincing to Spanish voters, who perceived little change in the party's internal modus operandi.

Leadership

As in the previous cases, a dominant theme in the political history of the Left during the 1970s was the competition between highly visible, assertive party leaders. Where France had its Mitterrand and Marchais and Italy its Craxi and Berlinguer, Spain had its González and Carrillo. From the standpoint of explaining their parties' strategic responses during the 1970s, the question is, What difference did leadership make? That is, what impact did these leaders have in determining their parties' responses? As in the previous two cases, the answer in the Spanish case is clearly, for better or for worse, a lot. As in the Mitterrand/Marchais contrast, the "better" aspect applied to the Socialist leader, the "worse" aspect to the Communist. Beyond the issues of media popularity, in which the suave "Felipe" contrasted favorably with the gruff Carrillo, González had something of Mitterrand's political savvy, namely, an ability to credibly combine dispassionate pragmatism with a vaguely idealistic personal image. González's own self-reflection at the beginning of this chapter—"I am a Socialist, but I am no fool"—nicely captures this dualism. This ability enabled Gónzalez, working with close associates such as Guerra and Redondo, to position the PSOE after 1977 as being both within and against the political establishment. On the one hand, the Socialists were a participant in the emerging democratic consensus; on the other hand, they were the most powerful opponent of and the most credible alternative to the Franco-tinged conservative UCD government headed by Suárez. Carrillo not only lacked González's political skills but also projected an ambiguous persona—that of a Eurocommunist who still practiced democratic centralism within his party—that did not ring true for the vast majority of Spanish voters.

Politics is never static, and thus one is not surprised that the Socialists and Communists experienced ebbs and flows in popularity, leadership struggles, and ideological and strategic shifts after 1979. What is striking, though, is how firmly the critical juncture of 1976–1979 set the template for the subsequent three decades in terms of the two parties' comparative electoral strength, overall political influence, and mutual relationship. On each of these aspects, there were no fundamental changes after 1979, and that outcome is the basis for identifying this period as a critical juncture for both parties. The strategic responses of the two parties in these years constituted, to recall the Colliers' definition from the introduction, the kind of political watershed that "establish[es] certain directions of change and foreclose[s] others in a way that shapes politics for years to come." During the late 1970s, the Socialists quickly emerged in Spain's new democracy as far more popular and powerful than the Communists to the point that Socialist leaders saw no pressing need to court the Communists for an alliance. Separation between the two parties is old story, a constant theme in their relationship since the 1920s. For much of the period since the initial split, the Socialists' animus derived from an unremitting anti-Communism. After 1980, that animus was largely replaced with a different attitude: indifference.

NOTES

1. Prieto (quoted in Payne 1985, 15); González (quoted in the *New York Times*, August 12, 1985).
2. The d'Hondt method of proportional representation is also known as the highest averages method. For elections to the Congress of Deputies, which has 350 seats, each of Spain's fifty provinces elects at least two representatives. In addition, Ceuta and Melilla have one seat each, for a total of 102. This fact alone gives disproportionate weight to less populated provinces, which are typically rural. The remaining 248 seats are distributed proportionally according to population. In general, the d'Hondt method of allocating seats tends to overrepresent the two largest parties. The system is also favorable to regional parties that can concentrate their votes in specific constituencies. By contrast, small national parties tend to be underrepresented in this system. One result of the Spanish electoral system is that it is possible for a party to obtain a majority of parliamentary seats with as little as 40 percent of the vote, as happened in 1989.
3. This analysis simplifies, for brevity's sake, a more complicated picture. Other important Socialist leaders who figure in all the essential histories of the period include Julian Besteiro (generally, a Prieto ally), Luis Araquistáin (a close Largo Caballero ally), Fernando de los Ríos (a Prieto collaborator), and Rodolfo Llopis. For useful discussions of internal leadership alignments, see Preston (1977), Gillespie (1989), and Heywood (1990).
4. Preston pinpoints the origin of their personal enmity in events during the Primo de Rivera dictatorship. The dispute was over the appointment of a labor representative to an advisory body, the Council of State. The UGT, on its own, appointed Largo Caballero to the Council. Prieto and his close ally within the PSOE, Fernando de los Ríos, opposed the appointment and accused Largo Caballero of opportunism. From that moment on, the UGT leader and Prieto (who ultimately lost on this issue) became archrivals within the party. Comments Preston (1977), "This division within the party was to have repercussions right up to the civil war, if only for the personal enmities created" (108).
5. For example, the agrarian reform of September 1932 expropriated all property from absentee landlords no matter how small their holdings or whether the lands were rented out or lay fallow. This blanket approach affected not only large landowners but also many people in the urban middle classes who supplemented their incomes by land rental. The effect was to greatly enlarge the group of those who felt aggrieved by the reform. Resistance to the law's implementation by these groups, as well as many local authorities who were under their influence, served to heighten the sense of disappointment and frustration among landless peasants expecting to gain access to rural property. The end result was a great sharpening of rural conflict. Comments Ranzato (2005), "Indeed, both the landowners and the peasant movement organizations seemed to try to outdo one another in their intransigence" (35). The most definitive study of rural conflict under the Second Republic remains Malefakis (1970).
6. The UGT went from approximately 200,000 members in 1930 to more than 1 million by 1933, with over 40 percent of its members in agriculture. The UGT continued to add members in 1934 and 1935, in the process becoming the largest political force in Spain. By contrast, the PSOE went from about 17,000 to 90,000 members in the same period (Gillespie 1989, 26–27).
7. As in Italy, a pro-Bolshevik faction constituted a strong minority within the Socialist Party, and the question of affiliation with the Communist Third International occasioned three separate PSOE congresses over an eighteen-month period in 1920–1921. In the final, definitive vote, the majority of delegates opted not to join the Comintern, thereby provoking the pro-Russian minority to walk out and organize the PCE.
8. During the 1936–1939 Civil War period, the PCE had only sixteen of the 271 Popular Front deputies (compared with the PSOE's total of ninety deputies), and the party never held more than two positions in the nine-person cabinet (Mujal-León 1983, 10; Payne 1985, 13).
9. This characterization of the POUM is made by Preston, who notes that the POUM was spearheaded by dissident anti-Stalinist Marxists, including one, Andreu Nin, who had been Trotysky's secretary in Moscow (Preston 2007, 7–8).
10. For the first time, Spain welcomed foreign capital and tourists while encouraging Spanish workers to emigrate elsewhere in Europe—a process that produced impressive growth.

Between 1960 and 1973, the country's gross domestic product (GDP) grew an annual average of 7.1 percent, compared with an average of 4.8 percent for other European nations (data compiled by Organisation for Economic Cooperation and Development).

11. Camiller (1994, 235) reports that the following data for number of working days lost in strikes (in millions): 1.5 in 1966, 8.7 in 1970, and 14.5 in 1975.

12. That the Carrillo leadership was pushing the envelope but still staying within the Soviet fold can be seen in the same document that condemned the Soviet's crushing of the Prague Spring. The document also denounced "any attempt to use the tragic error committed in Czechoslovakia to denigrate the glorious history of the CPSU and the Soviet people" (PCE Executive Committee, quoted in Preston 1981, 56).

13. The most infamous case of Carrillo's heavy-handedness in relation to internal dissent was his running feud with party leaders Fernando Claudín and Jorge Semprún over Carrillo's assessment of Spain's domestic situation. This conflict eventually led Claudín and Semprún to publicly criticize the lack of democracy within the party and Carrillo's authoritarian methods. The end result was that Carrillo eventually engineered the two leaders' expulsion from the party in 1965 (Preston 1981, 53).

14. It is customary in Spanish, when abbreviating a double name in the plural, to "double" the first letter of each name. Hence, "Comisiones Obreras" abbreviates as "CCOO."

15. For example, at the Second Congress of PSOE exiles held in Toulouse, France, in 1946, the largest delegations came from Mexico, Oran, Paris, Toulouse, Marseilles, Casablanca, and Bordeaux (Gillespie 1989, 75).

16. As an example of the *renovadores'* challenge to the exile leadership, the lead article in the group's publication, *El Socialista*, in May 1972 concluded the following: "Socialists have a double task to undertake: the struggle against the capitalist system that opposes them and the struggle against certain structures of their own organization whose sterile actions threaten the organization itself" (quoted in Preston 1986a, 365; author's translation).

17. Good accounts of this internal leadership struggle can be found in Maravall (1982), Gilmour (1985), Gunther et al. (1988), Gillespie (1989), Share (1989), and Juliá (1997).

18. Portions of this section have relied on the author's earlier work (see Smith 1998, especially chap. 3).

19. I will focus here only on the king's role in the transition process. He played perhaps an equally key role in consolidating Spain's fledgling democracy by firmly facing down a revolt by several army officers who stormed the Cortes in February 1981. For the most complete analysis of the King's actions, see Preston (2004).

20. See, inter alia, López-Pintor (1981, 20–21), McDonough, Barnes, and Pina (1981, 76; 1984, 680); and Barnes, McDonough, and Pina (1985, 716).

21. The literature on the Spanish democratic transition is enormous. Useful studies include Maravall (1982); Gilmour (1985); Preston (1986); Share (1986); Pérez-Díaz (1987); Gunther et al. (1988); Gunther (1992); Edles (1998); Aguilar (2002); Encarnación (2003); André-Bazzana (2006); and Gallego (2008).

22. The rule changes 1) required provincial delegations to vote en bloc rather than as individuals and 2) gave the Andalusian delegation 25 percent of all votes. These changes virtually assured the González–Guerra group the determining voice in party affairs. By contrast, the critical sector, which actually represented about 40 percent of the party's rank and file, could field only 10 percent of the delegates (Nash 1983, 46–47). Gillespie (1989) comments, "Moreover, the combination of indirect elections, a winner-takes-all list system for internal elections, and voting by delegations regardless of differences within them had the effect all along the line of filtering out representation of critical minority elements" (347).

23. This is not to say the PSOE adopted a bland document that completely negated its historical legacy. Whereas the 1976 document defined the PSOE as "a class party, and therefore of the masses, Marxist, and democratic," the "new, improved" 1979 version changed this statement to read, "a class party, of the masses, democratic, and federal." This version also claimed that Marxism was a useful "method of analysis" and labeled capitalist society as "intrinsically unjust and exploitative" (Gunther 1986, 46).

24. The reference is to the German Social Democratic Party's renunciation of Marxism at a 1959 congress in Bad Godesberg.

25.   The main push for this episode of cooperation came from the parliamentary elections held the previous month, in March 1979. In those elections, the Socialists failed to progress much beyond their 1977 performance, and Suárez's UCD easily won reelection. Meanwhile, the PCE marked a respectable advance, from 9.3 to 10.8 percent. From the Socialists' perspective, there was at least temporary doubt that they would be able to overtake the UCD without some level of cooperation with the Communists. This doubt disappeared during the subsequent two years as Suárez's coalition came apart, and he was forced to resign in early 1981.

26.   For example, a majority within the party's Catalan wing, the Partit Socialista Unificat de Catalunya (PSUC), rejected the Eurocommunist turn and went into open rebellion against the Madrid-based leadership. The leadership handled this dispute in time-honored form: by expelling the rebels (Mujal-León 1983, 215–17; Heywood 1994, 66).

27.   The IU's main constituent groups, other than the PCE, included the PASOC (party headed by Pablo Castellano, which had split from the PSOE over the 1986 referendum), the Partido Comunista de los Pueblos de España (party of PCE "Afghans" that had split off from the PCE in 1984), and the Progressive Federation (group organized in 1984 by former Communist Ramón Tamames). The IU also included several smaller groups, such as the Carlist Party, the Humanist Party, and the Republican Left, as well as a few "independent" personalities, such as Cristina Almeida (Heywood 1994, 70).

28.   The policy measures described in this paragraph are examined in detail in Smith (1998, especially chaps. 5 and 6).

29.   The Socialists' ministrations proved no miracle cure, however, and INI's losses mounted again in the recession years of the early 1990s. The government finally decided to liquidate INI in the late 1990s. Today, the old INI headquarters in the Plaza de Salamanca in Madrid has been taken over by the Foreign Affairs Ministry.

30.   All statistics reported in this paragraph come from OECD sources.

31.   Spain's average annual increase in gross fixed capital formation during this period was 12.9 percent compared with the EC mean of 6.5 percent.

32.   Various types of temporary and part-time employment created by the government's employment promotion programs increased from 1.1 million in 1985 to 2.3 million in 1990 (Smith 1998, 96).

33.   UGT leaders pointed to 1986 worker-delegate elections as a key factor. In those elections, the UGT gained in its vote percentage—from 36.7 percent in 1982 to 40.9 percent in 1986. The CCOO also increased but only marginally, from 33.4 to 34.5 percent, and thus the UGT actually increased its lead over the CCOO. The UGT, however, lost ground to the Comisiones in several important sectors and firms, especially in the public sector. This result apparently convinced UGT leaders that continued support of the government's policies would hurt the union. This conclusion was confirmed by Julian Ariza, a member of the CCOO executive committee in an interview with the author on October 27, 1993.

34.   According to a top UGT leader, "The conflict between the UGT and the government became, purely and simply, a personal fight between Redondo and González. Until their break, Redondo had supported the government's approach. He gradually saw, however, that the government was displacing him. But the government was doing this because of Redondo's own arrogance. He's the kind of leader who insists on being able to veto a decision if he doesn't like it. He always wants to be on top" (author interview with Antonio Puerta, former head of metalworkers federation, UGT, July 23, 1994).

35.   Astudillo (2001) argues, for example, that the break came largely from the UGT, for union competition reasons. Because economic conditions were improving in the late 1980s and wages were rising, the UGT would have been at a competitive disadvantage in relation to the CCOO by continuing to agree to wage restraint. Therefore, the UGT rejected further wage restraint and entered into a *unidad de acción* cooperation with the CCOO in order to maintain its relative position. Royo (2001), however, takes issue with this interpretation, imputing the impetus for the breakup to the Socialist government rather than the UGT. Given the centralization of power and cohesion within the PSOE, the UGT had become increasingly powerless within the organization (and, by extension, within the government). Thus, the UGT's "institutional dependence" on the PSOE government led the latter to "default repeatedly on promises made to the union, which brought about the collapse of concertation" (28). Instead of concerta-

tion and social pacts, the government concluded that its restrictive monetary policy should be the prime instrument for moderating inflationary pressures. Under these conditions, the UGT became an "expendable" partner. In my view, both authors make convincing arguments, and the issue of causation for the break is not an either/or question. Both the government and the UGT had reasons for ending their cooperation.

36. The ERM required all participating nations to maintain their currencies on a rough par with each other. In practice, this meant a restrictive monetary policy for all, given the large influence exercised by the inflation-phobic German Bundesbank. But even within the limited leeway that the ERM offered, Spanish authorities chose to peg the peseta in a strong position relative to the other currencies.

37. For example, between 1989 and 1993, overall government spending increased steadily from 40.9 to 46.9 percent of GDP, with most of the increase going for social programs. At the same time, the government's financial balances went from −2.8 to −7.2 percent of GDP.

38. Author interview with Luis de Velasco, June 5, 1992.

39. Along with various charges of illegal PSOE party financing, there were at least three major scandals during this period: 1) the government's creation of a secret counterterrorist organization, GAL, whose purpose was to murder suspected members of ETA, the Basque terrorist organization, who were living in France; 2) personal corruption on the part of the head of the Civil Guard, Luis Roldán; and 3) illegal enrichment and tax fraud on the part of Mariano Rubio, governor of the Bank of Spain. For a withering critique of the PSOE government's sense of public ethics, see Pérez-Díaz (1999, 70–102).

40. For example, Maravall (2008, 185) reports that whereas in 1990 66 percent of a national sample viewed the Socialists as a united party, that figure had dropped to 14 percent by 1994. Increasingly, the party's internal disputes were viewed as driven by the personal ambition of leaders rather than by the exercise of internal democracy.

41. That the IU's opposition to the Socialists was not always ideologically consistent could be seen in its behavior in Andalusia. Following the 1994 regional elections, the IU controlled twenty seats in that region, making it the decisive partner in any coalition. The IU refused to join the Socialists in government, opting instead to strike a deal with the Popular Party that gave the IU the speakership of the house (Bosco and Gaspar 2001, 370).

42. This assessment came from the author's interview on June 15, 1994, with Ignacio Fernández Toxo, who at that time was head of the CCOO metalworkers' federation. In 2008, Toxo was elected general secretary of the CCOO.

43. This distancing of the CCOO from the PCE can be detected at the grassroots level as well. Whereas in 1980 25 percent of CCOO members were also PCE members, by 1996 that figure had shrunk to 7.7 percent. By 2000 it was just 4.6 percent (Ramiro-Fernández 2004a, 288).

44. A good example concerned the case of the SEAT automobile firm in Barcelona. SEAT, initially a creation of the Franco-era INI, had been sold to Volkswagen in 1986, but it remained a brand with a Spanish identity and, more important, provided over 20,000 jobs in the Barcelona region. With SEAT running big losses, Volkswagen in 1994 threatened to absorb SEAT into VW, a move that would end SEAT's existence as a Spanish firm and terminate most if not all SEAT jobs. The CiU's leader, Jordi Pujol, was able to use the government's dependence on his party's votes in the Cortes to win a major government rescue package for VW/SEAT. For a full discussion, see Smith (1998, 199–205).

45. Average annual GDP growth for the 1994–1996 period was 2.52 percent versus 0.82 percent for 1991–1993. Inflation (average annual increase in consumer prices) for 1994–1996 was 4.09 percent, compared with 6.06 percent for 1991–1993. These positive trends were achieved at a slight cost to unemployment, which averaged 18.6 percent in 1994–1996 versus 15.3 percent for 1991–1993. All figures from the OECD.

46. Beginning in 1982 at a level of public spending below the OECD average—namely, 36.6 percent of GDP versus a 39.0 percent average for the OECD—Spain's figure for 1996 was 43.3 percent compared with the OECD average of 40.3 percent (data compiled by Organisation for Economic Cooperation and Development).

47. See the testimony of former party leader, Joaquín Almunia, in Iglesias 2005, vol. 2: 246–47.

48. Author interview with Dr. Mónica Méndez Lago, research director, Centro de Investigaciones Sociológicas, Madrid, March 26, 2009.

49. The following summary relies on Méndez Lago (2006) as well as on interviews with the following: Dr. Méndez Lago (see previous note), Professor Santos Juliá (Universidad Nacional de Educación a Distancia, Madrid, March 23, 2009), and Dr. Ignacio Urquizu-Sancho (Fundación Alternativas, Madrid, March 14, 2009).

50. In addition to Zapatero, there were three other candidates to succeed Almunia: José Bono (president of Castilla–La Mancha region (close to the González faction and thus hated by the Guerristas), Rosa Díez, and Matilde Fernández (the Guerristas' favored candidate). These three candidates were all of the "transition/González" generation, that is, born in the early 1950s and already active during the 1970s. By contrast, Zapatero, born in 1960, represented a younger generation of Socialist leaders. According to Professor Santos Juliá (see previous note), Guerra knew that his preferred candidate, Fernández, could not win, but he also wanted to block the "Felipista" candidate, Bono. Therefore, he instructed some of his supporters to support Zapatero. In the event, Zapatero edged Bono by a handful of votes (see also Méndez Lago 2006, 422).

51. Author interview with Professor José Ramón Montero, Universidad Autónoma de Madrid, March 11, 2009.

52. The following analysis is drawn from Ştefuriuc and Verge (2008).

53. This decrease was due to a decision to dilute the IU's "brand" from that of a Communist Party creation to that of an organization with a more generic leftist identity that emphasized ecological and peace issues. Thus, sympathizers were offered the option of direct membership in the IU itself rather than in the PCE or the other constituent groups (Ştefuriuc and Verge 2008, 159).

54. The Socialists' total vote in 2004 increased by about 3 million from its 2000 total. One estimate indicates that these additional voters came from the following groups: 1) previous nonvoters (1.5 million), 2) transfers from other parties (total of 1 million, with 700,000 coming from the PP and 300,000 from the IU), and 3) new voters (500,000) (see Michavila 2005).

55. The government's actual record of follow-through regarding the revision of autonomy statutes has been decidedly mixed (see Kennedy 2007, 198–200).

56. For example, in 2008, the regional parties totaled 7.6 percent of the vote and 7.0 percent of parliamentary seats. By contrast, the IU's 3.8 percent of the vote translated into a minuscule 0.6 percent of the seats.

57. As in the French and Italian cases, politics at the local level displayed considerable variety and was sometimes at odds with national-level trends. In municipal and regional governments, where the parties' overall programmatic and ideological orientations were less in play, the two parties often formed governing majorities.

III

Extensions

Chapter Five

Organization

In the life of political parties, organization precedes all else. In order to field candidates, mobilize voters, and build alliances, parties must first organize themselves. How they do so appears, at first glance, to be a mundane matter of setting the rules and procedures that regulate their activities. In reality, organization extends well beyond such formalities, for how parties organize themselves reflects fundamental choices and values. A given party may or may not be able to attract voters or build alliances, but it can decide how it will conduct its own internal affairs. A party decides, among other things, who can (or cannot) join the party, how its leaders and candidates are to be selected, and what its program will be. In so doing, a party defines its identity while expressing its goals and values.

How have Socialists and Communists in France, Italy, and Spain chosen to organize themselves? While organization has many dimensions, this chapter focuses on two key ones: membership and authority relations. First, parties vary enormously in the number and types of members that they recruit. Traditionally, political scientists have grouped parties into two broad types: small parties whose membership is restricted and large parties whose membership is extensive. Obviously, membership size is a relative concept; large in Luxembourg does not mean large in Germany. Thus, for comparative purposes, to explore membership size and trends, one needs a measure that takes the size of the electorate into account. Most commonly used in this regard is a measure employed here: the ratio of party members to the number of eligible voters in a society, a ratio that is often referred as the M/E ratio (Katz and Mair 1992, 330–32).

The second dimension explored here is authority relations, that is, how authority is "distributed" throughout a party. The term "authority relations" refers to the rules and practices by which parties make important decisions, including general strategy, party program, and leadership selection. The classic approach to characterizing authority relations dating back to the early days of political party research is in terms of oligarchy versus democracy. Here I reframe this idea in terms of the degree to which decision-making authority is *concentrated* within the party's main leadership group as opposed to being *diffused* throughout various levels of the party. There are many indicators that could be used to assess the relative degree to which authority is concentrated (or diffused). Three such indicators are leadership turnover, factionalism, and representation. To what extent does the party foster a regular "circulation of elites"? That is, does the party leadership group dominate the process of nominating and selecting party officials at national, regional, and local levels, or is leadership selection a competitive process? Does the party recognize and permit factions or currents that may oppose the leadership group, or are factions prohibited or discouraged? Finally, does the party take steps to ensure the representation of diverse societal interests on such dimensions as gender, class, age, and region?

This chapter examines how Socialists and Communists have approached these organizational issues, with a focus on the period since 1970. I do so in four steps. In the following section, I place the two dimensions of membership and authority relations in a larger European context. What have been the recent trends in party membership throughout European democracies, and how do the two main Left parties in our three countries compare with these trends? With regard to authority relations, has there been, as Roberto Michels predicted, a trend toward oligarchy and the concentration of authority in these parties during the past four decades? This section also proposes a simple graphic scheme for considering the co-variation of these two dimensions simultaneously over time. The two following sections analyze membership and authority relations across our cases, comparing, first, the three Socialist parties followed by the three Communist parties. Finally, in the conclusion, the organizational trajectories of these parties during the past four decades are related to this book's central argument.

MEMBERSHIP AND AUTHORITY RELATIONS: THE EUROPEAN CONTEXT AND A FRAMEWORK FOR ANALYSIS

Any consideration of membership trends and authority relations in the cases presented here needs to be placed within the context of broader tendencies affecting political parties in the established democracies, especially within Europe. Most generally, there has been a marked decline in partisanship across most of the European nations since the early 1970s. This decline has taken several forms, including ideological depolarization, the growth of "catchall" appeals by parties, a decline in partisan identification, increased voter volatility, decreasing voter turnout, a growing lack of trust in parties, and declining party membership (Mair 2008).

With respect to the last of these trends, party membership, a survey by Mair and Van Biezen (2001) finds "concrete and consistent evidence of widespread disengagement from party politics" during the 1980–2000 period (6). Of the nineteen European nations for which longitudinal data are available, fourteen countries experienced a decline in the M/E ratio, that is, the proportion of total party membership within the pool of eligible voters. On average, the M/E ratio in these nations decreased by over 40 percent. Party decline was concentrated among the older, established democracies; all but one of the fourteen "decliners" (the Czech Republic) have been democracies since the end of World War II. In these long-established democracies, the decrease has been not only in the percentage of party members relative to the electorate but also in the absolute number of party members. On average, the number of party members fell by 35 percent between 1980 and 2000. By contrast, all five of the nations experiencing an increase in the M/E ratio—namely, Greece, Hungary, Portugal, Slovakia, and Spain—are relative newcomers to democracy. Such a trend is not surprising. These nations had to build democratic institutions virtually from scratch in the 1970s and 1980s, so a rise in party affiliation relative to the eligible voting public would be expected. Although more recent data since 2000 are unavailable, there is little reason to believe that the overall trend toward partisan decline has reversed during the period since 2000; in all probability, it has continued.

Within this European context of generally declining party membership, the French, Italian, and Spanish cases stand at extremes. On the declining end, France and Italy have led the way. France experienced a decline in total party membership between 1980 and 2000 of nearly two-thirds: a drop from 1.7 million to 600,000. Italy's proportional decrease in total membership has been less than France's—just over 50 percent—but its numeric decline was even more dramatic: from over 4 million total members in 1980 to less than 2 million two decades later. At the other end of the scale, Spain is the European country with the largest percent increase in membership; during the two decades indicated, total party membership more than tripled from 322,000 to 1.1 million. Such an impressive increase can be deceiving, however, as Spain still remains well below the European average in terms of its overall M/E ratio. Thus, when one steps back from these changes and assesses the recent state of party affiliation in general, one finds all three countries at the lower end of the European scale. Of the twenty nations surveyed by Mair and Van Biezen, Italy's M/E ratio ranks eleventh, followed by Spain's (thirteenth) and France's (nineteenth).[1]

As for the second dimension of party organization, authority relations, one cannot with any confidence hypothesize a clear trend. Unlike research on issues such as partisan identity and membership, there is surprisingly scant empirical research in this area despite the fact that Michels's famous "iron law of oligarchy" almost single-handedly kick-started a major field of party research a century ago. In Mair's comprehensive survey of current trends in research on political parties cited earlier, the question of authority relations within parties is not even mentioned. Thus, recent studies give no clear indication about broad tendencies within European parties toward either the concentration or the diffusion of authority. In such a void, one could advance plausible hypotheses in either direction. On the one hand, one might reasonably suppose that parties are moving away from concentrating authority within the top leadership group. Given that the syndrome of trends mentioned above indicate that parties have lost much of their capacity to mobilize resources—specifically, to attract and activate voters—a likely outcome would be the diffusion of authority throughout levels and/or factions with party organizations. On the other hand, the "hollowing out" of party organizations, combined with the "presidentialization" of party politics—that is, the necessity for parties to emphasize the top leader's personality and personal appeal in an age of mass media—could work to concentrate authority within a fairly narrow leadership group (Ignazi and Ysmal 1998, 289; Mair 2008, 227). Lacking any comparative data, this chapter takes both hypotheses as alternate possible trends in its examination of six cases.

Given the European context just described, how can we analyze the organizational development—specifically, membership and authority relations—of Socialist and Communist parties during the past four decades? I propose to examine these two dimensions simultaneously, mainly because they can be expected to covary independently. There is no a priori reason to expect small parties to concentrate authority or mass parties to diffuse authority throughout the organization (or vice versa). To examine the covariation of these two dimensions over time, we can construct a graphic space, as in figure 5.1, in which, for heuristic purposes, we can place the parties under consideration.[2] Moreover, given that parties are constantly adapting organizations, we can expect to see shifts in a party's "coordinates" in this space over time. Figure 5.1 indicates two such stylized shifts. In the hypothetical example, a party in t_1 has relatively few members along with a highly diffused authority pattern. Then, in the period from t_1 to t_2, that party experiences membership growth simultaneously with a concentration of authority. Finally, in the period from t_2 to t_3, the party continues to grow steadily even as authority within the organization diffuses steadily. Using such a two-dimensional representation, we can plot how Socialists and Communists have constructed their organizations and how those organizations have changed over time.

SOCIALISTS: ROUTINIZING LEADERSHIP?

How have the three Socialist parties varied in terms of membership and authority relations since the early 1970s? Let us begin by examining membership trends in the Parti Socialiste (PS), the Partito Socialista Italiano (PSI), and the Partido Socialista Obrero Español (PSOE) during this period. Figure 5.2 presents a time series of standardized membership levels—that is, the M/E ratio—for the three parties from 1970 to 2005. First, one sees surprising differences among the parties, most notably the contrast between the French Socialists' generally low density levels compared with the Italian Socialists' much higher levels (at least until the PSI collapsed because of corruption scandals in the early 1990s). This contrast is especially striking given the French party's much greater electoral success; for example, in the parliamentary elections of the 1970s and 1980s, the PS's average score was nearly triple that of the PSI: 29.4 versus 10.9 percent. As we will also see when we compare French and Italian Communist memberships, this difference reflects a general systemic contrast: historically, party membership in general has been much higher in Italy than in France.

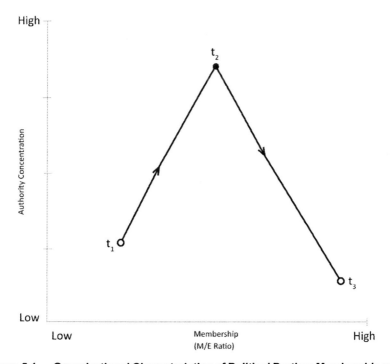

Figure 5.1. Organizational Characteristics of Political Parties: Membership and Authority Relations

Second, this figure demonstrates some interesting twists on the general European theme of membership decline. The French Socialists have largely but not completely followed the script, gradually increasing their numbers throughout the 1970s but beginning a slow but discernible decline in the 1980s. The party reached its nadir in 1995 but managed to stabilize and even increase its membership after that time. As for the Spanish Socialists, they have bucked the general European trend completely, increasing their membership more or less steadily from about 50,000 in 1977 to 460,000 in 2004. In this regard, as noted above, the PSOE is in line with the general Spanish trend of growing party membership since 1980. Finally, the now defunct Italian Socialists followed a kind of U pattern from 1970 until their demise in the early 1990s. Their membership dropped throughout the 1970s but climbed during the Craxi era in the 1980s.

How have membership levels covaried with changes in the parties' internal authority relations since the early 1970s? Using the graphic template outlined in figure 5.1, the following discussion analyzes this covariation across the three Socialist parties. As we shall see, all three parties were highly dynamic during the past four decades, experiencing not only significant fluctuations in membership levels but also shifts in authority relations. Moreover, as in the case of membership levels, there is no general trend in authority relations toward either greater concentration or diffusion of authority.

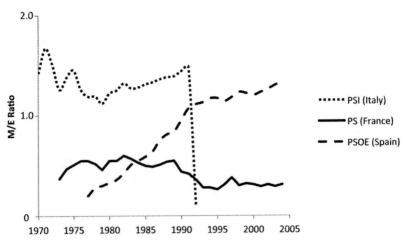

Figure 5.2.   Socialist Parties in France, Italy, and Spain: Membership, 1970–2005

French Socialists (PS)

Figure 5.3 indicates five significant movements or phases in the organizational fortunes of the PS.[3] The first phase, 1970–1981, began as the "new" French Socialist Party emerged as a resurrection project designed to revivify the traditional Socialist party, the Section Française de l'Internationale Ouvrière (Codding and Safran 1979, 215–21), which, never a mass party, had been one of the "inner-system" parties during the Fourth Republic, averaging about 15 percent of the vote in parliamentary elections during the 1950s and 1960s. In the aftermath of Gaston Deferre's disastrous run for president in 1969 as a center-leftist, however, a new leadership group led by Alain Savary took control of the party from the loyalists of longtime party head Guy Mollet. The goal of this group was to move the Socialist Party toward the left by enlarging the tent to include a number of smaller parties and clubs; indeed, Savary himself had most recently been a member of the "new left" Parti Socialiste Unifié. In short order, Savary may have regretted what he wished for. In 1971, the party brought in François Mitterrand and his small movement, the Convention des Institutions Républicaines, and Savary found himself replaced as first secretary by the newcomer.

In retrospect, Mitterrand looms as the towering figure of French Socialism of the second half of the twentieth century, serving as the de jure or de facto leader of the party for nearly twenty-five years (1971–1995). In reality, however, he inherited a party of factions and spent much of his time placating and compromising with disputatious *courants*. During Mitterrand's first and only decade as first secretary (1971–1981),[4] the reconstituted party was a work in flux, as leaders sought to carve out a distinctive left-leaning program that would both engage and challenge the Communists. This process of organizational self-definition took place in a context of internal struggle and renewal, as shifting factional alignments struggled to define the party's program even as new members and activists enlisted in the ranks.[5] Thus, this initial phase of the PS's organizational development featured two tendencies: on the one hand, steady and vigorous membership growth—from 80,000 members in 1971 to nearly 200,000 in 1981—and, on the other hand, a definite but fairly modest accretion of authority on the part of Mitterrand, who was certainly "first among equals" in the party but hardly an all-powerful figure.

This dynamic changed dramatically, and the second phase (1981–1990) began, with Mitterrand's election as president, followed by the Socialists winning a parliamentary majority. No longer feisty challengers, Mitterrand and his party stood at the top of the political system. Collective success often tends to mute internal bickering, and the Socialists were no exception in this regard. In this case, even though Mitterrand stepped down as the PS's titular leader, his dominance over the party increased exponentially virtually over-

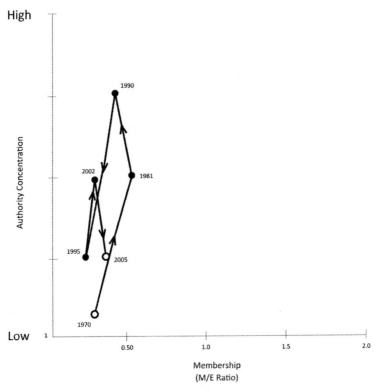

High

Low

Authority Concentration

1990

2002   1981

1995

2005

1970

1   0.50   1.0   1.5   2.0

Membership
(M/E Ratio)

Figure 5.3.   French Socialist Party: Membership and Authority Relations, 1970–2005

night. He consolidated that dominance by bringing his own team of rivals into the government, making ministers of some of the main party barons, including Pierre Mauroy (prime minister), Jean-Pierre Chevènement (minister of industry), and Michel Rocard (minister of economic planning and development). Throughout his first term (1981–1988) and into the early years of his second term (1988–1995), Mitterrand continued to control party affairs, largely with the close cooperation of the person he handpicked to manage the party, Lionel Jospin. Throughout this second phase, concentration of authority in the Mitterrand–Jospin group coincided with a peaking of membership in 1982 (at 214,000) and a stabilization of membership during the rest of the 1980s.

A third phase in the PS's organizational trajectory (1990–1995) reflects a growing entropy in the latter years of the Mitterrand presidency—a period of sharp membership decline and internal conflict. During these years, party membership diminished by over half—from 204,000 to 94,000—while a host of party barons struggled for power. The reasons for these trends are not hard to identify. Most generally, the heady days when Socialist promises to *"changer la vie"*—to change the way people lived—filled the air were long gone. Small, technical reforms, not grand transformations, characterized the minority government of Mitterrand's erstwhile rival, Michel Rocard. Demography also played a role in the PS's troubles: the party's activists were aging and not being replaced by new blood (Rey and Subileau 1991). In the three years following Rocard's resignation as prime minister in 1991, the party had no fewer than four leaders.[6] In the midst of this upheaval, the PS suffered a stinging defeat in the 1993 parliamentary elections. Adding to all these woes—indeed, in a fundamental sense, emblematic of them—was Mitterrand's own political and physical decline.

The period after 1995 was one that replayed, albeit in muted form, the party's up-and-down swing during the Mitterrand years, with Lionel Jospin, in effect, playing the Mitterrand role. The "up" cycle (1995–2002), the PS's fourth organizational phase, began with Jospin's reelection as first secretary and then his creditable albeit losing presidential campaign against Chirac. With a momentum-charged new leader, the Socialists' organizational fortunes began to reverse. Within two years, the party's membership increased by over 50 percent—from 94,000 to 143,000—and in 1997 Jospin led the PS to a surprise victory in legislative elections, at which point he was named prime minister. From this position, Jospin, in a lesser version of the Mitterrand ascendancy in the early 1980s, was able to unite the party around him for the next five years.

Alas, Jospin's humiliating loss in the 2002 presidential contest initiated a fifth phase, still in evidence as of this writing: a tailspin from which the PS has yet to fully recover. The Socialist leader's abrupt, unexplained departure from the political stage following his defeat left a power vacuum that gave rise to a series of leadership struggles among followers of Laurent Fabius, Ségolène Royal, Bertrand Delanoë, and Dominique Strauss-Kahn. Although Jospin's successor as first secretary, François Hollande, provided the party with steady if not charismatic leadership for over a decade (1997–2008), he was in no position to impose or concentrate his own personal power. By 2010, despite having been shut out of power in two major elections since 2002, the French Socialists remained France's second most popular party. On the other hand, the party's membership had stabilized at levels attained in the mid-1970s (despite a 50 percent growth in the electorate), and the party lacked a Mitterrand or a Jospin around whom the various factions could coalesce.

Spanish Socialists (PSOE)

The Spanish Socialists' organizational trajectory has diverged from the PS's experience in one major respect (see figure 5.4). Despite the party's fluctuating electoral performance and leadership struggles, the PSOE has never stopped growing in membership since its legalization in 1977. This is something of a paradox given the evidence of a bandwagon effect in the French case: when the PS attracted voters, it also attracted new members. Not so in the Spanish case, as the party continued to add members, albeit at a slower pace, in periods of electoral decline as well as increase. For example, between 1986 and 2000, the PSOE's vote decreased fairly steadily from 44.1 to 34.2 percent, yet the party's total membership nearly tripled from 158,000 to 408,000. Certainly, part of the explanation for the PSOE's steady growth is systemic. As discussed above, Spain's status as a relatively new democracy in which all political organizations had to basically start from scratch in 1977, and thus virtually all political parties have shown membership increases in the past three decades. (The one major exception is the Partido Comunista de España [PCE]—see below.) For example, during the period of the Socialists' first long run in office (1982–1996), the main opposition party, the Popular Party, also grew, from 85,000 to 504,000 members, despite *never* being in power.

While this systemic, "new democracy" effect is real, I would also suggest supplementary explanations that capture the nuances of the two main parties' circumstances. In the case of the Partido Popular (PP), a certain bandwagon effect did operate, as the PSOE lost popularity and the PP began mounting a serious challenge to the Socialists under their new leader, José María Aznar, in the late 1980s and early 1990s. For example, in the seven years between 1989 and 1996, the PP's vote increased from 25.1 to 38.8 percent; during the same period, the PP's membership nearly doubled from 263,000 to 504,000. As for the Socialists, their capacity to attract members even as their electoral performance slipped was related to the PSOE's dominance as a party of government not only at the national parliamentary level but also at regional and local levels. Put simply, PSOE membership could be very advantageous for any young, aspiring politician seeking and/or holding office. This instrumental motivation to join the PSOE is reflected in the marked "professionalization" of the middle and upper levels of the party. By 1990, more than 70 percent of PSOE delegates to party congresses drew their salaries from the government as either officeholders or civil servants. Indeed, González's stated goal was to raise that figure to 100 percent (Gillespie 1994, 53). Thus, even as the PSOE grew in numbers, it became increasingly organized around its elected officials rather than the ranks of voluntary grassroots activists.

As for the second organizational dimension, authority relations, it will be recalled that chapter 4 examined the waxing and waning of González's popularity and the impact of these shifts on the concentration of authority within the PSOE. As figure 5.4 indicates, there have been three "long cycles" of authority relations since the party's 1977 legalization. The first, the period from 1977 to 1989, represents the consolidation of authority around the

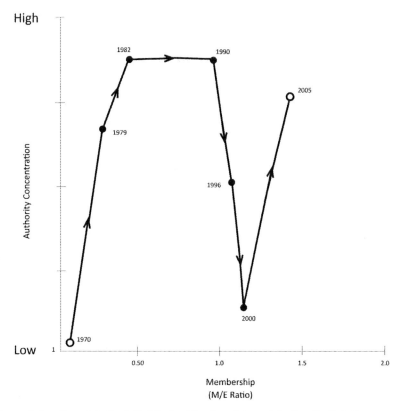

Figure 5.4.   Spanish Socialist Party: Membership and Authority Relations, 1970–2005

González–Guerra leadership. From the time he became party secretary in 1974, González never faced the degree of internal factionalism that Mitterrand confronted during the same era in France. Once his "interior" faction defeated the old-line "exiles" at the Suresnes congress in that year, González did not have to contend with organized factions built around ambitious, headstrong leaders such as Chevènement or Rocard. Yet the new PSOE leader did confront a restive Marxisant left wing that resisted his increasingly moderate positions, especially after the first elections in 1977. As we have seen, González successfully challenged his party's left-wing *sector crítico* in the 1979 congress, and, with the party's stunning 1982 victory, his position at the top of the party was secure. With González focused on governing and Guerra on running the party with a strong (some would claim authoritarian) hand, authority within the party remained concentrated throughout the 1980s.

This dynamic changed, and a second long cycle—a decadelong erosion of leadership authority—began in the early 1990s as scandals enveloped the

PSOE and tarnished González's image. This second long cycle witnessed the breaking apart of the González–Guerra tandem and the construction of rival factions based on personal loyalties as well as purported ideological differences between the moderate prime minister and his more leftist erstwhile partner. The diffusion of power away from the party's center continued even after the Socialists' defeat in 1996 as the party struggled to reconstitute cohesive leadership in the wake of González's resignation a year after the elections.

Finally, following the party's second defeat in 2000 and the subsequent selection of Zapatero as party chief, the PSOE moved into a third cycle of concentrating authority in the top leadership group. The key difference between this latest cycle and the first one is that although Zapatero did not face factional opposition per se, he did have to deal with the growing authority of regional party leaders, especially in regions such as Catalonia and Andalusia, where the PSOE has a governing stake (Méndez Lago 2006, 427). Thus, his authority within the party, although greatly enhanced compared with his immediate predecessor, Joaquín Almunia, was considerably more limited than was González's during the 1980s.

Italian Socialists (PSI)

The PSI followed a third distinct organizational trajectory, as depicted in figure 5.5. Like its Spanish counterpart, the PSI experienced steady membership growth in the 1970s under new leadership, namely, that of Bettino Craxi, who became party chief in 1976. That growth continued down to the moment when the party imploded because of corruption scandals in 1993–1994. In that respect, the PSI more closely resembles the PSOE pattern of an ever-expanding membership as opposed to the up-and-down fluctuations of the French Socialists. (There is little doubt, however, that much of the PSI's expansion was driven not by a growth in activism but by sheer clientelism, especially in the south, where the Socialists were gradually building a political machine built on favors and public contracts.) In contrast to both the Spanish and the French cases, however, Craxi and his leadership group were able to concentrate authority for over fifteen years without serious internal challenge, whereas authority relations in the PSOE and PS varied between periods of leadership dominance—Mitterrand between 1981 and 1990 and González from 1979 to 1991—and factional divisions. Thus, the PSI presents an unusual spectacle of a party that pursued a temporarily successful organizational model that ultimately proved unsustainable.

Craxi's spectacular rise and fall were hardly preordained. No one expected in 1976 that the forty-two-year-old Craxi would soon come to dominate not only his party but in fact the whole Italian political scene for much of the 1980s. As we saw in chapter 3, in the decade and a half prior to Craxi's

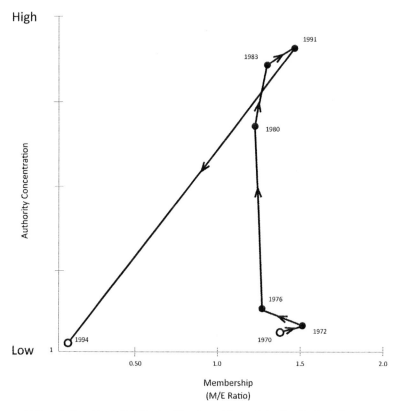

Figure 5.5. **Italian Socialist Party: Membership and Authority Relations, 1970–1994**

selection as party chief, the PSI had occupied an ambiguous role in Italian politics. Beginning in the early 1960s the PSI ended its long postwar cooperation with the Communists and, in 1963, joined a government led by the Democrazia Cristiana (DC). The PSI's partner switching proved frustrating, however; the party was unable to decisively affect DC policy, and its electoral support stagnated. A poor performance in the 1968 elections aggravated factional divisions within the party, forcing longtime leader Nenni to resign as party leader and to withdraw the PSI from the governing coalition. For the next eight years, the party failed to resolve its internal struggles or to reverse its electoral slide; by 1976, the party's share of the vote had declined by one-third compared with a decade earlier. In this context, Craxi's selection as leader represented a generational shift in leadership that brought the party new energy and direction. Endlessly ambitious both for his party and for himself, Craxi in the early 1980s was able to take advantage of the growing weakness of both the Partito Comunista Italiano (PCI) and the DC to become the linchpin of Italy's coalition-based parliamentary system, even though the PSI posted only modest electoral gains.

During his period as prime minister (1983–1987) and for another five years afterward (as the PSI remained in DC-dominated coalitions), Craxi concentrated power in his own hands and in those of his loyalists, many of whom were local or regional party bosses and/or elected officials. Organized factional activity was virtually eliminated, while the party apparatus, following the example of the Christian Democrats, turned its efforts toward generating spoils for its supporters. Here is the key difference in leadership between Craxi on the one hand and his contemporaries Mitterrand and González on the other: whatever their faults and weaknesses as leaders, the French and Spanish Socialist leaders did not view or use political power virtually exclusively in order to amass personal power or wealth. Craxi, by contrast, appeared to be a living example of Lord Acton's dictum about the corrupting nature of power. In the end, his authority within the PSI rested ultimately on his ability to exploit political office for private gain. Although Italians are long used to seeing their politicians abuse power, Craxi and the PSI ultimately went too far. By 1993, their exploitation of office had become too egregious for even the most long-suffering of Italians to bear, and the "Craxi model" unraveled within a few months.

The outset of this section noted that the Socialist parties considered here have followed no clear trends in terms of membership levels or authority relations. In terms of membership, whereas the PSOE has steadily added to its numbers over time, the PS has fluctuated within a fairly narrow range with a comparatively low membership. The PSI stands in a league of its own, with respectable growth that ended abruptly with the demise of the party itself in 1994. As for authority relations, one sees no general trend toward oligarchy à la Michels. Any such trend toward the concentration of authority in a single leader or a small leadership group appears to be transient and specific to that leader. A party leader's authority cannot be passed on to the leader's successor as one might transfer files and membership lists. The question of leadership succession recalls Weber's analysis of the difficulties in "routinizing charisma"—an organizational problem that might be rephrased in colloquial language as "He's a tough act to follow."

In the cases just reviewed, the problem of routinizing leadership is more complicated than merely stepping into a void left by a charismatic figure such as Mitterrand or González.[7] In those two instances, the inherently formidable task of following a dominant leader was made even harder by the fact that by the time of their departure, both leaders had largely exhausted much of their erstwhile charismatic authority. In the last three or four years of both Mitterrand's presidency and González's prime ministership, there was a palpable aura of intellectual and physical exhaustion, loss of enthusiasm, and even disillusionment among Socialist Party members, not to mention the public generally. What resulted within both the PS and the PSOE was not just a power vacuum but an escalating factional struggle. By the time each leader retired, the diffusion of authority was already well under way.

COMMUNISTS: CRISIS, CONTESTATION, TRANSFORMATION

Compared with the complexity of organizational change in our three Socialist parties, the fate of the Communist parties since 1970 has been fairly straightforward. As we have seen, for the first half of the 1970s, all three Communist parties appeared to be gathering or at least maintaining strength. In Italy, the PCI advanced to the point of seriously challenging the DC for primacy, while in France the Parti Comuniste Français (PCF) was holding its own with at least a 20 percent vote share. In Spain, the PCE was the leading opposition force to the Franco regime. New policy initiatives such as the PCI's Historic Compromise, the PCF's participation in the Union of the Left, and the PCE's support for democratization promised, for a time, to forge a specifically European variant of Communism. However, by the end of that decade, that promise had largely been erased, and the Communists' long decline had commenced. Since 1980, Communist parties have either withered as electoral forces (as in Spain and France) or transformed themselves into "post-Communist" parties that have severed all connections to their past (as in Italy). Accompanying this electoral decline has come organizational crisis, which has taken two main forms: on the one hand, dramatic drops in membership and activism and, on the other hand, internal disputes over classic Communist practices, notably the Leninist principle of democratic centralism. These trends have been remarkably similar in all three cases.

The trends in terms of membership can be seen in figure 5.6. The only obvious difference among the three cases is the relatively larger membership of the Italian Communist Party (and even its three post-Communist formations: the Partito Democratico della Sinistra [PDS], Democratici di Sinistra [DS], and Partito Democratico [PD]) compared with our other two cases. As we have noted, this reflects a systemic difference: Italian parties in general have enrolled proportionally greater numbers than their French and Spanish counterparts. Apart from this difference, membership levels since 1970 have followed a similar advance–retreat path in all three cases. All three parties experienced an influx of members in the early to mid-1970s. The experience of the Spanish Communists was, of course, distinctive, given that it became legalized just a few weeks before the first post-Franco elections in 1977 and had just a few thousand members at that time. By the end of that year, the PCE was reporting over 200,000 members. As for the PCI and PCF, although their percentage increase was not as impressive, each added several hundred thousand members during the 1970s.[8] At varying time points, however, the ascending line began to sink. Both the Spanish and the Italian Communist parties reached their high-water mark in members in 1977, whereas the French party's apogee came a few years later, in 1981. Since those maxima, the membership trend in all three cases has been steadily downward, with very few year-on-year increases. By 2004–2005, membership in each of the parties was well less than half of the level attained in the 1970s and early 1980s.[9]

Important organizational differences among these parties emerge only when one considers authority relations. As mentioned above, all three parties experienced challenges to the inherited pattern of democratic centralism as organizational decline set in during the late 1970s and early 1980s. What have varied in interesting ways are the timing, modes, and outcomes of these challenges.

French Communists (PCF)

As we saw in chapter 2, the longtime PCF secretary Georges Marchais sought to govern the party in the time-honored Stalinist tradition of centralized authority. Assuming his position in 1972, Marchais inherited leadership of a party that since 1930 had had only two leaders—Maurice Thorez (1930–1964) and Waldeck Rochet (1964–1972)—and was widely considered the most orthodox, pro-Soviet Communist Party in Western Europe. As a pure product of that system, Marchais was no innovator in conducting the party's internal affairs, and, like his predecessors, he brooked no challenges to his authority or that of the PCF's top body, the Bureau Politique. Throughout his first few years as party chief, Marchais faced few such challenges. There was a general consensus within the PCF behind the Union of the Left

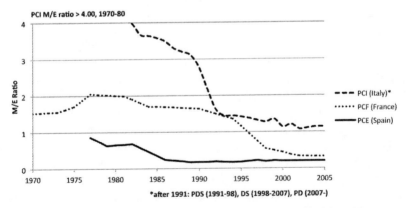

Figure 5.6.   Communist Parties in France, Italy, and Spain: Membership, 1970–2005

alliance strategy with the Socialists, and his Eurocommunist turn with Berlinguer and Carrillo proved popular within the party and, for a time, with the public. According to party figures, the PCF added over 350,000 members—an increase of nearly 80 percent—between 1972 and 1978, and even though the fledgling Eurocommunist discourse affirmed the PCF's commitment to democracy, that commitment did not extend to the party itself. Authority remained concentrated at the center (see figure 5.7).

This dynamic, combining the continued centralization of authority with membership growth, was shattered, however, with the PCF's decision to scuttle the Union of the Left in 1977–1978. The transparency of the leadership's decision to accept the Left's electoral defeat rather than participate in a Left government dominated by Socialists was evident to many party activists as well as to the public in general. This decision triggered a struggle within the party that would endure, in basic form, through the remainder of Marchais's tenure as party leader. At issue, in effect, was a struggle between two

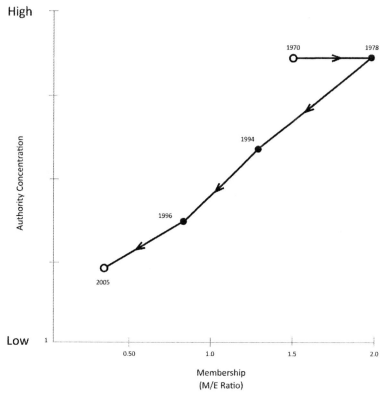

Figure 5.7.   French Communist Party: Membership and Authority Relations, 1970–2005

organizational logics. One side, that of Marchais and the top leadership, held fast to a "vanguard" view of the PCF: only the Communist Party was capable of defining and bringing about real change for the working class and its allies (Jenson and Ross 1984, 13). In this logic, the Union of the Left had become a dangerous trap and a political dead end; not only was the Socialist Party beginning to eclipse the PCF at the ballot box, but Socialist leaders, notably Mitterrand, had abandoned some of the core goals of the Common Program. Since the PCF was unable in such circumstances to perform its essential vanguard role, the party's (and the Left's) long-term interest was to end this alliance immediately. Explicit in this vanguard conception of the party was the overriding importance of maintaining party unity, which could be preserved only through the strict practice of democratic centralism. Internal dissent, factionalism, and the public questioning of the party's leadership were considered "disloyal" acts.

On the other side stood a vocal segment of party activists who rejected this essentially Leninist view. Being influenced by the Italian Communist example and interpreting Marchais's Eurocommunist embrace of democracy to include the party itself, these "renovators" openly criticized the PCF leadership for its excessive power, rigid internal practices, and damaging strategic decisions, notably the abandonment of Left unity. These critics pointed out that even the party's image-enhancing decision in 1976 to abandon the phrase "dictatorship of the proletariat" demonstrated that the party had not changed since the decision was made by Marchais alone (Lavabre and Platone 2003, 29–30).

These two perspectives essentially constituted the battle lines within the PCF from 1978 until Marchais's retirement in 1994. The basic dynamic between the party leadership and various cohorts of critics became a kind of scripted call-and-response. Renovators such as Henri Fizbin, François Hincker, and Pierre Juquin would call for greater freedom of expression within the party and more accountability on the part of the of the leadership. In response, Marchais would denounce such criticisms as attacks against the party itself and seek to have the dissidents removed from their party posts (Raymond 2005, 97–100). As we have seen, during the Gorbachev years, Marchais was never tempted to engage in any kind of PCF version of glasnost or perestroika. Virtually no changes in the party's internal operating practices were made during Marchais's tenure as party chief; democratic centralism remained the modus operandi. By the time he resigned, Marchais could certainly claim to have defended his particular vision of the French Communist Party and to have kept the party intact, even as other Communist parties throughout Europe were dissolved or transformed. From an organizational viewpoint, however, Marchais's insistence on concentrating authority within the top leadership proved a disaster. The PCF's electoral appeal plummeted throughout the 1980s and early 1990s along with membership.

French Communism in the post-Marchais era brought encouraging change along with depressing continuity. Under Marchais's successor, Robert Hue, who headed the party from 1994 to 2001, the PCF abandoned the practice of democratic centralism and instituted democratic elections within various levels of the party. Internal debate and dissent became "normal," not manifestations of disloyalty, and the PCF renewed a functioning alliance with the Socialists, which included the Communists' participation in Jospin's "plural left" government from 1997 to 2002. But for the great mass of French people, the Communist brand no longer had appeal, so the party's efforts to reform its internal practices and recast its public image failed to reverse the organization's slide. Communism in France, as virtually everywhere, lost its luster in the 1980s and early 1990s. For many reasons, there was no likelihood that the PCF could have maintained its organizational strength at the levels it had in the 1960s and 1970s. But Marchais's obdurate bunker mentality and refusal to reform from within only hastened that decline. He may have saved the "house" for Hue and his successors, but by 1994 the structure was largely empty.

Spanish Communists (PCE)

In Spain, the Communists' organizational story bears much resemblance to that of the PCF, although the Spanish leadership had a more flexible, creative response to decline than did its French counterparts. In the first few years following its legalization in 1977, the PCE appeared to be following in the PCF's footprints. In terms of membership, the Spanish Communists were initially able to take advantage of their leadership role in the anti-Franco opposition, increasing their numbers from 15,000 at the time of Franco's death in November 1975 to over 200,000 within two years. Although this early momentum quickly dissipated following the party's disappointing performance in the constituent assembly elections in 1977, the party managed to maintain its membership at slightly lower levels during the next five years. Meanwhile, although significant grumbling emerged over the leadership of Santiago Carrillo, the longtime party secretary continued to enforce the practice of democratic centralism even while fervently supporting Spain's new democracy (see figure 5.8).

Ultimately, as in France, the contradiction of maintaining a democratic public discourse while engaging in authoritarian internal practices caused the PCE to lose credibility as a force for reform. The breaking point came in the 1982 elections that swept the Socialists to power and virtually wiped the Communists off the map. With just 4 percent of the vote, the PCE became a marginal political entity; in less than a decade, the party had gone from being the most potent force on the Left to being almost irrelevant. Forced to resign as secretary, given the party's dismal results, Carrillo remained "in-house"

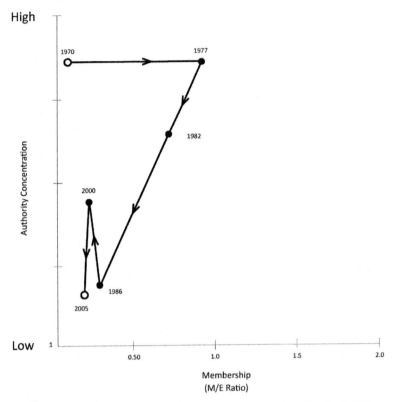

Figure 5.8. **Spanish Communist Party: Membership and Authority Relations, 1970–2005**

for a time, but he increasingly criticized the new reform-minded leader, Gerardo Iglesias, as did other groups dissatisfied with the party's direction. For the next four years, the PCE was in constant turmoil: a full-scale leadership struggle was accompanied by massive desertions. Between 1982 and 1986, party membership dropped by nearly two-thirds from 182,000 to 70,000. Iglesias was able to effect one big reform: the formation, in 1996, of Izquierda Unida (IU), a coalition of smaller left-wing parties led by the PCE. Although the IU's lackluster performance in the 1986 election forced Iglesias's replacement by Julio Anguita, the new coalition structure itself remained permanent.

What changed with the arrival of Anguita was both a reconcentration of party authority in the top leadership along with a strong tilt to the left. Assuming once again the classic Communist strongman role à la Carrillo, Anguita differed from his predecessor in being forthrightly Marxist and anti-Socialist. Anguita's forceful, centralized leadership did help revive a moribund party; as we have seen, the IU's vote more than doubled from 4.6 to 10.5 percent between 1986 and 1996; however, the PCE continued to lose members. Total membership eventually stabilized in the range of 60,000 to 70,000—a far cry from the late 1970s.

The final shift in authority relations occurred with Anguita's retirement in 1999 due to health reasons. In a scenario reminiscent of González's departure as Socialist leader, Anguita's resignation triggered a leadership succession struggle to the point that by the early 2000s, the IU coalition exercised a certain autonomy in relation to its main constituent, the PCE. By 2006, the Communist-dominated formation had a tense dual executive that pulled in opposing directions: the PCE secretary, Francisco Frutos, generally rejected coalitions with other parties, notably the Socialists, whereas IU leader Gaspar Llamazares (himself a Communist as well) favored coalitions. Although the days of democratic centralism in the PCE are long gone, this diffusion of authority has not led to a resurgence in membership. In 2008, the party's membership of about 70,000 was about the same as it was two decades before. Overall, even though the PCE undertook internal reforms at least a decade before its French counterpart, ultimately it arrived at roughly the same place: a marginal electoral presence of less than 5 percent and a greatly weakened organizational structure.

Italian Communists (PCI)

The Italian case presents a third variant in the adaptation of Communist parties to the upheavals that traversed their world during the past three decades. There is little variation, of course, in the long-term trend in membership. In all three cases, after a modest burst of growth in the 1970s, the parties began a long, steady slide in the late 1970s and early 1980s. The PCI's slide was especially marked because the party started at such a high level. During its heyday, between 1945 and 1985, the PCI was by far the largest Communist party in Western Europe. At no time during that period did the PCI's membership drop below 1.5 million. But by the early years of the twenty-first century, having abandoned Communism in favor of an amorphous center-left identity, the party saw two-thirds of its membership disappear (see figure 5.9).[10] The decline was due, in part, to the general decrease in partisan mobilization throughout Western Europe discussed above. There were also specific causes, including the split within the party over the transformation of the PCI into the "post-Communist" party of the Democratic Left and the subsequent departure of orthodox Communists and more radical leftists to form Rifondazione Comunista. Also contributing to the decline was the inability of the post-Communist versions of the PCI—the PDS, DS, and PD—to establish a stable identity that discouraged the kind of commitment that attracted earlier generations of Communists.

The Italian variation, then, comes not from membership trends but rather from differences in authority relations. Figure 5.9 notes a trajectory in authority relations roughly similar in form to the French: a concentration of authority in the 1970s due to strong leadership (Berlinguer and Marchais) followed by the growth of internal contestation and challenges to party leaders to the point where democratic centralism was abandoned and the party became more open and tolerant of dissent. (By contrast, we have noted a more up-and-down pattern of authority relations in the Spanish case because of Anguita's ability to reestablish a centralized leadership in the 1986–2000 period.) This apparent similarity is deceptive, however, because of the different way in which those shifts in authority relations occurred in the Italian and French cases.

Three aspects of these shifts are noteworthy. First, Berlinguer's dominance of the PCI—that is, his ability to concentrate authority in his own hands—did not approach that of Marchais. This difference in leadership

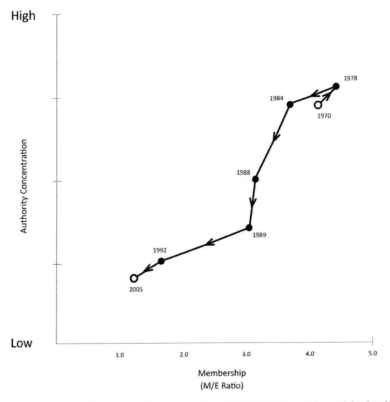

Figure 5.9.   Italian Communist Party (and Post-PCI): Membership and Authority Relations, 1970–2005

authority between the PCI and PCF has long been noted by observers, with the classic contrast being that of a "Bolshevized" French party compared with a more open, tolerant Italian party (Greene 1968). Throughout his tenure as PCI leader, from 1972 until his unexpected death in 1984, Berlinguer faced challenges to his leadership, notably following the abandonment of the Historic Compromise strategy of the late 1970s, when the party divided into three distinct camps. To recall, Pietro Ingrao and his followers favored a move toward a forthright anticapitalist stance, whereas Giorgio Napolitano espoused a social democratic, reformist line and Armando Cossutta urged a return to pro-Soviet orthodoxy. As much as Berlinguer may have wanted to squelch these dissenting voices, he was unable to do so given the PCI's tradition of allowing relatively free criticism of the leadership.

Second, the PCI's relative openness facilitated internal reform much earlier than in the PCF. In the early 1980s, for example, the PCI instituted secret voting on party business, including leadership elections and motions at party congresses. By contrast, Marchais's long tenure as party chief discouraged reform; only with leadership change in the mid-1990s did the French Communists begin to abandon democratic centralism. Finally, of course, the big difference in authority relations in the two cases is that a majority of the Italian party chose to abandon Communism, whereas the French party remained at least rhetorically committed to Marxism-Leninism.

These are not minor differences; the two organizational paths described above ultimately produced sharply contrasting outcomes. The PCF, because of Marchais's refusal to consider a fundamental reform of the party, bypassed the historical moment of Communism's worldwide demise and thus, in effect, painted itself into a corner from which it has still not escaped. Whatever Occhetto's failures (and there were many), he can be credited with the audacity to propose a painful change that, in the end, gave the most powerful party on the Left the possibility of reinventing itself. No one would argue that the PCI's "makeover" was a grand success. The successor party ultimately became something of an ideological and organizational hodgepodge, ever changing in name, identity, and leadership. Yet the decision to abandon its Communist roots at least allowed the PDS/DS/PD the chance to avoid the worst of all political fates: irrelevance. That the post-Communist party failed to make the most of its transformation does not gainsay the wisdom of making the transformation in the first place.

CONCLUSION

This review of how the major Left organizations have changed since 1970 enables us to make two generalizations. First, in terms of membership, five of the six parties experienced declines over the period surveyed. Only the

Spanish Socialists managed to increase their numbers over time. Beginning, of course, from a low base—an estimated 48,000 members during 1977, the year of legalization—the PSOE slowly but surely increased its membership to nearly 500,000 by 2004. In terms of the party's M/E ratio, the growth was over sixfold, from 0.20 to 1.33. Although this latter figure is still quite low compared with many other European Social Democratic parties, it is the highest among the six parties we are considering. The other five parties either disappeared (PSI) or dwindled in size. By the early 2000s, the M/E ratio of the PS, PCF, PCI (and successors), and PCE had declined, on average, 72 percent from their high points in the late 1970s or early 1980s.[11]

Second, in terms of authority relations, the general tendency was toward diffusion rather than concentration of authority over time. This was clearly the case for all three Communist parties, which, in the face of electoral decline beginning in the late 1970s, experienced strong internal challenges to traditional modes of democratic centralism. As we have just seen, this abandonment of highly centralized authority, often accompanied by the repression and/or expulsion of dissenters, did not occur evenly, easily, or automatically in any of the three parties. In the Spanish case, there was even a reassertion of central authority during Anguita's tenure. But the ultimate outcome was toward internal debate and decision making that was more open and democratic than before.

As for the Socialists, this trend was certainly not evident during Craxi's long period as chief of the Italian Socialists (1976–1993); however, his dramatic downfall was the exception proving the rule: highly concentrated authority within these political parties could not be sustained indefinitely. The two parties that have had the most success electorally during the past forty years, the French and Spanish Socialists, experienced cycles of concentration and diffusion of authority. By 2010, the two parties were at different points in their respective cycles. The French Socialists remained highly divided, still struggling to fill the void left by Jospin's abrupt departure following his disastrous 2002 showing in the presidential election. The Spanish Socialists, by contrast, had found renewed unity and vigor behind their reelected prime minister, Zapatero. Even in the latter case, however, the concentration of party authority under Zapatero's leadership did not approach that of the González–Guerra era in the 1980s. In summary, leaving aside the special case of the defunct Italian Socialists, in all of the parties surveyed, the general trend in authority relations is toward a lessening of control by top party leaders compared with the 1970s.

The organizational trends that we have examined in this chapter can be connected directly to the book's main thesis, namely, that all the Socialist and Communist parties under consideration experienced critical junctures at various points in the 1960s and 1970s. This is most obvious in the case of the Communists, where declines in membership, activism, and electoral popularity became evident by the end of the 1970s. This decline in organizational robustness, as in any collectivity undergoing stress, generated discontent and critiques of the top leadership not only from the grassroots but also from within the parties' governing circles. These critiques did not bring immediate changes in leadership or decision-making practices, but they ultimately served to undermine the key operating principle of the whole Communist enterprise—democratic centralism—and thus the parties' raison d'être. The data on both membership and authority relations presented in this chapter support the conclusion that, for the three Communist parties, the 1970s was a watershed period that definitively changed their trajectory from one of organizational growth and stable, centralized leadership to one of decline and divided, contested leadership.

For the Socialists, the 1960s and 1970s were also decisive, although the long-term outcomes were more variable than in the case of the Communists. From an organizational perspective, the chief importance of that decade for the Socialists was not so much in terms of membership as in authority relations. In terms of membership, as figure 5.2 demonstrates, there was no general trend during either the 1970s or thereafter. During the 1970s, the PS and PSOE advanced in numbers, whereas the PSI declined. After 1980, the PSOE continued to grow in membership, but the PS started a long cycle of diminishing membership that was only reversed, modestly, in the mid- to late 1990s. As for the PSI, its collapse in 1993 put an end to a period of modest growth during the Craxi heyday of the 1980s. Organizationally, the true impact of the 1970s was thus not in terms of membership but rather in the rise of strong, decisive leaders—Mitterrand, González, and Craxi—who not only concentrated authority within their respective parties but also served as the architects of new programmatic and/or alliance strategies that, for better or for worse, established their parties' trajectory for years to come.

NOTES

1. The M/E ratios for around the year 2000 are as follows: Italy (4.05 percent), Spain (3.42 percent), and France (1.52 percent). The twenty-nation mean is 4.99. See Mair and Van Biezen (2001, 9, 15–16).

2. I stress the term "heuristic" here. Whereas the horizontal dimension, the M/E ratio, is fairly precise, the vertical dimension of authority relations is much less so based on my own estimations and best judgments.

3. In this and subsequent graphs of trends in membership and authority relations, I use an M/E ratio scale of 0 to 3.0. The only exception to this is figure 5.9, where I use a scale of 0 to 4.0 in order to accommodate the initially much larger size of the Italian Communist Party.

4. On becoming elected president in 1981, Mitterrand relinquished this position, although he remained the de facto leader throughout his two terms from 1981 to 1995.

5. Factional alignments and dominant ideological tendencies went hand in hand during this period. Three factional alignments and three corresponding ideological orientations were evident in the 1971–1981 period. In each one, Mitterrand and his supporters were able to forge majorities at biennial party congresses. See Smith (1998, 52–53).

6. These were Pierre Mauroy (1988–1992), Laurent Fabius (1992–1993), Michel Rocard (1993–1994), and Henri Emmanuelli (1994–1995).

7. In the case of Craxi, of course, the "void" that he created was monumental, namely, the collapse of his party.

8. If one takes 1970 membership as the beginning reference point and the later year in which the party's maximum membership point was reached in this growth cycle, the PCI grew about 20 percent from 1.51 million to 1.81 million (in 1977), while the PCF advanced from 450,000 to 710,000 (in 1981), a gain of 58 percent. It should be noted that these are the parties' self-reported figures. Whereas most scholars believe that the PCI's membership figures are generally accurate, specialists have cast great doubt on the accuracy of the French party's numbers, believing them to be highly inflated (see, e.g., Andolfatto 2005, 245–46). Despite this probable bias, I have chosen, for the sake of consistent comparison, to base this analysis on the parties' self-reported figures in all cases.

9. PCF membership declined 81 percent (from 710,000 in 1981 to 133,000 in 2004), the PCI's decline was 69 percent (from 1.81 million in 1977 to 561,000 in 2005), and the PCE's membership decreased 66 percent (from 202,000 in 1977 to 68,000 in 2004). The figure for the post-PCI party does not include the membership of Rifondazione Comunista, but including this figure would lower the percentage decline only slightly.

10. Because the PCI was so much larger—in absolute size as well as M/E ratio—I have rescaled figure 5.9 to provide a maximum M/E ratio of 5.0 rather than 3.0 in the other figures. To give an idea of the differences in magnitude, the highest M/E ratios for the three Communist parties were as follows: PCI: 4.67 (in 1975); PCF: 2.05 (in 1977); and PCE: 0.86 (in 1977).

11. The change in M/E ratios are as follows:

PS: −50% (high point 0.60 in 1982; M/E ratio in 2004 = 0.31)
PCF: −84% (high point 2.05 in 1977; M/E ratio in 2004 = 0.32)
PCE: −77% (high point 0.86 in 1977; M/E ratio in 2004 = 0.20)
PCI (PDS etc.): −76% (high point 4.67 in 1975; M/E ratio in 2005 = 1.14)

Chapter Six

Alliances

François Mitterrand: You don't really have any other solution than to make an alliance with the Communists. I think it's the best way to reduce their influence.
Felipe González: Maybe. But it takes too long. I think we can rapidly eliminate the Communists—by refusing to finesse things, by fighting against them ideologically, and by showing that their proposals are ridiculous, dangerous, or obsolete.
Mitterrand: But you're running the risk of letting yourselves drift to the right and thereby create a new political space for the Communists.
González: So what? That's a risk I'll take. I prefer it to others.
—Conversation, May 24, 1975[1]

Figuratively and rhetorically, Left parties in France, Italy, and Spain have faced in two directions at once: toward the parliament building and toward the street. In the classic discourse of the Left, the pursuit of political power entails contesting elections in order to gain public office, but this is just part of the story. The other major task is to help mobilize society in favor of progressive social change, namely, reforms that will aid historically disadvantaged groups or achieve other long-term goals. This means sponsoring or working with social movement organizations such as labor unions, peace movements, and environmental organizations. Most Left parties have viewed their activities in the political and societal spheres as mutually reinforcing. By supporting social movements such as unions, parties can extend their influence throughout society and ultimately increase their electoral appeal. At the same time, grassroots action by social movements can help build mass pressure for governmental reforms championed by the Left.

In both the political and the social arenas, Left parties face strategic choices regarding alliances. In the political arena, for example, simple math suggests the need for allies among other parties. For more than a century, every Left party has recognized that achieving an electoral majority, on its own, was virtually impossible, especially given that the Left's core constituency, industrial workers, "never were and never would become a numerical majority in their respective societies" (Przeworski and Sprague 1986, 31). Even combining the votes of all Left parties would yield, at best, a bare and unstable majority. Given this reality, some parties have resigned themselves to permanent minority status, rejecting alliances and basically playing the electoral game for the sole purpose of representing their voting constituency. Other parties have aspired to become part of a governing majority and have sought various types of alliances with other parties. The question of *political* alliances, then, comes down to the choice of possible party allies. Does the party move to the left in order to ally with another left-wing party (or parties) or move toward the center to ally with more moderate parties?

In the sphere of civil society as well, Left parties face similarly difficult choices about potential partners. What organizations and movements make the best allies? What should be the nature of the relationship between the party and societal groups? While all Left parties give at least lip service to the need for what I term *social* alliances, they have engaged in a variety of relationships with organizations such as labor unions, ranging from hostility to close coordination and overlapping directorates.

Viewed from a strictly ideological viewpoint, the choice of alliance strategy would appear to separate Socialists from Communists. Socialist parties trace a major component of their heritage and lineage to the gradualist evolutionary tradition articulated by Eduard Bernstein in the early 1900s: the belief that Socialism could be achieved through a process of elections and incremental reforms (Bernstein 1961). All three of the countries considered here can point to their own native versions of Bernstein: Jaurès in France, Turati in Italy, and Prieto in Spain. This is not to deny the importance of revolutionary currents within Socialist thought, but it is to suggest that Socialists would seem, a priori, to be more open than Communists to both political and social alliances that move them toward the center of the political spectrum. By contrast, Communist parties, in accepting Lenin's and the Comintern's famous "Twenty-One Conditions," implicitly endorsed the Soviet model of revolution, thereby rejecting any prolonged, gradual transition to Socialism through electoral means. While such a stance did not exclude alliances with other parties, it did impose the condition that all alliances were temporary and conditional. At all times, the Communist Party had to remain the dominant force, the vanguard, in any alliance. Under such conditions, the likelihood of allying with centrist parties would be minimal.

Ideology, of course, is one thing and reality another. As we shall see, many factors besides ideology shape a party's alliance strategy; historically, there has been no systematic pattern of Communists seeking allies only on the Left, whereas Socialists ally with centrist as well as Left parties. To take only the most obvious example, Stalin, in an effort to fight the rise of Fascism in the 1930s, endorsed so-called Popular Front alliances with "bourgeois" parties, which were defined to include Socialist as well as middle-class parties. Thus, while Left parties need to build alliances, how and why they do so follows no set ideological script. As a careful reader of earlier chapters will have noted, there is no single "Socialist pattern" as opposed to a "Communist pattern" of alliances in our three countries.

This chapter, drawing on the case material of chapters 2 to 4, compares the alliance strategies engaged in by Socialist and Communist parties in France, Italy, and Spain, with a specific focus on the period since the 1960s. In line with this book's central thesis—namely, that during the 1960s and 1970s all of these parties experienced critical junctures—we focus on alliance strategies initiated during that period. The argument to be developed is straightforward: of all the strategic responses that these parties made during this period, the choice of alliances was the most significant in terms of long-term impacts. As in the previous chapter, we begin with an analysis of Socialist strategies, followed by the Communists.

SOCIALIST ALLIANCES

Socialist political alliances followed no set pattern. In the French and Spanish cases, as the Mitterrand–González exchange above indicates, the contrast was sharp: French Socialists sought to strike an agreement to their left, with the Communist Party, whereas Spanish Socialists rejected such a left-leaning move. Italian Socialists rejected a left-leaning move as well, but otherwise the Spanish and Italian parties parted company strategically, with Italian Socialists renewing their conflictual but functioning partnership with the Christian Democrats, whereas Spanish Socialists chose to preserve their independence and not ally with any other party. As for social alliances, all three Socialist parties sought to strengthen their ties with components of organized labor. These efforts were largely unsuccessful, however, not only because of the strong Communist presence in the largest union confederations but also because of divisions and crises within the labor movement itself. Of the three Socialist parties, the Partido Socialista Obrero Español (PSOE) was the most successful in building an alliance with organized labor given that it was able to reactivate its century-old historic ties with the Unión General de Trabajadores (UGT). But the party did so on terms that relegated the UGT to a subordinate position and laid the groundwork for a dramatic deterioration in PSOE–UGT relations in the late 1980s. In all three cases, Socialists failed to establish enduring social alliances with workers' organizations.

French Socialists (PS)

For French Socialists an alliance with the Communists in the early 1970s represented a departure from the preceding twenty-five years of distant relations. Although the Parti Comuniste Français (PCF) and Section Française de l'Internationale Ouvrière (SFIO) had cooperated extensively during the 1935–1938 Popular Front period and again during the Resistance, their relationship was one of the casualties of the Cold War. As we saw in chapter 2, it was actually a Socialist prime minister, Paul Ramadier, who sacked the Communists from his government in 1947, thereby sending the PCF into the political desert. Meanwhile, the Socialists became an essential element of the inner-party system of the Fourth Republic, participating in various coalition governments with left-center and center parties, including the Radical Socialists and the Catholic Popular Republican Movement.

The collapse of the Fourth Republic and the advent of the Fifth Republic in 1958 completely recast the party system and the alliance calculus of all parties, including the Socialists (Berstein 1989, 121–44). Specifically, de Gaulle's prestige and popularity, coupled with a new constitution providing for a strong president, threatened to relegate all leftist parties, including the Socialists, to permanent minority status. By excluding the Socialists from the possibility of power, the new Fifth Republic system provided the party an initial incentive to turn to its other leftist cohorts for cooperation. Further incentive was furnished by a two-ballot system for National Assembly elections as well as municipal elections. Given that the vast majority of district elections went to a runoff ballot among parties garnering at least 15 percent of the vote, there was a built-in incentive for Socialists and Communists to practice *désistement*, or "stand-down," agreements on the second ballot in order to help the better placed of the two parties in the first round. Such a cooperative arrangement began to be practiced as early as 1962 and was continued thereafter, although the parties refrained from agreeing on a common governing program (Bergounioux and Grunberg 2005, 275–94).

These tentative steps toward unity changed with the emergence of François Mitterrand as head of the "new" Socialist Party in 1971. Recognizing more astutely than any other Left leader the dynamics of the presidency-based system, Mitterrand set out to take both himself and his adopted party to the top. That meant establishing himself as *the* dominant candidate of the Left and the Socialist Party as a potential majority party. The road to these ambitious goals went straight through the Communist Party. Far from rejecting alliance with the PCF, Mitterrand embraced it, wagering that a PS–PCF alliance could enable him to achieve three goals: first, it could constitute a solid electoral base for his own presidential run; second, it could also build a parliamentary majority coalition; and, third, an alliance would work to the systematic advantage of the Socialists. Accordingly, Mitterrand led the Socialists in negotiating the 1972 cooperation agreement with the PCF that formalized the *désistement* principle for both parliamentary and local elections and established a governing platform, the Common Program of the Left (Tiersky 2000, 107–14).

Within a decade, this Union of the Left worked largely according to Mitterrand's calculus, although he could not have predicted the exact course that the Union would take. In the short term, the Union certainly played to the Socialists' advantage. Even though the PS–PCF alliance did not come close to a majority in the 1973 legislative elections, the two parties improved their combined score from the previous election in 1968 by nearly 5 percent. While the Communists did advance slightly (from 20.0 to 21.4 percent), the Socialists did so even more, increasing their previous vote by over 3 percent and pulling to within two points of the PCF. The benefits of the Socialists' alliance with the Communists proved even greater the following year. In presidential elections called in the wake of Pompidou's death, Mitterrand, with strong Communist backing in the second round, came close to defeating the conservative candidate, Giscard d'Estaing. The Socialists' alliance with the PCF was clearly bearing fruit—for the Socialists (Bergounioux 1996, 244–48).

From the Communists' perspective, however, the benefits were all one sided. For one thing, the *désistement* agreement was working against the PCF. While most Communist voters dutifully voted for the Socialist candidate in the second round, Socialist voters were not nearly so faithful. Asked to vote for a Communist candidate in the second round, many Socialist supporters refused to do so. Moreover, the PCF was starting to see sizable desertions to the PS from among their own voters. Finally, to the extent that Mitterrand and the PS came to appear as the stronger partner in the alliance, they were able to attract centrist voters who otherwise might have feared that the PCF would dominate the alliance. All of these trends were confirmed in local elections in 1977. Rather than allow the hemorrhaging to continue and to put the PCF in a secondary position in the likely event of a Union of the Left victory in the upcoming 1978 parliamentary elections, PCF leader Marchais chose to scuttle the alliance. The Left's subsequent loss in those elections definitively ended this attempt to build a formal Socialist–Communist alliance based on a shared governing plan (Lavabre and Platone 2003, 89–111).

The Union of the Left's demise did not end relations between the two parties, as those relations moved through cycles of tension and cooperation during the following three decades. The two parties even cooperated during two separate governing periods, in 1981–1984 and 1997–2002. But the Union of the Left experience had at least three long-term effects on the Socialists' alliance strategy. First, it made the Socialists averse to any formal, programmatic alliance with the PCF, certainly as long as Marchais remained head of that party (which was to last until 1994). From the Socialists' perspective, the Communists' unwillingness to continue the Union unless they could be the dominant partner demonstrated the vast gulf between the two parties. Henceforth, cooperation could only be ad hoc and based on contingent cost–benefit calculations, not on the prospect of a durable governing partnership.

Second, despite the eventual collapse of the Union, this experience demonstrated the wisdom of forging alliances toward the left, not toward the center. Voting strength, the Socialists recognized, could accrue by exploiting the bipolarizing effects of the new electoral arrangements, specifically the runoff provisions of presidential and legislative elections. By maintaining a clear Left identity as the "natural" alternative to Gaullists and other conservatives, the Socialists demonstrated their superior ability, in runoff situations, to attract voters across a wide spectrum of voters extending from the Communist Left to the center-left.

Finally, for the PS, the Communists' decline, while welcome, did complicate its overall party alliance strategy, especially insofar as many protest voters who had supported the PCF because it stood implacably against the status quo transferred their allegiance to the Far Right National Front. As a possible partner, the PCF was a shrinking resource, and thus the PS needed to cultivate other possible allies as well. Thus, by the mid-1990s, the Socialists' alliance strategy was much broader gauged than in the 1970s. From the two-party Union of the Left, the Socialists now sought to shepherd a "plural left"—a disparate coalition of Socialists, Communists, Greens, Left Radicals, and Chevènement's Citizens' Movement (Szarka 1999; Hanley 2003).

Along with these shifts in the French Socialists' political alliances came changes in their social alliances, especially with organized labor. To a significant extent, the PS's relations with organized labor became a casualty of the dissolution of the Union of the Left in the late 1970s. Prior to that time, although the PS had no formal ties with any of the three major labor confederations, the party was drawing close to the second-largest union, the Confédération Française Démocratique du Travail (CFDT). The formerly Catholic confederation openly endorsed Socialist candidates, and PS leaders let it be known that the CFDT was their favored labor organization. This harmonious dynamic was broken, however, with the dissolution of the Union. Corresponding with Union's demise was a long-term downward trend in overall union membership (Labbé 1996). Although organized labor's decline has structural economic roots as well, many observers linked the decline to the unions' excessive politicization in favor of the Union of the Left and to workers' subsequent disillusionment when the Union failed. This was, in essence, the analysis of the CFDT as well. For the CFDT, the lesson to be drawn from the Union's breakup was that the confederation had subjugated its everyday union activities to the prospect of a Left electoral victory.

Henceforth, the CFDT vowed to "recenter" its efforts on the workplace and labor market issues, a shift in priorities that obviously meant that the CFDT would distance itself from all political parties, including the Socialist Party (Hamon and Rotman 1982, 293–333; Groux and Mouriaux 1989, 205–22).

From 1978 on, therefore, the Socialists could count on no privileged allies within the labor movement (Howell 1992, 153–55). The CFDT leadership under Edmond Maire, while expressing sympathy for the Socialists, made it clear that the political sphere was largely "hands off" for his confederation. The union's priorities included reviving plant-level negotiations and pushing such initiatives as work sharing as a means of combating the unemployment problem. The growing separation between the PS and the CFDT continued throughout the Mitterrand presidency, especially once the Mauroy government took the famous economic policy U-turn in 1983. Whatever promise of a special relationship with organized labor that the Socialists hoped to cultivate in the 1970s evaporated along with the Union of the Left.

Italian Socialists (PSI)

Whereas the French Socialists wagered on a left-leaning alliance with the Communists in the 1970s, the Italian Socialists decisively rejected such a path. Instead, they opted for a strategy that would retain the party's independence while allowing for ad hoc alliances with center and center-right partners, especially the Christian Democrats. This turn is somewhat puzzling given the Italian Socialists' historically stronger ties with the Communists. Following the onset of the Cold War, the PSI and Partito Comunista Italiano (PCI) continued to cooperate for at least a decade, whereas the SFIO and PCF quickly went into opposing camps beginning in 1947. During the 1960s, the PSI decided to part company with the PCI and entered a government led by the Democrazia Cristiana (DC) in 1963. This move constituted the beginning of a critical juncture for the PSI in that it put the party on a new trajectory that was to have lasting consequences. This "opening to the Left" experience proved frustrating for the Socialists, however, and by the early 1970s, the party had left the government and was openly courting the PCI (Morel 1996, 266–70). Communist leader Berlinguer in 1972 rebuffed this overture, however, and announced the pursuit of his party's own alliance with the Christian Democrats. Thus, the 1968–1976 period—a period of great social unrest and political polarization—witnessed a curious stasis in the party system: Communists rebuffed Socialist efforts at an alliance, while Christian Democrats rejected similar attempts by the Communists (Galli 2004, 147–61).

The selection of Bettino Craxi as chief of the PSI in 1976 definitively changed this dynamic, for Craxi quickly made known his antipathy toward Berlinguer personally and the Communists collectively. The ambitious

Craxi—carefully studying his European Socialist counterparts, especially in France—sought to elevate his party over the historically dominant Communists, just as Mitterrand had done with the PS in France (Pasquino 1981, 143–51). Three factors, however, discouraged Craxi from attempting a Union of the Left style of strategy. The first was historical experience: the long period of alliance with the Communists in the late 1940s and 1950s had proven harmful to the PSI. The party's vote share dropped as the public increasingly perceived the Socialists as the subservient partner. Second, Italy's parliamentary system, coupled with a strict proportional representation system, closed off a Mitterrand (or de Gaulle) style of construction of a "presidential majority," that is, a broad-ranging, multiparty coalition behind a single left candidate. Thus, the electoral system did not permit Craxi or any other leader to pursue a role analogous to Mitterrand's as "the sole candidate of the Left." Finally, even assuming that Craxi had such a possibility, he faced an intractable obstacle: Enrico Berlinguer. Not only did Berlinguer evidence a personal antipathy toward Craxi that prevented him from deferring to the Socialist leader, but Berlinguer, unlike Marchais, had a following that extended well beyond the circle of convinced Communists. If any one person could pretend to embody and represent the Left, it was Berlinguer, not Craxi.

Even though the Socialist leader rejected an alliance with the PCI, he did not necessarily embrace the Christian Democrats. Rather, his goal was to maximize the PSI's maneuvering room and strategic indispensability during the crisis period of the late 1970s. This meant, above all, seeking to torpedo the PCI's Historic Compromise attempt. Thus, Craxi never missed a chance to engage in invidious comparison by denouncing the PCI's fealty to Moscow and its "antidemocratic" character. Even though he was unable to prevent several DC *monocolore* (single-party) governments from accepting PCI support between 1976 and 1979, he was eventually able to strike an agreement in March 1980 with the DC allowing the PSI back into the government (Hine 1979). This agreement resulted, above all, from the electoral decline and programmatic shift of the Communists in 1979 and early 1980. No longer could the DC rely on PCI support and hope to exercise power strictly on its own.

From that moment until the party's demise in 1994, the PSI participated in every government (with just one eleven-day exception in April 1987). Although the PSI was allied in government with the DC during this entire period, under Craxi's leadership the party was a prickly partner. Craxi's Machiavellian maneuverings were always aimed at increasing the PSI's power and leverage, not only at the expense of declared rivals such as the PCI but also putative partners such as the DC. Thus, during most of the 1980s, when both the PCI and the DC were losing popularity, the PSI successfully played the role of the DC's indispensable partner in the governing coalition. Craxi was even able to leverage the PSI's strategic position into his being named prime minister, a position he filled for nearly four years between 1983 and 1987.

Thus, Craxi took an approach to political alliances that was quite different from that of Mitterrand. Not only did Craxi reject any possible rapprochement with the Communists, despite strong voices in his own party who advocated a French-style Union of the Left, but he also rejected, at least in principle, a long-term alliance with any party. Thus, compared with Mitterrand, Craxi framed the question of alliances in a much more ad hoc, opportunistic way. His grand hope was to use the PSI's modest but mathematically essential voting bloc to become a permanent party of government that, over time, would draw votes away from both the PCI and the DC. To do that, of course, the PSI needed to be *in* the government, which implied negotiating a modus vivendi with the DC. But Craxi's strategy also implied that the PSI would never be a passive, secondary partner to the DC; the Socialists had to insist on a governing role out of proportion to its electoral weight. The main flaw in this alliance strategy was that it failed to produce the electoral big bang that Craxi envisioned. Despite all of his bluster, charisma, and even governing skill as prime minister, the PSI advanced only relatively modestly under his leadership—from 9.6 percent of the vote in 1976 to the party's high point of 14.3 percent in 1987. Even before his party, including himself, were engulfed in scandal in 1993–1994, Craxi had failed to realize his goal of establishing the PSI as the dominant force on the Left.

As for social alliances, even though Socialists were prominent in Italy's largest (Confederazione Generale Italiana del Lavoro [CGIL]) and third-largest (UIL) union confederations, the party itself, like its French counterpart, never had "organic" ties with organized labor. During the first three decades of the postwar period, the Communists and Socialists maintained an informal power-sharing arrangement within the CGIL. Communists always held a majority in the top bodies of the union, but Socialists were allotted strong minority representation (Lange, Ross, and Vannicelli 1981, 100–107). This friendly arrangement between the PSI and the CGIL ended when Craxi became the party's chief. Forever seeking to undermine the PCI wherever possible, Craxi opposed the CGIL, especially when he became prime minister in 1983. Most notably, he directly opposed the union on the issue of wage indexation in 1984 by pushing through a dramatic reduction in the *scala mobile*, one of the CGIL's sacred cows (Golden 1988b, 84–86).

From a long-term perspective, the PSI under Craxi in the 1980s was a far different organization than it had been in the heyday of Pietro Nenni in the 1950s. In Nenni's day, the PSI aspired to be a left-identifying, mass party with a strong base in the working class. Without great exaggeration, one could say that Nenni wanted the PSI to be a PCI without the Moscow connection and democratic centralism. In contrast, for Craxi the path to power entailed moving toward the center, engaging in temporary alliances where possible but remaining forever vigilant in protecting the party's autonomy, and demonstrating "toughness" against the mass organizations of the Left. This was the Socialist leader's vision of a "modern" version of Socialism, something that bore little relationship to the PSI's historic roots.

Spanish Socialists (PSOE)

The Spanish case presents a third variant on Socialist alliance strategies. For the five decades preceding 1970, the Socialists had maintained temporary alliances with the center-left (Left Republicans) as well as with the Communists. During the short-lived Second Republic (1931–1936), the PSOE cooperated both at the electoral and governmental levels with these parties, although the word "cooperation" is perhaps stretching the meaning of the term. Since the PSOE itself was bitterly divided between revolutionaries and reformists, the Socialists hardly made for a consistent partner. The Civil War and its aftermath demolished whatever goodwill existed between Socialists and Communists, so the long Franco dictatorship featured virtually no contact between the two parties. This began to change with the growth of opposition to the dictatorship by workers and students in the late 1960s. Between 1968 and 1974, Socialist activists operating clandestinely within Spain (as opposed to the party's leadership, who remained in exile) joined Communists in fighting the Franco regime. With their leadership of the only workers' defense organization, the Comisiones Obreras (CCOO), the Communists were clearly the stronger force, so Socialists were obliged to play a secondary role (Preston 1986a, 362–66).

Two main factors altered this tendency between 1974 and 1976. The first was the generational leadership shift in the PSOE. With the victory of Felipe González and his group of young *interiores*—young, educated activists operating within Spain—over the older generation of leaders living in exile, the PSOE took on new energy and assertiveness. Having thirty-year-olds as party leaders not only gave the PSOE a youthful public face but also meant that the Socialists no longer carried, at least visibly, the historical baggage of a party that had performed quite unsuccessfully during the 1930s and that still carried grudges and resentments from that period. This image of a new start by the Socialists proved enormously attractive to a broad spectrum of the population.

The second factor was the democratic transition launched by King Juan Carlos and Adolfo Suárez in 1975–1976. Reaching out to all the major political actors to build a consensus behind democratic reforms, the king and Suárez, in effect, placed the Socialists on an equal footing with the much larger Partido Comunista de España (PCE). Indeed, the PSOE was legalized some months before the PCE. The result of the events of 1974–1976 was to shift the momentum and initiative on the Left in the Socialists' favor, at the expense of the Communists (Preston 1986b, 103–21; Pérez-Díaz 1987, 175–82). The Socialists no longer had to settle for a secondary role. In their rise during this period, González and his team felt a decreasing need to collaborate with the Communists. They were doing just fine on their own.

The PSOE definitively affirmed its ascendancy in the constituent assembly elections of 1977, the first open vote in over forty years. Such was the PSOE's advantage over the PCE—nearly 30 percent of the vote versus the Communists' 10 percent—that the question for any Socialists contemplating an alliance with the PCE was, Why bother? Political alliances are, by definition, agreements struck out of some perception of utility if not necessity. After the 1977 elections, the Socialists felt no such benefit or need to cooperate with the Communists, at least at the parliamentary level. González made his party's strategy explicit in a February 1978 interview: "The PSOE aspires to obtain an absolute majority, and we are building our strategy on that basis" (quoted in Theuret 1996, 317). In any case, Spain's electoral rules, based on proportional representation, did not provide the kind of second-round, runoff opportunity that had encouraged Socialist–Communist cooperation in France. Such cooperation might be feasible or desirable in a postelection situation in which Socialists might need PCE votes in order to form a majority government, but this situation never arose in either of the next two elections. In 1979, all of the main parties roughly maintained their previous vote support levels, with the Unión de Centro Democrático under Suárez still commanding enough seats to form a government. Pooling their parliamentary support postelection, the PSOE and PCE made up only two-fifths of the seats—far short of a governing majority. In 1982, the Socialists' huge wave gave them an absolute majority of legislative seats, thus rendering a possible postelection alliance with the PCE unnecessary. To make matters worse for the Communists, their poor showing reduced them to virtual insignificance.

Once established in the late 1970s, the Socialists' largely go-it-alone political alliance strategy largely held through the next three decades. There have been just three notable exceptions to this pattern. The first concerns the subnational level, where, in local and regional elections and governments, the PSOE has cooperated on an ad hoc basis with Communists and regionalist parties. These arrangements have little to do with issues of general party strategy and broad policy positions and everything to do with securing a toehold on power in diverse local and regional contexts. Second, after 1989, the Socialists never regained an absolute majority of Cortes seats and thus had to rely on partners to cobble together working majorities. This was the case in 1993 and again in 2004 and 2008. In all cases, the partners were regionalist parties, notably from Catalonia and the Basque Country—not the Communists. Finally, the Socialists engaged in only one attempt, in the 2000 elections, to form an electoral agreement with the Communists (Izquierda

Unida [IU]), but the agreement was hastily composed and badly executed. In that election, both the PSOE and the IU saw their vote totals decline sharply. Such an agreement was not attempted again in 2004 or 2008.

In terms of social alliances, the PSOE's strategy contrasts with that of their French and Italian counterparts. Historically, unlike the latter two cases, Spanish Socialists maintained a formal relationship with the major union confederation, the UGT; indeed, the PSOE founded the union in 1888. During the Second Republic, the UGT was, in fact, the dominant component within the PSOE. Largo Caballero, as head of the UGT, led the largest mass organization in Spain, and this also gave him immense power within the PSOE itself. While the PSOE–UGT relationship lay dormant during the Franco years, it was revived with the PSOE's resurgence under González. Felipe, in fact, partly owed his victory over the exiled leader, Rodolfo Llopis, to support from the UGT leader in Bilbao, Nicolás Redondo. During the PSOE's drive for an electoral majority between 1977 and 1982, both the Socialist Party and the UGT participated together in the consensus-building politics of the period. Following the Socialists' victory in 1982, the UGT strongly supported the González government's economic policies, including the industrial reconversion program that resulted in tens of thousands of layoffs. Thus, unlike the PS and PSI, the PSOE had a long history of close relations with a major union confederation.

That historical tradition was definitively broken, however, in the mid-1980s as the fraternal ties between the PSOE and UGT dissolved in acrimony. Each organization had its rationale for ending their previously close relationship. On the one hand, the PSOE government was determined to reduce inflation, and this meant reducing wage pressures and budget deficits. These policies put the UGT on the defensive, especially in relation to its main union competitor, the CCOO, which from the outset took an antagonistic stance toward the Socialists' economic modernization policies (Maravall 2008, 73). From the viewpoint of organizational maintenance, the UGT by the mid-1980s had no further incentive to support the government's economic strategy, so it formed a working partnership with the CCOO focused on defending workers' economic interests. On the other hand, the Socialists, with a clear governmental majority and a determination to prepare the Spanish economy for full partnership in the European Union and the European Monetary Union, acted with little concern for the UGT's organizational dilemma and took no actions to salvage the relationship.

Once the two organizations severed their ties, they demonstrated no willingness to restore them. Since the general strike of December 1988, successive PSOE governments have worked out a new arm's-length relationship with the two major confederations. With the UGT and CCOO having maintained a close partnership on major economic questions for over two decades, PSOE and PP governments alike have engaged in peak-level bargaining rounds on such issues as labor flexibility, work time, and worker retraining (Hamann and Martínez Lucio 2003, 66–69). But the "special relationship" between the PSOE and the UGT is a thing of the past.

In summary, among Socialist parties in our three countries, one finds some distinct differences yet some intriguing similarities in alliance strategies since the 1960s. The main contrasts lie in political alliances, whereas social alliances have generally converged. With regard to the former, during the 1970s the three parties chose different routes. French Socialists opted to cooperate with the Communists, whereas Italian Socialists rejected such an alliance in favor of a series of ad hoc, opportunistic agreements with the DC and other inner-system parties. Spanish Socialists, emerging from the Franco period under new, young leadership, rejected national-level alliances altogether, instead striving to become a majority party on their own—a goal that proved attainable in 1982.

Whereas the Socialists' political alliance patterns diverged, their social alliance strategies eventually converged in that all three parties distanced themselves from the main elements of the labor movement. In the French case, the driving factor was the failure of the PS to develop tight, enduring relationships with any of the three main confederations: the Confédération Générale du Travail (CGT), CFDT, and Force Ouvrière. Although the PS sought to cultivate a favored relationship with the CFDT, that aspiration became a casualty, albeit an indirect one, of the collapse of the Union of the Left. The CFDT's leadership under Edmond Maire drew the conclusion that his organization had bet too heavily on a Left victory to the neglect of workplace and labor market issues. In "recentering" its action on these issues, the union implicitly drew away from the Socialist Party. In the Italian and Spanish cases, the distancing came as much or more from the parties' side. Craxi, in fact, wore his toughness toward the major unions as a badge of honor, while the González government eventually decided that its longstanding fraternal ties to the UGT served no useful political or policy purpose.

COMMUNIST ALLIANCES

As in the case of the Socialists, Communist parties in the 1970s embarked on new alliance strategies that had long-lasting effects on their parties' fortunes. In all cases, the effects were negative. In terms of political alliances, the Communists' strategies tended to mirror those of their Socialist counterparts. In France, the PCF, responding to the Socialists' overtures, pursued the Union of the Left alliance. As we have seen, however, the party abandoned the Union when it threatened to permanently harm the party's long-term interests. By contrast, Spanish Communists, given the Socialists' refusal to ally with them, eventually sought to rally other smaller left parties to their side in the United Left (IU) coalition; however, the IU only temporarily stanched the hemorrhaging of voter support. Certainly the most audacious strategy was that of the Italian Communists, whose Historic Compromise proposal represented a fulfillment of Togliatti's dream of a progressive bloc encompassing Communists and Catholics. Without abandoning its Marxist-Leninist ideological roots, the PCI behind Berlinguer attempted the unexpected and, as it turned out, the impossible: a reconciliation with a Christian-based party that maintained strong ties to the United States and the Western Alliance.

As for social alliances, all three Communist parties in the early 1970s dominated the largest labor confederations: the CGT in France, CGIL in Italy, and CCOO in Spain. This domination dwindled in the 1980s, however, along with the organizational decline of the Communists. By the early 1990s, all three confederations acted independently not only of Communist (or post-Communist) parties but also of all political parties. A combination of factors drove this separation between erstwhile Communist unions and their sponsoring parties. These included the Communists' organizational crises, an economic policy turn (abetted by Socialist-led governments as well as governments led by other parties), and the unions' own difficulties in attracting members and sustaining previous levels of worker activism.

French Communists (PCF)

Of the three Communist parties, the French party underwent more shifts in alliance strategy than their Italian and Spanish counterparts. For most of the post–World War II period prior to 1970, the PCF opposed the idea of a permanent alliance with any other party. After the Cold War drove a wedge between Socialists and Communists, the PCF, in fact, was openly hostile to its most likely ally, the SFIO. During the Fourth Republic, the PCF found a niche as a protest party and was able to sustain a strong membership base and social presence by systematically opposing various unstable parliamentary governments (Adereth 1984; Bell and Criddle 1994a).

This role was threatened by the consolidation of the Fifth Republic. On the one hand, the party's vote declined markedly in the first years of the new republic, as voters deserted the party for the Gaullist party, the "new left" Parti Socialiste Unifié, and other parties. From an average of nearly 27 percent in five elections between 1945 and 1956, the PCF averaged just 21 percent in four elections from 1958 to 1968. On the other hand, the new constitution included two innovations—namely, a strong presidency and a new electoral system based on single-member districts with a runoff provision—that changed the calculus for all parties, including the PCF. In all, electoral decline, coupled with institutional changes, provided the PCF with strong incentives to soften its resistance to political alliances. As early as

1962, the party began cooperating with Socialists in second-round legislative elections, and in 1965 it backed Mitterrand in the presidential runoff against de Gaulle.

Mitterrand's selection as head of a reorganized Socialist Party in 1971 set the stage for the next step in the Communists' alliance with the Socialists: the Union of the Left based on a "common program" for governing. In the context of the early 1970s, this strategy appeared to make sense. First, Mitterrand made all the correct, welcoming sounds, and he assented to most of the Communists' positions on such issues as nationalization of large firms and banks and new rights for workers. Moreover, he was backed by the CERES faction within his party, which was "unconditionally favourable towards whatever proposals the PCF put forward to advance the popular front" (Johnson 1981, 65). Third, the international climate of détente supported by the Soviet Union encouraged the PCF toward moderation and cooperation with other forces on the Left. Finally, the Union of the Left represented a plausible vehicle for redeeming the PCF's tarnished image in the wake of the May–June "events" of 1968, when the Communist leadership was roundly accused by others on the left (as well as many of their own members) of betraying the protests by workers and students (Touraine 1971).

Ultimately, the PCF's Union of the Left strategy, far from helping the party advance, decisively undermined it, resulting in a systematic movement of voters and parliamentary seats away from the Communists in favor of the Socialists. In breaking the alliance in 1977, the party reasserted its self-assigned vanguard role as the only party capable of leading the Left. Marchais and his inner circle reasoned that it was better to end the alliance, even if that led to the Left's defeat in the 1978 elections, than for the Union to triumph but with the PCF in a subordinate position. This abrupt shift in strategy produced maximum confusion within the party's ranks and triggered an internal *mise en cause* of Marchais's leadership (Jenson and Ross 1984, 309–26; Hazareesingh 1991, 161–67).

Over the next three years, Mitterrand remained at least rhetorically loyal to the Union of the Left, whereas the PCF denounced the Socialist leader and his party at every turn. In the 1981 elections, the Communists found themselves with the worst of all worlds. Far from having stopped or even slowed Mitterrand's momentum, the PCF achieved its lowest electoral score since 1936. When Mitterrand shrewdly offered the Communists four ministerial posts in the first Socialist government, the party was obliged to execute another about-face and ally with its former nemesis under humiliating conditions (Favier and Martin-Roland 1990, 83–89; Friend 1998, 27–28).

In the three decades following this *fausse alliance* with the Socialists, the PCF underwent another cycle of avoidance and approach. When the party left the Fabius government in July 1984 in protest over its economic policies, it embarked on a long period of hostility toward the Socialists that lasted until Marchais's retirement in 1994. With Marchais's successor, Robert Hue, bent on modernizing the party's image, the PCF gradually effected a rapprochement with the Socialists, joining Jospin's plural Left government from 1997 to 2002. By this time, the Communists could consider themselves fortunate to have such an option, given their continued electoral decline. But there was also irony in the Communists' circumstances. Even though the PCF was now drawing less than 10 percent of the vote, its contribution was essential to the Socialists' efforts to form a majority coalition. Thus, the party actually exercised more influence than it had twenty years earlier when, with a much larger vote share, the party was a largely superfluous appendage to the Socialist-dominated government.

In terms of social alliances, the PCF was long the dominant force in the largest union confederation, the CGT. From the time that it gained top leadership positions in the CGT during the early postwar period, the PCF largely set the parameters for the CGT's strategy. The CGT was never simply an extension of the PCF in the workplace, however. There were, to be sure, periods in which the PCF directed the CGT to support the party's political goals; for example, during the early Cold War period, the CGT became, in effect, the PCF's "political claque" by seeking to foment strikes that challenged the right-learning governments (Ross 1982, 85). But there were other periods in which the CGT exercised at least partial independence from direct party control and focused on labor market issues. The best example of this strategy was the "unity of action" period between 1966 and 1977, when the CGT cooperated closely with the CFDT not only at the peak national level but also within workplaces (Smith 1981, 1984). In both types of circumstances—"transmission belt" or "relative autonomy"—the party and the union maintained a close relationship based on overlapping executives and the massive presence of PCF *militants* among the CGT's rank and file.

As the PCF became beset by internal conflict and electoral decline in the mid-1980s, however, these close ties became frayed. For one thing, the same kinds of conflicts between the orthodox Marchais leadership and the various groups of *renovateurs* also beset the CGT, leading many union leaders to question the PCF's control over the confederation. Moreover, the PCF's sharp decline in members, material resources, and overall political clout, especially after the PCF left the Fabius government in 1984, limited the party's ability to manage not only its own affairs but also those of the CGT. Finally, the CGT had its own organizational challenges, as its membership and resources plummeted throughout the 1980s and 1990s. Thus, the confederation had dwindling incentive in being associated with much less controlled by an unpopular and failing party. Rather than having a single dramatic break, the two organizations gradually drifted apart, each preoccupied by its own difficulties (Andolfatto and Labbé 2006, 329–36).

Italian Communists (PCI)

The centerpiece of the Italian Communists' political alliance during the past forty years was the so-called Historic Compromise pursued by Berlinguer in the 1970s. The prospect of the largest Communist party in Western Europe collaborating in a government of national reconciliation with Christian Democrats struck many observers as unusual if not unnatural. In fact, the Historic Compromise strategy was in the broad ideological line laid down by Togliatti in his famous "*svolta di Salerno*" in 1944. Rejecting the revolutionary option and supporting Italy's new republican constitution, Togliatti built the PCI into a "*partito nuovo*," a new type of Communist party based on mass membership (as opposed to the Leninist model of an elite party of professional revolutionaries). Contesting elections and building up a mass presence in Italian society, not making revolution, were to be the PCI's main tasks (Hellman 1996, 73–75). Although DC prime minister De Gasperi shut the door on further cooperation with the PCI by ousting it (as well as the Socialist Party) from government in 1947, Togliatti continued to support Italy's parliamentary system, even as he also remained steadfast in his loyalty to the Soviet Union (Agosti 1996, 1999). With no possibility of cooperation with the DC in the early postwar period, the Communists maintained their wartime alliance with the Socialists under Nenni. But this alliance eventually dissolved in the late 1950s and early 1960s as Nenni grew disillusioned with the Soviet Union, especially after the Hungarian invasion in 1956 and indeed the Communist project in general. The end result was the PSI's joining the DC-led opening to the left in 1963 (Hine 1990, 75).

On becoming party chief in 1972, Berlinguer decided that the PCI's status quo needed to change; specifically, the party needed to break out of its political ghetto. Several factors drove Berlinguer to push for a cogoverning arrangement with the party's longtime nemesis, the Christian Democrats. The first was the party's reassessment of the DC. The PCI publicly recognized that the DC was not only a genuinely popular party, with strong roots in a largely Catholic culture, but also a diverse party with several factions, including a reform wing with which the PCI could collaborate. For the Historic Compromise to take place, this wing needed to gain the balance of power within the DC. Thus, the Compromise, in Berlinguer's view, was conditional on change within the DC itself (Urban 1986, 269). A second factor favoring a Historic Compromise was the PCI's surge in the early and mid-1970s. The party could make a credible claim that to exclude the PCI permanently from government was to disenfranchise nearly one-third of the Italian electorate. In a period wracked by the political and social crises of the late 1960s and early 1970s, such disenfranchisement only deepened the political system's legitimacy problems.

But why a collaboration with the DC and not the Socialists? Here was a third rationale for the Historic Compromise: what Berlinguer framed as the "51 percent problem." It was plausible to imagine that the PCI and PSI together could together total a bare majority, but such a government would not rest on a sufficient consensus to push through durable reforms. In the aftermath of the 1973 Chile coup, Berlinguer feared that a PCI–PSI alliance would push the DC into the arms of the extreme right and bring on a reactionary regime. The most logical resolution to Italy's crisis was a grand coalition of national unity formed by the two historic blocs, Catholics and Communists (Smith 1997, 459). The Socialists might join the coalition as well, Berlinguer argued, but only as a junior partner.

Following the PCI's strong showing in local and regional elections in 1975—in which the party gained control of six of Italy's twenty regions and most of the major cities from Naples northward—and in parliamentary elections in 1976, the PCI was in the strongest possible position to press for entry into a DC-led government (Kogan 1983, 289–90). Even though strong counterpressures came from several DC factions, the U.S. government, and even currents within the PCI itself, Berlinguer was finally able to strike an agreement with the DC in July 1977 to form a government of "national solidarity." The PCI took a decidedly secondary role, however, agreeing to support the government but without holding any ministerial positions. This was in no sense the historic compromise that Berlinguer envisioned, and party leaders explicitly recognized this, in large part because no leftward shift had taken place in the DC. Rather, this collaboration was conceived as an "interim stage" between the status quo and a true Historic Compromise (Urban 1986, 269–70).

Although PCI leaders viewed this move as a first step toward the PCI's eventual integration into the inner party system, the DC's flexibility and willingness to strike a partnership with the Communists ended with this arrangement. Thus, the PCI, lacking an official presence in the government yet universally viewed as part of the prime minister's team, exercised little real influence while being associated with the government's failings. Notable among these was the mishandling of the Moro affair, in which the PCI strongly backed Andreotti's hard line toward the Red Brigades, a stance that ultimately contributed to Moro's assassination in March 1978. Finally realizing that it had the worst of all worlds—policy impotence coupled with partial responsibility for policy failure—the PCI withdrew its support from the government in January 1979, thus ending a frustrating and politically costly eighteen-month collaboration with the Christian Democrats (Amyot 1981; Flores and Gallerano 1992).

The end of the limited experiment in PCI–DC cooperation effectively cut the Communists off from further prospects of forming a political alliance, at least at the national level. Even as the PCI was hardening its stance toward the Christian Democrats, Craxi was doing his utmost to marginalize the Communists (Spini 2006, 36–47). Reinforcing the PCI's isolation was its waning electoral support throughout the 1980s. Only the dramatic events of 1991–1994 altered this dynamic. A combination of changes—notably, the PCI's transformation into the Partito Democratico della Sinistra (PDS), the collapse of both the Socialists and the Christian Democrats, and the adoption of a new voting system—completely recast the party system in terms of principal actors and incentives. Once most of the PCI's erstwhile left wing deserted the PDS to form Rifondazione Comunista in 1991, the PDS was left with little more than a vague Social Democratic program that was largely indistinguishable from those of other center-left social democratic parties throughout Western Europe.

Such doctrinal vagueness was not without its strengths, however, as it fostered a catchall image for the PDS that helped attract former supporters of the PSI, the DC, and other, smaller parties who were suddenly available for recruitment (Rhodes 1996, 125–28). The new electoral system, which had elements of both proportional representation and single-member district voting, gave parties the incentive to form large multiparty electoral coalitions. Thus was formed the Olive Tree coalition in 1995, with the PDS as its largest component. To summarize an extremely complex process, although the Communist Party spent its final dozen years cut off from party alliance possibilities, the advent of the Second Republic served to integrate the PCI's post-Communist remnant fully into the system. In that sense, whatever its imperfections, the Second Republic ended one of the First Republic's most glaring weaknesses: the de facto permanent exclusion of over one-quarter of the Italian electorate from a voice in national government.

As for social alliances, the PCI's experience, in broad outline, paralleled that of its French counterpart in that the decline—and, in the Italian case, the transformation—of the Communist Party resulted in a loosening of historic ties between the party and its labor movement affiliate, in this case the CGIL. Although this outcome has been roughly the same in both cases, the dynamics of this shift toward an autonomous, arm's-length relationship between party and union have differed because of two factors: the history of postwar union–party ties and the contrasting trajectories of the two Communist parties.

First, PCI–CGIL ties never corresponded to the classic Leninist "transmission belt" model. Unlike the CGT, which was essentially taken over by the French Communist Party in the early postwar period, the CGIL was founded in 1944 as a shared project of the three main Resistance and Liberation elements—the Communists, Socialists, and Christian Democrats. Cold War divisions soon fractured the CGIL, with DC loyalists and dissident Socialists (who formed the Social Democratic Party) exiting by 1950 to form competing federations, the CISL and UIL, respectively. Despite this split,

Communists and Socialists continued to cooperate in leading the CGIL throughout the 1950s and 1960s. This fact alone, despite the PCI's far greater organizational strength compared with the PSI, meant that the PCI was never in a position simply to impose strategy on the union.

The CGIL's autonomy in relation to the PCI increased greatly during the late 1960s because of tensions in Italy's rapid growth that produced a surge in worker protest. Responding to grassroots pressures from industrial workers for union unity—especially among the metalworkers sector during the Hot Autumn strike wave of 1969—the CGIL and the two other major unions cooperated extensively throughout the 1970s and into the 1980s, even to the point of forming formal peak organizations to coordinate their actions; for example, in the early 1970s, the three unions established a "federation of confederations"—the Federation CGIL-CISL-UIL—as well as formal coordinating bodies in various industrial sectors, notably in the metallurgy industry (Golden 1988b, 20–21, 90–91; Locke 1995, 71–72). Along with growing union unity came the assertion of labor's voice as a political actor in its own right. Although the unions continued to focus on labor market issues such as wages and labor rights, they went beyond bread-and-butter questions to propose structural reforms in such areas as economic planning, full-employment policy, public housing, and tax reform (Lange et al. 1982, 131–80). Compared with the French CGT, whose strategy remained closely tied to the political goals of the PCF throughout the 1970s, the CGIL was able to carve out considerably more autonomy relative to the PCI.

A second major contrast with the French case is how the Communist parties and their "affiliated" unions have fared during the past two decades. As we saw above, in France the PCF–CGT tie dissolved out of the growing weakness of both the party and the union. For reasons related both to diminishing resources and to organizational survival, both the PCF and the CGT were unwilling and/or unable to maintain their historical relationship. In Italy, however, the Communist Party did not fade away as in France but rather cast off its Marxist heritage and transformed itself, ideologically at least, into a center-left "Social Democratic" party. Even though the post-Communist PDS of the 1990s did not compare with the 1970s PCI in terms of organizational resources, it still remained a potent organization, far more so than the PCF.

Thus, the PDS's incentive to loosen the ties with the CGIL derived less from organizational weakness than from the need for ideological consistency. With no pretense of being a party of protest or a "movement" party, the PDS sought equal, independent relations with all three of the major unions. As for the CGIL, we have just noted its considerable autonomy even prior to the PCI's transformation in the late 1980s and early 1990s. By 1994, with the Socialist Party having collapsed and the PCI having morphed into the PDS, CGIL leaders decided that it could no longer maintain a direct organizational link to any political party. (The same process was occurring simultaneously with the second-largest confederation, the CISL, which had historic ties with the DC party.)

Spanish Communists (PCE)

Political isolation marked the Spanish Communist Party for most of its first fifty years. From its formation in 1921 until the last decade of the Franco regime, the PCE knew only a brief period during the Popular Front (1934–1938) in which it actively cooperated with other parties, notably the Socialists. But even this short period was fraught with tension and mutual suspicion and ended in acrimony. The PCE and the PSOE had very little direct contact during most of the Franco era from 1939 to 1975; in any case, it is difficult to conceive of a working alliance when the leadership of both parties was living in exile and largely powerless to affect events back home.

This isolation began to end in the late 1960s when the PCE took the lead in opposing the Franco regime and in the process built both political and social alliances. By far, the most important alliance was with the labor movement. Working effectively at the grassroots through existing industrial relations institutions established by Franco, the PCE furnished many of the activists who led the CCOO, an organization that became one of the two main union confederations after 1975. As for political alliances, the PCE was less successful, although it spearheaded the formation, in June 1974, of the Junta Democrática, a coalition of smaller parties and influential intellectuals that became one of the main opposition groups to Franco prior to his death (Maravall and Santamaría 1986, 79–80).

PCE leader Santiago Carrillo strongly backed the democratic transition, and his party's participation in negotiations that ushered in a new democratic regime definitively ended the Communists' long exclusion from Spanish political life. But he was unsuccessful in establishing a working partnership with the Socialists. Much of the reason for this failure, as we have seen, rested with the Socialists. On the one hand, the PSOE's electoral dominance made an alliance unnecessary. The PCE's low voting score starting in 1977 never put it in a position to impose itself on the Socialists, as, for example, Craxi's Socialists had been able to do in relation to the Christian Democrats in Italy. On the other hand, the Socialists' rebuff stemmed from more than sheer electoral calculation. Given past experience, there was also ideological resistance within the party to an alliance with PCE. Although González himself, born several years after the end of the Civil War, was no visceral anti-Communist, many older Socialists still distrusted the Communists. In this respect, Carrillo, a PCE leader since the late 1930s, was certainly not the best public face for a party seeking to create a democratic image (Castro 2008, 75–76).

In the wake of the PCE's dismal performance in the 1982 election, the question for the Communists was not whether they would find allies but whether they would survive. The party sought to adapt to its post-Franco decline by forging the United Left (IU) coalition in 1986. The new party leader, Julio Anguita, managed to enlist several smaller parties and formations to join the coalition, which, in effect, filled a small but growing niche in the Spanish political space from the late 1980s to the mid-1990s, namely, that of a protest party to the left of the governing Socialists.

In a role somewhat analogous to that of the French Communist Party after it departed the Socialist-led government in 1984, the PCE sought to rally leftist voters who had become disillusioned with the Socialists' moderate economic policies. To do so, the party adopted an overtly Marxist, class warfare stance at odds with the moderate positions earlier preached by Carrillo (Taibo 1996). The party also added environmental and other "postmaterialist" themes to its program (Torcal and Montero 1997, 16–22). This strategy worked fairly well as long as the Socialists remained in power; in fact, the PSOE government in the early 1990s positively albeit inadvertently aided the PCE by becoming embroiled in scandals and factional fights such that by 1996 the PCE/IU had more than doubled its vote in the preceding decade.

That year proved to be the high point, however. With the PSOE cast back into the opposition in elections that year, the PCE/IU could no longer position itself as the progressive alternative to the Socialists, and its popularity waned. In the 2000 elections, the PCE/IU even forged a mutual support agreement with the Socialists, but the hastily constructed alliance worked poorly for both the Communists and the Socialists. Thereafter, the IU struggled to maintain a semblance of unity and electoral viability. Ironically, given the PCE's history of failing to maintain political alliances, the only bright spot for the IU has been its success in entering several regional governments as a minority partner.

As for the PCE's social alliances, the centerpiece was its close relationship with the CCOO, a unique hybrid within Western European labor movements. Whereas virtually all such movements, including the other main Spanish confederation, the UGT, trace their origins to a process of legal incorporation in the late nineteenth or early twentieth century, the CCOO was formed in the 1960s under the nose, as it were, of the Franco dictatorship. Initially a grassroots outgrowth of the official industrial relations system, the CCOO eventually became a national organization that was semilegal but tolerated by the Franco government. By the late 1960s, the CCOO had become, de facto, the main mass organization opposing the regime by virtue of its workplace militancy. From the beginning, Communist activists comprised the union's leadership, although the CCOO was officially nonpartisan and had leaders of other political persuasions as well. During the transition period (1975–1978), the PCE and CCOO worked closely together to support the democratization process (Fishman 1990, 178–80, 183–86).

The crisis in the PCE in the early to mid-1980s ultimately changed the relationship between the two organizations, resulting in the same dynamic of party–union separation that occurred in France and Italy. Not only did the PCE's loss of voters, activists, and resources make it increasingly difficult to control the CCOO, but two further developments reinforced this process, especially after 1985. One was the growing disaffection between the PSOE government and its own affiliated union, the UGT, which gradually came to openly oppose the government's economic policies. The UGT's move naturally moved it much closer to the CCOO's position, which had mobilized against the government's austerity and industrial reconversion programs from the outset. The great success of the December 1988 general strike, jointly led by the UGT and CCOO, solidified their commitment to joint action. Union unity made the labor movement a more formidable actor and led to a new round of concertation and peak-level bargaining between the government and the unions in the 1990s. In all, this dynamic focused the CCOO increasingly on labor market issues, not the organizational concerns of the PCE. Contributing to this process was a second factor: leadership conflicts. Specifically, after 1986, PCE/IU leader Anguita, seeking to consolidate his own power, tried to reassert the party's control over the union; however, CCOO head Gutiérrez fiercely resisted this move. In 1996, the CCOO officially cut all ties to the Communist Party.

The preceding overview indicates that by the end of the first decade of the twenty-first century, there was little left of historic Communism in France, Italy, and Spain. There are many reasons for this decline, but certainly a main one was the failure of these parties to build lasting alliances with other parties and movements. In terms of political alliances, whether the Communists tried a coalition with Socialists (as in France), with other non-Socialist parties of the Left (as in Spain), or with a dominant Catholic party (as in Italy), the results were in all cases disappointing, even disastrous. The reasons for these failures were specific to each case, but behind each one lay the indisputable fact that the Communist brand itself was a limiting factor: a diminishing resource that made the Communists either vulnerable to voter desertion (France), dispensable (Spain), or excessively cautious and deferential (Italy).

As in their political alliances, so also in their social alliances: all three Communist parties failed to maintain erstwhile close ties to an affiliated labor confederation. The party–labor divorce derived from several factors, but certainly a driving one was the Communists' growing organizational and political debility. In all three cases, the confederations drew away from the Communist Party because the latter could no longer provide a convincing rationale for maintaining the tie. Again, although the specifics differ in each case, all three confederations—the CGT, CCOO, and CGIL—found that their own organizational survival would be better served by severing their links with the Communists, asserting their own autonomy, and focusing pragmatically and, where possible, cooperatively with other unions on labor market issues rather than politics.

CONCLUSION

This chapter demonstrates that decisions about alliance strategies took place in contexts of uncertainty and flux on many levels—economic, social, and political. Moreover, Socialist and Communist leaders did not possess the freedom to craft new strategies willy-nilly. In each case, factors such as institutional arrangements and party culture shaped the range of alliance options. Despite such constraints, party leaders themselves did put their stamp on the outcome. As an exercise in counterfactual history, one might ask, What alliance strategy would the PS have followed without Mitterrand's vision of a Communist-embracing strategy designed to smother its target? Similarly, would another Spanish Socialist leader besides González have so firmly rejected—even while Franco was still alive and the Socialists and Communists were still illegal—any prospect of an entente with the PCE? Such questions could be posed about the alliance strategies of the other major party leaders of the 1970s: Craxi, Marchais, Carrillo, and Berlinguer.

Specific national conditions thus ensured that party alliance strategies would follow no uniform model. From the foregoing analysis, we can draw three main conclusions. The first is that Socialist–Communist alliances at the national level are both rare and fragile. Only in France was there a full-scale alliance, the Union of the Left, and it lasted barely five years, from 1972 to 1977. There were two subsequent episodes of cooperation between the two parties—Communist participation in the Mauroy government (1981–1984) and Jospin's "plural left" government from 1997 to 2002 that included Communists—but these periods bore little relationship to the initial Union of the Left experiment. Rather, these were uneasy governing partnerships in which a greatly weakened Communist Party, seeking to avoid political irrelevance, supported the much stronger Socialists. In Italy (after 1960) and Spain, there is virtually no record of formal cooperation between the two parties at the national level. Instead, the parties sought other alternatives, one of which was to seek alliances with other parties. In Italy, for example, both Communists and Socialists pursued governing arrangements with the Christian Democrats, whereas in Spain, the Communist Party sought to build the United Left coalition with other parties to the left of the Socialists. Another alternative was to reject alliances altogether, as in the case of the Spanish Socialists.

In all, in the broad perspective of the two parties' long coexistence since the early 1920s, what is striking is the immense difficulty, if not impossibility, of overcoming the breach opened by Lenin and the Third International nearly a century ago. Far from closing the breach, the two parties largely kept their distance from each other unless forced by crisis circumstances to cooperate. Their differences, initially rooted in ideological and strategic conflicts, quickly became institutionalized in distinct party cultures in which distrust of and even disdain for the other party was a given. Conflicting visions from within the Socialist "family" over how to achieve the end goal of a good society, in effect, turned brothers (and sisters) into enemies as those visions became transmuted into enduring organizational forms and practices that precluded permanent rapprochement.

The second main conclusion is that one of the bedrock bases of both Left parties in the past century—namely, the close identification between the party and the working class as represented by a major industrial union—has eroded away. In the early 1970s, all three Communist parties had a trade union ally, that is, a major confederation whose leadership was dominated by Communists. In all three cases, these confederations followed a general strategy that was either largely defined by the party, as in France and Spain, or at least supported by it, as in Italy. Of the three Socialist parties, the PSOE had a long-standing affiliate relationship with the UGT, the PSI had strong representation within the CGIL and many sympathizers in the UIL, and the PS had friendly relationships though no formal ties with the CFDT and the Force Ouvrière. In *every single case*, those strong links have been broken. All of the affiliated confederations have severed their formal links with the corresponding party, while the "friendly" confederations have distanced themselves from the Left parties.

The final conclusion is that alliance choices made in the 1960s and 1970s had lasting effects on the fortunes of all the parties we have examined. This conclusion connects directly to the book's main argument concerning critical junctures and thus merits some expansion. This we do in the following concluding chapter, which restates this argument and then briefly applies it to two other cases in which Socialist–Communist relations have been important in recent decades, Portugal and Greece.

NOTE

1. Quoted in Giesbert (1990, 96, author translation). For economy of presentation, I have slightly revised the "flow" of the conversation, but all sentences are in the quoted conversation.

Chapter Seven

Conclusion

Political scientists must be certain that attention to history precedes attention to theory, or we are bound to make a whole series of errors.
—Nancy Bermeo (1995, 452)

The past is never dead. It's not even past.
—William Faulkner, *Requiem for a Nun*

The chief aim of this book has been to compare and explain the relationship between Socialist and Communist parties in three Western European nations. This has meant, above all, paying attention to history. Specifically, it has meant identifying watershed historical moments—critical junctures—in which these parties made strategic decisions that had important long-term consequences both for the parties themselves and for relations between them. The concept of a critical juncture, it will be recalled from chapter 1, entails three elements: cause, response, and outcome. This book has argued that these elements can be identified for all of these parties at various moments during the 1960s and 1970s. Although we have sought to provide a full historical context going back to 1920, the focus has been on the period since the 1960s.

At stake, then, is the specification of cause, response, and outcome. Since these elements were discussed in some detail in chapter 1, they need only brief restatement here. The principal causes underlying the critical junctures were both general and case specific. At the most general level, beginning in the late 1960s, Left parties in France, Italy, and Spain—indeed, Left parties throughout Western Europe—faced new challenges stemming from fundamental economic changes; put simply, the economic growth model that had prevailed since the late 1940s began showing signs of slowdown and strain (Judt 2005, 453–83; Eichengreen 2007, 252–93). Throughout the following decade, Western economies went from crisis to crisis: Nixon's closing of the "Gold Window" in 1971, the first oil shock of 1973, the corrosive effects of stagflation, and the second oil shock of 1979. Predictably, economic disruptions produced political disruptions, so governments and parties everywhere had to wrestle not only with rising unemployment and inflation but also with the political tensions resulting from faltering economies (Bermeo 2000, 2001). Accompanying these disruptions were long-term structural and occupational shifts—including automation and diffusion and/or relocation of core manufacturing processes to new sites in the Third World—that tended to reduce the numerical importance of the Left's traditional demographic bastions within the industrial working class.

Left parties faced these general challenges within national contexts that varied in terms of governmental institutions, the strength and nature of political oppositions, the legitimacy of incumbent governments, and other aspects. Despite such differences, the Left in France, Italy, and Spain all confronted versions of "regime crisis" during the late 1960s and 1970s. In France, the Fifth Republic regime created by de Gaulle was shaken to its core by the Events of May–June 1968 and the resignation of de Gaulle himself a year later. Although the Right remained in power under de Gaulle's successors, there was widespread dissatisfaction with a political system that seemed centralized and stultified, incapable of reform. The Left's challenge was to somehow crack into a regime that had been designed to keep the Left out.

The Italian crisis was more profound, extending to an entire political and economic order. The dominant Democrazia Cristiana (DC) party had become increasingly entrenched, corrupt, and incapable of reform, even as the country was experiencing record postwar levels of inflation, unemployment, and worker militancy. One result was an alarming degree of political polarization reflected in the growth of violent acts by extremists of both ends of the political spectrum. For both Socialists and Communists, the dilemma was how to respond sympathetically to popular grievances without being tarred with the brush of irresponsibility and adventurism by the Right. Finally, in Spain the crisis stemmed from the imminent end of the Franco regime and the question of what type of government would follow the dictator's death. In all three cases, Left parties were excluded from power and on the defensive. All faced great uncertainty over the classic question: what is to be done?

Their responses were varied but fateful in the sense of decisively defining the parties' actions and fortunes for coming decades. A central argument of this book is that the parties' responses shifted their strategic and organizational trajectories in ways that proved lasting—the sine qua non of a critical juncture. The argument here accords with Katznelson's (2003) observation: "Key decisions at choice points produce outcomes that set history on a course whose mechanisms of reproduction make the initial selection unstoppable" (290). As indicated in chapter 1, Socialist and Communist parties in our three nations made such key decisions at various points during the 1960s and 1970s.

Of all the responses that Left parties made during these two decades, the choice of alliances, especially political alliances, was the most critical. In some cases, alliance strategy was innovative in the sense of breaking with past tradition. This was clearly the case for both the Parti Socialiste (PS) and the Parti Comuniste Français in France; never before 1972 had the two parties gone so far as to craft a shared platform for governing. Innovation in this sense can also be seen in Italy, albeit to a lesser degree. Although the Partito Comunista Italiano's (PCI's) proposed Historic Compromise with the DC had its roots in Togliatti's vision of a broad accommodation between Italy's Communist and Catholic subcultures, Berlinguer pursued this vision more vigorously than Togliatti ever did. Even the Socialists, by breaking with the Communists and joining the DC in government in 1963, can be considered innovative in their alliance strategy. The same can be said for the party under Craxi after 1976, although innovation came not from the party's courting of the DC but rather from its fervent anti-Communism. As we have seen, of the three Socialist parties, the Partito Socialista Italiano (PSI) was historically the most closely aligned with the Communists, and thus Craxi's strategy represented a complete departure from that tradition.

The Spanish case was the least innovative in that both parties, especially the Partido Socialista Obrero Español (PSOE) after 1977, essentially confirmed the post–Civil War pattern of mutual hostility. Once the PSOE established its dominance on the Left, it continued to reject reconciliation with the Communists. For its part, the Partido Comunista de España (PCE) eventually sought, by the mid-1980s, to build an alternative coalition with smaller parties and formations to the Socialists' left. The results for the PCE were mixed: initial electoral progress in the late 1980s and early 1990s but decline and internal division once the Socialists lost their governing majority in 1996.

How can differences in the parties' responses—notably their alliance strategies—be explained? Our case studies in chapters 2 to 4 emphasized three factors—institutional context, party culture, and leadership—that decisively shaped those strategies. While all three factors were at play in each country, their relative importance varied from case to case. This is, of course, to be expected, given significant cross-national differences in all three of these factors. For example, in France the most decisive factor was the institutional context of the Fifth Republic that featured both a new power center (the presidency) and an electoral system (two ballot with runoff). Both of these new constitutional elements tended to encourage the formation of coalitions on the Left that, in the event, greatly favored the Socialists over the Communists. In Italy, although the institutional context—a parliamentary system based on proportional representation—gave both the PCI and the PSI incentives to pursue a coalition with the dominant DC, the factors of party culture and leadership ultimately were crucial in determining the two parties' mutual antipathy and divergent paths in the 1970s.

Lastly, in Spain all three factors were of roughly equal importance. The post-Franco electoral system—proportional representation using the d'Hondt method—favored the much larger Socialists over smaller parties such as the Communists, and this advantage grew even larger in the contrast between the parties' leaders, González and Carrillo. Just as crucially, the cultures of both parties had been transformed by nearly four decades of underground survival; specifically, the PSOE and PCE had engaged in a process of social learning that made them amenable to moderation and compromise with the new regime. The impact of these factors was to put the Socialists in a position to become a majority party in their own right, without need of the Communists.

What is distinctive about the alliance strategies adopted by these parties in the 1960s and 1970s—and what enables us to specify critical junctures according to the third element of outcome—is their long-term impact. In all cases, the choice of alliances had a decisive effect on the parties' subsequent trajectory. With the benefit of hindsight, one can conclude that the French and Spanish Socialists' strategies—the former embracing an alliance with the Communists, the latter rejecting it—were easily the most successful in electoral and organizational terms. Even though Mitterrand and González held diametrically opposed views on how to deal with the Communists, history proved both leaders to have been remarkably prescient. History was not nearly so kind to the other four parties. In both France and Spain, the Communist parties enjoyed dominance on the Left in the early 1970s, but by the end of the decade both parties were dramatically diminished and effectively marginalized, in large part because of their own alliance choices. In Italy, the PCI's Historic Compromise strategy in the late 1970s ended in frustration and disappointment that hastened that party's decline during the following decade, while the PSI's alliance maneuverings under Craxi beginning in the late 1970s failed to put the Socialists in a position to challenge the Communists' supremacy on the Left. While many factors shaped the fortunes of all of these Left parties in the decades following the critical junctures I have identified, no other factor was as important in the long run as the choices these parties made about alliances.

EXTENDING THE ARGUMENT: GREECE AND PORTUGAL

The test of any explanatory scheme is how well it travels beyond the specific cases for which it was constructed. As a final step in this study, then, let us assess how well the critical juncture argument developed herein applies to two other Mediterranean cases in which Socialist and Communist parties have played important roles—Greece and Portugal. Both countries, of course, emerged from dictatorships in the 1970s and so in that sense bear a closer resemblance to the Spanish experience than to the French or Italian cases. Moreover, as in Spain, the Socialist parties in Greece and Portugal have outperformed the Communists since democratization, especially since the dissolution of the Soviet system in the late 1980s and early 1990s (see appendix A and appendix B). Finally, as in the Spanish case, the Greek and Portuguese Communist parties continue to function under their original name. Despite internal conflicts and various splits, these parties have undergone no metamorphosis to a "post-Communist" party as did the Italian Communists.

Despite these similarities with the Spanish case, the experiences of the Left in Greece and Portugal since the end of dictatorship have carried their own dynamics, and we need to assess these with the book's main argument in mind. To do so, we ask three questions. First, can one identify critical junctures for the Socialists and Communists? Second, what alliance strategies have the two parties adopted? And, finally, how well do the factors of institutional context, party culture, and leadership explain the choice of those strategies?

Greece

The experiences of military dictatorship (1967–1974) followed by a democratic transition constituted a critical juncture for Greece's Left parties and, indeed, for Greece's entire political order. In July 1974, the ruling "Colonels' regime," following their inept and disastrous handling of the Cyprus crisis, decided to return power to a civilian government after seven years of harsh repression. The subsequent return to democracy brought a refashioning of the political system. Although Greece, unlike Portugal, had much historical experience with democracy, all political organizations had to be legalized and reconstituted or even, as in the case of the non-Communist Left, created de novo. As a prime demonstration of the nation's lack of ready and able civilian leaders, the new interim president, Konstantin Karamanlis, was called on to return from an eleven-year, self-imposed exile in Paris. Nonetheless, within four months of the junta's resignation, Greece held new legislative elections featuring five major parties and/or coalitions and a voter turnout of nearly 80 percent. Although Karamanlis's New Democracy Party obtained a clear majority, a Communist-led coalition and a newly formed Socialist party led by fifty-five-year-old Andreas Papandreou managed to attract a combined total of 23 percent of the vote (Clogg 1987, 59–60).

Papandreou's party, officially named the Panhellenic Socialist Movement (PASOK), drew only 13.6 percent of the vote in the November election;

however, given that the Greek Communist Party (KKE) had historically dominated the Left and given that *no* Socialist party had ever existed in Greece before the previous July,[1] the PASOK's showing was quite respectable (Petras, Raptis, and Sarafopoulos 1993, 166–67). Papandreou himself was a compelling figure, combining a long and heroic political pedigree, intellectual brilliance, and a charismatic public presence.[2] More than any other public figure, Papandreou embodied both a break from and continuity with pre-1967 Greek politics, and thus he appealed to various political tendencies (Spourdalakis 1988, 277).

Initially adopting a staunchly Left program denouncing Greece's dependent status in relation to the United States, NATO, and the European Community while espousing extensive nationalizations and other economic reforms, PASOK under Papandreou sought to occupy a political space that was unambiguously leftist but distinct from the Communists (Achimastos 1996, 354). PASOK's program also entailed a repudiation of Karamanlis's governing center-right New Democracy Party for being too aligned with the disgraced dictatorship as well as a nationalistic stance against Turkish "aggression" in the Aegean (Clogg 1987, 76). These positions, coupled with Papandreou's personal popularity, produced a near doubling of the Socialists' electoral performance in the next elections in 1977. (PASOK's surge also owed much to New Democracy's inability to spark the economy during the post-1974 recession.) Thus, within three years of its founding, PASOK was drawing over 25 percent of the vote, thereby establishing itself as the main opposition party.

For the Socialists, the 1974–1977 period was a watershed—and therefore a critical juncture—because it put them on a trajectory to contend directly for power on their own. The two elections during this period demonstrated two things. The first was that the Communist Left had hit a ceiling of about 12 percent of the vote. To increase its own vote share, PASOK would need to capture votes toward the center; a Mitterrand-style attempt to turn Communist voters into PASOK supporters held little promise. In addition, these elections, especially the 1977 contest, showed that PASOK indeed possessed a catchall appeal, with the party's electoral support coming fairly proportionally from virtually all sociodemographic groups (Moschonas 1999, 118). In all, these elections revealed PASOK's capacity to mobilize left-leaning voters while also attracting centrist voters. For party leaders, the lesson was clear: PASOK would likely not need the KKE—or any other party—in order to form a governing majority (Diamondouros 1991, 23). Pushing their momentum in the next elections, PASOK gained an absolute majority of parliamentary seats in 1981 and proceeded to govern until 1989. Since their defeat in the latter year, the Socialists have been the chief party of the opposition on two occasions and have returned to power twice. In all, in the thirty years between PASOK's 1981 victory and 2011, the party has held parliamentary power a total of twenty-two years.[3]

This electoral performance had straightforward implications for the Socialists' alliance strategy. As in Spain, Socialist dominance in the early years of democracy meant that the party did not need to rely on any other party. This is not to say that PASOK has categorically rejected all cooperation with the Communists. Since the first elections in 1974, there have been at least two occasions—in 1975 and 1989—when Socialists pushed for either an electoral alliance or a governing coalition. In both instances, however, the two parties failed to reach agreement.[4] In general, however, PASOK's stance toward alliances has remained what it was in the wake of the 1977 elections. That stance was described by one scholar, writing prior to PASOK's first victory in 1981, as follows: "[PASOK] concentrated its energies on its own autonomous political and organizational growth, taking advantage of its status as the official opposition, of the political weight of its ninety-three deputies, and of its image as the only viable alternative to Karamanlis" (Elephantis 1981, 129). In terms of the Socialists' view of possible alliances with the Communists, the parallels between PASOK and the PSOE are indeed striking.

In accounting for PASOK's approach to alliances, all three of our main factors carry some explanatory weight. PASOK party culture, for example, helped shape the party's approach to alliances. Although PASOK was indeed a new formation created in 1974 and thus had no "culture" in the sense of well-established practices, customs, and ideological references, it did reflect several extant tendencies within the Greek Left and Greek politics generally. These included a motley mix of populism, nationalism, anti-imperialism, Marxism, and anti-Right/anti-Fascist ideology (Featherstone 1987, 123–25; Moschonas 1999, 110). While appealing to a broad spectrum of voters, this broad ideological tent also ensured that the party would host a range of factions and tendencies (Spourdalakis 1988, 206–7; Gunther, Diamondouros, and Puhle 1995, 30).

The one ideological element that could unite all of these factions was a determination to assert Greece's (and PASOK's) autonomy in relation to both superpowers, automatically inducing a certain distrust of the Moscow-friendly KKE. Adding to this tendency was that a major faction within PASOK—including Papandreou *père et fils*—came from the Center Union Party, which had fractious relations with the Communists from the Union's founding in 1961 until the 1967 military coup. As in Spain, the non-Communist Left's historical memory ran deep when it came to dealing with Communists. The same could be said for any possible alliance with the new center-right party, New Democracy, many of whose leaders, the Socialists believed, had been complicit with the military dictatorship (not to mention the Central Intelligence Agency).

The factor of leadership also influenced PASOK's alliance strategy, and here it is hard to exaggerate the role of the party's founder and leader for twenty-two years (1974–1996), Andreas Papandreou. Somewhat in the manner of Mitterrand in France, Papandreou in the early 1980s embodied both a vague concept of transformation—the slogan "*Allagi*" ("Change") was the all-purpose campaign slogan—and the reassurance of continuity by virtue of his family's long involvement in politics. Even more than Mitterrand, however, Papandreou played on his personal popularity in developing a populist style that centralized party power in his hands (Elephantis 1981, 129; Diamondouros 1991, 33; Kalyvas and Marantzidis 2003, 17). This tendency to concentrate power carried over to Papandreou's long tenure as prime minister from 1981 to 1989; the term "alliance" did not appear to be part of his vocabulary. While critics variously criticized Papandreou for fostering a clientelistic spoils system and abandoning his commitment to progressive structural reforms,[5] there is no denying his capacity to control PASOK while keeping the party free of all constraining alliances. Subsequent changes in party leadership since Papandreou's resignation in 1995 brought a less autocratic leadership style, but PASOK's founder decisively set the template for the party's go-it-alone alliance strategy (Moschonas 1999, 116; Dinas 2008, 600).

Even though party culture and leadership are important to explaining the Socialists' alliance behavior, by far the most consequential factor has been the institutional context. Two characteristics of Greece's 1975 postdictatorship constitution have especially shaped PASOK's (and all parties') alliance strategies. The first is the particular nature of Greece's "semipresidential" system that was modeled on Fifth Republic France. Designed to avoid the kind of parliamentary paralysis and breakdown that led to the colonels' coup in 1967, the new constitution provides, à la France, a dual executive—a president and a parliamentary leader (prime minister). Unlike France, however, the president is elected not directly by the public but rather by parliament. Therefore, whichever party controls parliament also determines, in effect, who will be president (Clogg 1987, 82). The Greek presidency, therefore, lacks the electoral importance that it has in France, thereby obviating the need for any party to build a broad coalition capable of capturing the presidency in a popular vote. Put simply, the Mitterrand-style strategy of building a united Left coalition behind a single person capable of being elected president makes little sense in Greece.

The second important element in Greece's institutional context is the type of electoral system, which is termed "reinforced proportional representation." The complicated calculation method—designed initially in the 1950s to reduce the Left's strength, which at that time was concentrated in urban areas and a few regions—has the effect of giving the winning party a disproportionately high number of seats, while the runner-up party receives a number of seats roughly proportional to its vote. All other parties receive dispro-portionately low seat shares relative to their vote.[6] As with the fairly similar d'Hondt proportional representation (PR) method used in Spain, the Socialist Party has benefited greatly by this system. For example, in the eleven parlia-mentary elections held between 1981 and 2009, PASOK won a majority of seats in six of them. In *none* of those six elections did PASOK win a majority of the popular vote. (The party's vote range in those contests was 41.5 to 48.1 percent, with an overall average of 45.0 percent.) Taken together, the institu-tional arrangements embodied in the 1975 constitution have given the Social-ists scant incentive to cooperate with other parties.

As the foregoing indicates, the Communist party has not been able to rival the Socialists as an electoral force since the 1974 return to democracy, and for that reason there have been precious few instances of cooperation be-tween the two parties. This is not to say, however, that the KKE has been totally isolated, lacking political friends or influence. Even though the party was outlawed in 1947, it remained engaged, from 1949 to 1967, as a key albeit behind-the-scenes element in a legal party, the United Democratic Left—the only unabashedly Left organization during that period (Papayanna-kis 1981, 141–43; Kapetanyannis 1987, 150). In the postdictatorship period, even though, as mentioned, the electoral system disadvantages small parties such as the Communists, the KKE managed to elect between ten and twenty members of Greece's 300-person parliament in every election between 1974 and 2009—a performance that gave the party constant visibility and viability.

From its stolid position on the Far Left, the KKE has sought to rally other groups to the left of PASOK into various coalitions and united fronts. The results of these coalition efforts have been largely negative, however. Begin-ning in the dictatorship period and then carrying over into the early years of the new democracy, the Greek Communists experienced a fundamental split within their own ranks that has limited the movement's electoral perfor-mance and hampered its ability to form a cohesive rival bloc to the Socialists. For that reason, we can identify the KKE's critical juncture as the period 1968–1974.

Historically, the Greek Communist Party, in its fealty to Moscow, was more akin to French comrades than to its Italian and Spanish counterparts (Smith 1993, 88). In the late 1960s, however, a significant minority within the KKE came to question not only the party's dependence on the Soviets but also its organizational methods, lack of democracy, and ambivalent role in the last democratically elected governments before the 1967 coup (Papayan-nakis 1981, 148). This intraparty conflict, coming during the first years of the dictatorship when most of the KKE leadership had gone into exile, had an exterior/interior dimension reminiscent of the Spanish Socialists in that the critical faction was composed primarily of Communists who had remained within Greece. Unable to resolve its differences with the party's pro-Moscow leadership, the critical faction split off in 1968 to form a rival Communist group, the Greek Communist Party of the Interior (KKE-I). Thereafter, Greek Communism had two competing faces: an orthodox, pro-Soviet party (the KKE) and a more autonomy-minded, reformist, PCI-style party (KKE-I) (Kalyvas and Marantzidis 2003, 16).

This split, by permanently dividing the Communist camp into two rival blocs, constituted a watershed moment in itself; however, the severity of the split would not become evident until the first postdictatorship elections in 1974. In those elections, the two Communist parties managed to put together a common United Left list of candidates. But persisting ideological differences between the two organizations, coupled with the United Left's lack-luster 9.5 percent, discouraged further cooperation. During the following decade, the two parties contested every election as rivals. For that reason, the 1974 election marks the end of the Communists' critical juncture because by then the die was cast: the Greek Communist movement was not only electorally anemic but also fundamentally divided.

Although the history of the non-PASOK Greek Left after the mid-1970s is full of complexity, the basic pattern of division remained. Complexity within the KKE camp included another major split within the party, in 1991, over the question of reform following the collapse of the Soviet Union (Smith 1993, 90–97). Yet, despite the loss of many younger, educated cadres in this split, the KKE endured as an organization, retaining the Leninist practice of democratic centralism while replacing orthodox Communist ideology with a combination of nationalism (antiglobalization, anti–United States, anti-NATO, and anti–European Union) and social protest (Kalyvas and Marantzidis 2003, 22–23).

As for the KKE-I , its history has been even more complex. After performing poorly as a party that had neither the discipline and rigid ideology of the KKE nor the broad appeal of PASOK, the KKE-I eventually voted, in 1986–1987, to abandon the Communist brand and rename itself the Greek Left (EAR). This new party went on to form an electoral alliance with the KKE under the name Synaspismos (the Greek word for "Coalition"), which ran a common list of candidates in the two elections in 1989. But the new coalition evidenced the same kinds of tensions that we saw in Spain with respect to the PCE and Izquierda Unida, namely, conflicts over the relative balance of power between the Communist Party and the other components of the coalition. The prospect of a possible merger between Synaspismos and the KKE was abandoned, and since the early 1990s the two organizations have competed as left-wing alternatives to PASOK. In the 2009 elections, they drew a combined total of 12.1 percent of the vote, with the KKE taking about two-thirds of that total (Dinas 2010, 390).

What explains the KKE's alliance strategy? Institutional context and party culture can account for much of the Communists' behavior. As we have seen, the institutional context—specifically Greece's electoral system—vastly overrewards large parties such as PASOK and New Democracy while greatly underrewarding smaller parties such as the KKE and Synaspismos. Given PASOK's dominance and therefore its indifference toward potential coalition partners, the KKE has had basically two choices: go it alone or seek partnerships with other small Left parties. In the unending search to expand its electoral base since 1974, the KKE has followed each of these paths at various times. The second factor, party culture, can help explain why going it alone has proven to be the general default mode. Once the reform-minded faction exited from the KKE in 1968 to form KKE-I, the remaining party loyalists were by and large reflexively orthodox. Party culture emphasized loyalty to Moscow (and hence an automatic anti-Americanism), internal discipline, and an attitude of vanguardism in relation to other leftist groups. This party culture did not, of course, suddenly emerge during the critical juncture we have identified; it was created and nurtured during the civil war and the long period of banishment. But the possibility that the KKE could develop an Italian or even a Spanish type of autonomous, ideologically flexible Communism was effectively choked off with the 1968 split.

Portugal

At first glance, the recent histories of both Portugal and Greece as well as that of their respective Left parties appear to have much in common. Both countries experienced the end of dictatorship in the same year, 1974, and Socialist and Communist parties in both nations quickly became important actors in the construction of a new political system. Although the two parties initially shared many programmatic affinities—notably opposition to the dictatorship and to the social groups supporting dictatorship, coupled with a nascent nationalism that sought to cast off the imperialist yoke of the United States—they soon parted company over the direction of their respective new regimes. Perhaps most important in terms of similarities, the Socialist Party in both Greece and Portugal quickly surpassed the Communists electorally and found decreasing need for a lasting alliance. The history of Socialist–Communist relations in both countries since the mid-1970s is largely one of mutual hostility and avoidance that resembles the Spanish case. In neither Greece nor Portugal was there a sustained period of cooperation as in France (1962–1977) or Italy (1946–1960).

This summary, while accurate in broad outline, fails to convey some crucial differences between the Greek and Portuguese cases. First, whereas Greece's seven-year military dictatorship ended in 1974 with the whimper of disgraced colonels surrendering their power, the long-running Salazar–Caetano dictatorship (1926–1974) in Portugal terminated with a bang: a full-scale mutiny in that same year by a revolution-minded group of disaf-

fected junior military officers formed into a small group called the Armed
Forces Movement (MFA) (Chilcote 2010). This fact alone established a very
different dynamic in postdictatorship politics. Moreover, whereas Greece
proceeded, in effect, to resume—albeit with major modifications—a long
democratic tradition, Portugal had to start one largely from scratch. Taken
together, these contrasts virtually ensured that democratic transition and consolidation in Portugal would be more protracted, fluid, contested, and inde-
terminate than in Greece.

The trajectory of the Portuguese revolution—a process that played out
between the April 1974 military overthrow and the first elections under a
democratic constitution in May 1976—defined a critical juncture for both
Socialists (PSP) and Communists (PCP). During this period, a wide range of
political actors contended to define a new political order. Among the major
actors—the MFA, the two major Left formations, and various moderate
groups—the only principle they shared can be stated as, We will not go
back—Portugal will not revert to strongman rule. Beyond that, there was
little consensus, even within individual groups themselves. This was especially true within the trigger force of the revolution, the MFA, which, even
though it was fairly small (fewer than 200 members), lacked a clear goal
other than to rid Portugal of a political elite that had sent the army to Africa
on a fool's mission in order to retain a vestige of colonial glory (Maxwell
1978, 272–74). There was certainly not, as in the Greek case, a general
consensus that Portugal would become a "normal" European democracy.[7]
Although there were strong pressures pushing in that direction—including
the country's recent socioeconomic modernization that had generated a new
middle class of activist students and young professionals—there were also
groups advocating radical economic reforms along Socialist lines. Within
this chaotic context, Socialists and Communists began as cosympathizers
with the April 1974 military overthrow but ended, by the time of the May
1976 elections, as antagonists. By then, the two parties' ideologies and political goals had diverged drastically, and a lasting pattern of division had
emerged.

The central factor behind this division was a fundamental difference in
how the two parties responded to the uncertainty unleashed by the military
coup.[8] More specifically, the PSP and PCP adopted diametrically opposed
alliance strategies that put them on a collision course. Since neither party
played a part in bringing down the previous regime, both parties initially
adopted a cautious, wait-and-see stance, expressing general support for the
officers' revolution while seeking to cultivate support within friendly factions of the MFA. There was at least the appearance of amity between the
two parties.[9] Above all, the parties tried to avoid statements and actions that
might provoke a right-wing reaction. The PCP's main effort during the fall of
1974 and the early months of 1975 was to create—and then to convince the

MFA to recognize—a single labor confederation, InterSindical (IS), that the party would control. In this endeavor, the PCP was successful, but the move, unsurprisingly, generated the first major split between the PCP and the Socialists (Antunes Sablosky 1997, 66; Cunha 1997, 24–25; Royo 2002, 195–203).

An even more important event during the year following the April 1974 military takeover put the Communists and Socialists on diverging alliance paths: a counterrevolutionary coup attempt on March 11, 1975. Although the attempt was thwarted, the threat that it represented emboldened the most radical elements within the MFA to push ahead with revolutionary reforms, including massive nationalizations of large firms and redistribution of land to favor smallholders and landless peasants (Bermeo 1987, 217). In response to the MFA's initiative, the PCP "went with the tide" in support of this radical faction (Mujal-León 1978b, 126). Over the course of the following six months, the PCP sought to push the revolution to the left, notably by seeking to mobilize and channel land seizures in the southern Alentejo region.

In the midst of this radicalization wave, the MFA regime, having committed itself from the outset to holding constituent assembly elections, reluctantly allowed the elections to go forward in April 1975. In this first test of its general popularity, the Communists performed poorly, gaining just over 12 percent, with its base largely limited to the Alentejo region and industrial areas around Lisbon. The Socialists, by contrast, garnered 38 percent, with relatively even support throughout the country. The Communists' response to these elections was dismissive. Revealing his disdain for standard democratic practices, PCP leader Cunhal declared, "If you believe the constituent assembly will be transformed into a parliament, you are very much mistaken. In Portugal there will be no parliament" (quoted in Maxwell 1978, 291).

Thus, within a year of the MFA coup, the Communists had decisively thrown in with the most radical elements of the MFA; however, the 1975 elections provided prima facie evidence of the PCP's lack of broad support. In Maxwell's (1978) apt phrase, "The [1975 election] returns provided a geography for counterrevolution" (288). At the same time, the Socialists, having received nearly two-fifths of the popular vote in the first open election, had every reason to espouse a gradual transition to parliamentary democracy.[10] Cooperation between these parties was no longer on the agenda.

The inevitability and intractability of the two parties' diverging trajectories by the summer of 1975 can be seen in the struggle over land reform, which became a casualty of PSP–PCP competition.[11] Key to understanding the dynamic whereby relations between the two parties broke down is the fact that the Socialist Party was not reflexively opposed to major economic reforms such as nationalizations and land redistribution. Given the delegitimation of the previous regime, many groups—not just the Communists—gave at least lip service to such reforms, and the Socialists were no exception. In the case of land reform, the Socialists in 1975–1976 were even in a position to determine the course of reform since a Socialist leader, Lopes Cardoso, was minister of agriculture. Although sympathetic to reform, Cardoso also had to deal with a Communist party that sought to establish "facts on the ground" by pushing land seizures and the creation of production units largely dominated by PCP activists.

The Communists' aggressive actions quickly alienated small and medium-size farmers, who in turn pressured the Agriculture Ministry to stop what they perceived as Soviet-style collectivization. The Socialist minister became caught between two increasingly mobilized and vociferous rural camps. By mid-1976, Cardoso had lost the support not only of the newly elected president, General Antonio Eanes, but also of other leaders in his own party, and land reform featuring worker-controlled production units was abandoned. As Bermeo (1986) summarizes,

> Searching for the support of the numerically powerful small and medium farm community, pressured by anti-Communist forces abroad, and unable to compromise with its competition on the Left, Portugal's Socialist party turned against the agrarian reform. The articulation of participation structures at the national level and the base thus proved impossible—not because the Socialists were opposed to workers' control but because a rival party seemed so closely associated with it. (201)

The upshot of these complicated events was a reaction against radical change that pushed the MFA, along with the entire Portuguese revolution, toward growing moderation (Maxwell 1978, 270; Villaverde Cabral 1983, 195). Given its strong support for radicalization, the PCP found itself not only increasingly distanced from the Socialists but isolated generally, whereas the Socialists had little choice but to seek allies among other prodemocratic parties toward the center and even center-right. Such a pattern became clear in May 1976 in the very first elections under a new constitution. Even though, compared with the constituent assembly elections a year earlier, the PSP did somewhat worse and the PCP somewhat better, the two parties together totaled nearly 50 percent of the vote. Conceivably, they could have formed a governing coalition. But the Socialists chose initially to form, by themselves, a minority government and then later struck a coalition with a center-right party, the CDS. A PSP–PCP alliance remained off the agenda. By and large, this has been the template for post-1976 Portuguese politics, and thus the 1974–1976 period indeed stands out as a watershed defining a critical juncture for both Left parties.

The foregoing does not imply that after 1976 the Portuguese Communists withered away or rejected all alliances with the Socialists. Although the PCP's electoral support dropped significantly after 1990, the party continued to draw between 7 and 10 percent of the vote in legislative elections during the next two decades. Much in the manner of Spanish and Greek Communists, the PCP sought to strike electoral alliances with the Green Party and other Left groups, albeit with limited success (Cunha 1997, 40; 2003, 102). The arena of greatest Communist impact was not at the ballot box, however, but rather at the workplace. As mentioned earlier, the PCP had an important presence within the first labor confederation, IS, that was recognized by the postdictatorship government. Initially granted a representational monopoly, IS eventually faced union competitors, but it remained one of the two largest labor organizations, and the PCP kept its strong ties with IS (later renamed the CGTP); as one observer remarks, "It is virtually impossible to decide where the trade union branch ends and the party cell begins" (Van Biezen 2003, 67). As for relations with the Socialists, the PCP—in manner of its counterparts in the other countries studied—has managed to keep some bridges from burning, notably at the local level. For example, in the late 1980s, Socialist leader Jorge Sampaio ran successfully for the presidency of the Lisbon city council with PCP backing (Lisi 2006, 391–92). On the whole, however, the pattern set by 1976 remained in place well into the twenty-first century: no national cooperation between Socialists and Communists at the national level.

As for the Socialists, their post-1976 fortunes broadly paralleled those of their comrades in Spain and Greece in that the PSP became one of the primary inner-system parties. While the PSP did not enjoy quite the hegemonic position of its Spanish and Greek counterparts, the party held the prime ministership in seventeen of the thirty-five years between 1976 and 2011, usually with the support of one or more centrist or center-right parties. Moreover, in Portugal's semipresidential system—a model that was inspired, as in Greece, by the French Fifth Republic—Socialist leaders Mario Soares and Jorge Sampaio successively held the presidency for twenty consecutive years from 1986 to 2006.[12]

In essence, the PSP's alliance strategy after 1976 was an outgrowth of what one might term the party's "identity formation" during the democratic transition that we have reviewed. On the one hand, as we have seen, the PSP stood against the radicalism of the PCP and other groups on the extreme left in 1975–1976. This experience basically established a bright line of distrust and antagonism between the two parties that did not fade. On the other hand, lacking compatible allies on the Left, the Socialists quite logically sought them toward the center. These responses created a durable dynamic that is well summarized by Lisi (2006): "The underlying features of the competitive strategy adopted by the PS are the strengthening of the competition towards the centre of the political spectrum and the refusal to form any kind of alliance with the left-wing parties (PCP, BE) at the national level" (391).

How to account for these contrasting alliance strategies? Again, let us return to our three main explanatory factors: institutional context, party culture, and leadership. For the Socialist Party, all three factors had a marked, mutually reinforcing impact. Party culture, for reasons just explained, is probably the most important given that the PSP virtually defined its organizational being *in opposition to* the Communists. This is not to say that the PSP has always been reflexively procapitalist or moderate, at least ideologically. On the contrary, for more than a decade after its 1974 founding, the party continued to claim Marxism as a centerpiece of its intellectual heritage (Costa Lobo and Magalhaes 2004, 85). Nevertheless, a kind of "genetic" imprint distrustful of Communism permeated the PSP from the outset.

Leadership has also been an important influence on Socialist alliance strategy. Since 1974, the three most powerful party leaders have been Mario Soares (party leader 1974–1987), Jorge Sampaio (1987–1991), and António Guterres (1992–2005). Although there were ideological and stylistic differences among these leaders—notably Sampaio's more favorable inclination toward an alliance with the PCP compared with Soares and Guterres—all three leaders sought to position the PSP as a party in favor of economic modernization and European integration. Guterres, especially, as prime minister (1995–2001), embraced a Blair-style Third Way model (without naming it as such) stressing education and government efficiency. Such a stance fostered collaboration with the center-right Social Democrats while continuing to put the PSP at odds with the Communists, who denounced this approach as neoliberal (Costa Lobo and Magalhaes 2004, 90–94; Lisi 2006, 386).

Finally, the institutional context also influenced the Socialists' alliance behavior. As in the Greek and Spanish cases, the new postdictatorship constitution established both electoral systems and governmental structures that shaped party strategies. Of particular importance are the electoral rules. Although Portugal adopted a proportional representation system, as did Greece and Spain, the Portuguese system is distinctive in that it much more faithfully "translates" each party's vote percentage into that party's percentage of parliamentary seats.[13] (Recall that the Spanish and Greek PR systems, in effect, reward the larger parties at the expense of smaller ones.) The upshot is that the Socialists do not receive the kind of "bump" in terms of parliamentary seats that their counterparts in Spain and Greece do. This means, in turn, that the PSP only rarely has been in a position to garner a majority of seats on its own (Gunther 2007, 39).[14] Thus, the electoral system keeps the PSP in a position of constantly needing to find allies in order to boost its influence within parliament. Given that a PSP–PCP alliance is permanently off the table, the electoral system thus induces a center-moving dynamic for the Socialists because that is where allies are more likely to be found.[15]

As for the Communists, our three factors also help explain much of their alliance strategy. The institutional context, for example, has shaped the opportunities and incentives for Communist alliances. Just as Portugal's PR electoral system has encouraged the Socialists to seek allies toward the center, so has it served to keep the PCP fairly isolated from the mainstream parties. Of more importance are the other two factors, party culture and leadership. Communist parties everywhere have emphasized internal discipline ("democratic centralism"), the self-appointed role as working-class "vanguard," and opposition to capitalism, but, as this study has shown, there is considerable national variation in how Communist parties approach issues of internal organization, alliances, and program. In a comparative context, the Portuguese Communist Party must be placed among the most orthodox Communist parties in Western Europe (Bosco 2000; Van Biezen 2003, 75). Historically, the party was staunchly loyal to the Soviet Union until the end, while party leadership discouraged factionalism and internal dissent. Thus, the PCP's closed, dogmatic culture—formed in nearly five decades (1926–1974) as an illegal, underground party[16] —has discouraged cooperation with other groups on the Left, notably the Socialists (Villaverde Cabral 1983, 180–81; Patricio and Stoleroff 1993, 81).

Communist leadership both created and reinforced this orthodoxy, most notably the tenure of Alvaro Cunhal, who served as party leader for over fifty years (1941–1992). Under Cunhal's leadership, the PCP tolerated little internal dissent while remaining adamant on the need for forceful revolution. To the end, Cunhal remained steadfast in his belief in the Soviet system, declaring that it was the principal force for "peace and progress throughout the world" and that its existence "is like sunlight on the earth." (quoted in Mujal-León 1978b, 139). Given such a mind-set that governed the PCP well into the democratic period, it is not hard to grasp the gulf that separated the two left parties.

GOOD ENOUGH: ON THE STATUS OF CRITICAL JUNCTURES

The preceding overviews of the recent history of the Left in Greece and Portugal demonstrate, it is hoped, the further utility of the critical juncture framework that we employed for the French, Italian, and Spanish cases. The framework "travels" pretty well, at least to neighboring nations that share a Mediterranean location and heritage. A final question, then, is, Where does this leave the overall analysis, specifically the theoretical and/or explanatory reach of a critical juncture approach? In concluding, I think it wise to restate the humbling words of the fortune cookie quoted in this book's introduction: "It could be better, but it's good enough."

To be explicit: a critical juncture perspective such as the one developed here is not a theory per se but rather a methodological approach. More specifically, it is a way of studying historical change. As such, following Bermeo's useful advice that heads this chapter, it pays attention to history before it pays attention to theory. In paying attention to history, one is ever sensitive to specific events and sequences of events—in effect, the "what happened?" that pertains to a particular period in a specific place (a family, a village, a region, a nation, a world system). But a critical juncture perspective does not stop there. It takes a step back to inquire about *patterns* in those events and sequences. One then asks a series of questions. What pattern is one observing; that is, how do the events being analyzed fit into their larger historical context? Moreover, can one identify specific historical moments when a particular pattern shifts? Can one detect those instances when events create (to requote Collier and Collier from chapter 1) "watersheds in political life, . . . transitions [that] establish certain directions of change and foreclose others in a way that shapes politics for years to come"? If the answer to that question is yes, then the analytical task is straightforward: to examine the nature, causes, and consequences of those "watersheds." That, in essence, has been the goal of this book.

A critical juncture approach will always be subject to the timeless wisdom of the fortune cookie—"It could be better, but it's good enough"—for one simple reason: history is ever changing. The past may not even be past, as Faulkner suggests, but neither is it static. This means that any particular critical juncture has finite duration. Just as individuals face various turning points—critical junctures—in life, so do societies. The European economic crisis since late 2008 underscores this obvious point. Since that time, Social-ist-led governments in Spain, Portugal, and Greece have struggled mightily but vainly to maintain popular support, not to mention domestic tranquillity, while keeping their economies tied to the eurozone. A safe hypothesis is that Left parties in these countries are facing critical junctures comparable to those identified in this book. As the cliché goes, time will tell, or, perhaps better stated, history will decide. Thus, a critical juncture approach when applied to contemporary history can take us only so far: to the next critical juncture. In the meantime, that will be good enough.

NOTES

1. The Greek Left is distinctive within Europe in that the Communist Party resulted not from a classic split within the main existing Socialist Party but rather from the unification of several small Left groups in the early 1920s. From that period on, the Communist Party was the hegemonic party on the Left, a fact that helps explain a strong culture of vanguardism within the PCP (Papayannakis 1981, 135).

2. Andreas's father, Giorgio Papandreou, had led an important predictatorship party, the Center Union. Born in 1919, Andreas had been briefly imprisoned for antiregime activities in the late 1930s, but on his release he went to the United States, earned a doctorate in economics at Harvard, and then had a distinguished academic career at several American universities. Returning to Greece in 1959, he became active in Greek politics and was elected to parliament in 1964. At the time of the colonels' coup in 1967, he was strongly identified with the Left faction of the Center Union (Featherstone 1987, 117).

3. The dates of PASOK's tenure as majority party are 1981–1989, 1993–2004, and 2009–2011 (as of this writing).

4. The first occasion, in late 1975, came as PASOK and other parties began to position themselves for the next elections. With less than 14 percent of the vote, compared with the Communists' 9.5 percent, PASOK leaders viewed some kind of alliance with the KKE and other Left groups as necessary. According to one analyst, however, PASOK sought to dictate the terms of the alliance, and the KKE and other parties pulled out of negotiations (Papayannakis 1981, 153). The second attempt came after the June 1989 elections when neither PASOK nor New Democracy won a majority of seats. PASOK proposed a governing alliance with the KKE, which held the balance of power. In an extraordinary case of how politics can make strange bedfellows, the KKE refused this offer and threw its support to New Democracy, a party the KKE had been denouncing for the previous decade and a half (Petras et al. 1993, 213; Linz, Stepan, and Gunther 1995, 115).

5. As an example of the kinds of critiques that became common among scholars and other relatively neutral observers by the end of the Socialists' first terms (1981–1985 and 1985–1989), consider the following: "The legislation that made the right to strike almost impossible to exercise, the crude colonization of the state apparatus, the party's scandalous relations with business interests, which resulted in unprecedented instances of corruption, and, finally, its fickle and erratic foreign and especially European policy are some of the most striking examples of [the PASOK government's] programmatic and value changes" (Spourdalakis and Tassis 2006, 500). For useful accounts of PASOK's policies while in power in the 1980s, see Petras et al. (1993) and Kalyvas (1997).

6. This system is explained in detail by Vegleris (1981, 33–36); see also Legg and Roberts (1997, 132). The calculation method involves three separate "distributions" of seats at the constituency, regional, and national levels. There is a threshold of 17 percent for parties to receive seats in the second and third distributions, which "ensures a systematic and organic overrepresentation of the larger parties and underrepresentation or nonrepresentation of the smaller ones" (Vegleris 1981, 35).

7. Timing also played a role in the relative lack of consensus. It will be recalled that the April 1974 military coup in Portugal preceded both the downfall of the Greek dictatorship (July–August 1974) and Franco's death (November 1975). Thus, initially Portugal had no "role models" for a peaceful democratic transition.

8. A detailed analysis of the "April Revolution" is beyond the scope of the present discussion. Needless to say, its underlying causes were complex, including two futile and enormously expensive colonial wars in Angola and Mozambique, massive emigration of Portuguese workers due to a poor labor market at home, and other factors. One observer notes that "the April Revolution was the culmination of the protracted process of modernization and liberalization which the country had undergone in the previous decade" (Villaverde Cabral 1983, 193). For a useful summary of the social changes that Portugal was experiencing at the time of the revolution, see Hamann and Manuel (1999, 77–78). The most comprehensive and insightful study of the revolution itself is Maxwell (1995).

9. In one famous albeit fleeting moment of unity just after the military coup, PSP leader Mario Soares (who had returned from exile in Paris) and PCP chief Alvaro Cunhal (who had returned from exile in Prague) posed together for photographs, holding a red carnation between them (Maxwell 1978, 282).

10. An intriguing question is why the PCP moved so strongly to the left in what would appear to have been a risky strategy. Mujal-León (1978b) argues that the Communists did not "have much to lose" in any case given their weak showing in the April 1975 constituent assembly elections, which indicated that the PCP would play at best a minor role in a parliamentary system (126). Desperation is not the whole story, however. Maxwell claims that PCP leader Cunhal wanted at all costs to avoid a Chilean scenario, and thus he sought a close alliance, at any given moment, with the dominant group within the MFA. After the failed counterrevolutionary coup attempt in March 1975, that dominant group was the MFA's most radical faction (Maxwell 1978, 281).

11. The following account is based on Bermeo's excellent study of the agrarian struggle during the 1974–1976 period (Bermeo 1986).

12.   Soares served two consecutive five-year terms as president (1986–1991 and 1991–1996), as did Sampaio (1996–2001 and 2001–2006). Soares also served two terms as prime minister (1976–1979 and 1983–1985).

13.   Portugal, like Spain, adopted the d'Hondt method of PR to award parliamentary seats; as we saw in chapter 4, this system generally tends to disproportionally reward the larger parties at the expense of smaller parties. This bias is true for Portugal as well as Spain; however, there is a major difference in the two systems because of the number and size (i.e., the number of parliamentary representatives) of electoral districts. The basic contrast is that Spain has a relatively large number of small districts compared with Portugal. The result is that the Spanish system greatly accentuates the "majoritarian" effects of the d'Hondt method, whereas Portugal's comparatively higher number of larger districts reduces those effects. One illustration of Portugal's relatively weak majoritarian bias (and Spain's strong one) can be seen in "electoral disproportionality" scores for seventeen Western democracies. With scores ranging from a high disproportionality score of 11.8 (France) to a low of 1.3 (the Netherlands), Spain's score of 8.2 was substantially higher than Portugal's 4.0 (Greece's score was 8.1). See Gunther and Montero (2009, 108).

14.   In none of the seven elections before 1995 did the PS win more than 41 percent of the seats. Since 1995, the party has performed markedly better; however, of the five elections between 1995 and 2009, in only one (2005) did the party gain more than 50 percent of the seats and thus was able to govern as a single party. In that election, the PS received a 45.0 percent vote share, translating into 52.6 percent of the parliamentary seats (Lisi 2010, 385).

15.   Portugal's semipresidential system featuring a dual executive—a directly elected president and a prime minister heading parliament—has also shaped the PS's alliance strategy although to a lesser extent than in France. As in France, there is an incentive for the larger parties such as the PS to put together a "presidential majority" of voters, especially in the second-round runoff; however, the persistent division between Socialists and Communists, as well as the PCP's growing electoral weakness over time, has removed any incentive for the Socialists to pursue a French-style Union of the Left strategy (Costa Lobo 2001, 650).

16.   Villaverde Cabral (1983, 188) notes that in 1974, the twenty members of the PCP's Central Committee had spent a total of 300 years in jail for antiregime activities.

Afterword

The [euro crisis] is not primarily one of profligate public sectors or broken private sectors in debtor countries. It is rather the result of a fundamental disequilibrium within the single currency zone, which applies a single monetary policy and a single exchange rate to a diverse group of countries.
—Andrew Moravcsik, *Foreign Affairs*, May/June 2012

The phrase "two-speed Europe" hardly does justice to the bifurcation. There are in fact now two Europes: a Teutonic core and a Latin periphery.
—Niall Ferguson, *Newsweek*, June 11, 2012

While this study has stressed the importance of, in Bermeo's words, attention to history, it goes without saying that we ignore the present at our peril. A critical juncture always occurs in *some* present, although that historical moment may not be widely recognized as a watershed as it unfolds, nor may its consequences be immediately clear. That said, sometimes events occurring before our eyes are so obviously momentous and fate changing that we cannot turn away—attention must be paid. In such moments, engaged citizens as well as political analysts try to gauge the nature and likely impact of a new critical juncture. As even a casual observer of current events knows, the European Union is now experiencing such a juncture.

This book was researched and written largely between 2008 and 2011, a period marked by the onset and development of a full-blown crisis over the euro. As this book goes to press (June 2012), legislative elections are occurring in France and Greece that will likely nudge the crisis in one direction or another. It is unclear how this crisis will play out, and publishers' deadlines do not wait for denouements. Yet for a book that purports to understand the dynamics of Left politics in some of the major nations involved in the euro crisis, it is a propos to conclude with some observations, however provision-al, on Left parties in the current crisis.

Let us begin with the obvious: the crisis has severely limited the policy options of the seventeen euro zone nations. As *The Economist* (May 26, 2012) recently stated, "A consensus is slowly emerging that . . . there will have to be a greater level of integration in the euro zone, with tighter con-straints on the freedom of national governments" (23). This is especially true for the governments of the zone's "southern tier": Greece, Spain, Portugal, Italy, and, to a lesser extent, France. As the two quotes heading this after-word suggest, these nations are on the negative end of a "fundamental dis-equilibrium" within the euro zone. Collectively, these nations, which consti-tute over half of the euro zone in terms of population and economic output, have sharply diverged in economic performance from what Ferguson calls the "Teutonic core."[1] That divergence, the driver of the current crisis, has now boxed these nations into a limited set of options that is sapping their policy autonomy while choking off growth.

The euro crisis has multiple causes, beginning with, as Moravcsik indi-cates, a structural imbalance: a one-size-fits-all monetary policy for nations with diverse political economies. Aside from such design issues—including the lack of a pooled fiscal regime to accompany monetary pooling—the euro crisis also stems from two unintended consequences of German economic might. On the one hand, Germany, in the negotiations over the 1992 Maas-tricht Treaty to create a monetary union, insisted that the new monetary authority, the European Central Bank (ECB), not only be headquartered in Frankfurt but also operate in accord with Germany's historical preference for a low-inflation strategy. One result was that after the introduction of the euro in 1999, the ECB's conservative monetary approach convinced financial markets that the classic practices of borrowing and lending were largely risk free throughout the euro zone, and so a kind of irrational exuberance drove both private investors and governments to take on growing levels of debt. For a time at least, to most investors and lenders, a Greek or Portuguese borrower looked more or less like a German borrower—a by-product of German eco-nomic credibility.

On the other hand, Germany has been highly protective of its economic dominance. Specifically, the country has been reluctant to assume full re-sponsibility for the imbalances the monetary arrangement created. After the 2008 crisis hit and credit markets largely froze, it became apparent that the southern-tier nations, in particular, had assumed unsustainable debt loads. In reaction, the strongest creditor nations within the euro zone, foremost among them Germany, were resistant to providing relief without restrictions. Some analysts referred to Germany's "transfer fatigue"—an unwillingness to as-sume, once again, the costs of economic stabilization as it had done in reuni-fying the two Germanys in the early 1990s. In the post-2008 context, Chancellor Merkel's consistent mantra to the southern-tier nations has been, Do not expect us to bail you out. You must first put your own fiscal house in order by cutting government spending and raising taxes.

This German-prescribed austerity cure has only worsened economic conditions in the southern tier, even if one grants that Merkel is right in claiming that Germany alone cannot rescue these nations from their economic hole. The upshot is that an ostensibly virtuous cycle of respectable growth, stabilized unemployment, and tolerable levels of government deficits and debt that held for these nations during the early 2000s has turned vicious since 2008. Although there is some cross-national variation in economic performance, all five nations of the southern tier have experienced marked deterioration in the measures just mentioned to the point that international financial investors have increasingly lost faith in the viability of the euro itself.

THE SOUTHERN TIER: EURO CRISIS AND THE LEFT

Since 2008, Greece has become the focal point for speculative attacks on the euro. Popular authors such as Michael Lewis and others have made Greece— not without reason—the whipping boy for establishing or allowing lavish retirement regimes, tax evasion, cronyism, and profligate government borrowing and spending. Such hallmarks of Greece's political economy—including a widely known tendency to cook the financial books when reporting to external entities—were tolerated as long as international credit flowed freely and the national economy was growing. Greece, in fact, grew nearly twice as fast as the euro zone average between 2000 and 2008.[2] But the severe recession that first struck the United States in September 2008 utterly reversed the growth trend, and the Greek economy has sharply contracted; between 2009 and 2012, the country's GDP shrank an annual average of 4.6 percent (vs. the euro zone's average of −0.3 percent).[3]

Along with contraction have come other negative consequences, most notably rising unemployment, which more than doubled from under 8 percent in 2009 to over 20 percent in 2012, along with public deficits and debt that have spun seemingly out of control.[4] The upshot—after downgrading of its sovereign debt rating to "junk" status, two major bailouts by the ECB and the International Monetary Fund, five austerity packages, and more or less continuous waves of street protests and riots—was a hopeless short- and medium-term economic prospect and polarized political deadlock.

Legislative elections on May 6, 2012, revealed the true state of political paralysis and public disaffection with the status quo, beginning with a record-high abstention rate.[5] Most notably, the elections reflected a strong center-fleeing trend, as the two dominant inner-system parties—the center-left Socialists, PASOK, and the center-right New Democracy—experienced massive defections. Whereas these two parties captured a combined 77 percent of the vote in 2009, that figure in 2012 was just 32 percent. The result was downright devastating for PASOK, which went from 44 percent of the vote and an absolute parliamentary majority in 2009 to just 13 percent of the vote and a roughly corresponding percentage of seats. In the space of a few months, as a direct result of PASOK Prime Minister Papandreou's failure to deal with Greece's economic crisis, the Socialists' support collapsed.

The logical counterpoint to the centrist parties' decline was a surge of the extremes. On the nationalistic and even xenophobic Right, three parties—ANEL, XA, and LAOS—attracted one-fifth of the total vote and a slightly smaller proportion of legislative seats. This performance contrasts with the previous 2009 election, when only one of these parties (LAOS) even fielded candidates and received less than 6 percent of the vote. A somewhat similar push came on the Left, with three formations—Syriza (a coalition of disparate leftist groups), the KKE, and Dimar (a 2010 split-off from Syriza)—garnering over 34 percent of the vote and about one-third of the seats. By comparison, these parties drew only 12 percent in the previous election. Because no party held anything close to a majority and no party leader could muster a majority, a caretaker prime minister (the country's most senior judge) was selected to run the government until new elections could take place. At the time of this writing—between the two elections—Greece has a complete political vacuum and no consensus on the way forward. The big surprise of the May elections was the rise of Syriza and its charismatic thirty-seven-year-old leader, Alexis Tsipras, who claims that he wants Greece to remain within the European Union (EU) and the euro zone yet rejects the austerity plans being imposed on the country. Whether he or any other leader can square that circle remains to be seen. Policy constraints? Greece has them on all sides, and for the foreseeable future, a distinctive yet viable leftist approach to the nation's crisis is far from apparent.

Portugal, after Greece, has often been referred to as "the next domino": a nation under speculative attack because its economic fundamentals have deteriorated precipitously since 2008. One sees in the Portuguese experience since 2008 a similar—albeit less extreme—version of Greek economic performance: overall economic contraction, a doubling of unemployment and the government deficit, and a sharp rise in government debt.[6] Slow (or no) growth and heavy borrowing led, as in Greece, to a series of increasingly harsh austerity measures enacted by a minority government headed by Socialist José Sócrates. The proposal of fourth austerity package in May 2011 triggered the collapse of Sócrates's government and new elections the following month. Those elections, marked by the Socialists' loss of one-quarter of their erstwhile voter support—from 37 percent in 2009 to 28 percent—produced a coalition government led by the center-right Social Democratic Party. On taking office, that government faced the challenge of implementing a €78 billion ($97.5 billion) bailout from the European Union and the International Monetary Fund negotiated by Sócrates in his last weeks in office. The classic, seemingly ineluctable pattern was set: in return for loans and debt forgiveness, the government was committed to enact hundreds of reform measures, including increases in health charges, liberalization of labor markets, and privatization of public firms. As in Greece, the Left finds itself both internally divided and politically marginalized in the face of the current crisis.

The same can be said for the Spanish Left, although Spain's economic crisis is of a different order than that of Greece and Portugal and, in turn, has created a different political dynamic. Compared with the latter two cases, the Spanish crisis is distinctive in three respects. First, Spain's trouble is primarily one of the private as opposed to the public sector. During the 2000–2008 period, the nation's largely private banks, taking advantage of euro-facilitated low interest rates, went on a massive lending spree, much of it to the construction sector. When the housing bubble burst in 2007–2008, the banks faced equally massive losses. By contrast, government debt is comparatively slight.[7] In this context, although the government has had to enact austerity measures, it has faced relatively less pressure from Germany and the ECB to get its fiscal house in order; rather, negotiations between Madrid and these actors have focused on how to manage bank losses and recapitalize the sector.

Moreover, when comparing Spain's position in the current crisis with that of Greece and Portugal, size matters; according to one report, Spain is "too big to fail and possibly too big to steamroll."[8] Whereas it is at least imaginable that the euro zone could survive without the small economies of Greece and Portugal, that is not the case with Spain. This reality has given Spanish leaders a certain leverage in relation to Germany and the ECB, enabling them to partially deflect demands for fiscal reform in favor of bank bailouts.

A third aspect of Spain's crisis, however, undermines this leverage and curtails the government's options, namely, the country's abysmal labor market. Since 2008, Spain has experienced a sharp rise in unemployment. After averaging 10.3 percent for the 2000–2008 period, Spain's unemployment rate doubled to an average of 20.2 percent for 2009–2012—the highest in the euro zone. As of mid-2012, about one-fourth of the working population is unemployed, with the burden especially falling on the youngest cohort who have enormous difficultly finding jobs in a highly dualistic labor market of protected permanent workers on the one hand and temporary contract workers on the other.[9]

The economic context just described came increasingly to preoccupy Socialist prime minister Zapatero after his party's reelection in 2008. As discussed in chapter 4, Zapatero's first term (2004–2008) stressed noneconomic issues such as civil and gender rights, historical memory, and church–state relations. This emphasis changed, of course, when the construction and housing bubble burst in 2008–2009, but the Zapatero government proved incapable of stemming job loss and the rise in unemployment. The eventual, predictable result was declining public favor, punctuated by the poor showing of the Partido Socialista Obrero Español (PSOE) in legislative elections in late 2011. With just 29 percent of the vote—compared with 44 percent in the previous election—the PSOE was reduced to a sideline player in the Cortes. Every other party increased its vote, including the Communist-led Izquierda Unida and other smaller leftist formations. Profiting most from the PSOE's misfortunes was the center-right Popular Party, which captured an outright parliamentary majority.

The Greek, Portuguese, and Spanish experiences share one evident outcome: incumbent center-left governments dominated by Socialist parties have fared poorly in the post-2008 crisis both in economic results and in popularity. Placed in broader European perspective, however, these cases demonstrate the dangers of incumbency rather than a partisan turn away from the Left. While it is true that some Left and center-left parties in Europe have lost voters and shares of power since 2008, such as in the United Kingdom, the Netherlands, Sweden, and Finland, the same is also true of some conservative governments, such as in Ireland, Denmark, and, most notably, Italy and France. In neither of the two latter cases, however, did a leftist insurgence have anything to do with conservatives' loss.

In Italy, Berlusconi's scandal-plagued tenure as prime minister since 2008 came to an end in late 2011 via the breakup of his parliamentary coalition rather than defeat at the polls. That breakup was triggered by a combination factors, including Berlusconi's scandalous personal behavior, his inept and vacillating attempts to reform Italy's increasingly bleak economy and public finances, and, in the end, opposition to a proposed pension plan from one of Berlusconi's own coalition partners, the Northern League. Without calling for new elections, Berlusconi resigned and was replaced by a "technocratic" government headed by economics professor and former European commissioner, Mario Monti. During the long spectacle of Berlusconi's final act, the left-center Democratic Party (PD), with just one-third of the seats in the Chamber of Deputies, remained a marginal actor. The most effective opposition to Berlusconi came not from the PD but from its labor ally, the Confederazione Generale Italiana del Lavoro, which organized several one-day strikes and demonstrations; however, Berlusconi ultimately left the stage because he had squandered all credibility and lost his following.

A leadership change in France in May 2012 produced a different dynamic, at least in the short term. Somewhat in the manner of Italians becoming fatigued by the "Berlusconi show," the French eventually tired of their frenetic, erratic President Nicolas Sarkozy. In presidential elections, Sarkozy was defeated in his reelection bid by Socialist leader François Hollande, who had never held national office. Consciously modeling himself on the "first François"—Mitterrand—Hollande took office in a context bearing no resemblance to the euphoric expectations surrounding Mitterrand's victory in 1981. Whereas Mitterrand initially sought to assert France's economic autonomy with a *volontariste* policy of reflation and nationalizations, Hollande had no such option. Although France's economic fundamentals were certainly stronger than those of the other southern-tier nations, the country faced many of the same tendencies: stagnant growth, rising unemployment, and worsening government deficits and debt. Still, Hollande sought to push back against Merkel's reluctance to pursue a growth strategy as opposed to continued austerity. Even with a favorable showing of the Socialist Party in the follow-on legislative elections in June, it was not clear, as of this writing, that the new president would be able to bend a policy trajectory that was eroding the euro zone's viability and solidarity by the day.

CONCLUSION

Any speculation on how the euro crisis will play out will doubtlessly be rendered obsolete by unfolding events. Within the context of this study of Socialist–Communist relations, however, the foregoing overview permits three observations. First, as the Spanish, Portuguese, and Greek cases indicate, governing left-leaning parties have not escaped public blame for unraveling economic conditions. All three Socialist parties suffered resounding electoral defeats in 2011–2012 directly as a result of a broad perception that governments they controlled had failed to anticipate and/or confront the recession and its impact on employment and living standards. Was this because these parties lacked an effective alternative strategy, or was it because their policy options were too constrained to permit any such strategy? One can plausibly argue that, in fact, the answer to both questions is yes. In any case, the clear evidence is that, politically speaking, the euro crisis ultimately comes home to roost on those parties in charge of managing the crisis.

Second, the flip side of the previous point is that being in the opposition has its electoral advantages. The French Socialists and their leader Hollande, benefiting from Sarkozy's unpopularity and ineffectual economic management, convinced a critical mass of voters that a change of approach—specifically, a more activist progrowth strategy—would be preferable to the status quo. The Italian case, to date, is unclear on this point since no national electoral contest has taken place since 2008; however, the dissolution of the Berlusconi coalition has given the post-Communist Democratic Party a favorable position going into parliamentary elections in 2013. Whether the PD and its allies can overcome their innate reflex to fragment and present a united front remains to be seen.

Finally, recent experience demonstrates that although the classic lines of division between Socialists and Communists are largely passé, a comparable tension remains between center-left parties and what might be termed "Left alternative" parties. The best example is the split between the moderate socialists, PASOK, and the hard-left Syriza Party in Greece. Other examples include the French Parti Socialiste and the newly formed Front de Gauche (a coalition of Communists and dissident Socialists), the Portuguese PSP and two left blocs (the CDU and BE), and the Spanish PSOE and Izquierda Unida. In various ways, these formations echo the age-old debates pitting reformers versus revolutionaries, *possibilistes* versus *maximalistes*. No doubt there will always be conflict within the Left between two broad camps: on the one hand, those who refuse, in Voltaire's formulation, to let the perfect be the enemy of the good and are therefore open to compromise and gradual reform of the status quo and, on the other hand, those who demand "the perfect": immediate, fundamental change in the status quo.

What is striking about the current crisis is its polarizing effect, which has tended to reenergize the latter tendency (as well as more radical tendencies on the Right). Despite—or perhaps because of—the huge constraints that governments face, parties and movements refusing to bear the costs of austerity have mobilized new sources of support. Whether that momentum will last and set the stage for another critical juncture in the history of the Left is an open question. For the present, though, one can conclude that while the specter of Communism no longer haunts Europe, the public's willingness to contest the human consequences of the continent's response to global capitalism—its noble but flawed adoption of a shared currency—is on the rise.

NOTES

1. As a rough gauge of this divergence, consider the annual national averages for the period 2009–2012 on such indicators as real growth in gross domestic product (GDP), government fiscal balance (as percent of GDP), and government debt (as percent of GDP). The following table contrasts the "southern tier" with what one can take as the eight nations of the "Teutonic core" (Austria, Belgium, Denmark, Finland, Germany, Luxembourg, the Netherlands, and Sweden). (Note: Even though Denmark and Sweden are not in the euro zone, I have included them as being largely within the German economic sphere.) All figures reported in this afterword come from the European Union's statistical unit, Eurostat.

	Real GDP Growth	Fiscal Balance	Government Debt
Southern tier	−1.7 %	−8.1%	110.6%
Teutonic core	+0.2%	−2.6%	57.2%

2. Greece's real GDP averaged 3.6 percent annually during this period, compared with the euro zone's 2.0 percent.

3. All figures for 2012 are Eurostat estimates.

4. Greece's annual average government deficit (as a percent of GDP) ballooned from 5.9 percent for 2000–2008 to 11.7 percent for 2009–2012. By 2012, after three years of govern-

ment austerity measures that incited riots, the deficit was still running at nearly 10 percent of GDP. Government debt (as a percent of GDP) averaged 103.5% for 2000–2008 but ballooned every year after 2008, averaging 146.6 percent for the 2009–2011 period.

5. Although high by American standards, Greek voter turnout of 65 percent confirmed a participation rate decline of about one-fourth during the past two decades.

6. Portugal's annual averages for the periods indicated were as follows:

	2000–2008	2009–2012
Real GDP (annual % change)	1.3	−1.6
Unemployment (%)	6.9	12.3
Government fiscal balance (% GDP)	−3.7	−8.1
Government debt (% GDP)	59.3	94.7

7. Thus, as of early 2012, Spanish private debt was 227 percent of GDP—among the highest in Europe—whereas public debt was just 68 percent of GDP, well below the euro zone average of 87 percent. Figures are from Eurostat and the *New York Times*, March 23, 2012.

8. *New York Times*, June 6, 2012.

9. According to the Organization for Economic Cooperation and Development (OECD), about 25 percent of all Spanish workers are on temporary contracts, a figure that is more than twice the OECD average. See *OECD Economic Surveys: Spain* (December 2010, 97).

Appendix A

Socialist and Communist Components of the Left Vote in Western Europe, 1945–1990

Country	Average Vote %: Main Socialist/ Social Democratic/ Labor Party	Average Vote %: Communist Party	Average Vote %: Main Socialist + Communist Party[a]
Austria	43.5	2.4	45.9 (14)
Belgium	27.4	3.9	31.3 (15)
Denmark	36.0	3.1	39.1 (20)
Finland	24.8	18.9	43.7 (13)
France	21.8	21.1	42.9 (14)
Greece	35.9	12.5	48.4 (10)
Italy	12.2	27.3	39.5 (9)
Luxembourg	32.5	9.6	42.1 (11)
Netherlands	29.1	4.1	33.2 (14)
Norway	42.3	3.2	45.5 (12)
Portugal	29.6	15.5	45.1 (7)
Spain	38.3	7.6	45.9 (5)
Sweden	45.5	4.9	50.4 (14)
Switzerland	24.4	2.5	26.9 (11)
United Kingdom	41.5	—	41.5 (13)
West Germany	37.3	1.3	38.6 (12)
Average (%)	32.6	8.6	41.2

[a] Total number of legislative elections in parentheses.
Source: Compiled from *Parties and Elections in Europe* (http://www.parties-and-elections.de).

Appendix B

Socialist and Communist Components of the Left Vote in Western Europe, 1991–2010

Country	Avg. Vote %: Main Socialist/ Social Democratic/ Labor Party	Avg. Vote %: Communist (and Post-Communist) Party	Average Vote %: Main Socialist + Communist Party[a]
Austria	31.1	0.4	31.5 (6)
Belgium	12.1	—	12.1 (6)
Denmark	30.2	—	30.2 (5)
Finland	23.8	10.2	34.0 (5)
France	22.5	7.1	29.6 (4)
Greece	42.2	5.9	48.1 (5)
Italy[b]	7.9	28.8	36.7 (6)
Luxembourg	33.9	1.3	35.2 (4)
Netherlands	23.3	—	23.3 (5)
Norway	32.3	0.1	32.4 (4)
Portugal	41.8	8.2	50.0 (5)
Spain	39.4	6.9	46.3 (5)
Sweden	38.9	7.4	46.3 (5)
Switzerland	21.1	0.9	22.0 (5)
United Kingdom	38.4	—	38.4 (4)
West Germany	37.5	—	37.5 (4)
Average (%)	31.2	3.2	34.4

[a] Total number of legislative elections in parentheses.

[b] Because of extensive changes in the party system in the 1990s, Italy is omitted from the overall category averages. The percentage for the Italian Socialist Party (PSI) is based on the 1992 and 1994 elections only since the PSI was basically dissolved after that date. The percentage for the Communist (and post-Communist) Party includes both the post-Communist Party (PDS, DS, PD) and Rifondazione Comunista.

Source: Compiled from *Parties and Elections in Europe* (http://www.parties-and-elections.de).

Bibliography

Abse, Tobias. 2001. "From PCI to DS: How European Integration Accelerated the 'Social Democratization' of the Italian Left." *Journal of Southern Europe and the Balkans* 3, no. 1 (May): 61–74.

Achimastos, Myron. 1996. "Le mouvement socialiste panhellénique et l'implantation de l'idéologie populiste dans un régime pluraliste." In *La gauche en Europe*, edited by Marc Lazar. Paris: Presses Universitaires de France, 347–65.

"Addio, Dolce Vita: A Survey of Italy." 2005. *The Economist*, November 24.

Adereth, Maxwell. 1984. *French Communist Party: From Comintern to the Colors of France: A Critical History, 1920–1984*. London: Palgrave Macmillan.

Adler, Franklin Hugh. 2005. Review of Michael Mann, *Fascists*. Cambridge: Cambridge University Press, 2004. *Comparative Political Studies* 38, no. 6 (August): 731–36.

Agosti, Aldo. 1996. *Palmiro Togliatti*. Turin: UTET.

———. 1999. *Storia del Partito Comunista Italiano, 1921–1991*. Rome: Laterza.

Aguilar, Paloma. 2002. *Memory and Amnesia: The Role of the Spanish Civil War in the Transition to Democracy*. New York: Berghahn.

Amyot, G. Grant. 1981. *The Italian Communist Party: The Crisis of the Popular Front Strategy*. New York: St. Martin's Press.

Anderson, Perry. 2004a. "Dégringolade." *London Review of Books*, September 2 (part 1 of 2).

———. 2004b. "Union Sucrée." *London Review of Books*, September 23 (part 2 of 2).

———. 2009a. "An Entire Order Converted into What It Was Intended to End." *London Review of Books* 31, no. 4 (February 26): 3–8.

———. 2009b. "Italy's Invertebrate Left." *London Review of Books* 31, no. 5 (March 12): 12–18.

Anderson, Perry, and Patrick Camiller. 1994. *Mapping the West European Left*. London: Verso.

Andolfatto, Dominique. 2005. *PCF: De la mutation à la liquidation*. Monaco: Éditions du Rocher.

Andolfatto, Dominique, and Dominique Labbé. 2006. *Histoire des syndicats: 1906–2006*. Paris: Éditions du Seuil.

Andreatta, Filippo, and Robert Leonardi. 2003. "The Victory of the Ulivo in the 1996 Campaign and Its Defeat in 2001: An Insider's View." In *Italy: Politics and Policy*, vol. 2, edited by Robert Leonardi and Marcello Fedele. Aldershot: Ashgate, 11–34.

André-Bazzana, Bénédicte. 2006. *Mitos y mentiras de la transición*. Madrid: El Viejo Topo.

Antunes Sablosky, Juliet. 1997. "The Portuguese Socialist Party." In *Political Parties and Democracy in Portugal: Organizations, Elections, and Public Opinion*, edited by Thomas Bruneau. Boulder, CO: Westview, 55–76.

Astudillo, Javier. 2001. "Without Unions, but Socialist: The Spanish Socialist Party and Its Divorce from Its Union Confederation (1982–1996)." *Politics and Society* 29, no. 2 (June): 273–96.

Baccetti, Carlo. 1996. "Ruptures et continuités en Italie: Le Parti démocratique de la gauche." In *La gauche en Europe depuis 1945: Invariants et mutations du socialisme européen*, edited by Marc Lazar. Paris: Presses Universitaires de France, 293–307.

———. 2003. "After PCI: Post-Communist and Neo-Communist Parties of the Italian Left after 1989." In *The Crisis of Communism and Party Change: The Evolution of West European Communist and Post-Communist Parties*, edited by Joan Botella and Luis Ramiro. Barcelona: Institut de Ciències Polítiques I Socials, 35–52.

Barbagli, Marzio, and Piergiorgio Corbetta. 1982a. "After the Historic Compromise: A Turning Point for the PCI." *European Journal of Political Research* 10, no. 3: 213–39.

———. 1982b. "The Italian Communist Party and the Social Movements, 1968–1976." In *Political Power and Social Theory: A Research Annual*, vol. 3, edited by Maurice Zeitlin. Greenwich, CT: JAI, 77–112.

=

Barbagli, Marzio, Piergiorgio Corbetta, and Salvatore Sechi. 1979. *Dentro Il PCI*. Bologna: Il Mulino.

Bardi, Luciano. 2006. "Arena elettorale e dinamiche parlamentari nel cambiamento del sistema partitico italiano." In *Partiti e sistemi di partito*, edited by Luciano Bardi. Bologna: Il Mulino.

Bardi, Luciano, and Leonardo Morlino. 1994. "Italy: Tracing the Roots of the Great Transformation." In *How Parties Organize: Change and Adaptation in Party Organizations in Western Democracies*, edited by Richard S. Katz and Peter Mair. London: Sage, 242–77.

Barnes, Samuel H. 1966. "Italy: Oppositions on Left, Right, and Center." In *Political Oppositions in Western Democracies*, edited by Robert A. Dahl. New Haven, CT: Yale University Press, 303–31.

———. 1967. *Party Democracy: Politics in an Italian Socialist Federation*. New Haven, CT: Yale University Press.

Barnes, Samuel H., Max Kaase, et al. 1979. *Political Action: Mass Participation in Five Western Democracies*. Beverly Hills, CA: Sage.

Barnes, Samuel H., Peter McDonough, and Antonio López Pina. 1985. "The Development of Partisanship in New Democracies: The Case of Spain." *American Journal of Political Science* 29, no. 4 (November): 695–720.

Barreiro, Belén. 2002. "La progresiva desmovilización de la izquierda en España: Un análisis de la abstención en las elecciones generales de 1986 a 2000." *Revista Española de Ciencia Política* 6 (April): 183–205.

———. 2004. "14-M: Elecciones a la sombra del terrorismo." *Claves de Razón Práctica* 141: 14–22.

Bartolini, Stefano. 2000. *The Political Mobilization of the European Left, 1860–1980: The Class Cleavage*. Cambridge: Cambridge University Press.

Bartolini, Stefano, Alessandro Chiaramonte, and Roberto D'Alimonte. 2004. "The Italian Party System between Parties and Coalitions." *West European Politics* 27, no. 1 (January): 1–19.

Bauchard, Philippe. 1986. *La guerre des deux roses: Du rêve à la réalité*. Paris: Grasset.

Becker, Jean-Jacques, and Gilles Candar, eds. 2005. *Histoire des gauches en France. Volume 2 XXᵉ siècle: À l'épreuve de l'histoire*. Paris: La Découverte.

Bedani, Gino. 1995. *Politics and Ideology in the Italian Workers' Movement*. Oxford: Berg.

Bell, Daniel A. 1973. *The Coming of Post-Industrial Society: A Venture in Social Forecasting*. New York: Harper Colophon.

Bell, David S., ed. 1993. *Western European Communists and the Collapse of Communism*. Oxford: Berg.

———. 2005. *Francois Mitterrand: A Political Biography*. Oxford: Polity.

Bell, David S., and Byron Criddle. 1988. *The French Socialist Party: Resurgence and Victory*. 2nd ed. Oxford: Oxford University Press.

———. 1994a. *The French Communist Party in the Fifth Republic*. Oxford: Oxford University Press.

————. 1994b. "The French Socialist Party: Presidentialised Factionalism." In *Conflict and Cohesion in Western European Social Democratic Parties*, edited by David S. Bell and Eric Shaw. London: Pinter, 112–32.

Bell, David S., and Eric Shaw, eds. 1994. *Conflict and Cohesion in the Western European Social Democratic Parties*. London: Pinter.

Bellucci, Paolo, Marco Maraffi, and Paolo Segatti. 2001. "The Democrats of the Left." In *Italian Politics: A Review, Volume 16. Emerging Themes and Institutional Responses*, edited by Mario Caciagli and Alan S. Zuckerman. New York: Berghahn, 53–65.

Bergounioux, Alain. 1996. "Les fragilités du Parti Socialiste Français." In *La gauche en Europe depuis 1945: Invariants et mutations du socialisme européen*, edited by Marc Lazar, with the collaboration of Francine Simon-Ekovich. Paris: Presses Universitaires de France, 237–62.

Bergounioux, Alain, and Gérard Grunberg. 2005. *L'ambition et le remords: Les socialistes français et le pouvoir (1905–2005)*. Paris: Fayard.

Berlinguer, Enrico. 1973. "Riflessioni sull'Italia dopo I fatti del Cile." *Rinascita* 30 (October 12): 3–5.

Berman, Sheri. 2006. *The Primacy of Politics: Social Democracy and the Making of Europe's Twentieth Century*. Cambridge: Cambridge University Press.

Bermeo, Nancy. 1986. *The Revolution within the Revolution: Workers' Control in Rural Portugal*. Princeton, NJ: Princeton University Press.

————. 1987. "Redemocratization and Transition Elections: A Comparison of Spain and Portugal." *Comparative Politics* 19, no. 2 (January): 213–31.

————. 1995. "Classification and Consolidation: Some Lessons from the Greek Dictatorship." *Comparative Politics* 110, no. 3 (Fall), 435–452.

————, ed. 2000. *Unemployment in Southern Europe: Coping with the Consequences*. Essex: Frank Cass.

————, ed. 2001. *Unemployment in the New Europe*. Cambridge: Cambridge University Press.

Bernstein, Eduard. 1961. *Evolutionary Socialism: A Criticism and Affirmation*. New York: Schocken. (orig. German ed. 1899)

Berstein, Serge. 1989. *La France de l'expansion. I. La République gaullienne 1958–1969*. Paris: Éditions du Seuil.

Blackmer, Donald L. M., and Sidney Tarrow, eds. 1975. *Communism in Italy and France*. Princeton, NJ: Princeton University Press.

Bobbio, Norberto. 1995. *Ideological Profile of Twentieth-Century Italy*. Princeton, NJ: Princeton University Press.

Bodin, Louis, and Jean Touchard. 1986. *Front Populaire, 1936*. 4th ed. Paris: Armand Colin.

Boggs, Carl, and David Plotke, eds. 1980. *The Politics of Eurocommunism: Socialism in Transition*. Boston: South End.

Boix, Carles. 1998a. "Las elecciones primarias en el PSOE: Ventajas, ambigüedades y riesgos." *Claves de Razón Práctica* 83: 34–38.

————. 1998b. *Political Parties, Growth and Equality: Conservative and Social Democratic Economic Strategies in the World Economy*. Cambridge: Cambridge University Press.

Bordandini, Paola, Aldo Di Virgilio, and Francesco Raniolo. 2008. "The Birth of a Party: The Case of the Italian Partito Democratico." *South European Society and Politics* 13, no. 3 (September): 303–24.

Bosco, Anna. 2000. *Comunisti: Trasformazioni di partito in Italia, Spagna e Portogallo*. Bologna: Il Mulino.

Bosco, Anna, in collaboration with Carlos Gaspar. 2001. "Four Actors in Search of a Role: The Southern European Communist Parties." In *Parties, Politics, and Democracy in the New Southern Europe*, edited by P. Nikoforos Diamondouros and Richard Gunther. Baltimore: Johns Hopkins University Press, 329–87.

Bosco, Anna, and Leonardo Morlino. 2007. *Party Change in Southern Europe*. London: Routledge.

Bosworth, R. J. B. 1998. *The Italian Dictatorship: Problems and Perspectives in the Interpretation of Mussolini and Fascism*. London: Arnold.

————. 2006. *Mussolini's Italy: Life under the Dictatorship, 1915–1945*. New York: Penguin.

Botella, Joan. 1988. "Spanish Communism in Crisis: The Communist Party of Spain." In *Communist Parties in Western Europe: Decline or Adaptation*, edited by Michael Waller and Meindert Fennema. Oxford: Basil Blackwell, 69–85.

Botella, Joan, and Luis Ramiro, eds. 2003. *The Crisis of Communism and Party Change: The Evolution of West European Communist and Post-Communist Parties*. Barcelona: Institut de Ciències Polítiques I Socials.

Boy, Daniel, Françoise Platone, Henri Rey, Françoise Subileau, and Colette Ysmal. 2003. *C'était la gauche plurielle*. Paris: Presses de Sciences Po.

Boyer, Robert. 1986. *La théorie de la régulation: Une analyse critique*. Paris: Éditions la Découverte.

Bracke, Maud, and Thomas Ekman Jørgensen. 2002. "West European Communism after Stalinism: Comparative Approaches." EUI Working Paper HEC No. 2002/4. Badia Fiesolana, San Domenica: European University Institute.

Brenner, Robert. 1998. *The Economics of Global Turbulence: A Special Report on the World Economy, 1950–1998*. New Left Review 229 (special issue): 1–264.

Brower, Daniel R. 1968. *The New Jacobins: The French Communist Party and the Popular Front*. Ithaca, NY: Cornell University Press.

Bull, Martin J. 1994. "Social Democracy's New Recruit? Conflict and Cohesion in the Italian Democratic Party of the Left." In *Conflict and Cohesion in Western European Social Democratic Parties*, edited by David S. Bell and Eric Shaw. London: Frances Pinter, 31–49.

———. 1995. "The West European Communist Movement in the Late Twentieth Century." *West European Politics* 18, no. 1 (January): 78–97.

———. 2003. "Italy: The Crisis of the Left." *Parliamentary Affairs* 56, no. 1: 58–74.

Bull, Martin J., and Paul Heywood, eds. 1994. *West European Communist Parties after the Revolutions of 1989*. London: Macmillan.

Bull, Martin J., and James Newell. 2005. *Italian Politics*. Oxford: Polity Press.

Bunce, Valerie J. 1984. "The Empire Strikes Back: The Evolution of the Eastern Bloc from a Soviet Asset to a Soviet Liability." *International Organization* 39 (Winter): 1–46.

Burgess, Katrina. 2004. *Parties and Unions in the New Global Economy*. Pittsburgh, PA: University of Pittsburgh Press.

Calise, Mauro. 1994. "The Italian Particracy: Beyond President and Parliament." *Political Studies Quarterly* 109, no. 3: 441–60.

Cameron, David R. 1984. "Social Democracy, Corporatism, Labour Quiescence and the Representation of Economic Interest in Advanced Capitalist Society. In *Order and Conflict in Contemporary Capitalism: Studies in the Political Economy of Western European Nations*, edited by John H. Goldthorpe. Oxford: Oxford University Press, 143–78.

———. 1988. "Colors of the Rose: On the Ambiguous Record of French Socialism." Cambridge, MA: Harvard University, Center for European Studies Working Paper.

Camiller, Patrick. 1994. "Spain: The Survival of Socalism?" In *Mapping the West European Left*, edited by Perry Anderson and Patrick Camiller. London: Verso, 233–65.

Cammett, John McKay. 1967. *Antonio Gramsci and the Origins of Italian Communism*. Stanford, CA: Stanford University Press.

Carrillo, Santiago. 1977. *Eurocomunismo y estado*. Barcelona: Editorial Crítica.

Castro, Carles. 2008. *Relato electoral de España (1977–2007)*. Barcelona: Institut de Ciències Polítiques I Socials.

Cayrol, Roland. 1974. "Les militants du Parti Socialiste: Contribution à une sociologie." *Projet* 88 (September–October): 929–40.

———. 1978a. "Les attitudes des électorats de gauche: Changement social, liberté, alliances politiques." In *Sofres, L'opinion française en 1977*. Paris: Presses de la FNSP, 43–68.

———. 1978b. "Le Parti Socialiste à l'entreprise." *Revue Française de Science Politique* 28, no. 2 (April): 296–312.

Chari, Raj S. 2005."Why Did the Spanish Communist Strategy Fail?" *Journal of Communist Studies and Transition Politics* 21, no. 2 (June): 296–301.

Charzat, Michel, et al. 1975. *Le C.E.R.E.S.: Un combat pour le socialisme*. Paris: Calmann-Levy.

Chilcote, Ronald H. 2010. *The Portuguese Revolution: State and Class in the Transition to Democracy.* Lanham, MD: Rowman & Littlefield.

Clift, Ben. 2005. *French Socialism in a Global Era: The Political Economy of the New Social Democracy in France.* New York: Continuum.

Clogg, Richard. 1987. *Parties and Elections in Greece: The Search for Legitimacy.* Durham, NC: Duke University Press.

Coates, David, ed. 2005. *Varieties of Capitalism, Varieties of Approaches.* Basingstoke: Palgrave Macmillan.

Codding, George A., Jr., and William Safran. 1979. *Ideology and Politics: The Socialist Party of France.* Boulder, CO: Westview.

Collier, Ruth Berins, and David Collier. 1991. *Shaping the Political Arena: Critical Junctures, the Labor Movement, and Regime Dynamics in Latin America.* Princeton, NJ: Princeton University Press.

Colton, Joel. 1966. *Léon Blum: Humanist in Politics.* New York: Knopf.

Costa Lobo, Marina. 2001. "The Role of Political Parties in Portuguese Democratic Consolidation." *Party Politics* 7, no. 5: 643–53.

Costa Lobo, Marina, and P. Magalhaes. 2004. "The Portuguese Socialists and the Third Way." In *Social Democratic Politics in Contemporary Europe*, edited by G. Bonoli and M. Powell. London: Routledge, 83–101.

Courtois, Stephane, and Marc Lazar. 2000. *Histoire du Parti Communiste Français.* 2nd ed. Paris: Presses Universitaires de France.

Crouch, Colin. 2008. "Change in European Societies since the 1970s." *West European Politics* 31, no. 1–2 (January–March): 14–39.

Crow, John A. 1985. *Spain: The Root and the Flower.* 3rd ed. Berkeley: University of California Press.

Cunha, Carlos. 1997. "The Portuguese Communist Party." In *Political Parties and Democracy in Portugal: Organizations, Elections, and Public Opinion*, edited by Thomas Bruneau. Boulder, CO: Westview, 23–54.

———. 2003. "Mais Portugal! mais CDU!" . . . mais PCP? The Portuguese Communist Party at the Turn of the 21st Century." In *The Crisis of Communism and Party Change: The Evolution of West European Communist and Post-Communist Parties*, edited by Joan Botella and Luis Ramiro. Barcelona: Institut de Ciencies Politiques I Socials, 99–127.

D'Alimonte, Roberto. 1999. "Party Behavior in a Polarized System: The Italian Communist Party and the Historic Compromise." In *Policy, Office, or Votes? How Political Parties in Western Europe Make Hard Decisions*, edited by Wolfgang C. Muller and Kaare Strom. Cambridge: Cambridge University Press, 141–71.

Dalton, Russell D. 2004. *Democratic Challenges, Democratic Choices: The Erosion of Political Support in Advanced Industrial Democracies.* Oxford: Oxford University Press.

De Grand, Alexander. 1989. *The Italian Left in the Twentieth Century: A History of the Socialist and Communist Parties.* Bloomington: Indiana University Press, 1989.

Di Palma, Giuseppe. 1977. "Eurocommunism? A Review Article." *Comparative Politics* 9, no. 3 (April): 357–75.

Di Scala, Spencer M. 1988. *Renewing Italian Socialism: Nenni to Craxi.* New York: Oxford University Press.

———, ed. 1996. *Italian Socialism: Between Politics and History.* Amherst: University of Massachusetts Press.

Diamondouros, P. Nikiforos. 1991. "PASOK and State-Society Relations in Post-Authoritarian Greece (1974–1988)." In *Greece on the Road to Democracy: From the Junta to PASOK, 1974–1986*, edited by Speros Vryonis Jr. New York: Aristide Caratzas, 15–35.

Diamondouros, P. Nikiforos, and Richard Gunther, eds. 2001. *Parties, Politics, and Democracy in the New Southern Europe.* Baltimore: Johns Hopkins University Press.

Díez Medrano, Juan. 1995. *Divided Nations: Class, Politics, and Nationalism in the Basque Country and Catalonia.* Ithaca, NY: Cornell University Press.

Dinas, Elias. 2008. "The Greek General Election of 2007: You Cannot Lose If Your Opponent Cannot Win." *West European Politics* 31, no. 3 (May): 600–607.

———. 2010. "The Greek General Election of 2009: PASOK—The Third Generation." *West European Politics* 33, no. 2 (March): 389–98.

Dubois, Pierre, et al. 1971. *Grèves revendicatives ou grèves politiques?* Paris: Éditions Anthropos.

Duggan, Christopher. 2007. *The Force of Destiny: A History of Italy since 1796.* London: Allen Lane.

Duverger, Maurice. 1959. *Political Parties: Their Organization and Activity in the Modern State.* 2nd English ed. New York: Wiley.

Edles, Laura Desfor. 1998. *Symbol and Ritual in the New Spain: The Transition to Democracy after Franco.* Cambridge: Cambridge University Press.

Eichengreen, Barry. 2007. *The European Economy since 1945: Coordinated Capitalism and Beyond.* Princeton, NJ: Princeton University Press.

Einaudi, Mario, Jean-Marie Domenach, and Aldo Garosci. 1951. *Communism in Western Europe.* Ithaca, NY: Cornell University Press.

Elephantis, A. 1981. "PASOK and the Elections of 1977: The Rise of the Populist Movement." In *Greece at the Polls: The National Elections of 1974 and 1977*, edited by Howard R. Penniman. Washington, DC: American Enterprise Institute, 105–29.

Eley, Geoff. 2002. *Forging Democracy: The History of the Left in Europe, 1850–2000.* Oxford: Oxford University Press.

Encarnación, Omar G. 2003. *The Myth of Civil Society: Social Capital and Democratic Consolidation in Spain and Brazil.* New York: Palgrave Macmillan.

———. 2008. "Reconciliation after Democratization: Coping with the Past in Spain." *Political Science Quarterly* 123, no. 3: 435–59.

Eubank, William Lee, Arun Gangopadahay, and Leonard B. Weinberg. 1996. "Italian Communism in Crisis: A Study in Exit, Voice and Loyalty." *Party Politics* 2, no. 1: 55–75.

Evans, Jocelyn A. J., ed. 2003. *The French Party System.* Manchester: Manchester University Press.

Favier, Pierre, and Michel Martin-Roland. 1990. *La décennie Mitterrand. Tome 1: Les ruptures (1981–1984).* Paris: Éditions du Seuil.

———. 1991. *La décennie Mitterrand. Tome 2: Les épreuves (1984–1988).* Paris: Éditions du Seuil.

———. 1996. *La décennie Mitterrand. Tome 3: Les défis (1988–1991).* Paris: Éditions du Seuil.

Featherstone, Kevin. 1987. "PASOK and the Left." In *Political Change in Greece: Before and after the Colonels*, edited by Kevin Featherstone and Dimitrios K. Katsoudas. London: Croom Helm, 112–34.

Feenberg, Andrew, and Jim Freedman. 2001. *When Poetry Ruled the Streets: The French May Events of 1968.* Albany: State University of New York Press.

Ferraresi, Franco. 1996. *Threats to Democracy: The Radical Right in Italy after the War.* Princeton, NJ: Princeton University Press.

Fishman, Robert M. 1990. *Working Class Organization and the Return to Democracy in Spain.* Ithaca, NY: Cornell University Press.

———. 2004. *Democracy's Voices: Social Ties and the Quality of Public Life in Spain.* Ithaca, NY: Cornell University Press.

Flores, Marcello, and Nicola Gallerano. 1992. *Sul PCI: Un'interpretazione storica.* Bologna: Il Mulino. http://www.iue.it/LIB/About/webfloorplanfinal.swf.

Fonteneau, Alain, and Pierre Muet. 1985. *La gauche face à la crise.* Paris: Presses de la Fondation Nationale des Sciences Poltiques.

Fourastié, Jean. 1979. *Les trente glorieuses: Ou, la révolution invisible de 1946 à 1975.* Paris: Fayard.

Fowerwaker, Joe. 1989. *Making Democracy in Spain: Grass-Roots Struggle in the South, 1955–1975.* Cambridge: Cambridge University Press.

Freeman, Richard. 2006. "Learning in Public Policy." In *The Oxford Handbook of Public Policy*, edited by Michael Moran, Martin Rein, and Robert E. Goodin. Oxford: Oxford University Press, 367–88.

Friend, Julius W. 1998. *The Long Presidency: France in the Mitterrand Years, 1981–1995.* Boulder, CO: Westview.

Fuentes, Juan Francisco. 2005. *Francisco Largo Caballero: El Lenin español.* Madrid: Editorial Síntesis.

Gaffney, John. 1989. *The French Left and the Fifth Republic: The Discourses of Communism and Socialism in Contemporary France.* New York: Palgrave Macmillan.

Gallego, Ferran. 2008. *El mito de la transición: La crisis del Franquismo y los orígenes de la democracia (1973–1977).* Barcelona: Crítica.

Galli, Giorgio. 2004. *I partiiti politici italiani (1943–2004).* Milan: Rizzoli Libri.

Gallie, Duncan. 1983. *Social Inequality and Class Radicalism in France and Britain.* Cambridge: Cambridge University Press.

Gardner, Richard N. 2005. *Mission Italy: On the Front Lines of the Cold War.* Lanham, MD: Rowman & Littlefield.

Giannetti, Daniela, and Rosa Mulé. 2006. "The Democratici di Sinistra: In Search of a New Identity." *South European Society and Politics* 11, no. 3–4 (September–December): 457–75.

Giesbert, Franz-Olivier. 1990. *Le Président.* Paris: Éditions du Seuil.

Gilbert, Mark. 1995. *The Italian Revolution: The End of Politics Italian Style?* Boulder, CO: Westview.

Gillespie, Richard. 1989. *The Spanish Socialist Party: A History of Factionalism.* Oxford: Oxford University Press.

———. 1990. "The Break-up of the 'Socialist Family': Party-Union Relations in Spain, 1982–89." *West European Politics* 13, no. 1 (January): 47–62.

———. 1994. "The Resurgence of Factionalism in the Spanish Socialist Workers Party." In *Conflict and Cohesion in the Western European Social Democratic Parties,* edited by David S. Bell and Eric Shaw. London: Pinter, 50–69.

Gillespie, Richard, and William E. Paterson, eds. 1993. *Rethinking Social Democracy in Western Europe.* London: Frank Cass.

Gilmour, David. 1985. *The Transformation of Spain: From Franco to the Constitutional Monarchy.* London: Quartet.

———. 2011. *The Pursuit of Italy: A History of a Land, Its Regions, and Their Peoples.* New York: Farrar, Straus and Giroux.

Ginsborg, Paul. 2003a. *A History of Contemporary Italy: Society and Politics 1943–1988.* New York: Palgrave Macmillan.

———. 2003b. *Italy and Its Discontents: Family, Civil Society, State: 1980–2001.* New York: Palgrave Macmillan.

———. 2004. *Silvio Berlusconi: Television, Power and Patrimony.* London: Verso.

Giovagnoli, Agostino. 1996. *Il partito italiano: La Democrazia Cristiana dal 1942 al 1994.* Rome-Bari: Laterza.

Glyn, Andrew, ed. 2001. *Social Democracy in Neoliberal Times: The Left and Economic Policy since 1980.* Oxford: Oxford University Press.

Gold, Thomas W. 2003. *The Lega Nord and Contemporary Politics in Italy.* New York: Palgrave Macmillan.

Golden, Miriam A. 1988a. "Historical Memory and Ideological Orientations in the Italian Workers' Movement." *Politics and Society* 16, no. 1 (March): 1–34.

———. 1988b. *Labor Divided: Austerity and Working-Class Politics in Contemporary Italy.* Ithaca, NY: Cornell University Press.

Gordon, David M., Richard Edwards, and Michael Reich. 1982. *Segmented Work, Divided Workers: The Historical Transformation of Labor in the United States.* Cambridge: Cambridge University Press.

Gramsci, Antonio. 1971. *Selections from the Prison Notebooks of Antonio Gramsci.* Edited by Quintin Hoare and Geoffrey Nowell Smith. New York: International Publishers.

Greene, Nathanael. 1969. *Crisis and Decline: The French Socialist Party in the Popular Front Era.* Ithaca, NY: Cornell University Press.

Greene, Thomas H. 1968. "The Communist Parties of Italy and France: A Study in Comparative Communism." *World Politics* 21, no. 1 (October): 1–38.

Griffith. William E., ed. 1979. *The European Left: Italy, France, and Spain.* Lexington, MA: D. C. Heath.

Groux, Guy, and René Mouriaux. 1989. *La C.F.D.T.* Paris: Economica.

Grunberg, Gérard. 2007. "Les elections françaises de 2007." *French Politics, Culture and Society* 25, no. 3 (Winter): 62–73.

Guiat, Cyrille. 2003. *The French and Italian Communist Parties: Comrades and Culture.* London: Frank Cass.

Gunther, Richard. 1986. "The Spanish Socialist Party: From Clandestine Opposition to Party of Government." In *The Politics of Democratic Spain*, edited by Stanley G. Payne. Chicago: Chicago Council on Foreign Relations, 50–110.

———. 1992. "Spain: The Very Model of the Modern Elite Settlement." In *Elites and Democratic Consolidation in Latin America and Southern Europe*, edited by John Higley and Richard Gunther. Cambridge: Cambridge University Press, 38–80.

———. 2007. "Portuguese Elections in Comparative Perspective: Parties and Electoral Behavior in Southern Europe." In *Portugal at the Polls*, edited by Andre Freire, M. Costa Lobo, and P. Pagalhaes. Lanham, MD: Lexington Books, 11–47.

Gunther, Richard, P. Nikiforos Diamandouros, and Hans-Jürgen Puhle, eds. 1995. *The Politics of Democratic Consolidation: Southern Europe in Comparative Perspective.* Baltimore: Johns Hopkins University Press.

Gunther, Richard, P. Nikiforos Diamandouros, and Deimitri A. Sotiropoulos, eds. 2006. *Democracy and the State in the New Southern Europe.* New York: Oxford University Press.

Gunther, Richard, and José Ramón Montero. 2009. *The Politics of Spain.* Cambridge: Cambridge University Press.

Gunther, Richard, José Ramón Montero, and Joan Botella. 2004. *Democracy in Modern Spain.* New Haven, CT: Yale University Press.

Gunther, Richard, Giacomo Sani, and Goldie Shabad. 1988. *Spain after Franco: The Making of a Competitive Party System.* Berkeley: University of California Press.

Hall, Peter A. 1986. *Governing the Economy: The Politics of State Intervention in Britain and France.* Oxford: Polity.

———. 1993. "Policy Paradigms, Social Learning, and the State: The Case of Economic Policymaking in Britain." *Comparative Politics* 25, no. 3 (April): 275–96.

Hamann, Kerstin, and Miguel Martínez Lucio. 2003. "Strategies of Union Revitalization in Spain: Negotiating Change and Fragmentation." *European Journal of Industrial Relations* 9, no. 1 (2003): 61–78.

Hamann, Kerstin, and Paul Christopher Manuel. 1999. "Regime Changes and Civil Society in Twentieth-Century Portugal." *South European Society and Politics* 4, no. 1 (Summer): 71–96.

Hamon, Hervé, and Patrick Rotman. 1980. *L'effet Rocard.* Paris: Éditions Stock.

———. 1982. *La deuxième gauche: Histoire intellectuelle et politique de la CFDT.* Paris: Éditions Ramsey.

Hanley, David. 1986. *Keeping Left? Ceres and the French Socialist Party: A Contribution to the Study of Fractionalism in Political Parties.* Manchester: Manchester University Press.

———. 2003. "Managing the Plural Left: Implications for the Party System." In *The French Party System*, edited by Jocelyn A. J. Evans. Manchester: Manchester University Press, 76–90.

———. 2008. *Beyond the Nation State: Parties in the Era of European Integration.* Basingstoke: Palgrave Macmillan.

Hazareesingh, Sudhir. 1991. *Int ellectuals and the French Communist Party: Disillusion and Decline.* Oxford: Clarendon Press.

———. 1994. *Political Traditions in Modern France.* Oxford: Oxford University Press.

Heclo, Hugh. 1974. *Modern Social Policies in Britain and Sweden.* New Haven, CT: Yale University Press.

Hellman, Stephen. 1975. "The PCI's Alliance Strategy and the Case of the Middle Classes." In *Communism in Italy and France*, edited by Donald L. M. Blackmer and Sidney Tarrow. Princeton, NJ: Princeton University Press, 373–419.

————. 1988. *Italian Communism in Transition: The Rise and Fall of the Historic Compromise in Turin, 1975–1980*. New York: Oxford University Press.

————. 1993. "The Left and the Decomposition of the Party System in Italy." In *Real Problems, False Solutions: Socialist Register 1993*, edited by Ralph Miliband and Leo Panitch. London: Merlin, 190–210.

————. 1996. "Italian Communism in the First Republic." In *The New Italian Republic: From the Fall of the Berlin Wall to Berlusconi*, edited by Stephen Gundle and Simon Parker. London: Routledge, 72–84.

Heywood, Paul. 1990. *Marxism and the Failure of Organised Socialism in Spain (1879–1936)*. Oxford: Oxford University Press.

————. 1994. "The Spanish Left: Towards a 'Common Home'?" In *West European Communist Parties after the Revolutions of 1989*, edited by Martin J. Bull and Paul Heywood. London: Macmillan, 56–89.

Hine, David. 1979. "The Italian Socialist Party under Craxi: Surviving but Not Reviving." *West European Politics* 2, no. 4 (October): 133–48.

————. 1990. "The Consolidation of Democracy in Post-War Italy." In *Security Democracy: Political Parties and Democratic Consolidation in Southern Europe*, edited by Geoffrey Pridham. London: Routledge, 62–83.

————. 1993. *Governing Italy: The Politics of Bargained Pluralism*. Oxford: Clarendon.

Hobsbawm, Eric J., and Giorgio Napolitano. 1977. *The Italian Road to Socialism*. Westport, CT: Lawrence Hill.

Howell, Chris. 1992. *Regulating Labor: The State and Industrial Relations Reform in Postwar France*. Princeton, NJ: Princeton University Press.

————. 2003. "Varieties of Capitalism: And Then There Was One? A Review Essay." *Comparative Politics* 36, no. 1 (October): 103–24.

Iglesias, María Antonia, ed. 2005. *La memoria recuperada: Lo que nunca han contado Felipe Gonález y los dirigentes socialistas*. 2 vols. Madrid: Punto de Lectura.

Ignazi, Piero. 2002. *Il potere dei partiti. La politica in Italia dagli anni sessanta a oggi*. Roma-Bari: Laterza.

Ignazi, Piero, and Colette Ysmal, eds. 1998. *The Organization of Political Parties in Southern Europe*. New York: Praeger.

Jackson, Gabriel. 1974. *A Concise History of the Spanish Civil War*. New York: John Day.

Jackson, Julian. 1988. *The Popular Front in France: Defending Democracy, 1934–38*. Cambridge: Cambridge University Press.

Jenson, Jane, and George Ross. 1984. *The View from Inside: A French Communist Cell in Crisis*. Berkeley: University of California Press.

Johnson, R. W. 1981. *The Long March of the French Left*. London: Macmillan.

Joravsky, David. 1994. "Communism in Historical Perspective." *American Historical Review* 99 (June): 837–57.

Judt, Tony. 1982. "Une historiographie pas comme les autres: The French Communists and Their History." *European Studies Review* 12: 445–78.

————. 1986. *Marxism and the French Left*. Oxford: Oxford University Press.

————. 2005. *Postwar: A History of Europe since 1945*. New York: Penguin.

Juliá, Santos. 1989. "The Origins and Nature of the Spanish Popular Front." In *The French and Spanish Popular Fronts: Comparative Perspectives*, edited by Martin S. Alexander and Helen Graham. Cambridge: Cambridge University Press, 24–37.

————. 1991. "The Ideological Conversion of the Leaders of the PSOE, 1976–1979." In *Elites and Power in 20th Century Spain*, edited by Frances Lannon and Paul Preston. Oxford: Clarendon Press, 269–85.

————. 1997. *Los socialistas en la política de España, 1879–1982*. Madrid: Taurus.

July, Serge. 1986. *Les années Mitterrand: Histoire baroque d'une normalisation inachevée*. Paris: Grasset.

Kalyvas, Stathis. 1997. "Polarization in Greek Politics: PASOK's First Four Years, 1981–1985." *Journal of the Hellenic Diaspora* 23, no. 1: 83–104.

Kalyvas, Stathis, and Nikos Marantzidis. 2003. "The Two Paths of the Greek Communist Movement (1985–2001)." In *The Crisis of Communism and Party Change: The Evolution of*

West European Communist and Post-Communist Parties, edited by Joan Botella and Luis Ramiro. Barcelona: Institut de Ciencies Politiques i Socials, 15–32.

Kapetanyannis, Vassilis. 1987. "The Communists." In *Political Change in Greece: Before and after the Colonels*, edited by Kevin Featherstone and Dimitrios K. Katsoudas. London: Croom Helm, 145–73.

Katz, Richard S., and Peter Mair. 1992. "The Membership of Political Parties in European Democracies, 1960–1990." *European Journal of Political Research* 22: 329–45.

———. 1995. "Changing Models of Party Organization and Party Democracy: The Emergence of the Cartel Party." *Party Politics* 1, no. 1 (January): 5–28.

Katznelson, Ira. 2003. "Periodization and Preferences: Reflections on Purposive Action in Comparative Historical Social Science." In *Comparative Historical Analysis in the Social Sciences*, edited by James Mahoney and Dietrich Rueschemeyer. Cambridge: Cambridge University Press, 270–301.

Kennedy, Paul. 2007. "Phoenix from the Ashes. The PSOE Government under Rodríguez Zapatero 2004–2007: A New Model for Social Democracy?" *International Journal of Iberian Studies* 20, no. 3: 187–206.

Kertzer, David I. 1980. *Comrades and Christians: Religion and Political Struggle in Communist Italy*. Cambridge: Cambridge University Press.

———. 1996. *Politics and Symbols: The Italian Communist Party and the Fall of Communism*. New Haven, CT: Yale University Press.

Kesselman, Mark. 1983. "France: Socialism without the Workers." *Kapitalistate* 10/11: 11–41.

———, ed. 1984. *The French Workers Movement: Economic Crisis and Political Change*. London: George Allen & Unwin.

Kesselman, Mark, Joel Krieger, et al. 2009. *European Politics in Transition*. 6th ed. Boston: Houghton Mifflin.

Kitschelt, Herbert. 1994. *The Transformation of European Social Democracy*. Cambridge: Cambridge University Press.

Knapp, Andrew. 2004. *Parties and the Party System in France: A Disconnected Democracy?* New York: Palgrave Macmillan.

Koelble, Thomas A. 1991. *The Left Unraveled: Social Democracy and the New Left Challenge in Britain and West Germany*. Durham, NC: Duke University Press.

Kogan, Norman. 1983. *A Political History of Italy: The Postwar Years*. New York: Praeger.

Kowalski, Ronald. 2006. *European Communism: 1848–1991*. New York: Palgrave Macmillan.

Kriegel, Annie. 1972. *Les communistes français*. Paris: Éditions du Seuil.

Kurth, James, and James Petras, with Diarmuid Maguire and Ronald Chilcote. 1993. *Mediterranean Paradoxes: The Politics and Social Structure of Southern Europe*. Providence, RI: Berg.

Labbé, Dominique. 1996. *Syndicats et syndiqués en France depuis 1945*. Paris: L'Harmattan.

Labbé, Dominique, and Dominique Andolfatto. 1997. *La CGT: Organisation et audience depuis 1945*. Paris: Decouverte.

Ladrech, Robert. 2003. "The Left and the European Union." *Parliamentary Affairs* 56: 112–24.

Ladrech, Robert, and Philippe Marlière, eds. 1999. *Social Democratic Parties in the European Union*. Basingstoke: Macmillan.

Lago, I., and José Ramón Montero. 2005. "Los mecanismos del cambio electoral: Del 11-M al 14-M." *Claves de Razón Práctica* 149: 36–44.

Lancaster, Thomas D. 1994. "A New Phase for Spanish Democracy? The General Election of June 1993." *West European Politics* 17, no. 1 (January): 183–90.

Lane, David. 2004. *Berlusconi's Shadow: Crime, Justice, and Pursuit of Power*. London: Penguin.

Lange, Peter. 1986. "The End of an Era: The Wage Indexation Referendum of 1985." In *Italian Politics: A Review*, vol. 1, edited by Robert Leonardi and Raffaella Y. Nanetti. London: Frances Pinter, 29–46.

Lange, Peter, Cynthia Irvin, and Sidney Tarrow. 1990. "Mobilization, Social Movements and Party Recruitment: The Italian Communist Party since the 1960s." *British Journal of Political Science* 20, no. 1 (January): 15–42.

Lange, Peter, George Ross, and Maurizio Vannicelli. 1982. *Unions, Change and Crisis: French and Italian Union Strategy and the Political Economy, 1945–1980.* London: George Allen & Unwin.

Lange, Peter, and Maurizio Vannicelli, eds. 1981. *The Communist Parties of Italy, France, and Spain.* London: George Allen & Unwin.

LaPalombara, Joseph. 1987. *Democracy Italian Style.* New Haven, CT: Yale University Press.

Lavabre, Marie-Claire, and François Platone. 2003. *Que reste-t-il du PCF?* Paris: Éditions Autrement.

Lavau, George. 1981a. "The Effects of Twenty Years of Gaullism on the Parties of the Left." In *The Impact of the Fifth Republic on France,* edited by William G. Andrews and Stanley Hoffman. Albany: State University of New York Press, 91–116.

———. 1981b. *A quoi sert le Parti Communiste Français?* Paris: Fayard.

Lazar, Marc. 1992. *Maisons rouges: Les partis communistes français et italiens de la Libération à nos jours.* Paris: Aubier.

Lazar, Marc, with the collaboration of Francine Simon-Ekovich, ed. 1996. *La gauche en Europe depuis 1945: Invariants et mutations du socialisme européen.* Paris: Presses Universitaires de France.

Lefranc, Georges. 1965. *Histoire du Front Populaire, 1934–1938.* Paris: Payot.

Legg, Keith R., and John M. Roberts. 1997. *Modern Greece: A Civilization on the Periphery.* Boulder, CO: Westview.

Levy, Jonah. 1999. *Toqueville's Revenge: State, Society, and Economy in Contemporary France.* Cambridge, MA: Harvard University Press.

———. 2000. "France: Directing Adjustment?" In *Welfare and Work in the Open Economy: Vol. II. Diverse Responses to Common Challenges,* edited by Fritz W. Scharpf and Vivien A. Schmidt. Oxford: Oxford University Press, 308–50.

———. 2005. "Economic Policy and Policy-Making." In *Developments in French Politics 3,* edited by Alistair Cole, Patrick Le Galès, and Jonah Levy. Basingstoke: Palgrave Macmillan, 170–94.

———, ed. 2006. *The State after Statism: New State Activities in the Age of Liberalization.* Cambridge, MA: Harvard University Press.

Lewis-Beck, Michael S., ed. 2000. *How France Votes.* New York: Chatham House.

Lichtheim, George. 1966. *Marxism in Modern France.* New York: Columbia University Press.

Linz, Juan J. 1973. "Opposition to and under an Authoritarian Regime: The Case of Spain." In *Regimes and Oppositions,* edited by Robert A. Dahl. New Haven, CT: Yale University Press, 171–259.

Linz, Juan J., Alfred Stepan, and Richard Gunther. 1995. "Democratic Transition and Consolidation in Southern Europe, with Reflections on Latin America and Eastern Europe." In *The Politics of Democratic Consolidation: Southern Europe in Comparative Perspective,* edited by Richard Gunther, P. Nikiforos Diamandouros, and Hans-Jürgen Puhle. Baltimore: Johns Hopkins University Press, 77–123.

Lipset, Seymour Martin, and Stein Rokkan. 1967. *Party Systems and Voter Alignments: Cross-National Perspectives.* New York: Free Press.

Lisi, Marco. 2006. "The Importance of Winning Office: The PS and the Struggle for Power." *South European Society and Politics* 11, no. 3 (September): 381–97.

———. 2010. "The Renewal of the Socialist Majority: The 2009 Portuguese Legislative Elections." *West European Politics* 33, no. 2 (March): 381–88.

Locke, Richard M. 1995. *Remaking the Italian Economy.* Ithaca, NY: Cornell University Press.

López-Pintor, Rafael. 1981. "El estado de la opinion pública española y la transición a la democracia." *Revista Española de Investigaciones Sociológicas* 13 (January–March): 7–47.

———. 1985. "The October 1982 General Election and the Evolution of the Spanish Party System." In *Spain at the Polls 1977, 1979, and 1982,* edited by Howard R. Penniman and Eusebio Mujal-Léon. Durham, NC: Duke University Press, 293–313.

Lorusso, Mino. 1992. *Ochetto: Il comunismo italiano da Togliatti al PDS.* Firenze: Ponte Alle Grazie Editori.

Luebbert, Gregory M. 1991. *Liberalism, Fascism, or Social Democracy: Social Classes and the Origins of Regimes in Interwar Europe.* New York: Oxford University Press.

Mahoney, James. 2001. *The Legacies of Liberalism: Path Dependence and Political Regimes in Central America*. Baltimore: Johns Hopkins University Press.

Mahoney, James, and Dietrich Rueschemeyer, eds. 2003. *Comparative Historical Analysis in the Social Sciences*. Cambridge: Cambridge University Press.

Mair, Peter. 2008. "The Challenge to Party Government." *West European Politics* 31, no. 1–2 (January–March): 211–34.

Mair, Peter, and Stefano Bartolini, eds. 1990. *Identity, Competition, and Electoral Availability: The Stabilisation of European Electorates 1885–1985*. Cambridge: Cambridge University Press.

Mair, Peter, and Ingrid Van Biezen. 2001. "Party Membership in Twenty European Democracies, 1980–2000." *Party Politics* 7, no. 1: 5–21.

Malefakis, Edward E. 1970. *Agrarian Reform and Peasant Revolution in Spain: Origins of the Civil War*. New Haven, CT: Yale University Press.

Maravall, José María. 1978. *Dictadura y disentimiento político: Obreras y estudiantes bajo el Franquismo*. Madrid: Ediciones Alfaguara.

———. 1982. *The Transition to Democracy in Spain*. New York: St. Martin's.

———. 1985. "The Socialist Alternative: The Policies and Electorate of the PSOE." In *Spain at the Polls 1977, 1979, and 1982*, edited by Howard R. Penniman and Eusebio Mujal-Léon. Durham, NC: Duke University Press, 129–59.

———. 1992. "From Opposition to Governnment: The Politics and Policies of the PSOE." In *Socialist Parties in Europe*. Barcelona: Institut de Ciències Politiques i Socials, 7–34.

———. 2008. "The Political Consequences of Internal Party Democracy." In *Controlling Governments: Voters, Institutions, and Accountability*, edited by José María Maravall and Ignacio Sánchez-Cuenca. Cambridge: Cambridge University Press, 157–201.

Maravall, José María, and Marta Fraile. 1998. "The Politics of Unemployment. The Spanish Experience in Comparative Perspective." Working Paper 1998/124. Madrid: Centro de Estudios Avazados en Ciencias Sociales, Instituto Juan March de Estudios e Investigaciones.

Maravall, José María, and Julián Santamaría. 1986. "Political Change in Spain and the Prospects for Democracy." In *Transitions from Authoritarian Rule: Southern Europe*, edited by Guillermo O'Donnell, Philippe C. Schmitter, and Laurence Whitehead. Baltimore: Johns Hopkins University Press, 71–108.

Marglin, Stephen A., and Juliet B. Schor, eds. 1990. *The Golden Age of Capitalism: Reinterpreting the Postwar Experience*. Oxford: Clarendon Press.

Martin, Andrew, and George Ross, et al. 1999. *The Brave New World of European Labor: European Trade Unions at the Millennium*. New York: Berghahn.

Maxwell, Kenneth. 1978. "Portuguese Communism." In *Eurocommunism: The Ideological and Political-Theoretical Foundations*, edited by George Schwab. Westport, CT: Greenwood, 269–99.

———. 1995. *The Making of Portuguese Democracy*. Cambridge: Cambridge University Press.

McDonough, Peter, Samuel H. Barnes, and Antonio López Pina. 1981. "The Spanish Public in Political Transition." *British Journal of Political Science* 11, no. 1 (January): 49–79.

———. 1984. "Authority and Association: Spanish Democracy in Comparative Perspective." *Journal of Politics* 46, no. 3 (August): 652–88.

———. 1986a. "Economic Policy and Public Opinion in Spain." *American Journal of Political Science* 30, no. 2 (May): 446–79.

———. 1986b. "The Growth of Democratic Legitimacy in Spain." *American Political Science Review* 80, no. 3 (September): 735–60.

———. 1998. *The Cultural Dynamics of Democratization in Spain*. Ithaca, NY: Cornell University Press.

Méndez Lago, Mónica. 2006. "Turning the Page: Crisis and Transformation of the Spanish Socialist Party." *South European Society and Politics* 11, no. 3–4 (September–December): 419–37.

Mendras, Henri, with Alistair Cole. 1991. *Social Change in Modern France: Towards a Cultural Anthropology of the Fifth Republic*. Cambridge: Cambridge University Press.

Michavila, Narcisco. 2005. "Guerra, terrorismo y elecciones: incidencia electoral de los atentados islamistas en Madrid." Madrid: Real Instituto Elcano, Working Document 13 (March), 34 pp.

Montero, Alfred. 2002. *Shifting States in Global Markets: Subnational Industrial Policy in Contemporary Brazil and Spain.* University Park: Pennsylvania State University Press.

Montero, José Ramón. 1999. "Stabilizing the Democratic Order: Electoral Behavior in Spain." In *Politics and Policy in Democratic Spain: No Longer Different?*, edited by Paul Heywood. London: Frank Cass, 53–79.

Moore, Barrington. 1966. *Social Origins of Dictatorship and Democracy: Lord and Peasant in the Making of the Modern World.* Boston: Beacon.

Morel, Laurence. 1996. "Du marxisme au craxisme: Le socialisme italien à la recherche d'une identité." In *La gauche en Europe depuis 1945: Invariants et mutations du socialisme européen*, by Marc Lazar, with the collaboration of Francine Simon-Ekovich, ed. Paris: Presses Universitaires de France, 263–91.

Morlino, Leonardo. 1986. "Consolidamento democratico: Definizione e modelli." *Revista Italiana di Scienza Politica* 16: 197–238.

Morlino, Leonardo, and Anna Bosco, eds. 2007. *Party Change in Southern Europe.* London: Routledge.

Moschonas, Gerassimos. 1999. "The Panhellenic Socialist Movement." In *Social Democratic Parties in the European Union: History, Organization, Policies*, edited by Robert Ladrech and Philippe Marlière. London: Palgrave Macmillan.

———. 2002. *In the Name of Social Democracy: The Great Transformation, 1945 to the Present.* London: Verso.

Mouriaux, René. 1982. *La CGT.* Paris: Èditions du Seuil.

———. 1983. *Les syndicats dans la société française.* Paris: Presses de la Fondation Nationale des Sciences Politiques.

Mujal-León, Eusebio M. 1978a. "Communism and Revolution in Portugal." In *Eurocommunism and Détente*, edited by Rudolf L. Tőkés. New York: New York University Press, 271–313.

———. 1978b. "Portuguese and Spanish Communism in Comparative Perspective." In *The Many Faces of Communism*, edited by Morton A. Kaplan. New York: Free Press, 122–45.

———. 1979. "The Spanish Left: Present Realities and Future Prospects." In *The European Left: Italy, France, and Spain*, edited by William E. Griffith. Lexington, MA: D. C. Heath, 81–108.

———. 1983. *Communism and Political Change in Spain.* Bloomington: Indiana University Press.

Mulé, Rosa. 2007. *Dentro i DS.* Bologna: Il Mulino.

Nash, Elizabeth. 1983. "The Spanish Socialist Party Since Franco: From Clandestinity to Government: 1976–82." In *Democratic Politics in Spain: Spanish Politics After Franco*, edited by David S. Bell. London: Frances Pinter, 29–62.

Newell, James L. 2006. "The Italian Election of May 2006: Myths and Realities." *West European Politics* 29, no. 4 (September): 802–13.

Noland, Aaron. 1956. *The Founding of the French Socialist Party, 1893–1905.* Cambridge, MA: Harvard University Press.

Nora, Pierre. 1996. "Gaullists and Communists." In *Realms of Memory: Rethinking the French Past. Vol. 1: Conflicts and Divisions*, edited by Pierre Nora. New York: Columbia University Press, 205–39.

Novelli, Diego. 2006. *Com'era bello il mio PCI.* Milan: Melampo Editore.

Ortuño Anaya, Pilar. 2002. *European Socialists and Spain: The Transition to Democracy, 1959–77.* London: Palgrave Macmillan.

Padgett, Stephen, and William E. Paterson. 1991. *A History of Social Democracy in Postwar Europe.* London: Longman.

Panebianco, Angelo. 1988. *Political Parties: Organisation and Power.* Cambridge: Cambridge University Press

Papayannakis, Michalis. 1981. "The Crisis in the Greek Left." In *Greece at the Polls: The National Elections of 1974 and 1977*, edited by Howard R. Penniman. Washington, DC: American Enterprise Institute, 130–59.

Pappalardo, Adriano. 2006. "Italian Bipolarism and the Elections of 2006: End of the Line or Just a Connecting Stop?" *Journal of Modern Italian Studies* 11, no. 4: 472–93.

Pasquino, Gianfranco. 1981. "The Italian Socialist Party: Electoral Stagnation and Political Indispensibility." In *Italy at the Polls, 1979: A Study of the Parliamentary Elections*, edited by Howard R. Penniman. Washington, DC: American Enterprise Institute for Public Policy Research, 141–71.

———. 1988. "Mid-Stream and under Stress: The Italian Communist Party." In *Communist Parties in Western Europe: Decline or Adaptation?*, edited by Michael Waller and Meindert Fennema. Oxford: Basil Blackwell, 26–46.

———. 2005. "In the Italian Senate: A Personal Memoir." *European Political Science* 4: 129–40.

———. 2008. "The 2008 Italian National Elections: Berlusconi's Third Victory." *South European Society and Politics* 13, no. 3 (September): 345–62.

Paterson, William E., and Alastair H. Thomas, eds. 1986. *The Future of Social Democracy: Problems and Prospects of Social Democratic Parties in Western Europe*. Oxford: Clarendon.

Patricio, Maria Teresa, and Alan Stoleroff. 1993. "The Portuguese Communist Party: Loyalty to the 'Communist Ideal.'" In *Western European Communists and the Collapse of Communism*, edited by David S. Bell. Providence, RI: Berg, 69–85.

Payne, Stanley G. 1985. "Representative Government in Spain: The Historical Background." In *Spain at the Polls 1977, 1979, and 1982*, edited by Howard R. Penniman and Eusebio Mujal-Léon. Durham, NC: Duke University Press, 1–29.

Pérez, Sofía A. 1999. "From Labor to Finance: Understanding the Failure of Socialist Economic Policies in Spain." *Comparative Political Studies* 32, no. 6 (September): 659–89.

Pérez-Díaz, Victor. 1980. *Clase obrera, partidos, y sindicatos*. Madrid: Fundación del INI.

——— . 1987. *El retorno de la sociedad civil: Respuestas sociales a la transición política, la crisis económica y los cambios culturales de España 1975–1985*. Madrid: Instituto de Estudios Económicos.

——— . 1993. *The Return of Civil Society: The Emergence of Democratic Spain*. Cambridge, MA: Harvard University Press.

——— . 1999. *Spain at the Crossroads: Civil Society, Politics, and the Rule of Law*. Cambridge, MA: Harvard University Press.

Petras, James. 1993. "Spanish Socialism: The Politics of Neoliberalism." In *Mediterranean Paradoxes: The Politics and Social Structure of Southern Europe*, edited by James Kurth and James Petras, with Diarmuid Maguire and Ronald Chilcote. Providence, RI: Berg, 95–127.

Petras, James, Evangelos Raptis, and Sergio Sarafopoulos. 1993. "Greek Socialism: The Patrimonial State Revisited." In *Mediterranean Paradoxes: The Politics and Social Structure of Southern Europe*, edited by James Kurth and James Petras. Providence, RI: Berg, 160–224.

Pfister, Thierry. 1986. *La vie quotidienne à Matignon au temps de l'Union de la Gauche*. Paris: Hachette.

Piccone, Paul. 1983. *Italian Marxism*. Berkeley: University of California Press.

Pickles, Dorothy. 1982. *Problems of Contemporary French Politics*. London: Methuen.

Pierce, Roy. 1995. *Choosing the Chief: Presidential Elections in France and the United States*. Ann Arbor: University of Michigan Press.

Piore, Michael J., and Charles F. Sabel. 1984. *The Second Industrial Divide: Possibilities for Prosperity*. New York: Basic Books.

Piven, Frances Fox, ed. 1992. *Labor Parties in Postindustrial Societies*. New York: Oxford University Press.

Pizzorno, Alessandro. 1978. "Political Exchange and Collective Identity in Industrial Conflict." In *The Resurgence of Class Conflict in Western Europe since 1968*, edited by Colin Crouch and Alessandro Pizzorno. New York: Holmes & Meier, 277–98.

Platone, François, and Jean Ranger. 1985. "Les communistes au gouvernement: Une expérience complexe et contradictoire." *Revue Politique et Parlementaire* 914 (January–February): 28–49.

Pons, Silvio. 2006. *Berlinguer e la fine del comunismo*. Turin: Giulio Einaudi Editore.

Portelli, Hugues. 1980. *Le socialisme francais tel qu'il est*. Paris: Presses Universitaires de France.

Prasad, Monica. 2006. *The Politics of Free Markets: The Rise of Neoliberal Economic Policies in Britain, France, Germany, and the United States*. Chicago: University of Chicago Press.

Preston, Paul. 1977. "The Origins of the Socialist Schism in Spain, 1917–1931." *Journal of Contemporary History* 12, no. 1 (January): 101–32.

———. 1981. "The PCE's Long Road to Democracy 1954–77." In *In Search of Eurocommunism*, edited by Richard Kindersley. New York: St. Martin's, 36–65.

———. 1983. "The PCE in the Struggle for Democracy in Spain." In *National Communism in Western Europe: A Third Way to Socialism?*, edited by Howard Machin. London: Methuen, 154–79.

———. 1986a. "Decadencia y resurgimiento del PSOE durante el regimen franquista." In *El socialismo en España: Desde la fundación del PSOE hasta 1975*, edited by Santos Juliá. Madrid: Editorial Pablo Iglesias, 349–66.

———. 1986b. *The Triumph of Democracy in Spain*. London: Methuen.

———. 2004. *Juan Carlos: Steering Spain from Dictatorship to Democracy*. New York: Norton.

———. 2007. *The Spanish Civil War: Reaction, Revolution, and Revenge*. New York: W.W. Norton.

Przeworski, Adam, and John Sprague. 1986. *Paper Stones: A History of Electoral Socialism*. Chicago: University of Chicago Press.

Puhle, Hans-Jürgen. 1986. "El PSOE: Un partido predominante y heterogeneo." In *Crisis y cambio: Electores y partidos en la España de los años ochenta*, edited by Juan J. Linz and José Ramón Montero. Madrid: Centro de Estudios Constitucionales, 289–344.

Ramiro-Fernández, Luis. 2004a. *Cambio y adaptación en la izquierda: La evolución del Partido Comunista de España y de Izquierda Unida (1986–2000)*. Madrid: Centro de Investigaciones Sociológicas.

———. 2004b. "Electoral Competition, Organizational Constraints and Party Change: The Communist Party of Spain (PCE) and United Left (IU), 1986–2000." *Journal of Communist Studies and Transition Politics* 20, no. 2 (June): 1–29.

Ranzato, Gabriele. 2005. *The Spanish Civil War*. Northhampton, MA: Interlink.

Raymond, Gino G. 2005. *The French Communist Party during the Fifth Republic: A Crisis of Leadership and Ideology*. London: Palgrave Macmillan.

Regalia, Ida, and Emilio Reyneri. 1978. "Labour Conflicts and Industrial Relations in Italy." In *The Resurgence of Class Conflict in Western Europe since 1968: Volume 1. National Studies*, edited by Colin Crouch and Alessandro Pizzorno. New York: Holmes & Meier, 101–58.

Rey, Henri. 2004. *La gauche et les classes populaires: Histoire et actualité d'une mésentente*. Paris: Presses de Sciences Po.

Rey, Henri, and Françoise Subileau. 1991. *Les militants socialistes à l'épreuve du pouvoir*. Paris: Presses de la Fondation Nationale des Sciences Politiques.

Rhodes, Martin. 1995. "Reinventing the Left: The Origins of Italy's Progressive Alliance." In *Italian Politics: A Review, Vol. 9. Ending the First Republic*, edited by Carol Mershon and Gianfranco Pasquino. Boulder, CO: Westview, 113–34.

———. 1996. "The Italian Left between Crisis and Renewal." In *Italy: Politics and Policy*, vol. 1, edited by Robert Leonardi and Raffaella Y. Nanetti. Aldershot: Dartmouth, 108–33.

Ross, George. 1982. *Workers and Communists in France*. Berkeley: University of California Press.

———. 1992. "Party Decline and Changing Party Systems: France and the French Communist Party." *Comparative Politics* 25, no. 1 (October): 43–61.

———. 2006. "Communism." In *The Columbia History of Twentieth-Century French Thought*, edited by Lawrence D. Kritzman. New York: Columbia University Press, 18–23.

Ross, George, Stanley Hoffman, and Sylvia Malzacher, eds. 1987. *The Mitterrand Experiment: Continuity and Change in Modern France.* Oxford: Polity.

Ross, Kristin. 2002. *May '68 and Its Afterlives.* Chicago: University of Chicago Press.

Royo, Sebastián. 2001. "The Collapse of Social Concertation and the Failure of Socialist Economic Policies in Spain." *South European Society and Politics* 6, no. 1 (Summer): 27–50.

———. 2002. *"A New Century of Corporatism?" Corporatism in Southern Europe—Spain and Portugal in Comparative Perspective.* Westport, CT: Praeger.

———. 2008. *Varieties of Capitalism in Spain: Remaking the Spanish Economy for the New Century.* New York: Palgrave Macmillan.

Sa'adah, Anne. 2003. *Contemporary France: A Democratic Education.* Lanham, MD: Rowman & Littlefield.

Salavadori, Massimo L. 1999. *La sinistra nella storia italiana.* Rome: Editori Laterza.

Salvati, Michele. 1981. "May 1968 and the Hot Autumn of 1969: The Responses of Two Ruling Classes." In *Organizing Interests in Western Europe: Pluralism, Corporatism, and the Transformation of Politics*, edited by Suzanne D. Berger. Cambridge: Cambridge University Press, 329–63.

Santamaría, J. 2004. "El azar y el contexto: Las elecciones generales de 2004." *Claves de Razón Práctica* 146 (October): 28–40.

Sartori, Giovanni. 1966. "European Political Parties: The Case of Polarized Pluralism." In *Political Parties and Political Development*, edited by Joseph La Palombara and Myron Weiner. Princeton, NJ: Princeton University Press, 137–76.

———. 1976. *Political Parties: A Framework for Analysis.* Cambridge: Cambridge University Press.

Sassoon, Donald. 1990. "The Role of the Italian Communist Party in the Consolidation of Parliamentary Democracy in Italy." In *Securing Democracy: Political Parties and Democratic Consolidation in Southern Europe*, edited by Geoffrey Pridham. London: Routledge, 84–103.

———. 1996. *One Hundred Years of Socialism: The West European Left in the Twentieth Century.* New York: HarperCollins.

———. 2003. "Reflections on a Death Foretold: The Life and Times of the Italian Communist Party." In *Italy: Politics and Policy* , vol. 2, edited by Robert Leonardi, Marcello Fedele, and Raffaella Y. Nanetti. Aldershot: Ashgate, 35–54.

Sawicki, Frédéric. 1998. "The Parti Socialiste: From a Party of Activists to a Party of Government." In *The Organization of Political Parties in Southern Europe*, edited by Piero Ignazi and Colette Ysmal. New York: Praeger, 70–87.

Scase, Richard. 1977. *Social Democracy in Capitalist Society: Working-Class Politics in Britain and Sweden.* London: Croom Helm.

Schain, Martin. 1985. *French Communism and Local Power: Urban Politics and Political Change.* London: Frances Pinter.

———. 1990. "The French Communist Party: The Seeds of Its Own Decline." In *Comparative Theory and Political Experience*, edited by Peter Katzenstein, et al. Ithaca, NY: Cornell University Press, 119–43.

Scharpf, Fritz. 1991. *Crisis and Choice in European Social Democracy.* Ithaca, NY: Cornell University Press.

Schmidt, Vivien A. 1996. *Between State and Market: The Transformation of French Business and Government.* Cambridge: Cambridge University Press.

Seidman, Michael. 2004. *The Imaginary Revolution: Parisian Students and Workers in 1968.* Oxford: Berghahn.

Share, Donald. 1986. *The Making of Spanish Democracy.* New York: Praeger.

———. 1988a. "Dilemmas of Social Democracy in the 1980s: The Spanish Socialist Workers Party in Comparative Perspective." *Comparative Political Studies* 21, no. 3 (October): 408–35.

———. 1988b. "Spain: Socialists as Neoliberals." *Socialist Review* 18 (January–March): 38–68.

———. 1989. *Dilemmas of Social Democracy: The Spanish Socialist Workers Party in the 1980s.* Westport, CT: Greenwood.

Singer, Daniel. 1970. *Prelude to Revolution: France in May 1968.* New York: Hill and Wang.

———. 1988. *Is Socialism Doomed? The Meaning of Mitterrand.* New York: Oxford University Press.

Smith, Dennis Mack. 1976. *Mussolini's Roman Empire.* New York: Penguin.

———. 1997. *Modern Italy: A Political History.* Ann Arbor: University of Michigan Press.

Smith, Ole L. 1993. "The Greek Communist Party in the Post-Gorbachev Era." In *European Communists and the Collapse of Communism,* edited by David S. Bell. Oxford: Berg.

Smith, Timothy B. 2004. *France in Crisis: Welfare, Inequality, and Globalization since 1980.* Cambridge: Cambridge University Press.

Smith, W. Rand. 1981. "Paradoxes of Plural Unionism: CGT-CFDT Relations in France." *West European Politics* 4, no. 1 (January): 38–53.

———. 1984. "Dynamics of Plural Unionism in France: The CGT, CFDT, and Industrial Conflict." *British Journal of Industrial Relations* 22, no. 1 (March): 15–33.

———. 1987. *Crisis in the French Labor Movement: A Grassroots Perspective.* New York: St. Martin's.

———. 1990. "Nationalizations for What? Capitalist Power and Public Enterprise in Mitterrand's France." *Politics and Society* 18, no. 1 (March): 75–99.

———. 1995. "Industrial Crisis and the Left: Adjustment Strategies in Socialist France and Spain." *Comparative Politics* 28, no. 1 (October): 1–24.

———. 1998. *The Left's Dirty Job: The Politics of Industrial Restructuring in France and Spain.* Pittsburgh, PA: University of Pittsburgh Press.

———. 1999. "Unemployment and the Left Coalition in France and Spain." *South European Society and Politics* 4, no. 3 (Winter): 111–34.

Solinger, Dorothy J. 2009. *States' Gains, Labor's Losses: China, France, and Mexico Choose Global Liaisons, 1980–2000.* Ithaca, NY: Cornell University Press.

Spini, Valdo. 2006. *Campagni, siete riabilitati! Il grano e il loglio dell'esperienza socialista 1976–2006.* Rome: Editori Riuniti.

Spotts, Frederic, and Theodor Wieser. 1986. *Italy: A Difficult Democracy.* Cambridge: Cambridge University Press.

Spourdalakis, Michalis. 1988. *The Rise of the Greek Socialist Party.* London: Routledge.

Spourdalakis, Michalis, and Chrisanthos Tassis. 2006. "Party Change in Greece and the Vanguard Role of PASOK." *South European Society and Politics* 11, no. 3–4 (September–December): 497–512.

Ştefuriuc, Irina, and Tània Verge. 2008. "Small and Divided Parties in Multi-Level Settings: Opportunities for Regional Government Participation, the Case of Izquierda Unida in Spain." *South European Society and Politics* 13, no. 2 (June): 155–73.

Stille, Alexander. 2006. *The Sack of Rome: How a Beautiful European Country with a Fabled History and a Storied Culture Was Taken Over by a Man Named Silvio Berlusconi.* New York: Penguin.

Szarka, Joseph. 1999. "The Parties of the French 'Plural Left': An Uneasy Complementarity." *West European Politics* 22, no. 4 (December): 20–37.

Taibo, Carlos. 1996. *Izquierda Unida y sus mundos: Una visión crítica.* Madrid: Libros de la Catarata.

Tamames, Ramón. 1992. *Introducción a la economía española.* 20th ed. Madrid: Allianza Editorial.

Tarrow, Sidney G. 1983. "Historic Compromise or Bourgeois Majority? Eurocommunism in Italy 1976–9." In *National Communism in Western Europe: A Third Way to Socialism?,* edited by Howard Machin. London: Methuen, 124–53.

———. 1985. "The Crisis of the Late 1960s in Italy and France: The Transition to Mature Capitalism." In *Semiperipheral Development: The Politics of Southern Europe in the Twentieth Century,* edited by Giovanni Arrighi. Beverly Hills, CA: Sage, 215–41.

Tezanos, José Félix. 1983. *Sociología del socialismo español.* Madrid: Editorial Tecnos.

———, ed. 2004. *PSOE 125: 125 años del Partido Socialista Obrero Español.* Madrid: Fundación Pablo Iglesias.

Theuret, Patrick. 1996. "Le Parti Socialiste Ouvrier Espagnol de l'exil au pouvoir." In *La gauche en Europe*, edited by Marc Lazar. Paris: Presses Universitaires de France, 309–28.

Thomas, Hugh. 1961. *The Spanish Civil War*. New York: Harper and Row.

Thomson, Stuart. 2000. *The Social Democratic Dilemma: Ideology, Governance, and Globalization*. London: Macmillan.

Tiersky, Ronald. 1974. *French Communism, 1920–1972*. New York: Columbia University Press.

———. 2000. *François Mitterrand: The Last French President*. New York: St. Martin's.

Torcal, Mariano, and José Ramón Montero. 1997. "Party Change and Cleavage Formation: The Effects of Value Change on the Spanish Party System." Working Paper 132. Barcelona: Institut de Ciències Polítiques I Socials.

Torcal, Mariano, and Guillem Rico. 2004. "The 2004 Spanish General Election: In the Shadow of al-Qaeda?" *South European Society and Politics* 9, no. 3: 107–21.

Tortella, Gabriel. 2000. *The Development of Modern Spain: An Economic History of the Nineteenth and Twentieth Centuries*. Cambridge, MA: Harvard University Press.

Touraine, Alain. 1971. *The May Movement: Revolt and Reform: May 1968*. New York: Random House.

Urban, Joan B. 1986. *Moscow and the Italian Communist Party: From Togliatti to Berlinguer*. Ithaca, NY: Cornell University Press.

Van Biezen, Ingrid. 1998. "Building Party Organisations and the Relevance of Past Models: The Communist and Socialist Parties in Spain and Portugal." *West European Politics* 21, no. 2 (April): 32–62.

———. 2003. *Political Parties in New Democracies: Party Organization in Southern and East-Central Europe* . Basingstoke: Palgrave Macmillan.

———. 2008. "Party Development in Democratic Spain: Life-Cycle, Generation, or Period Effect?" In *Democracy and Institutional Development: Spain in Comparative Theoretical Perspective*, edited by Bonnie N. Field and Kerstin Hamann. Basingstoke: Palgrave Macmillan, 23–43.

Vegleris, Phaedo. 1981. "Greek Electoral Law." In *Greece at the Polls: The National Elections of 1974 and 1977*, edited by Howard R. Penniman. Washington, DC: American Enterprise Institute, 21–48.

Verge Mestre, Tània. 2007. *Partidos y representación política: Las dimensiones del cambio en los partidos políticos españoles, 1976–2006*. Madrid: Centro de Investigaciones Sociológicas.

Villaverde Cabral, Manuel. 1983. "The Portuguese Communist Party: The Weight of Fifty Years of History." In *National Communism in Western Europe: A Third Way to Socialism?*, edited by Howard Machin. London: Methuen, 180–99.

Waller, Michael, and Meindert Fennema, eds. 1988. *Communist Parties in Western Europe: Decline or Adaptation*. Oxford: Basil Blackwell.

Weinberg, Leonard. 1995. *The Transformation of Italian Communism*. New Brunswick, NJ: Transaction.

Weitz, Eric D. 1992. *Popular Communism: Political Strategies and Social Histories in the Formation of the German, French, and Italian Communist Parties, 1919–1948*. Ithaca, NY: Institute for European Studies, Cornell University.

Weitz, Peter. 1975. "The CGIL and the PCI: From Subordination to Independent Political Force." In *Communism in Italy and France*, edited by Donald L. M. Blackmer and Sidney Tarrow. Princeton, NJ: Princeton University Press, 541–71.

Western, Bruce. 1997. *Between Class and Market: Postwar Unionization in the Capitalist Democracies* . Princeton, NJ: Princeton University Press.

Willard, Claude. 1965. *Les Guesdistes: Le mouvement socialiste en France (1893–1905)*. Paris: Éditions Sociales.

Wilson, Frank L. 1971. *The French Democratic Left, 1963–1969: Toward a Modern Party System*. Stanford, CA: Stanford University Press.

———. 1993. *The Failure of West European Communism: Implications for the Future*. New York: Paragon House.

———. 2002. "After the Deluge: The French Communist Party after the End of Communism." *German Policy Studies* 2, no. 2: 259–89.

Wohl, Robert. 1966. *French Communism in the Making, 1914–1924.* Stanford, CA: Stanford University Press.

Wright, Vincent. 1983. "The French Communist Party during the Fifth Republic: The Troubled Path." In *National Communism in Western Europe: A Third Way to Socialism?*, edited by Howard Machin. London: Methuen, 90–123.

Index

281

About the Author

W. Rand Smith is the Irvin L. and Fern D. Young Presidential Professor of Politics and Associate Dean of the Faculty at Lake Forest College. He is the author of two previous books, *Crisis in the French Labor Movement: A Grassroots Perspective* (1987) and *The Left's Dirty Job: The Politics of Industrial Restructuring in France and Spain* (1998), as well as articles on French and Spanish politics and political economy published in *Comparative Politics*, *Politics & Society*, *West European Politics*, and other journals. He has received research fellowships from the Fulbright program and the German Marshall Fund of the United States. Smith received his B.A. (Honors) from the University of North Carolina at Chapel Hill and M.A. and Ph.D. from the University of Michigan.